Iran–Europe Relations

This book provides an assessment, and history, of relations between Iran and Europe. With an account of their development since the early years of the twentieth century, this book shows that, despite the recent deterioration of relations between Iran and the West, Iran has enjoyed a long history of cultural, economic, and political ties with many European nations.

The book examines pivotal historical episodes: Iran's support of Germany before the First World War; cooperation and close trading relations between the two countries in the interwar years; the Islamic revolution in 1979; and Iran's attempts to strengthen ties with Europe in the aftermath of the Iran–Iraq War.

The book closely examines recent issues of conflict: disputes over weapons of mass destruction; allegations of Iranian support for terrorist groups in Afghanistan, Bosnia, Iraq, and Lebanon; human rights issues; and the Arab–Israeli conflict and the Middle East peace process. It concludes by suggesting ways in which Iran–Europe relations could develop positively, overcome current obstacles, and take advantage of the opportunities and common interests that lie beneath the surface.

Dr Seyyed Hossein Mousavian is currently Vice President of the Centre for Strategic Studies, Tehran, Iran. He was Chairman of the Supreme National Security Council's (SNSC) Foreign Policy Committee from 1997 to 2007 and was also the foreign policy advisor to the Secretary of the SNSC until September 2007. From 1990 to 1997 he served as Iranian Ambassador to Germany.

Durham Modern Middle East and Islamic World Series

Series Editor: Anoushiravan Ehteshami

University of Durham

Iran–Europe Relations

Challenges and opportunities

Seyyed Hossein Mousavian

LONDON AND NEW YORK

First published 2008 by Routledge
2 Park Square, Milton Park, Abingdon, Oxon, OX14 4RN

Simultaneously published in the USA and Canada
by Routledge
270 Madison Avenue, New York, NY 10016

Routledge is an imprint of the Taylor & Francis Group, an informa business

Typeset in Times New Roman 10/12 pt
by SPi Publisher Services, Pondicherry, India
Printed and bound in Great Britain
by TJI Digital, Padstow, Cornwall

British Library Cataloguing in Publication Data
A catalogue record for this book is available from the
British Library

Library of Congress Cataloging in Publication Data
Mousavian, Seyyed Hossein, 1967–
    Iran–Europe relations : challenges and opportunities / Seyyed Hossein
    Mousavian. – 1st ed.
        p. cm. – (Durham modern Middle East and Islamic world series)
    Includes bibliographical references and index.
    ISBN 978-0-415-44756-0 (cloth : alk. paper) – ISBN 978-0-203-92889-9
(ebook) 1. Iran–Foreign relations–Europe. 2. Europe–Foreign
relations–Iran. 3. Iran–Foreign relations–Germany. 4. Germany–Foreign
relations–Iran. I. Title.

    DS274.2.E85M87 2008
    327.5504–dc22
    2007039664

ISBN 10: 0-415-44756-9 (hbk)
ISBN 10: 0-203-92889-X (ebk)

ISBN 13: 978-0-415-44756-0 (hbk)
ISBN 13: 978-0-203-92889-9 (ebk)

Contents

Foreword

An accurate analysis of the development of Iran's foreign policy and its relations with the international community since the fall of the Pahlavi dictatorship in 1979 reveals an important chapter in the history of Iran's Islamic revolution. In this light, Iran's relations with Germany stand out in importance. Historical and traditional interactions between the two countries had a great impact on regional developments and international equations during the First and Second World Wars. With the collapse of the strategic alliance between the two countries during the Second World War, the Allies were able to divide Germany into eastern and western parts and set out to strengthen their political and security grip over the divided country. During the same period, Iran was also technically under the influence of foreign powers.

After the victory of the Islamic revolution of Iran in 1979, Iran regained its political independence, but was immediately guided by big powers through the dictatorial and aggressive regime of Iraq. The war was in fact the price that Iran paid for its political independence. After the end of the war, which coincided with my first term as president, reengineering Iran's foreign policy started concurrently with scientific, cultural, social, and economic reconstruction of the country. In this period we were also witness to major international upheavals, namely, the end of the Cold War. The most important development of this period was the shattering of the Berlin Wall and the reunification of East and West Germany into a sovereign, politically independent Germany in 1990.

That juncture provided leaders of both countries with a suitable opportunity to take steps toward the revival of historical ties and the adoption of a new diplomatic approach. In the viewpoint of German leaders, Iran's geopolitical position, bordering the former Soviet republics and sharing a common history with many of them, its potential for having a far-reaching influence within the sensitive regions of the Persian Gulf and the Middle East, its vast energy reserves, and, above all, its ideological force, serve as important factors that are needed to regulate Germany's position in the region. On the other hand, the Iranian leaders looked upon Germany as a good model for relations with Europe and paid special attention to its role in defying economic sanctions imposed on Iran by the United States and its support for the transfer of credits and modern technology for the reconstruction of the country after the end of the imposed war. Expansion of relations with the West, excluding the United States, was one of the main features of Iran's national diplomacy and the quality and quantity of relations with Germany and Europe could have been influential in promoting that diplomacy.

The current research by Dr Seyyed Hossein Mousavian, a prominent Iranian diplomat and the then-ambassador of Iran to united Germany, has addressed the two nations' diplomatic approach in those years in a proper manner. In this research, Iran–Germany relations have been examined since their inception up to the victory of the Islamic revolution and from that time to the reunification of Germany from different political, economic, security, cultural, and military viewpoints. Drawing upon facts and authentic historical documents, as well as memories of his diplomatic mission, the author has managed to comprehensively analyze a number of salient issues within Iran–Germany relations. These include Iran's dealings with Europe and the West in such fields as human rights, terrorism, and weapons of mass destruction; the Middle East peace process and regional security; the influence of foreign players, including the United States, Britain, and Israel, on Iran–Germany relations since the reunification of Germany up to the Mykonos crisis; and the role of those countries in creating that crisis.

It is hoped that this study will facilitate a better understanding of the most important challenges facing Iran's relations with the West, provide solutions for those challenges, and draw the attention of researchers and decision makers within Iran's diplomatic structure.

His Excellency Hojjatoleslam Ali Akbar Hashemi Rafsanjani
Chairman of the Expediency Council of Iran
December 2006

Introduction: Putting forth the argument

Analyzing relations between Iran and the West requires a political, economic, and social framework that can be developed through the analysis of the development of Iran's relations with Germany. This model provides one with the necessary historic platform upon which further examination can be fully conducted. Understanding the current issues of contention between Iran and the West will only be made possible through the full breakdown of how relations between Iran and Western countries, such as Germany, have developed over the years and what factors, both internal and external, have impacted relations. Therefore, the first section of this study will set forth the overall framework of Iran–Germany relations and will provide an inside view of the development of that relationship after the fall of the Berlin wall.

Having been posted as Ambassador of Iran to Germany at the crucial time of opening of relations, I had a firsthand grasp of the issues and process that made possible the development and growth of the relationship between the two countries. It is also important to recount the major differences that existed between the two sides throughout the period and how external powers and actors moved to undermine the strengthening relations of the two countries in different ways. This section will provide an overall analysis along with a detailed breakdown of the different crises that challenged the improvement of relations and derailed positive steps that had been taken.

Throughout Iran's history of political ties with foreign countries, its relationship with Germany has always been regarded as especially significant. From the time of Bismarck and the visit to Germany of the Qajari King Nasseruddin Shah, up to the present day, friendship between Iran and Germany has remained almost uninterrupted.[1] At the same time economic ties between the two have grown so much that today some 30 percent of Iran's industrial base has been built by German technology. During the Second World War, the close ties between Tehran and Berlin became an issue of worldwide concern and aroused the objections of the Allies, with the consequence that Iran was occupied by the USSR and Britain in 1941. After 1945 Iran remained under Western control, as did much of Germany.[2] Following the victory of the Islamic revolution in 1979, Iran was able to break free of American domination, but during the 1980–8 war with Iraq, initiated by

Baghdad, Iran was confronted with many new difficulties. At such critical times, Germany remained the only Western diplomatic intermediary for Iran.[1]

The development of relations between Germany and Iran after 1990 built in certain important ways on the long and diverse history of links between the two states. Germany was not a haphazard choice for Iran in the latter's search to improve relations with the West: A century of contact, based on strategic, political, economic, and cultural interests, had made Germany the most enduring of European interlocutors, just as for Germany the wealth and location of Iran had merited particular attention. The purpose of this chapter, necessarily schematic and wide-ranging, is an attempt to survey this diverse bilateral inheritance.

With the coming to power of Akbar Hashemi Rafsanjani's government and the acceptance of a cease-fire between Tehran and Baghdad in 1988, a period of Iran's history began that was characterized by internal reconstruction and consolidation of foreign relations. At the same time, on October 3, 1990, West and East Germany were reunified, a historic development that enabled Germany to throw off the last traces of the political and military hegemony of the Second World War Allies.[3] At this time the relationship between Iran and Germany was of considerable significance: After several decades of stagnation the two countries now found an opportunity to build a new kind of relationship in the context of full sovereignty.[4]

This new context promoted bilateral relations. Diplomatic ties between the two states were so invigorated that between October 1990 and 1996 more than 300 political, economic, cultural, judicial, and parliamentary delegations at different levels exchanged visits between the two countries. Almost half of them involved German and Iranian Cabinet ministers.[5] In the context of post-revolution relations between Iran and Germany the two states set up for the first time joint delegations relating to economics, the environment, conservation, transportation, culture and interparliamentary affairs.[6] The balance of trade between the two countries leaped to an unprecedented figure of around DM 10 billion. Iran's Ali Fallahian, the then Information (Intelligence) Minister, and his German counterpart, exchanged visits for the first time in 1992 and 1993, and laid the foundation for an exchange of intelligence between the two states.[7] At all the summits of the heads of state of the world's industrialized countries held during the period, Germany either rejected or sought to moderate resolutions critical of Iran sponsored by the United States. During a period when Iran was suffering from a foreign debt crisis, particularly in 1994 when it underwent its most critical post-revolutionary international financial crisis, Germany took the lead in supporting Tehran by rescheduling billions of marks of its debts, and encouraged other countries to follow suit.[8] During the early 1990s, for the first time since the victory of Iran's Islamic revolution, the heads of state of Iran and Germany regularly contacted each other to discuss important regional and international issues.[9]

The expansion of relations between Tehran and Bonn in the 1990s was given extensive coverage by the press, to the extent that the international news media began to describe it as a "special relationship."[10] However, simultaneously with the unprecedented growth of relations between Iran and Germany during the period from 1900 to 1996, others challenged the amicable ties between the two countries. During the years 1996 and 1997, the relationship confronted a serious crisis. The driving factors of this crisis can be categorized as: (1) opposition of Britain, Israel, and the United States to improved relations between Iran and Germany;[11] (2) incidents such as the assassination of Kurdish leaders at the Mykonos restaurant in Berlin, the assassination of former Iranian minister Reza Mazlooman in Paris, the detention and trial of German subjects in Iran, the detention of Faraj Sarkuhi on the charge of espionage for Germany; and (3) eventually the Berlin court verdict in the Mykonos Trial.

In light of the general trend toward the improvement of relations between Iran and Germany from 1990 to 1996, and taking into account the fact that both sides believed that these better ties would be of benefit to them, the sudden onset of the crisis of 1996–7 and the consequent deterioration of German–Iranian relations lead to the question, what were the main factors that led to such a crisis? It is this question, the background to Iranian–German relations in the 1990s, the course of these relations, and the factors that led to the crisis of 1996–7, that this thesis seeks to examine. As a participant in the events, the author hopes to add an original contribution to this issue.

After the reunification of Germany, relations between Iran and Germany became a topic of interest for the international media, and for writers and researchers in the academic and policy fields. However, an examination of the existing works suggests that no writer has yet carried out a systematic review of German–Iranian relations during the given period. So far, not even one book has been published on the subject, either in Persian or in any other language. Of course, the international news media, including radio and TV, have sporadically published reports about the events of the period, and these will be referred to in this study. Nevertheless, no work or article exists, which has analyzed and scrutinized the overall relationship between Iran and Germany after the reunification of East and West Germany. Reports published by the international media cover only individual incidents at particular periods. The only book the author is aware of about relations between Iran and Germany prior to the period under consideration was published in 1989 by the Institute for Trade Studies and Research (ITSR) in Tehran, affiliated to the Department of Planning and Information Dissemination of Iran's Commerce Ministry. In this work the relationship between the two countries is discussed from the earliest days up to 1989.

In attempting a description of the crisis in the relations between Iran and Germany in 1997, it is possible to enumerate many variables. These would include the following:

The influence of external actors and foreign policy constraints: The United States, the United Kingdom, and Israel

The expansion of ties between Iran and Germany aroused protests from Washington, London, and Tel Aviv. The issue took on such significance that during the visit of the German Chancellor to Washington in 1995, the difference of opinion between Germany and the United States about Iran became the main item in the agenda for the talks between the American and German leaders. This difference of opinion was clearly reflected in the official statements of the two Heads of State. During his visit to Israel in 1995, the German Chancellor faced protests from the Israeli leadership as well. The Israeli press reported that the existence of friendly ties between Germany and Iran was the sole point of difference between Germany and Israel, and gave prominence to the protests lodged by the Israeli leadership over the maintenance of Bonn's friendly relationship with Tehran.[12] Iran's policy of rejecting Israel's right to exist, and its opposition to the peace process, together with the level of hostility in Iran–US relations, were complicating factors. For its part, Germany gave priority to its relationships with the United States, the European Union (EU), and Israel, which further complicated the issue of bilateral relations between Iran and Germany.

Differences of opinion on the issues of human rights, weapons of mass destruction, and the Middle East peace process: Moves by German opposition parties against relations between Tehran and Bonn

The issue of human rights was one of the most fundamental points of difference between Tehran and Bonn during the period in question. This was particularly so with regard to the British author Salman Rushdie, to the extent that Rushdie made repeated trips to Germany, met German officials, and continually called on Bonn to scale down its ties with Iran.[13] In addition, every year the German Parliament passed a resolution condemning Iran's behavior in one way or another over human rights issues. The Middle East peace process and weapons of mass destruction (WMD) were also important points of dispute between the two countries, to the extent that in their official declarations, German statesmen, the leaders of the major political parties, and parliamentarians, all spoke out from time to time against Iran. Controversial reports were published from time to time in the German media about the purchase by Iran of WMD from Germany, which damaged political ties between the two sides.[14] Another difficulty arose from the antagonistic attitude of the German Social Democratic Party (SPD), the biggest German opposition party, and by the Green Party, Germany's third largest party. These two parties cooperated in their opposition to the broad concept of links between Germany and Iran.

The pursuit and assassination of opponents of the Iranian government in Germany and Europe, the detention and trial of German citizens in Iran, charges of espionage by both sides, and the provocative behavior of the terrorist Mujahedin-i Khalq Organization

The issue of the assassination of Kurdish leaders in Berlin in 1992 was not the only impediment to the relations between the two countries: The murders of Fereidoon Farrokhzad in Bonn and Reza Mazlooman in Paris, The detention of a suspicious figure apparently linked with the assassination in Bonn,[15] the assassination of

Shahpur Bakhtiar in Paris in 1991,[16] and the killing of Iranian Kurdish leader Qassemlu in Vienna in 1989[17] were all incidents that were not only raised in the German courts but were also widely reported in the German press. All these issues damaged the political relations between the two countries. The detention and trial of German citizens in Iran in the period from 1992 to 1995 also created an unprecedented situation in the history of Iran–Germany relations. The arrest and trial of a number of German citizens, Szimkus,[18] Bakhman, Fersch,[19] and Schleger, aroused much indignation in the German press. It not only prevented officials of the two countries from maintaining good relations but also caused a further deterioration of ties.

At the same time, the German press and government repeatedly accused the Iranian Embassy and other Iranian representative offices in Germany of espionage and Iran, for its part, arrested and tried people such as Faraj Sarkuhi on charges of espionage for Germany.[20] These mutual allegations, mingled with a series of retaliatory measures by the two countries, led to political problems and cast a cloud over the hitherto good relations between the two sides. Dozens of small groups opposing the Iranian government, including the Mujahedin-i Khalq Organization (MKO) and the royalists, succeeded through their activities in Germany in marring relations between the two countries. These activities continued to such an extent that each separate incident was raised by German officials in their meetings with Iranian officials, or publicized through demonstrations. Moreover all such events were in general reflected in the German news media. Actions by these small groups were often undertaken in a provocative manner and sometimes involved the use of arms. The attacks on Iran's diplomatic missions in Bonn, Hamburg and Munich,[21] on the Iranian foreign minister's car,[22] on Iran's parliamentary vice-speaker, and an assault on the Iranian Minister of Culture and Islamic Guidance, were all evident examples of uncivil behavior, which created problems in the relations between the two states.

The Mykonos trial

The verdict issued in what was termed the Mykonos Trial in Germany on April 10, 1997, led the German government to issue a statement in which it downgraded its diplomatic relationship with Iran. In the official statement issued on this date, the German government announced a series of steps to reduce the level of its diplomatic ties with Iran, which included the recall of the German ambassador to Tehran for consultation, the suspension of the ongoing critical dialogue, and the cancellation of the exchange of visits by political dignitaries between the two countries at the ministerial level.[23] In response, Iran took retaliatory action by recalling its ambassador and reducing its political and economic ties with Germany.[23]

These are, in summary, the four factors that led to the crisis of 1996–7. Based on these four factors and taking into account the explanations given about each of them, one can put forward, as follows, four hypotheses about the crisis in the relations between Iran and Germany. Of these, the fourth is to be seen as the principal hypothesis, while the first three are to be seen as alternative possibilities:

1. It could be argued that in light of the role of external actors and foreign policy constraints, the influence of the United States, the United Kingdom, and Israel was the main cause of the deterioration of relations between Iran and Germany.
2. It is possible that the main reason for the deterioration of the relationship was the existence of differences of opinion—about human rights issues, WMD sales to Iran, the Middle East peace process, and the activities of German opposition parties antagonistic to Tehran–Bonn relations.
3. Terrorism and security issues, including the pursuit and assassination of the opponents of the Iranian government in Germany and Europe, together with allegations of espionage, and the arrest and trial of citizens, worsened the relations between the two countries.
4. The verdict in the Mykonos Trial played a decisive role in the crisis in Iran–Germany relations.

The first three factors were aggravations but were not decisive in the crisis of 1996–7. It was the verdict of the German court in the Mykonos Trial that created a real crisis in the relations between Iran and Germany. The following facts can serve as indicators justifying this supposition:

1. The recall of the ambassadors of the two countries by the governments.
2. The cancellation of the two countries' exchange of visits at the ministerial level.
3. The expulsion of a number of diplomats from both countries.
4. The suspension of the policy of critical dialogue between Iran and Germany, and, as a natural consequence, between Iran and the EU as a whole.
5. The effects of these measures and the resulting crisis on relations between Iran and Europe in general.

It is therefore our main hypothesis that the verdict in the Berlin court case, known as the Mykonos Trial, must be seen as the most important factor that disrupted relations between Iran and Germany in the period in question.

The first section of the book essentially paves the way for a broader examination of Iran–West relations, since many issues addressed in Iran–Germany relations can be transformed to the grander picture of Iran–West relations. Issues such as human rights, WMD, the Middle East peace process, and the ongoing debate over Iran's nuclear activities can all be understood within the framework set up in the first section and are addressed in detail in the second section of the book.

Naturally, the most important of the above-mentioned issues is Iran's nuclear dossier, which has transformed into the most pressing foreign policy challenge the Islamic Republic has been faced with since the Islamic revolution of 1979. For the first time, this book examines the extent of this challenge and puts into perspective the different policy approaches examined and implemented by the Iranian decision-making apparatus. While there has been and continues to be a national consensus on the necessity of having and benefiting from a peaceful nuclear energy program, it cannot be denied that Iranian nuclear diplomacy has undergone different phases under the administration of President Khatami and President Ahmadinejad. Having served as a member of the previous negotiating team charged with resolving the crisis has allowed me a good insight into the different tactics used and the overall dynamics of the challenge Iran's nuclear dossier poses for Iran–West relations.

Since the Islamic revolution, Iran's relation with the West has undergone dramatic ups and downs. This book highlights these challenges to present the reader with a wider perspective of the overall factors impacting the relations and concludes with strategic recommendations for enhancing Iran–West understanding and cooperation.

Part I

Case study: Iran–Germany relations

1 History of Iran–Germany relations

Relations between Iran and Germany before the First World War[1]

Iran–Germany relations can draw on a rich premodern heritage. The first encounter between Iranians and Germans took place some 2,000 years ago. At that time, German soldiers who formed part of the Roman army fought against the Parthian warriors who were the defenders of the original Pahlavi state, and on their return to Germany they related their reminiscences. However, until 1427, the German people had little accurate information about Iran. In that year a German traveler, Hans Johann Schiltberg, visited Iran and later published his notes in German. In 1523, the founder of Iran's Safavid dynasty, Shah Ismail I, sent a Hungarian priest who was resident in his court in Tabriz as his representative to the German territories. The aim of the mission was to meet the then ruler of the region, the Holy Roman Emperor Maximilian II, to persuade the Holy Roman Empire to sign a treaty of alliance with Iran against the Ottoman Empire. It was two years before the envoy succeeded in meeting the Emperor and conveying the Shah's message. Emperor Maximilian then sent a delegation to Tabriz with his reply to the Iranian ruler. However, the delegation arrived after Shah Ismail's death, and his successor, Shah Tahmasb Safavi, showed no interest in responding to the Emperor's proposals.

During the sixteenth and seventeenth centuries, European rulers sought to make alliances with the Ottoman Empire's eastern neighbors. It was at this time that the strategic logic of Iranian–German concern at shared foes began to emerge. In this period, envoys were exchanged between Iran's Shah Abbas I and Germany's rulers. However, the first real and official relations between Iran and Germany were inaugurated during the reign of the Safavid Shah Abbas I in Iran, and the reign in Germany of the Holy Roman Emperor Rudolph II. In 1599, a delegation led by Hussein Ali Beig and Sir Anthony Shirley, an English adventurer, was dispatched by the Shah to Prague, where they met the German ruler in 1600. In that year the draft of a treaty uniting Iran and the Holy Roman Empire against the Ottoman Empire was signed. According to the terms of this treaty the two states undertook to remain in contact and consult with each other on issues of mutual concern. Some years later, Rudolph II sent another team of envoys led by Stefan Kakaseh Zalakoemeny to Iran. Before his arrival in Iran, Zalakoemeny died and the leadership of his mission was transferred to his deputy, George Tectander von der Jabel. Shah Abbas received Jabel but no record exists of the result of their negotiations. The Shah sent Jabel back to Europe, accompanied by an Iranian envoy, Mehdi Qoli Beig, whose mission was equally inconclusive. Following this, Shah Abbas sent a further envoy, Sir Robert Shirley, Anthony Shirley's brother, to negotiate once more with Rudolph II. Although Shirley endeavored to forge a bond between Iran and Germany and to unite the two against the Ottomans, and even received the verbal endorsement of the then German ruler, he ultimately failed in his mission. On the succession to the throne of Shah Suleiman, Iran adopted a less belligerent attitude toward the Ottoman Empire, and as a result relations between the rulers of Iran and Germany became less warm.

From that time up to the reign in Iran of Nasseruddin Shah Qajar in the nineteenth century, relations between Iran and Germany were apparently not strong. However, in the 1870s, as Russia and Britain had begun to interfere in Iran's domestic affairs, Nasseruddin Shah decided to boost ties between Iran and other European countries with the aim of diminishing the influence exercised in Iran by Moscow and London. As a consequence, during his second trip to Europe in 1873, the Iranian ruler visited Germany, by this time effectively unified, to negotiate with Emperor Wilhelm I and his chancellor Bismarck, who had founded the German state in 1871. The result was a treaty of friendship between the two countries.[2]

In March 1883, confidential letters were exchanged between Nasseruddin Shah and Bismarck, and in 1885, Mirza Reza-Khan Moyeduldoleh, as the first Iranian plenipotentiary ambassador to Germany, established the first Iranian Embassy in Berlin. Bismarck, who was not unwilling to secure an ally in the Middle East, also sent Ernest von Braunschweig as German plenipotentiary ambassador to Tehran. Meanwhile in January of the same year, and in order to be able to navigate in the Persian Gulf, Nasseruddin Shah purchased from Germany a 600-ton ship named *Persepolis* and a second 250-ton ship named *Shush*, which were crewed by Germans, while orders for several other ships were placed with German shipyards. At the same time, thanks to the efforts of the German ambassador, a German school was established in Tehran and henceforth the Dar ul-Funun (technical center) school began to conduct German language courses. In addition, confidential talks were held between the two sides on collaboration in the construction of a railway line toward northern Iran but because of strong British and Russian opposition to the project the decision was later reversed.

During the reign of Mozaffaruddin Shah Qajar, the German authorities, who were increasingly aware of the significance of the Persian Gulf, decided to investigate the possibility of setting up a shipping line from the Gulf to Hamburg. In 1896, the German company Wenghaus opened a branch office at the southern Iranian port of Bandar Lengeh and began to trade in seashells and pearls. In the following year, Germany established its first Consulate in the southern port of Bushehr. By 1901 Wenghaus, which was receiving financial aid from the German government, was able to open more branches, including one in another southern Iranian port, Bandar Abbas. Finally, in 1904, the first German shipping line between Hamburg and the Persian Gulf was inaugurated. Through such measures Germany succeeded in making, in comparison with other European countries, a strong impression on the Iranian people, and imports from Germany increased considerably. In 1904, a number of German engineers built the first sugar factory in Iran and in the same year Wilhelm von Friedrich founded the Islamic Art Museum in Berlin, which was recognized as the best Islamic museum outside the Islamic world. A few years later, in 1910, a German Consulate was opened in Tabriz.

Relations between Iran and Germany during the First World War

At the beginning of the First World War, the sympathy of the Iranian people was with Germany, and Iran's hope was that with the assistance of the strong German government they would be able to contain the imperialist aspirations of Great Britain and Russia. (The Russian Empire was located north of Iran, and the British Empire, whose Indian possessions included the area at present occupied by Pakistan, was considered an eastern neighbor of Iran.) Nevertheless, with the start of the war in 1914, Iran declared itself neutral, although a number of deputies from the Democratic Party in the Third National Consultative Assembly (the Majlis) believed that, like the Ottoman Empire, Iran should, as an ally of Germany, go to war with Russia and Britain. However, another group of deputies regarded as moderates, whose view prevailed, believed that Iran should opt for neutrality. During the early years of the war, Germany conducted a constant and vigorous campaign within Iran against the influence of Britain and Russia. Germany's aim was to persuade Iran to follow the lead of the Ottoman Empire and become the second independent Islamic state in alliance with Germany, and to join the battle with Britain and Russia. They had two plans for Iranian involvement: first, that German officials and representatives would supply large amounts of money and arms to nomadic tribesmen throughout Iran to encourage them to revolt against the British and the Russians; and second, that Russian and British subjects should be expelled from Iran, after which Iran would be obliged to ally itself formally with Germany.

In March 1915, Prinz Durwitz, the German plenipotentiary ambassador, together with his Austrian counterpart and a number of officers, provided with large amounts of money and gold, arrived in Tehran. They assembled the former German prisoners who had fled from Russian prisons in the embassy grounds and turned the German embassy into a military camp. In May 1915, Wassmus, the German consul in Bushehr, succeeded in converting the Tangestani and Qashqayi tribesmen to the German cause. These tribes dealt a heavy blow to the British and Indian armed forces in Iran's southern Fars Province: They captured the British Consulate in the provincial capital of Shiraz, and brought almost the whole province under their control. Simultaneously with these unprecedented developments, as there was a fear that Tehran could be occupied by the Allies, the German ambassador encouraged the Prime Minister, Mostofi ul-Mamalek, to transfer the royal household and the seat of government to the southern city of Isfahan, which seemed likely to be more secure than the capital. Britain, however, threatened to depose the Shah from his throne if such a move were to be made. Ahmad Shah Qajar therefore rejected the proposal of moving to Isfahan.

Prinz Durwitz himself, however, with his Austrian counterpart, as well as a number of Democratic Party leaders, moved to the central city of Qom. They converted the town into a military bastion and formed an administration under the title of the National Defense Committee. When Russia attacked Qom they retreated to the western province of Kermanshah and set up a provisional government in Kermanshah city, the provincial capital, headed by the provincial Governor Nezamolsaltaneh Mafi. Under this government an army was formed, comprising some 4,000 Mujahids and nomadic warriors, which later, under the supervision of German officers, attacked British and Russian interests. Nezamolsaltaneh, under the tutelage of his German colleagues, also signed a treaty with the German Field Marshal Von der Gultz, who represented Germany's military interests in the Ottoman Empire. In January 1916, Gultz and his headquarters staff, along with a number of Turkish combatants, arrived in Kermanshah and began to train the German and Iranian forces there. However, from the beginning of 1917, the tide of the world war changed to the benefit of the Allies. The Russian General Partuv, following a sharp attack on Hamedan and Kermanshah, succeeded in reoccupying the former positions of his forces to the west of Tehran. The day after the fall of Baghdad to British forces, the Germans evacuated Kermanshah.

Iran–Germany relations up to and during the Second World War[1]

Germany's defeat in the First World War contributed to a period of stagnation in relations between Tehran and Berlin. This began to change with the reign of Reza Shah Pahlavi in 1925. At this time, because Iran's undeveloped industrial sector was compelled to look to the West for help, and the government's efforts to approach the United States had been unsuccessful, Tehran turned its attention once more toward Germany: The relationship with Germany appealed to Iran as Berlin was free of any colonial ambitions in the region. In 1927, Iran contracted the development of its postal service to the German Junkers Airline. In the following year, it brought in German contractors to undertake the construction of the railway to its northern provinces with German collaboration, and in 1930, German experts were appointed to manage the Bank Melli Iran, the National Bank of Iran.

At this time there was also a development that represented a significant change in relations between Iran and Germany. Hitherto the basis for relations between the two countries had been the treaty signed by them in May 1873. Chapter 19 of this treaty embodied the so-called law of capitulation, under which German consular officials were authorized to exercise jurisdiction over German subjects in Iran. In 1929, the Prime Minister, Mostofi ul-Mamalek, notified the German embassy that such privileges were no longer in force. This was accepted by

Germany, and in March 1929, three new protocols of friendship relating to residence permits, trade, and navigation were concluded. This opened a new chapter in the fields of economic, commercial, and scientific cooperation between the two states. In February 1930, a contract was signed in Tehran between the two countries' representatives, which protected patent rights, trademarks, and industrial ownership. In January 1933, Adolf Hitler became chancellor of Germany and attempted to reconcile relations between Iran and Germany with his racial theories, launching extensive propaganda about common Aryan descent between Iranian, Afghan, and German nationals.

In 1934, following a visit to Tehran by the German Economic Minister Hjalmar Schacht, economic and commercial agreements were made between the two countries. In the following five years, German exports to Iran multiplied fivefold and Germany became the biggest importer of Iranian raw materials, ranking first among Iran's foreign trade partners. In 1937, two years before the outbreak of the Second World War, Germany ranked second in foreign trade with Iran. In 1939, it regained the leading position. Britain and the Soviet Union, however, were very wary of the close relationship between Tehran and Berlin: When the Second World War began in September 1939, although Iran had declared itself neutral, Britain nevertheless prevented German goods from reaching Iranian ports by sea. It went so far as to confiscate a ship, which was transporting parts from Hamburg for use in Iranian steel mills. The German government, which still had a nonhostile relationship with the Soviet Union, persuaded the Russians to transport German goods to Iran through Russian territory. But, with the expansion of war and the outbreak of hostilities between Germany and the Soviet Union in June 1991, Britain and the Soviet Union issued an ultimatum to Reza Shah demanding the expulsion of German citizens from Iran. In August 1941, Allied armies occupied Tehran, and the Pahlavi king was deposed. On January 29, 1942, after the replacement of Reza Khan by his son Mohammad Reza Pahlavi, a tripartite pact was signed between Iran, Britain, and the Soviet Union. Following an attempt by the German government to instigate a revolt by Iranian tribesmen against the central government and the Allies, in a repeat of the events of the First World War, Iran officially declared war against Germany on September 9, 1943. With this announcement all relations and commercial agreements between the two countries were suspended.

Iran–Germany relations after the Second World War[1]

The defeat of Nazi Germany led to another hiatus in Iranian–German relations. However, in 1951 Iran and Germany resumed their diplomatic ties with the opening of Iran's Consulate at Stuttgart as well as a representative office at the Allied Supreme Headquarters Council. On November 14, 1954, while validating former agreements, the two countries signed a protocol to permit the opening of manufacturing subsidiaries, and to establish cooperation in the fields of commerce, customs, shipping, and education. In 1954, a former colonel in the German Army was employed as a military attaché by the Iranian government; and in 1955 the diplomatic missions exchanged by the two countries were upgraded to the ambassadorial level. Iranian Consulates General were subsequently opened, first in Hamburg and then in Munich and Berlin. These closer relations led to the following agreements between the two countries:

1. November 4, 1954: Accord on economic and technical collaboration.
2. December 22, 1959: Accord signed in Bonn covering the settlement of out-standing balances relating to former barter accounts.
3. 1961: Agreement between Iran and Germany on air transportation and commerce (cancelled in 1971).
4. 1965: Agreement signed in Tehran to encourage and support mutual capital investment—containing 14 articles and two protocols (which laid the foundation for mutual investment by citizens and commercial companies in the two countries).
5. 1968: Technical agreement signed in Bonn committing the two sides to cooperate with each other in technical issues.
6. 1968: Agreement signed in Bonn prohibiting dual taxation on income and property.

In addition to these accords, other agreements were concluded between the two sides to establish colleges for agricultural studies, as well as training and experimental centers in the field of agriculture, and the development of sugar beets cultivation and sugar production. In 1957, Germany's Chancellor Adenauer and his deputy, Vice-Chancellor Professor Ludwig Erhard, visited Iran. After a visit to Tehran in 1963 by Heinrich Lübke, the then German head of state, relations between the two countries were further consolidated. With the visit of the deposed Shah to Germany in 1965, relations between Tehran and Bonn entered a new stage and, in June 1967, the Shah and his Queen visited the country once more. Between 1967 and 1974, numerous Iranian dignitaries made visits to Germany. In 1967, a friendship society, the Iranian–German Association, was formed. A financial agreement was concluded in 1968, when ties were consolidated between Germany and Iran's National Bank. A further cultural agreement was made in the same year. In addition, a contract establishing the extension of credit for trade was signed between Tehran and Bonn in 1969 and a German company was commissioned to prospect for copper deposits in Iran.

During the period 1970–2, there were more visits in both directions by senior dignitaries of the two countries. In 1973, the first session of a joint Iran–Germany Ministerial Commission was held in Bonn and this led to the signing of a protocol to establish a petroleum refinery in Iran. The broadening of cooperation between Iran and Germany, with the exchange of visits by senior politicians of both sides and the signature of bilateral economic and trade agreements, continued until 1978. In that year, and during the first manifestations of the Islamic revolution in Iran, Walter Scheel, the German head of state, visited Iran and expressed Germany's full support for the Shah's regime. In that same year, in various interviews with the news media, German officials showed concern over developments in Iran and continued to support the Shah's policies. However, a month before the victory of the Islamic revolution in Iran, Iranian demonstrators in Germany attacked the Iranian Embassy in Bonn and called on the Embassy to rename itself "the Embassy of the Islamic Republic of Iran."

Prerevolutionary ties

In contrast with the practice of other countries such as Britain and France, Germany had hitherto imposed limitations on the sale of weapons to Middle Eastern states. However, from the winter of 1973, German arms sales grew and entered a new stage. This development coincided with a slowdown in Germany's economic growth and with a rise in world fuel prices, which led Germany to view an increase in its arms sales as a principal source of export income for the country. In the period ranging from 1973 to 1976, German sales of munitions increased by 145 percent. The value of arms sold in 1971 amounted to $25 million, which increased to $138 million in 1975. During these years, despite tough competition from European rivals, Germany sold 75 percent of its weapons to developing nations, of which 48 percent were placed in the Middle East. Meanwhile, Germany's defense budget increased considerably and its weapons exports became a source of income to cover the country's budget deficit. However, in accordance with the existing law, Germany's arms manufacturers were not permitted to export weapons to belligerent states, or to states that were regarded as unable to control the use to which arms might be put. Nevertheless, under pressure from the arms manufacturers, and after advice from economic experts, a number of amendments were made to the law by the German Parliament, which relaxed the rules and regulations restricting Germany's arms exports.

This development of German arms exports was particularly relevant to Iran. The origin of Iran's military industry (now 50 years old) was German. The first batch of German military hardware delivered to Iran was 100 fighter airplanes, which were purchased from Germany before the Second World War by Reza Khan Pahlavi. After that date, Germany laid the foundations of Iran's own modern arms industry. From 1966, Germany included Iran among the list of recipients of German military aid. In 1969, Bonn agreed to manufacture Leopard tanks for Iran. In 1978, it was announced that the largest German aircraft manufacturer and the Iranian Army would jointly establish a company known as the Iranian Institute for Management and Systems. Alongside these major contracts a quantity of light arms and other equipment were dispatched to Iran, including items of all kinds. In November 1978, for example, some 1,521 pairs of handcuffs were purchased from Germany. However, from 1979, the scale of the orders received by German tank and airplane manufacturers from the North Atlantic Treaty Organization (NATO) and the German Army meant that they were unable to take new orders from Iran. On the other hand, the German shipbuilding industry was in difficulties and welcomed new contracts. The deposed Shah of Iran had ordered a number of military submarines from the German HDW shipbuilding company and had made some advance payments. But with the eruption of the Islamic revolution in Iran, HDW refused to deliver the submarines: This has been a source of friction between the two countries ever since.

From revolution to reunification

From the time of the Islamic revolution in Iran up to German reunification, diplomatic relations between Iran and Germany were maintained at the ambassadorial level. The diplomatic and political stance adopted by the German government toward Iran during the 1980–8 Iran–Iraq war can be considered as somewhat independent of the position of the Western bloc in general. With the onset of attacks on Iran by the Baathist regime in Iraq, the German government declared its neutral stance. Several years after the start of the fighting, however, Germany officially declared that Iraq was in its view the aggressor, though it refused to condemn Iraq's actions. Germany's constitution does not permit the country to interfere in the affairs of belligerent states, and under no circumstances is the German government permitted to sell arms to warring countries.

However, even though Bonn had officially declared its neutral stance in the war, it finally established an economic boycott that covered only Iran. Of course, German official sources insisted that they were ignorant of any sale of arms to Iraq, and Germany refused to publish any official information on this issue. The German Chancellor and Minister of Defense had evidently concluded that, were Iran to be victorious in the war, European interests, including those of Germany, would be in jeopardy. However, claims that Germany had not sold arms to Iraq were not true, while the distorted and conflicting information published about Germany's attitudes during the war did not allow Iran to learn the exact position of that country toward the belligerent parties. However, it should not be forgotten that Germany is fundamentally part of the Western bloc and might have found it difficult to deviate from the general Western view.

The position of the German government toward the Iraqi regime could best be described as optimistic. Bonn repeatedly condemned Baghdad for employing chemical weapons and announced that this practice was contrary to international norms. Meanwhile the German head of state sent a message to his Iranian counterpart in which he said the German government had closely studied the reports published by the United Nations about the use of chemical weapons by Iraq and condemned these actions. Nevertheless, during the course of the war, German companies supplied massive amounts of chemical weapons to Iraq, which were used on a large scale by Baghdad to kill both Iranian citizens and Iraqis opposed to Saddam Hussein's policies. On September 16, 1984, following a missile attack by Iraqi fighters against a small German ship in the Persian Gulf, the German government in Bonn officially condemned Baghdad for the attack and the consequent deaths of two German nationals. According to the German news media, the German Foreign Ministry summoned the Iraqi ambassador concerning this issue and conveyed Germany's protest, informing him that Germany would demand damages for the Iraqi attack and a full explanation of the incident.

There was a marked contrast in Germany's reactions to the use of its missile technology in the cases of Iran and Israel. During the 1980–8 war, Iraq fired more than 1,800 Scud B missiles at Iranian cities. During Iraq's war with Kuwait, Baghdad fired around 25 similar missiles at Israel. After the latter event, the German government sent its foreign minister to Tel Aviv and apologized for the incident, while Germany paid DM 250 million in damages to Israel in compensation for the missile attack. It was rumored in Bonn that this apology and the payment of damages by the German government took place because Bonn had supplied missile technology to Iraq. However, throughout the Iran–Iraq war, the German government never apologized to Iran for Iraqi missile attacks, nor did it pay any damages to Tehran.

After the outbreak of the Iran–Iraq war, there were no official exchanges of visits by Iranian or German political figures until 1984. A number of Iranian dignitaries made unofficial trips to Germany, including Deputy Prime Minister, Mir-Hussein Musavi, during his period as foreign minister (1980–1), and also Ali-Akbar Velayati during his term as foreign minister (1981–7). Velayati repeatedly stopped over in Germany on his way to New York to attend the U.N. General Assembly. Unofficial visits to Germany were also made by Kazempour-Ardabili, the Deputy Foreign Minister for International and Economic Affairs (1983), and Ahmad Azizi, the Chairman of the Majlis Foreign Policy Committee (1984–8). During these trips, the Iranian statesmen discussed matters of mutual interest with German officials. In July 1984, the German Foreign Minister Hans-Dietrich Genscher, heading a senior economic delegation, made an official visit to Tehran and held discussions with Iranian officials. During his two-day visit, he met the then Iranian President, as well as the speaker of the Majlis, the Prime Minister, the Foreign Minister, and the Minister of Economy and Finance. The following year, in February 1985, the political director of the German Foreign Ministry made an unofficial visit to Iran, where he met and held negotiations with the director of economic relations at Iran's foreign ministry.

With the end of the war in August 1988, relations took a turn for the better. On December 30, 1988, the German Foreign Minister Hans-Dietrich Genscher once more visited Tehran, on this occasion at the head of a senior delegation of German business executives. On his arrival in Iran, Genscher made a declaration to the effect that Iraq was the aggressor in its war with Iran, a statement that was reported widely in the international news media. He was the first Western Foreign Minister officially to make such a statement about the Iran–Iraq War. Genscher also signed a cultural agreement with Iran,[3] and conferred with Iran's Foreign Minister Velayati and Deputy Foreign Minister Larijani. During the war, regular secret meetings had been held between Genscher and Larijani, mostly in Germany, about the cease-fire. These meetings played an important role in the framing of U.N. Resolution 598. On this occasion, he also met Ayatollah Khamenei, the then President of Iran,[4] and the speaker of the Parliament, Mr Hashemi-Rafsanjani. The German Foreign Minister discussed with Iranian officials the question of Iranian and German hostages in Lebanon, the convening of a joint Iranian–German economic commission, Germany's participation in the postwar rehabilitation of Iran, and the human rights issue. The two sides expressed their satisfaction over the progress of the talks.[5,6] On January 5, 1989, the German Housing Minister Schneider traveled to Tehran on the invitation of his Iranian counterpart Kazerooni. During that trip, Schneider held discussions with Mr Kazerooni, as well as with Iran's Prime Minister and Foreign Minister, on Germany's participation in the reconstruction of the war-torn country of Iran.[7] During these meetings, the Iranian Prime Minister thanked Germany for its previous declaration that Iraq had been the aggressor.

At the beginning of the 1960s, trade between the two countries achieved a balance and in 1962 the volume of trade between Iran and Germany climbed to DM 670 million. In 1964, Germany was the principal exporter to Iran. During that year, imports from Germany made up 19.22 percent of Iran's total imports. In the same year, Germany was the second biggest importer of Iranian goods and 13.9 percent of Iran's total exports went to German destinations. By 1965, the volume of German exports to Iran far exceeded its imports. In 1967, Germany was the leading exporter to Iran, and bought 15.08 percent of its total imported goods from the Iranian market, ranking as the second largest importer of Iranian goods. By supplying 20.75 percent of Iran's imports, Germany once again became the leading supplier to Iran in 1970, and continued to be the second largest purchaser of Iranian goods other than oil.

In comparison with other countries, it could be said that from 1971 to 1974 Germany's economic relationship with Iran continued to be close. During the first ten months of 1971, more than half of the volume of Iran's exports to Germany was made up of oil (worth DM 490 million), against a total value of exports to Germany of DM 918 million. The volume of trade in 1973 was DM 3.6 billion, which jumped to 6 billion in 1974 and to 8.8 billion in 1975. This figure again rose in 1976 to DM 10.83 billion. In 1976, Germany was the biggest exporter to Iran and the most important importer of Iranian goods. In other words, from 1973 to 1977 approximately one-fifth of Iran's imports came from Germany. Meanwhile, the most important Iranian investment in Germany during these years was made in the German company Friedrich Krupp, when in 1974, Iran purchased 25.3 percent of Krupp's stock.

After the victory of the Islamic revolution, however, Iranian–German trade relations were adversely influenced by the new political climate. In 1981, exports to Iran formed just 9 percent of the total volume of German exports and imports from Iran, including oil, formed only 0.4 percent of Germany's total imports. This situation showed no improvement in 1982. Although Germany was buying more oil than in previous years, the overall volume of trade between the two countries slumped a little. In 1982, the volume of trade between the two countries amounted to DM 5.1 billion. Total German exports to Iran were DM 3.4 billion, which represented a 5.8 percent decline compared with that of 1981, when Germany exported DM 3.61 billion worth of goods to Iran. In that year, Germany imported goods worth DM 1.7 billion, a rise of 13.9 percent compared with the DM 1.5 billion of imports the previous year. Thus the volume of exports from Germany to Iran was twice that of Iran's exports to Germany.

One of the problems that stood in the way of better economic relations between the two countries was the existence of unsettled disputes concerning commercial dealings interrupted by the Islamic revolution or during the 1980–8 war, which had led to conflicting claims by the two countries in international tribunals. A crucial case was that of the Bushehr Nuclear Plant: Germany had undertaken to complete the construction of this project, but during the war, and particularly in 1986, Bonn refused to deliver the parts that had been purchased by Iran, thus failing to comply with its contractual obligations. As a whole, German exports to Iran by the end of 1983 amounted to approximately DM 7.7 billion against the DM 1.5 billion worth of goods imported from Iran. This showed an increase of 127 percent compared with a year earlier, while in that year Iranian exports to Germany declined. The reason for this imbalance was the reduced purchase of Iranian oil by Germany. A glance at the volume of trade in 1984 between the two countries reveals a big gap in the volume of exports and imports to Iran's disadvantage. Of course, it should not be forgotten that the figure of DM 6.5 billion for exports from Germany to Iran in 1984 represents a 16.2 percent decline compared with 1983, and by exporting goods worth DM 1.8 billion to Germany, Iran's exports jumped by 27.6 percent. High officials from the two sides discussed the imbalance in trade between the two countries in the course of numerous visits. The visits of the German Deputy Economic Minister to Iran and the Iranian Deputy Minister of Economy and Finance to Germany in 1984 were undertaken in connection with the trade imbalance. However, no substantial measures were taken to improve the situation.

During 1984, Iran purchased bus and minibus spare parts worth DM 45 million from Germany. In light of the vast profits made by German companies from trading with Iran, it can easily be seen why Germany was so eager to boost its trade with Tehran. A glance at export–import figures in Germany in 1984 shows that Bonn exported goods worth DM 488 billion and imported good worth DM 435 billion, registering a DM 50 billion trade surplus. Of this, DM 4.7 billion was achieved from transactions with Iran. Therefore, although only 1.3 percent of German exports were destined for Iran, actually one-tenth of that country's trade surplus was gained from Iran. In 1984, the total of German exports to and imports from Iran amounted to DM 6.5 billion and DM 1.84 billion, respectively.

Before the victory of the Islamic revolution, no contract for the delivery of crude oil had been concluded between the National Iranian Oil Company (NIOC) and the German oil companies. In these years, crude oil was mostly exported by the consortium or was directly purchased by a number of non-German buyers (under a sales contract from NIOC) and then delivered to the German market. However, by 1978, with the supply of 18 percent of Germany's total oil needs, Iran was already the biggest exporter of oil to Germany. Following the victory of the Islamic revolution, numerous contracts for the delivery of crude oil were signed between the NIOC and various major oil firms such as BP, Shell, Exxon, Mobil, and Texaco, as well as independent German oil refining companies such as Weber and Union Rheinische, which operated in the German oil markets. Thus, with the resumption of the export of crude oil in March 1979 until the cessation of oil exports to the United States on November 14, 1979, large amounts of Iranian crude were purchased by these companies. However, until the end of 1979, Iranian oil continued to be exported to the German market through companies such as BP, Shell, and Union Rheinische, as well as other buyers of Iranian oil. From the beginning of March 1979 until the end of the year, Iran's oil output declined by comparison with that of the year before, falling to 3.5 million barrels per day.

2 Development of bilateral relations, 1990–7

Expansion of political, economic, social and cultural ties after German reunification: The political field

The Iranian Foreign Minister's 1991 trip to Germany

The Iranian Foreign Minister, Dr Ali Akbar Velayati, made his first visit to the newly united Germany in mid-February 1991. During the visit, Germany and Iran expressed their mutual hope that Iraq would comply with the Security Council resolutions on the basis of which the Gulf War could be brought to a conclusion. The German Foreign Minister Hans-Dietrich Genscher, together with his Iranian counterpart, Dr Velayati, announced their concurrence that after the war, as they expressed it, "Iraq's territorial integrity must not be damaged." Foreign Minister Velayati also met the German Chancellor Helmut Kohl. The Chancellor assured Dr Velayati that he would do everything possible to convince the Iraqi President, Saddam Hussein, of the necessity of an immediate and unconditional withdrawal of Iraqi forces from Kuwait.

A German Foreign Ministry statement said that Mr Genscher had agreed that, to create a peaceful and stable system in the Middle East region, Germany in particular, and Europe in general, must play a responsible role. Among the issues on which agreement was reached were the expansion of relations between Iran and Germany, the improvement of economic relations, the opening of a dialogue on renewed cultural exchanges, and the continuation, within a systematic framework, of meetings between the foreign ministers of the two countries and between high-ranking officials. Mr Genscher also reported back to the foreign ministers of the European Union (EU) regarding his discussions in Bonn with Dr Velayati.[1] The author, who was present in his capacity as ambassador at the meeting between the German President Richard von Weizsäcker and Dr Velayati, recollects that President von Weizsäcker said that if within the next few hours there were to be no signs of action on the part of Iraq with respect to withdrawing from Kuwait, the United States would invade, at the risk of the annihilation of the Iraqi people. Immediately after his meeting with the German president, Dr Velayati relayed President von Weizsäcker's warning to President Rafsanjani in an urgent and confidential telegram. The Iranian president at once passed the message on to Baghdad, and subsequently informed Dr Velayati of Baghdad's response, indicating Iraq's readiness to withdraw from Kuwait. Dr Velayati quickly conveyed this message to the Germans, and the news that Iraq was prepared to withdraw unconditionally from Kuwait made headlines in the world media.

Frankfurter Allgemeine reported the incident as follows: "According to a statement from the Iranian Foreign Minister, Dr Velayati, Iraq is prepared to act on Security Council resolution 660 calling for an unconditional withdrawal from Kuwait. In a press conference, Dr Velayati referred to his talks with the Iraqi Foreign Minister Tariq Aziz. Dr Velayati added that what Iraq has put on the table as its preconditions for carrying out the above-mentioned resolution – namely, Israel's withdrawal from occupied regions, and Syria's withdrawal from Lebanon – must not be interpreted as Iraq's conditions for withdrawing from Kuwait." The newspaper report went on to say that Dr Velayati expressed Iran's desire for the preservation of security in the Persian Gulf region, which must be secured by the countries of the region themselves. In response to the question whether or not Iran is prepared to officially recognize Israel, and what role Israel should play, the newspaper reported the Iranian foreign minister's view that, according to Iran's interpretation of the situation, the problem at issue is a matter only for the countries of the Persian Gulf region. The Iranian foreign minister was reported as saying that—as the newspaper puts it—"questions pertaining to Israel must also be clarified."

Frankfurter Allgemeine also reported that after talks with senior officials Dr Velayati said that "all efforts must be focused on a peaceful solution to the war." The newspaper added that as the result of talks held with Tariq Aziz, Dr Velayati believed that Iraq was prepared to withdraw from Kuwait, and that he confirmed his country's position that "any military solution would result in an increase of tension in the region," saying that a political solution must include Iraq's withdrawal from Kuwait, as well as the withdrawal of Allied forces from the region. The report also noted that Germany's Chancellor Helmut Kohl had expressed his appreciation of Iran's efforts for a peaceful solution to the current conflict, which he would like to see continued. The paper also spoke about Irano-German relations in general, saying that "it has become clear that relations between Germany and Iran will intensify from both an economic and a cultural point of view, and Chancellor Kohl has voiced Germany's interest in the expansion and deepening of relations between Germany and Iran." Mr Genscher and Dr Velayati expressed their agreement on the continuation of talks in the near future. The report also recorded the Irano-German agreement on the desirability of the reopening of cultural centers, referring particularly to the reestablishment of a Goethe Institute in Tehran, and that the two sides had agreed on the formation of a joint commission.[2]

Direct talks between political leaders

On March 4, 1991, for the first time since the Islamic revolution, a telephone conversation took place between the political leaders of Germany and Iran. For 30 minutes Chancellor Helmut Kohl and President Hashemi Rafsanjani discussed the crisis between Iraq and Kuwait and bilateral relations between their two countries, while agreeing to remain in direct contact. Telephone contacts between the political leaders of the two countries have subsequently occurred two to three times a year.

Foreign Minister Genscher's visit to Tehran and the provision of German aid for Iraqi refugees in Iran

In May 1991, the German Foreign Minister Hans-Dietrich Genscher visited Tehran at the head of a high-ranking delegation, an event that received wide publicity in Germany. The newspaper *Suddeutsche Zeitung* reported that Germany had not been slow to remind Iran of the support Bonn had offered Tehran in the past, at a time when the United States and most European countries supported the Iraqi leader Saddam Hussein: "German Foreign Minister Hans-Dietrich Genscher has not lost any opportunity to remind us that alone among Western diplomats, during the first Persian Gulf War, he was the only Western diplomat to name Iraq … as the initiator of the war against Iran and as a user of chemical weapons." This circumstance has given Germany credit in its present dealings with Iran, notes *Suddeutsche Zeitung*, which summed up the aims of the current visit: "Mr Genscher's visit has three goals, of which the first is to demonstrate that on the subject of aid to Kurdish refugees it appears that Bonn has outstripped all others. The second goal is the normalization of relations between Iran and Germany, for which substantial preparation is being made. The final goal is to demonstrate that in the Middle East, from a political point of view, Germany is capable of taking action. Chancellor Helmut Kohl and Mr Genscher, who share the same view, have for some time assiduously courted their Iranian interlocutors, Iran's President Hashemi Rafsanjani and Foreign Minister Ali Akbar Velayati. This has led Tehran to having a preference for this country's demonstrated revival of its traditionally good relations with Germany."

Suddeutsche Zeitung continued by remarking that "much has to be done to create the necessary trust," commenting that what it called realistic policies in Iran would be matched by German acquiescence in relegating past disagreements to the sphere of history, especially in the field of human rights and in the liberalization of relations. The paper referred specifically to the closure of the Goethe Institute in Iran under Ayatollah Khomeini's regime, and to the fact that Western hostages were still held captive in Beirut by Shiite fundamentalists under the sway of Iran's influence. The West in general, the paper noted, has called for direct Iranian participation in a future system of peace in the Middle East, but it also commented that there was apprehension on this score in the region. Countries such as Egypt and Syria, as well as the states of the Gulf region, according to

Suddeutsche Zeitung, would prefer theocratic Iran to remain aloof because of their fear of fundamentalism, the same unease that led them during the Iran–Iraq war to support Iraq. Another consideration, said the paper, was that Russia took the view that though Iran's influence should be enhanced, it should also be carefully controlled. Meanwhile, the paper added, though the United States was also toying with the idea of improved relations with Iran, Germany had evidently been cultivating Tehran with assiduity, and Iran had been drawn by economic considerations to contemplate its own rapprochement with Bonn. In June, the paper pointed out, the German Economy Minister, Jürgen Möllemann, was to travel to Iran as head of a joint economic commission, a kind not seen since the time of the Shah.[3]

Suddeutsche Zeitung also reported on May 11, 1991 on Hans-Dietrich Genscher's visit to refugee camps in Iran, noting that he made an appeal for German medical help for the refugees. During his talks in Tehran, Mr Genscher had already negotiated with Iran with the aim of allowing Germany to take a leading role in the provision of international aid to Kurdish refugees on the Iran–Iraq border. The paper reported Mr Genscher's visits to a number of refugee camps, in the town of Bakhtaran and the Jigaran region, where German aid workers were active. The paper noted the scale of German involvement, reporting a visit by Mr Genscher to a German army field hospital where 15 German physicians were due to begin work. About 30 tons of aid was being flown in daily, reported the paper, which was being distributed by German soldiers using 20 helicopters.[4]

German television extensively covered this visit. The German television network's Channel 2 looked at the possibility of renewed relations between Iran and the United States in the light of Mr Genscher's tour: "The German foreign minister discussed possible future relations between Iran and the United States, but Mr Velayati considered such a development impossible." The TV station pointed out that though Germany's expectations were limited, the atmosphere was good: "Due to the granting of a sum of DM 87 million to Kurdish refugees, a friendly atmosphere prevails over this visit. By encouraging Iranian cooperation with Europe, Mr Genscher is attempting to create a secure region in northern Iraq for Kurdish refugees, where Tehran must agree to the dispatch of a United Nations peacekeeping force." The report went on to look at the prospects for future contacts, in light of the crucial importance of the Iranian clergy: "During this visit, Iran's President Hashemi Rafsanjani accepted an invitation to the Federal Republic of Germany, and the German Economy Minister Jürgen Möllemann is to visit Tehran in late June. Thereafter, the economic commission set up by the two countries will consult on whether or not Iran can cope with a higher level of credit."[5]

The German TV station Channel 1 also reported the foreign minister's visit: "Iran is opening its doors to the West, and in this respect, Mr Genscher's visit is being evaluated as the beginning of a new phase in relations.... Chancellor Helmut Kohl is also to visit Iran in the current year." The reporter added that the German army's efforts in aiding the Kurdish refugees were crucial in building good relations between the two countries: This was the first time Iran had allowed the troops of a NATO country to be active on Iranian territory. In addition to political contacts, the TV report commented, large-scale exchanges had begun with Iran in the fields of economics and culture. During his talks with his Iranian counterpart, Mr Genscher had been successful in making major improvements in bilateral relations, so that a joint economic commission was to be formed in late June, and the Goethe Institute was soon to be opened. The report also touched on Iran's role in regional stability: "The two sides are in agreement that Iran plays a significant role in creating peace in the Persian Gulf region. Mr Genscher, speaking to reporters, said: 'Saddam Hussein's policy is still considered a threat to the people of his own country as well as to stability. Thus, we consider it imperative that Security Council resolutions be observed.'" Finally the reporter added that Mr Genscher had agreed in accordance with Iran's wishes that Germany should be responsible for coordinating all European aid activity in support of the Kurds.[6]

Visit to Iran by the Head of the German Federal Parliament

Mr Stärken, the Head of the German Parliament's Foreign Policy Committee, traveled to Tehran on October 23, 1991. During his visit he met his counterpart, Dr Rowhani, Iran's Foreign Minister, as well as the speaker of parliament and other Iranian officials. Representatives of the leading parties in the German parliament accompanied Mr Stärken on this trip. Mr Stärken took the opportunity during his meetings in Iran of raising in confidence the issue of the German hostages in Lebanon and the Hamadi brothers, currently imprisoned in Germany.

Germany's position on Iraq's aggression against Iran and UN resolution 598

On January 15, 1992, the author, acting in his capacity as Iran's ambassador in Bonn, met German Foreign Minister Genscher and requested that Germany extend its explicit support to the report presented to the Security Council on December 11, 1991 by the outgoing UN secretary-general Javier Perez de Cuellar, in which the secretary-general had deemed Iraq to be the aggressor in the Iran–Iraq war and had raised the issue of war reparations to be made by Baghdad. After the meeting, the German Foreign Ministry issued a statement to the effect that in a meeting with Mr Mousavian, the ambassador of Iran, Hans-Dietrich Genscher, had said that "from the onset of the Iran–Iraq war, the German government has considered Iraq to be the aggressor, and Germany has given its immediate support to UN Security Council resolution 598 as soon as the resolution was passed."[7]

At the same meeting the issue of the two remaining German hostages in Lebanon was raised. The author confirmed that the Iranian government would continue its efforts for the unconditional release of the two hostages and expressed the view of the Iranian authorities that the hostages would soon be freed. It is notable that Hans-Dietrich Genscher was the first Western foreign minister to characterize Saddam Hussein as the aggressor in the Iran–Iraq war, and he now became the first Western foreign minister to announce his country's support for the UN secretary-general's report, affirming that Iraq was the aggressor in the war and should make war reparations to Iran.

Visit to Tehran by the German Minister of Justice

The then German Minister of Justice, Klaus Kinkel, arrived in Tehran on January 29, 1992 and met with his counterpart, Mr Shooshtari, as well as the Head of the Judiciary, Ayatollah Yazdi, Foreign Minister Velayati, and President Hashemi Rafsanjani. On this occasion, the first memorandum of understanding in the field of judicial cooperation to be drafted since the Islamic revolution was signed by the two countries. In the course of a three-day visit to Iran, Mr Kinkel discussed foreign policy and familiarized himself with issues relating to Islamic legal principles. In this context, after talks with the Iranian president, as well as with Foreign Minister Velayati, and other political officials of the country, Mr Kinkel said that he was aware that Iran wished to expand its relations with Europe by way of its links with Germany. But Mr Kinkel made the point candidly that, while he was fully aware of the specific demands of Islam, Iran will be judged by the international community according to its observation of human rights. He also pointed out that if Iran were to be subjected to continued censure because of its perceived failure to observe human rights, this would not serve the improvement of relations. However, the German Minister of Justice left no doubt that Germany nevertheless wished to expand its relations with Iran. During his visit, President Rafsanjani assured Mr Kinkel that he would do all he could to free the two German hostages, Thomas Kemptner and Heinrich Strübig, who were by now the last Western hostages in Lebanon.[8]

Establishment of security relations

On May 31, 1992, Bernd Schmidbauer, the Minister of State in the Chancellor's office responsible for the German Federal Intelligence Service, arrived in Tehran at the head of a high-ranking intelligence delegation and delivered a written message to President Rafsanjani from Chancellor Kohl. Mr Schmidbauer also met Foreign Minister Velayati and Information Minister Fallahian. This visit laid the foundations for cooperation between the two countries in the field of intelligence. Mr Schmidbauer's visit was the first to Iran by a senior representative of a Western intelligence service in the period since the Islamic revolution.

The release of the German hostages in Lebanon

On June 8, 1992, the author met the new German Foreign Minister Klaus Kinkel and informed him of the ongoing efforts on Iran's part to free the German hostages. It was determined that two senior German officials would go to Lebanon. Minister of State Bernd Schmidbauer, the responsible official in the Chancellor's office for the German Federal Intelligence Service, and Mr Schlagenweit, the Political Director General of the German Foreign Ministry, went to Beirut on June 13, 1992. The author informed the two officials that the hostages in Lebanon would most probably be freed, with the qualification that conditions in Lebanon were such that nothing could be predicted for certain. The diplomats and officials involved coordinated the efforts of the UN secretary-general, Iran, Syria, Germany, Lebanon, and the leaders of Islamic groups in Lebanon, leading to increasing hope regarding the prospects for the hostages' release. Unfortunately, an Israeli air attack on the headquarters of Hezbollah, with the deaths of some of its leaders, hardened the attitude of those opposed to it.[9]

However the visit of Minister of State Bernd Schmidbauer on June 13, 1992 to Beirut, together with Iran's goodwill and humanitarian aid, secured the release of the German hostages on Wednesday June 17, 1992, after which they traveled to Bonn accompanied by the German delegation. Public opinion in Germany was very positive about this outcome, which received unprecedented coverage in the German media. All the German officials concerned formally thanked Iran. At a press conference at Bonn airport, with the hostages standing at his side, Mr Schmidbauer expressed his appreciation for the key role played by President Hashemi Rafsanjani and Foreign Minister Velayati, and said the efforts of the Iranian ambassador had been a significant factor.

Visit to Germany by the Iranian Foreign Minister

On July 14, 1992, the Iranian Foreign Minister Ali Akbar Velayati arrived in Germany on an official visit at the invitation of the German Foreign Minister Klaus Kinkel to undertake bilateral talks with the German Chancellor Helmut Kohl, as well as with Mr Kinkel himself, and with his colleagues Jürgen Möllemann, the Economy Minister, and Mr Schmidbauer, the Intelligence Chief and Minister of State at the Chancellor's office. The former foreign minister Hans-Dietrich Genscher, as well as Hans Ulrich Klose, Head of the parliamentary group of the German Social Democratic Party (SPD) also met Dr Velayati on his arrival in Bonn.[10] On July 15, 1992, the German ZDF television network quoted Mr Kinkel as saying: "The German foreign ministry has been reminded that, without Iran's help, German hostages would not have been freed from captivity in Lebanon."

Release of Abbas Hamadi from prison in Germany

During the previous year, the author, in his role as Iran's ambassador, had held repeated talks with German officials aimed at obtaining the release of the Hamadi brothers from prison. In a meeting with Mr Stärken, Head of the German Parliament's Foreign Policy Committee, held on July 2, 1992, a promise was made to release one of the brothers, Abbas Hamadi. During Mr Velayati's trip, most German television networks broadcast reports to the effect that Abbas Hamadi would probably soon be released, and that he would renounce his German citizenship. Abbas Hamadi had already served almost half his 13-year sentence at a prison in Saarland, the reports noted, and could be allowed to leave Germany after his release. Radio Germany [Deutschlandfunk] quoted the state minister of justice in Saarland to similar effect: "The Hamadi brothers, who are held in prison in Saarland, are to be provided with better facilities. The minister of justice for the state of Saarland, Mr Arno Walter, announced that these actions were connected with the release of the two German hostages named as Thomas Kemptner and Heinrich Strübig in Lebanon."[11]

Appointment of special representatives for relations between Iran and Germany

In July 1992, in a telephone conversation between the two political leaders, Chancellor Kohl proposed to President Hashemi Rafsanjani the appointment of special representatives whose role would be to promote better Irano-German relations and to facilitate the resolution of difficulties between the two states. Chancellor Kohl nominated Minister of States and Intelligence Chief Bernd Schmidbauer to play this role. President Rafsanjani concurred with the proposal. Chancellor Kohl thus in effect took direct control of relations between Iran and Germany.

Seminar on human rights

On September 23, 1992, a seminar on Human Rights in Islam and Christianity was convened jointly by Iran and Germany in Hamburg, with the participation of 50 prominent Iranian and German scholars. The seminar was attended by Islamic scholars from Iran, including Mohammad Mojtahed Shabestari, Mohaghegh Damad, Mohammad Javad Hojjati Kermani, Dr Abdolkarim Soroush, Dr Mehrpour, Dr Gorgi, Dr Rajai Khorassani, and Dr Mahmoud Kashani. The German Minister of State for Foreign Affairs gave the opening address.

Visit to Germany by the Deputy Head of the Iranian Judiciary

On November 2, 1992, the Deputy Head of the Iranian Judiciary, Dr Bijani, arrived in Bonn at the head of a judicial delegation that included the Iranian Deputy Minister of Justice. In meetings with the German Minister of Justice, the head of the Supreme Constitutional Court, the prosecutor-general, the head of the Foreign Policy Committee, and the state minister at the Chancellor's office, Dr Bijani reviewed cooperation between the two countries and signed a protocol covering legal and judicial cooperation.

Revival of Iran–Germany friendship associations

The year 1991 saw the revival of the Iran–Germany Friendship Association in Bonn, headed by the late Mr Kai-Uwe von Hassel, the former speaker of the parliament of the German Federal Republic. The Iran–Hamburg Friendship Association came officially into existence in March 1993, when Mr Funke, the parliamentary deputy of the minister of justice, became its president. In 1993, Iran–Berlin and Iran–Munich Friendship Associations were also formed and began operation.

Visit to Germany by the Head of the Iranian Parliamentary Foreign Policy Committee

On April 26, 1993, Dr Hassan Rowhani, the Head of the Foreign Policy Committee of the Islamic Consultative Assembly (parliament) visited Germany. Dr Rowhani, who was also Vice Speaker of the Iranian Parliament and a member of Iran's Supreme National Security Council, met senior officials in Bonn, including Chancellor Helmut Kohl. Dr Rowhani also held meetings with Foreign Minister Kinkel and Minister of State Schmidbauer, as well as Mr Stärken, the Head of the Foreign Policy Committee of the German Parliament. Meanwhile, a high-ranking three-member Iranian parliamentary delegation under Dr Rowhani's leadership held talks over a period of four days with prominent members of the German parliament and government regarding the broadening of cooperation between the two countries. It was rumored in Bonn that the agenda would include talks regarding the fate of a German national named Helmut Szimkus, who had been sentenced to death in Iran, having been arrested in 1989 on charges of spying for Iraq. However, according to information provided by the Iranian Judiciary, the current position regarding Mr Szimkus was that his file had been referred to the Supreme Court for review and final judgment.[12]

In a press conference, Dr Rowhani told reporters that Iran was seeking the completion of the Bushehr nuclear power plant, whose construction by one of the subsidiaries of the Siemens company of Munich had begun in 1975, and in which, according to Dr Rowhani, DM 8 billion had thus far been invested. He said Iran was prepared to accept any kind of supervision required by the Vienna-based International Atomic Energy Agency (IAEA). This could include the presence of German inspectors, who could be based permanently at Bushehr, at the expense of the Iranian government. Dr Rowhani pointed out that Iran held no weapons of mass destruction, and asserted that, on the contrary, Tehran would like to cooperate with Bonn to secure the Middle East as a region free from nuclear, biological, and chemical weapons.[13] The construction of the Bushehr plant, which had a projected capacity of 2,400 MW, came to a halt following the Iranian revolution in 1979, when the German government halted the supply of components for the plant's construction.

Dr Rowhani's talks with the German Foreign Minister Klaus Kinkel were reportedly very open and friendly. Mr Kinkel, a member of the Free Democratic Party (FDP) "emphatically" expressed Germany's appreciation of the Iranian government's efforts in relations between the two countries, which were founded, he said, on an appreciation of the benefits that would ensue in future. Mr Kinkel discussed a number of human-rights-related issues with Dr Rowhani, including the Salman Rushdie affair and the Szimkus case. Dr Rowhani assured the German minister that Tehran was prepared to cooperate in the struggle against terrorism. Iran, he said, would not send any commandos abroad to kill Salman Rushdie. However, he pointed out that it could not be forgotten that Salman Rushdie had insulted and deeply hurt the religious sensibilities of Muslims and suggested that Iran found it hard to understand why the West was defending him. With regard to the *fatwa* on Rushdie's life, Rowhani said the declaration of such an edict is in accordance with the right of an Islamic jurisprudent to express freely his ideas. In contrast, Dr Rowhani argued, Salman Rushdie appears to wish to assert the claim of an individual freely to express any ideas, whatever the consequences. Mr Kinkel asked Dr Rowhani to ensure that the sentence of execution on Helmut Szimkus should not be carried out, and Dr Rowhani promised to use his considerable influence in the case after his return to Iran. However, he added that Szimkus had been convicted of spying for Iraq, and that Iran could not simply let such a matter go.[13] In a telephone conversation with Chancellor Kohl on May 13, 1993, President Rafsanjani endorsed Dr Rowhani's talks with the Chancellor.

German parliamentary delegation visits Tehran

Two German parliamentarians Burkhard Hirsch and Gerhard Baum, members of the FDP, traveled to Tehran in mid-May 1993 for talks on human rights. While meeting with parliamentary, political, and judicial officials, the two German parliamentarians also visited Evin Prison, and spoke to prisoners, including the German national Helmut Szimkus.

The trip of the German Deputy Foreign Minister to Tehran

On June 23, 1993, the German Deputy Foreign Minister Dieter Kastrup left for Tehran with a written message from the German Chancellor for the Iranian President. In Iran, he delivered the message to the president and held talks on relations between the two countries. Mr Kastrup also met and spoke with Foreign Minister Velayati and Deputy Foreign Minister Vaezi, as well as with Dr Rowhani, and the Governor of the Central Bank, Mr Nourbakhsh.

High-level dialogue on debt deferment

Iran's foreign debts, amounting to about $30 billion, had become the greatest political and economic problem facing President Hashemi Rafsanjani's government. Because of pressure from the United States, no creditor country was willing to take the first step in rescheduling Iran's liabilities. The intention of the Americans was to put political pressure on President Rafsanjani's government by subjecting it to an international economic boycott, which would have the effect of preventing Iran from embarking on its second reconstruction plan. However, as ambassador to Bonn, the author had already begun extensive talks with Germany on debt rescheduling, and requested Bonn to take the first step in the deferment of Iran's debts. The part of Iran's debt to Germany covered by Hermes credit insurance was approximately DM 4.2 billion, while the debt to Germany not covered by Hermes was about a further DM 4 billion. In a telephone conversation between the political leaders of Iran and Germany on September 22, 1993, when President Rafsanjani discussed the topic with Chancellor Kohl, the German Chancellor offered some encouragement. The author invited the deputy of the

Central Bank of Iran, Mr Kashan, for specialized talks, and in a meeting held on September 27, 1993, he opened discussions with the Director General of the German Economy Ministry, Mr Lorenz Schomerus. We arranged a visit to Tehran on October 1, 1993, for the Deputy Economy Minister Mr von Würtzen. Thus, after Germany took the initiative, the process of dialogue on the deferment of Iran's debts began.

Controversial visit to Germany by the Iranian Minister of Information

On October 6, 1993, at the invitation of his German counterpart, the Iranian Information Minister Ali Fallahian arrived in Bonn to hold important talks on intelligence and security relations between the two countries with officials at the highest level in Germany's intelligence and security organizations. However, the issue of Mr Fallahian's trip to Germany was soon to cause the biggest media uproar in the history of Iran–Germany relations. The visit also led to the most major political controversy over Middle East relations since German reunification between Germany on the one hand, and the United States, the United Kingdom, and Israel, on the other.

The newspaper *Die Welt* reported Mr Fallahian's press conference in Bonn, during which he disclosed that the German Federal Intelligence Service (BND) had agreed with Iran's intelligence service to cooperate in combating international terrorism and the smuggling of narcotic drugs. The paper noted that during two visits to Bonn, Mr Fallahian had held confidential talks with Bernd Schmidbauer, the Minister of State responsible for the German Federal Intelligence Service, and with the Head of the BND, Konrad Pörtzner, as well as with another senior intelligence official, Gerhardt Werthebach, Head of the Office for the Protection of the Constitution. *Die Welt* quoted Mr Fallahian as saying that "terrorism and drug smuggling are a danger to all, and we should jointly struggle against them." The paper said that Iranian embassy sources in Bonn had been unaware of what Mr Fallahian would reveal to the press. Further astonishment was apparently caused to the media by a statement from the head of Iran's intelligence service, accompanying the minister, who disclosed that the Iranian and German intelligence services had already been cooperating for two years, and that any new moves would only build on an existing situation. The Iranian intelligence chief, according to the newspaper report, said that both countries were opposed to terrorism of whatever kind, and wished, as he put it, "jointly to struggle against it." He also emphasized that both Iran and Germany had agreed to refrain from any action, which might prejudice the other country's interests on Iranian or German soil. Meanwhile, the paper reported that Mr Fallahian had spoken out against international drug smugglers, commenting that "they use Iran's soil as a path to transport narcotic drugs from Afghanistan to the West." He added that Iran was determined to struggle against them, but needed Western cooperation.[14]

In another article on Mr Fallahian's visit, *Frankfurter Allgemeine* commented that, as the paper put it, "The German Foreign Ministry has been perplexed by the recent diplomatic behavior of the United States and Britain." The paper noted that anger had already been expressed by the US Secretary of State, Warren Christopher and the British Foreign Secretary, Douglas Hurd, who were concerned at the apparently close relations that have evolved between the intelligence services officials of Germany and Iran. The paper noted that Mr Hurd had summoned the German ambassador in London to remind him of the agreement signed three weeks previously by the European Community in Edinburgh, according to which a greater observance of human rights and the lifting of the *fatwa* threatening the life of British writer Salman Rushdie must be regarded as central issues in any talks with Iran. Mr Christopher, the paper added, was also concerned. But the paper went on to make the point that Western concern about relations between Germany and Iran ran deeper than the intelligence cooperation, which was the immediate cause of the row, intimating that Germany had already repeatedly been accused, as Iran's largest trading partner, and because of the close economic relations it enjoyed with Iran, of assisting Iran to acquire weapons.

Frankfurter Allgemeine quoted a *Wall Street Journal* article to the effect that the Clinton administration was angry with Bonn because of the way Germany's rapprochement with Iran undermines US efforts to isolate what the American source called *the Tehran regime*. The same source also suggested that Iran appeared to have obtained indirect help from the Siemens company, after a meeting between Mr Fallahian and Siemens representatives, to complete the construction of the nuclear plant at Bushehr, broken off after the Islamic revolution. The US Central Intelligence Agency's belief was that Siemens would enable Iran to purchase nuclear fuel rods of German origin through the intermediary of a Slovak company, Skoda Energo. However, according to *Franfurter Allgemeine*, a spokesman for Siemens denied this report.

Frankfurter Allgemeine continued by saying that the Western powers were alarmed at Iran's intention to play a role in the Middle East, and suspected its motives and its plans: "Presently, Washington, London, and especially Tel Aviv have expressed horror at the fact that Tehran will not stand aside in the face of the Middle East peace process. Rather, it will immediately attempt to engage in terrorist activities." However, the paper went on, there was a range of opinion on this issue, and while Warren Christopher, Douglas Hurd, and Israel's Shimon Peres were opposed to any sort of cooperation with Tehran, this contrasted with the German view that relations with Iran could increase the influence of moderate elements in the country. The German Foreign Ministry, the paper said, was well aware that during the Iran–Iraq war all the states of Western Europe, with the exception of Germany, recalled their ambassadors from Tehran, lending their support to Iraq. Today, however, countries such as France and Britain try to play down their past relationship with Iraq, but Tehran had not forgiven their policies and actions. All this was conducive, said the paper, to the German view that the Federal Republic should take advantage of its good standing with Iran, which is a regional power in the Middle East.[15]

Meanwhile, the German government was led to make its own response to the crisis stirred up by the visit of Mr Fallahian, and Minister of State Bernd Schmidbauer issued a statement: "During the past week German officials and

I have held talks with the Iranian Minister of Information and Security. In the face of the general criticism of these talks, emanating from various quarters, including friendly countries, I strongly and emphatically defend myself. The focal points of our talks were humanitarian issues, which in the first place were related to the protection of and the provision of aid for individuals from a friendly country. In so far as our talks have not yet ended, the Government of the Federal Republic is not yet prepared to divulge details regarding the individuals or governments concerned, because in that case the aim of the talks and, along with it, the lives of individuals may be endangered. The Government of the Federal Republic has decided to continue these humanitarian discussions, regardless of the inappropriate criticism which is taking place, in a suitable manner and within the framework of a 'critical dialogue' with Iran. In addition, with respect to certain press reports published abroad, I wish to make it plain that the goal of Germany's policy with respect to Iran is that international efforts be made for a peaceful relationship founded on international laws and norms, and this plan will be pursued, particularly with respect to the Middle East. The accusation which has been made by British officials that these talks are in contradiction with the agreement reached at the European Council in Edinburgh on December 12, 1992 is totally false. According to that agreement, dialogue with Iran has not been prohibited; rather, on the contrary, it has been emphasized that a dialogue with the Iranian government must be held."[16]

Visit to Tehran by the Head of the Human Rights Commission of the German Federal Parliament

On Friday October 8, 1993, Mr Vogel, the Head of the Human Rights Commission of the Parliament of Germany, began a visit to Tehran, holding talks on parliamentary cooperation between the two countries in the area of human rights with his Iranian counterpart, Dr Rajai Khorassani, and other Iranian parliamentary and political officials. A German member of the European parliament, Mr Schnitzel, also arrived in Tehran on the same day.

Visit by the Head of the Iran–Germany Parliamentary Friendship Group to Germany

Dr Mohammad Javad Larijani, the Iranian Head of the Iran–Germany Parliamentary Friendship Group, arrived in Bonn on Monday, January 10, 1994, for the first joint meeting of the parliamentary groups of the two countries. He met the Speaker of the Federal parliament, Mr Süssmuth, the German Head of the Iran–Germany Parliamentary Friendship Group, Mr Matschi, Deputy Foreign Minister, Mr Kastrup, the former Foreign Minister, Hans-Dietrich Genscher, and the Minister of State in the Chancellor's office, Bernd Schmidbauer. This visit saw a further move toward the resolution of the Szimkus affair. *Frankfurter Allgemeine* reported that "the Iranian Government has informed the Chancellor's office that it will not carry out the sentence of death on 59-year-old Helmut Szimkus. Information to this effect had been conveyed to Mr Schmidbauer last year."[17] Mr Matschi, a deputy for the German SPD, who also met Dr Larijani, confirmed this information. In his meeting with Schmidbauer, Dr Larijani alluded to the probability that Helmut Szimkus would receive a pardon from Ayatollah Khamenei, the Iranian spiritual leader, and added that this could take place within the next three to four months.

Frankfurter Allgemeine went on to report allegations in the American press that during the meeting between the Iranian Information Minister Mr Fallahian and the German Minister of State Bernd Schmidbauer, which had taken place in October the previous year, a number of Israeli officials were seated in nearby rooms to speak indirectly with the Iranian minister about the release of Israeli prisoners held by Shiites in Lebanon. According to the paper, Dr Larijani said, "The Israelis were not only a few rooms apart but rather, technologically, were only a few centimetres apart, eavesdropping on the talks – not in person but by means of wiretapping devices."[17] Dr Larijani expressed his wish that, despite setbacks, Iran–Germany relations would resume their positive trend, and said that a way of resolving the issue of the delay in the repayment of Iran's current debts would be found, suggesting that the fault lay in a weakness in the management of the Iranian banking system. The paper also reported Dr Larijani as expressing his regret over Germany's reluctance to complete the construction of the Bushehr nuclear power plant. With regard to the religious edict, or *fatwa*, calling for the death of Salman Rushdie, he warned that this issue should not be allowed to become political. The paper also noted that the SPD deputy Mr Matschi claimed that the *fatwa* could be regarded as having lapsed, saying that "Ayatollah Khomeini has written in his own book on Islamic government that the *fatwa* of a *marja'a* (a source of emulation) who has passed away is no longer valid. Therefore, this *fatwa* can be revoked by Iran."

Expansion of relations with various individual German states

As Iranian ambassador, the author regularly visited and spoke with the prime ministers and parliamentary speakers of various German states within the Federal Republic. These talks were an effective means toward the improvement of relations with individual German states. Reporting the visit paid by the author to Gerhard Schröder, the then prime minister of Niedersachsen, the *Jomhuri Islami* daily wrote as follows: "Mr Hossein Mousavian, the ambassador of the Islamic Republic of Iran in Germany, met and talked with Mr Gerhard Schröder, the prime minister of the German state of Niedersachsen, in Hanover yesterday. Cooperation between Iran, Germany, and the state of Niedersachsen were the focal point of the talks." The paper went on to say that Mr Schröder, who is considered to be the second most influential figure in the SPD, welcomed the expansion of relations between Iran and Germany, especially regarding his own state, and announced his readiness for further improvement. Mr Schröder was also reported to have laid stress on Germany's high estimation of the regional importance of Iran. The paper then quoted the author's statement as follows: "Mr Mousavian said that the Islamic Republic of Iran was prepared to set aside an appropriate share for Germany in its second Five-Year Reconstruction and Development Plan."

According to the paper, Mr Mousavian added that in his view the United States was the main obstacle in the attainment of a collective and comprehensive political, economic, cultural, defensive, and security cooperation between the countries of the Persian Gulf region for the preservation of regional peace and stability, and also made the point that, as he put it, "Iran does not have a policy of competition with Turkey; rather it is prepared for cooperation with that country in Central Asia. The Islamic Republic of Iran will also take advantage of all opportunities for the expansion of relations between member states of the ECO (Economic Cooperation Organization) and the European Community."[18]

Visit to Germany by the Mayor of Tehran

On April 26, 1994, at the invitation of Gerhard Schröder, Prime Minister of the state of Niedersachsen, the Mayor of Tehran, Mr Gholamhussein Karbaschi, arrived in Germany on an official three-day visit, which began with a meeting with the Mayor of Frankfurt, Mr Andreas von Schüler. The Mayor of Tehran explained to his German counterpart the challenges facing the city of Tehran during the transformation it was currently undergoing, such as the issues of air pollution, traffic, and the inadequacy of municipal transportation, as well as problems in the preservation of the environment and difficulties arising from the unmethodical expansion of the city and from industrial development. The two mayors agreed to make their knowledge and experience available to each other and to promote cooperation between the cities of Tehran and Frankfurt by means of the exchange of experts in municipal affairs. In the city of Mainz the Mayor of Tehran met Reiner Brüderle, the Deputy Prime Minister of the state of Rheinlandpfalz. At these talks, attended by a number of local industrialists, economic cooperation with Tehran in the field of municipal transportation was discussed and an agreement in principle was reached on ways to assist Tehran in the reconstruction and renovation of its bus service. The issues of garbage recycling and the reduction of environmental pollution also came under discussion. Mr Brüderle endorsed a proposal for the transfer of technology and training by the state of Rheinlandpfalz to the municipality of Tehran. Mr Karbaschi's visit to Germany was the first step in the direction of cooperation at the municipal level between Iran and Germany.[19]

Visit to Germany by the Head of the Human Rights Commission of the Islamic Consultative Assembly (the Iranian parliament)

On Monday, May 16, 1994, in reciprocation of the visit to Tehran by his German counterpart, Mr Vogel, and in response to Mr Vogel's official invitation, Dr Rajai Khorassani arrived in Bonn. He met and held talks with some 20 political and parliamentary figures, including the speaker of the Federal parliament, the head of the parliamentary Foreign Policy Committee, and the leaders of the major parties represented in the German parliament, as well as the deputy minister of justice, the deputy minister of the interior, and the deputy foreign minister. This visit was a notable development toward mutual understanding between the two countries over the difficulties on human rights issues between Iran and Europe, as well as a contribution toward wider cooperation between the two countries.

Visit by Minister of State Bernd Schmidbauer to Tehran (representing Chancellor Kohl)

On Friday, July 1, 1994, by order of Ayatollah Khamenei, the leader of the Islamic revolution of Iran, the German national Helmut Szimkus was released. He left for Germany by a Lufthansa flight the same evening. The German Minister of State in the Chancellor's office arrived in Tehran on July 2, to express Germany's gratitude to Ayatollah Khamenei and to President Rafsanjani. Mr Schmidbauer, acting in his capacity as Chancellor Kohl's special representative for Iran–Germany relations, held discussions with President Rafsanjani, Dr Rowhani, in his capacity as a member of the Supreme National Security Council, Mr Fallahian, the Minister of Information, Mr Velayati, the Foreign Minister, and Mr Vaezi, the Deputy Foreign Minister. He communicated the deepest gratitude of the German government to Iranian officials and also discussed other bilateral and regional issues.

Iran–Germany Human Rights Conference

In April 1995, the Fourth Conference on Human Rights in Iran and Germany convened in Tehran, with the participation of Iranian and German scholars. On this occasion, the conference was on a larger scale and covered a broader range of issues than previously. The Head of the Institute for Oriental Studies in Hamburg, Professor Udo Steinbach, wrote a lengthy report in the March 28, 1995 issue of the *Frankfurter Allgemeine*, which drew attention to the significance and comprehensiveness of this conference.

Prohibition of the entry into Germany of Maryam Rajavi, Elected President of the Mujahedin Khalq Organization

In 1995, in the largest auditorium in Germany, in Dortmund, the dissident Iranian Mujahedin Khalq Organization (MKO) planned to organize the largest gathering to date of its members and supporters outside the country. The organization had spent several million marks on propaganda and payment of the travel expenses of its members and supporters. Posters for the gathering had appeared throughout Germany. Over a period of about two weeks, unreported by the press, the author had held in his capacity as Iranian ambassador, a number of meetings with German political, security, and parliamentary officials, with the effect that just one day before the planned opening of this gathering, on June 13, 1995, the German government issued an instruction that Maryam Rajavi was prohibited from entering Germany, which carried the implication that the MKO would henceforth be regarded by Germany as a terrorist group. In its official announcement of the ban the German government set out three reasons, as follows:

1. "Maryam Rajavi has declared herself to be the President of the Islamic Republic of Iran, a title which she claims illegitimately.
2. Maryam Rajavi has acted as the deputy commander of the National Liberation Army, the armed wing of the Mujahedin Khalq, and even today she believes in changing the system in Iran by violence. The Mujahedin Khalq have engaged in a series of violent attacks against Iranian associations outside the country.
3. The German Government has consistently refused to accept violence as a tool for political change. Therefore, the presence of Maryam Rajavi in the city of Dortmund, as well as any political activities which may take place within the framework of the Iranian National Council of Resistance, are in conflict with the Federal Republic of Germany's foreign policy interests and its obligations with regard to international human rights."

The German government's statement continued: "The Federal Republic of Germany has an overriding duty to struggle against terrorism, by whomsoever it may be perpetrated. Therefore, if we give official sanction to groups in Germany which support the violent overthrow of another country's government, great damage would be inflicted on Germany's credibility."[20]

The imposition of this ban was a considerable diplomatic success for Iran, as it was the first official expression of opposition on the part of a powerful Western country against the MKO and the National Council of Resistance of Iran, and was widely covered in the German and world media.

Visit to Tehran by the vice Speaker of the German Parliament

At the invitation of Dr Rowhani, the Vice Speaker of the Federal Parliament, Hans Klein, went to Tehran in mid-October 1995, where he met the President, the Speaker, and Vice Speaker of the Iranian Parliament, the Head of the Parliamentary Friendship Group, the Economics and Finance Ministers, and the Head of the Parliamentary Economic Committee. Mr Klein described as very constructive his talks with Iranian officials, which related to regional changes and bilateral relations. This was a visit that opened the way for further expansion of Iran–Germany relations.[21]

Visit to Tehran by the Head of the German–Central Asian/Caucasus Parliamentary Group

On January 14, 1995, the deputy president of the parliamentary assembly of the Organization for Security and Cooperation in Europe (OSCE) Willy Wiemer, who was also Head of the Joint Parliamentary Group for Germany, Central Asia, and the Caucasus, made a visit to Tehran. He held talks concerning the crisis in

Afghanistan and other issues regarding Central Asia and the Caucasus with Dr Rowhani, in his capacity as Vice Speaker of the Iranian Parliament, and with the Iranian Deputy Foreign Ministers Mr Vaezi and Mr Boroujerdi, and also discussed cooperation between Iran and Germany. Mr Wiemer said the role of Iran in relation to the Central Asian countries was crucial, because of its geographic situation in the region, and suggested that tripartite cooperation by Germany, Iran, and the states of Central Asia would be beneficial and practicable.[22]

Visits to Germany by the Iranian Deputy Foreign Minister

On February 21, 1996, the Deputy Foreign Minister of Iran, Mr Vaezi, arrived in Bonn for an official visit. The Islamic Republic News Agency (IRNA) reported on the trip as follows: "Mahmoud Vaezi, deputy minister for European and American Affairs of the Iranian Foreign Ministry, met high-ranking political officials in Germany and held talks on important bilateral, regional and international issues. Mr Vaezi met Helmut Schäfer, minister of state for foreign affairs, Dr Hermann Otto Solms, Head of the parliamentary group of the FDP, and Christof Zöpel, a member of the board of Germany's SPD. In his meeting with Helmut Schäfer, Mr Vaezi said, 'Iran is ready to cooperate with the EU in freeing the region from nuclear weapons and weapons of mass destruction, as well as in the struggle against terrorism and the traffic in narcotic drugs'."[23] Mr Vaezi made another trip to Germany on April 21, 1996, when he met German officials such as Hans-Dietrich Genscher.[24] At his meeting with Mr Vaezi, deputy Günter Verheugen, in charge of foreign policy for the SPD, said, "Iran is an important country to us; one with which we have traditional, cultural, political and economic relations. Iran plays a role in the region and in the world."[25]

Visit to Tehran by Chancellor Kohl's special envoy

On May 11, 1996, Willy Wiemer once more arrived in Tehran, on this occasion acting as a special envoy for Chancellor Kohl, from whom he delivered a confidential verbal message to President Rafsanjani. In a further meeting with the Speaker of Parliament, Nateq Nouri, together with Vice Speaker, Dr Rowhani, Dr Larijani, the Deputy Chairman of the Parliament's Foreign Policy Committee, Mr Bouroujerdi, and Mr Maleki, he discussed bilateral relations and parliamentary cooperation as well as developments in Central Asia and the Caucasus.

Visit by Minister of State Bernd Schmidbauer to Tehran

On May 26, 1996, Bernd Schmidbauer, the Minister of State in the Chancellor's office for the German Federal Intelligence Service, held talks in Tehran on bilateral and regional issues with President Rafsanjani, Foreign Minister Velayati, and Deputy Foreign Minister Vaezi, together with the Vice Speaker of Parliament, Dr Rowhani. The two sides reached an agreement on cooperation between Iran and Germany with the aim of obtaining the return to Israel of the bodies of two deceased Israeli captives held by Hezbollah in exchange for the Hezbollah prisoners and the bodies of Lebanese martyrs in Israel's possession, and for the return of Lebanese prisoners held by the forces of Antoine Lahad in exchange for members of Lahad's militia held by Hezbollah, together with a framework for Iran's assistance in this process.

These negotiations were the subject of an article in *Focus* magazine, which described as "strange and extraordinary" the Middle East missions carried out by Bernd Schmidbauer. The German authorities, says *Focus*, were attempting to play down the importance of Mr Schmidbauer's diplomatic endeavors as of little significance. However, commented the magazine, Mr Schmidbauer's so-called *humanitarian diplomacy* was far from uninteresting, in view of Germany's involvement with what it called the "triangular connection" of Israel, Hezbollah, and Tehran. Meanwhile, the magazine said, Germany was attempting to limit the damage to relations with its Western allies, which may have resulted from its connections with Iran. As *Focus* puts it: "Officials in Bonn are following a 'half-open' style of publishing information so as to reduce the impact of concerted attacks by the United States, Britain and Israel against Germany's diplomacy with Iran."[26]

Following the agreement made by Mr Schmidbauer, the author was delegated to undertake a diplomatic mission to Damascus on behalf of President Rafsanjani, where he met Seyed Hassan Nasrollah, the leader of Hezbollah, and Mr Akhtari, the Iranian ambassador in Damascus, to make the preliminary arrangements for the exchange of prisoners and bodies. On Friday, July 20, 1996, Mr Schmidbauer went to Beirut, and on Sunday the exchange took place. Sixteen of Antoine Lahad's men were exchanged for 20 Hezbollah fighters and 25 Lebanese soldiers, and 2 Israeli corpses were exchanged for 120 corpses of Lebanese martyrs. In its live coverage on July 22, 1996, the CNN network called this exchange the biggest human exchange in the past 14 years. The operation was covered as the lead story of the day by most of the international radio and television networks. The two Israeli corpses were carried to Israel by a German military aircraft, the first German military plane to land on Israeli soil since the Second World War. Both Israeli and German officials admitted that, while the initiative that had led to the exchange had been taken by Chancellor Kohl, without Iran's help it would not have been possible. Cooperation between Iran and Germany thus became for the first time a significant factor in the Middle East. In an interview, the spokesman for the Iranian Foreign Ministry conveyed his felicitations to the families of the martyrs and the released captives, as well as the leaders of the Islamic Resistance in Lebanon, on the successful completion of the exchange, and thanked Germany for its role as mediator.[27]

Visit to Tehran by German Chancellor Kohl's envoy

On August 13, 1996, in his capacity as the German Chancellor's envoy, Willy Wiemer yet again arrived in Tehran. On this occasion he conveyed to President Hashemi Rafsanjani Chancellor Kohl's gratitude for Iran's exercise of humanitarian goodwill in the achievement of the largest human exchange in the Middle East in the past 14 years, and informed him of the Chancellor's wish to see the continuation of cooperation between Iran and Germany in the Middle East.

Foreign ministers' meeting in New York

On September 26, 1996, the Iranian Foreign Minister Ali Akbar Velayati and Germany's Foreign Minister Klaus Kinkel met in New York, where they discussed bilateral and multilateral issues of mutual concern to Iran and Germany. Noting the improved relations between the two countries, the two sides expressed their political will for the resolution of the remaining problems in the relations between Bonn and Tehran. It was arranged for the German Deputy Foreign Minister to travel to Iran to look more closely at the issues involved and to attempt to resolve the outstanding problems of concern to Iran and Germany, as well as to plan the mutual exchange of further delegations between the two countries.[28]

In the wake of this agreement, the German Deputy Foreign Minister Peter Hartmann arrived in Tehran on November 4, 1996. The German Foreign Ministry made the following official statement about the visit: "On 4 and 5 November 1996, Dr Peter Hartmann, the German deputy foreign minister, and Mr Mahmoud Vaezi, the deputy foreign minister of Iran, held political talks. Dr Klaus Kinkel, German foreign minister, and Dr Ali Akbar Velayati, Iranian foreign minister, had agreed on the agenda at their previous meeting, which took place during the 51st session of the United Nations General Assembly in New York. Mr Hartmann also held talks with the vice speaker of the Iranian Parliament and the head of the Parliamentary Foreign Policy Committee, Dr Hassan Rowhani, as well as with Dr Ali Akbar Velayati, the Iranian foreign minister, and Dr Mohammad Javad Larijani, deputy head of the Parliament's Foreign Policy Committee. The subject matter of the talks was the examination and regulation of bilateral relations, in the course of which outstanding difficulties and current issues came under discussion. In the field of legal issues, the discussions concerned the state of human rights in Iran and the desirability of holding a further seminar on human rights. Within the framework of a wider discussion of regional international problems, Dr Hartmann emphasized the importance of the Middle East peace process for the stability and development of the region as well as the role played by Iran. With respect to the legal process concerning the so-called 'Mykonos affair', on which the Iranian side placed some emphasis, Mr Hartmann stressed the independence of the German judicial system. Dr Hartmann and Mr Vaezi agreed on the continuation of similar talks in the future."[29]

The indictment of Iranian officials by the German Prosecutor-General

On Tuesday, November 12, 1996, an event occurred, which was momentous in the history of Iran–Germany relations and which threatened the process of steady improvement that had been under way. At the close, after three years of legal proceedings, of the so-called Mykonos trial, which related to the murders of Kurdish–Iranian dissidents at the Mykonos restaurant in Berlin in September 1992, the German Prosecutor-General in his closing speech accused the most senior Iranian officials of approving the plan for the murders. The prosecutor named the Supreme Leader of the Revolution, Ayatollah Khamenei; the President of the Republic, President Rafsanjani; and the Iranian Ministers of Foreign Affairs and Information, Dr Velayati and Mr Fallahian; and described the Berlin murders as "state terrorism." The result was that an upheaval occurred in relations between the two countries as well as in the media of the two countries and the world, a subject that will later be treated separately.

Chancellor Kohl's letter to President Rafsanjani

As a result of the intense crisis that occurred after the Prosecutor-General's closing address, the German Chancellor Helmut Kohl wrote a letter to Iran's President Rafsanjani, asking the President to use his influence to prevent an already difficult situation from becoming more acute. In his letter, Chancellor Kohl stressed the fruitful nature of the cooperation that existed between the two countries and requested President Rafsanjani to take measures to preserve the good state of Irano-German relations. Prior to the dispatch of the letter, the German Cabinet had met to look at the issues and had decided to strive to maintain good relations between the two countries, preventing if possible the Mykonos affair from overshadowing Germany's links with Iran.[30] Chancellor Kohl also emphasized that the German government and the judiciary had no intention of insulting the honor of the Iranian nation and leadership. In his Friday prayer address on November 23, 1996, President Hashemi Rafsanjani spoke about the crisis and drew a distinction between the responsibility of the German government and the actions of the judicial branch of the state, endorsing the view that good relations should be maintained.[31]

Cultural and scientific exchanges

Visit to Germany by Iran's Vice President Mr Mirsalim

The Iranian Vice President for Research and Technology, Mr Mirsalim, began a visit to Germany on January 23, 1991, during which he held talks with the German Minister of Research and Technology regarding bilateral cooperation in research and technology.

Iranian Art and Culture Festival

On September 12, 1991, the first major festival of Iranian Art and Culture since the Islamic revolution, was inaugurated in the German city of Düsseldorf, with opening speeches by the Iranian Minister of Culture and Islamic Guidance Mohammad

Khatami and the German Minister of Education. This was the largest festival of Iranian Art and Culture ever held outside the country, either before or after the revolution. For the space of an entire month, the principal art galleries of Düsseldorf were devoted to this major endeavor: One mounted an exhibition of Iranian paintings while another displayed fine Persian carpets. Around 500 people visited the Iranian art exhibitions and programs each day, a figure that rose to almost 3,000 on holidays. Meanwhile, concerts of Iranian music, in the Persian, Kurdish, and Baluchi styles, were held in Dusseldorf's auditoria. The Iranian Ministry of Culture and Islamic Guidance paid the expenses incurred by the festival in Iranian rials, while the hard currency expenses, which amounted to about DM 3 million, were met by the German Thyssen company.[32]

The festival was covered extensively both by the Iranian and German media. Some 600 policemen were responsible for maintaining 24-hour security at the festival's various centers in Düsseldorf. During this trip, Mr Khatami met with German Foreign Minister Hans-Dietrich Genscher, who proposed the expansion of cultural relations between Iran and Germany. During the final ceremonies of the festival, Mr Genscher expressed his profound regret at the occurrence of a demonstration against Mr Khatami by the terrorist group Mujahedin Khalq after the festival's inaugural ceremonies, when demonstrators threw eggs and chanted insulting slogans, as Mr Khatami and his entourage were leaving the hall.

Training camp for the Iranian National Football Team

On April 17, 1992, the author welcomed the Iranian National Football Team to Frankfurt for its first training session outside Iran, which was undertaken as part of the team's preparations for the preliminary sessions of the World Cup. Dr Ghafourifard, the President of Iran's Physical Education Organization, and Mr Noamouz, President of the Football Federation, had asked the Iranian embassy in Germany to arrange training for the team. This was a matter which the author was in his capacity as ambassador eager to pursue, and was able to achieve the satisfactory result that the Iranian National Football Team, consisting of about 40 members, spent three weeks in Germany's best training camp, used by the world's most prominent teams. The Iranian team played matches against German and Swiss teams, and benefited from a world-class sports clinic and physical therapy, while receiving training and advice from prominent German football experts. The lesson was learned that Iran should make an appropriate investment in the development of sports. The Iranian football team was once the best in Asia, and those who are concerned with sport should take steps to restore Iran's former level of performance.

The cost of the training camp was about DM 300,000, which was met by the German Siemens company. No budget was available in Iran for such expenses, and in the difficult circumstances of economic reconstruction in Iran, the embassy was anxious not to impose any additional expenses on the Iranian authorities. There were many such instances of German generosity during the author's term of office as ambassador. For example, the Siemens company also provided funds of

DM 4 million for equipment for the Centre for Technical and Professional Education in Fars and Isfahan provinces. The Mannesmann company provided DM 300,000 for education and training in Bonn, while Volkswagen gave DM 100,000 to purchase the equipment for a center for education and technical training for motor mechanics. Over a period of three years, we received DM 6 million from various German companies, including Daimler-Benz, Siemens, Krupp, Mannesmann, Busch, and Szell.[33] *Salam* daily published critical articles on this issue, which caused a row in the domestic press in Iran, but most of the media, especially the sports media, supported these actions, and at a press conference the Iranian President also gave his support.

Visit to Germany by the Head of Seda-va-Seema (Iranian radio and TV)

On September 8, 1993, Mr Mohammad Hashemi Rafsanjani, the Head of the Iranian radio and TV organization *Seda-va-Seema* and the brother of President Rafsanjani, began a visit to Germany. He held talks on bilateral relations with Mr Schäfer, Minister of State for Foreign Affairs, Mr Stärken, Head of the Parliamentary Foreign Policy Committee, Mr Vogel, the German Government Spokesman, and Bernd Schmidbauer, the Minister of State in the Chancellor's office responsible for the German Federal Intelligence Service. In a meeting with Chancellor Kohl on September 10, 1993, Mr Mohammed Hashemi Rafsanjani delivered an important oral message from President Rafsanjani to Chancellor Kohl. In the course of this diplomatic visit, the Head of *Seda-va-Seema* also signed a memorandum of understanding for cooperation between Iran's *Seda-va-Seema* and the German television network ZDF.

Persian language studies and academic relations between Iran and Germany

A two-day seminar directed at the promotion of Persian language studies and the enhancement of academic relations between Iran and Germany in other fields was held in Bonn on November 27 and 28, 1993, with the attendance of a substantial number of Iranian scholars who were teaching at German universities. Dr She'rdoost, the secretary of the Council for the Expansion of the Persian Language, under the supervision of the Ministry of Islamic Guidance and Mr Mohammad Javad Kamalian, supervisor of the group for the Expansion of the Persian language in Iran, also participated. The seminar culminated in the formation of a standing association and the election of an administrative board, after an extensive discussion of appropriate strategies for the promotion of scholarly cooperation between Iranian and German universities and the preservation and establishment of chairs in the Persian language and in Iranology at German universities.

The opening speaker was Dr Shams-Anvari, professor of the Persian language at Cologne University. With regard to Iranology and the activities of German professors in this field, he took a critical view, suggesting that some German scholars took an exploitative attitude toward their studies, and that their intention was, as he put it, "profit-oriented." Professor Shams-Anvari emphasized that Iranians must reevaluate their own heritage and take steps to preserve it, while also adopting a new approach. The difficulties inherent in scholarly cooperation between Iranian and German universities also came under examination. The Professor of Iranology at Hamburg University, Dr Khaleghi-Motlagh, said two separate councils should be formed, one for academic study in general and the other for the study of the Persian language. Members of these councils should visit Iran to familiarize themselves with the situation in the country, and to devise ways in which cooperation with Germany could be improved.

Professor Mahmoud Torkban, the professor of mining studies at the University of Hamburg, drew attention to the necessity of cooperation in science and scientific research between Iranian and German universities. He noted that Iran is not only an oil-rich country but also, in contrast to the other oil-rich countries in the Persian Gulf region, the possessor of many other mineral resources, which should be exploited. He pointed out the value of enhanced cooperation between Iran and Germany in scientific research, for example in mining and in earth sciences, and suggested that Iranian doctoral students studying in Germany in the field of earth sciences should complete their dissertations on a subject relevant to Iranian interests, so that Iranian society would derive direct benefit from their work. Another speaker at the seminar was Professor Khakzar, professor of electronics at Stuttgart University, who emphasized the value of cooperation between Iranian and German universities in technological fields. Professor Khakzar said that instead of increasing the number of students, Iran should raise the quality of its universities. Closer links should also be established between industry and university departments in Iran.

In the author's own address at the seminar, delivered in his capacity as ambassador, ways in which Iran could derive benefit from German scholarship were discussed and he pointed out that in the previous two years much had been achieved from the exchange of views between Iranian and German delegations. An important goal was the establishment of professional colleges and educational centers, as well as cooperation between academic bodies and industry. With the support of the Iranian government, measures had been taken to set up professional training establishments in the Iranian provinces, in instances where German industrial companies were prepared to assume responsibility for the provision and installation of the necessary equipment and facilities.

The author emphasized that Iran would provide facilities and amenities for German scholars who wish to carry out scholarly research in Iran or to undertake missions in connection with academic cooperation. It was pointed out that the establishment of direct relations between German and Iranian universities was a key issue, and while it was to be borne in mind that German universities were independent entities, they were nevertheless sympathetic to the efforts toward the expansion of Irano-German academic cooperation in the academic field.

Following a vote, the administrative board of the Association for Scholarly and University Cooperation between Iran and Germany was formed with seven members. The seminar was a unique gathering of scholars concerned with Persian language and literature and of other Iranian experts based in Germany.[34]

Visit to Tehran by the Head of the Cultural Committee of the German Federal Parliament

The Head of the Cultural Subcommittee of the Federal Republic's Parliament, Mr Kohl, visited Tehran in early July 1994, where he held satisfactory talks with cultural and political officials of the Iranian parliament on issues concerned with the advancement of relations between the two countries in the cultural, scientific, and educational fields.

Visit to Germany by the President of Seda-va-Seema (Iranian radio and TV)

On September 25, 1994, at the head of a high-ranking delegation, the President of *Seda-va-Seema* (the Iranian radio and TV organization), Dr Ali Larijani, arrived in Bonn. He held talks on bilateral cooperation in the cultural aspect of radio and television with the Minister of State for Foreign Affairs, Mr Schäfer; the Chairman of the FDP, Mr Hans-Dietrich Genscher; the Head of the Parliamentary Foreign Policy Committee, Mr Stärken; and the heads of some of Germany's radio and television networks, including Deutschlandfunk and the ZDF television network.

Visit to Germany by the Head of the Association for Unity Among Iranian Women

Ms Fatemeh Hashemi, the Head of the Association for Unity Among Iranian Women, began a visit to Germany on January 25, 1995, where she met the German Minister for Youth and the Family, Ms Nölte, and held talks on the strengthening of relations between the two countries in the spheres of women and family affairs.

Joint German–Iranian cultural meetings

On October 2, 1995, the third joint cultural meeting between Iran and Germany took place with a visit to Tehran by Mr Wittmann, the Cultural Director General of the German Foreign Ministry. The visit was reported by *Die Welt*: "In the next few days, Mr Lothar Wittmann, head of the Department for Cultural Policy of the German Foreign Ministry, is to travel to Tehran to talk with Iranian government officials regarding the German language, which is to be taught in Iranian high schools as the first foreign language." The paper's report noted that projects to raise the level of German teaching abroad had recently not met with great success, particularly in Eastern Europe, where in spite of an apparent will to extend the scope of German teaching the results had been weak because of insufficient support provided by the Federal Government of Germany, both in funding and in the provision of teaching staff. Another problem was the persistent primacy of English as an international language, a tendency exacerbated, according to the paper, by the fact that German institutions themselves had begun often to use English as a means of international communication. The paper expressed concern that the same difficulties might be experienced in Iran.[35] Nevertheless, during Mr Wittmann's trip to Tehran, a cultural protocol between Iran and Germany was signed.

Visit to Tehran by the Head of the German Archaeological Institute

On October 18, 1995, the President of the German Archaeological Institute began a visit to Tehran, where he reached agreements with Mr Kazerouni, the President of Iran's Cultural Heritage Organization, on the revival of archaeological activities and cooperation between the two countries in this field. While reviewing the new protocol for cooperation between the two countries in archaeology, Mr Kleis was installed as the new President of the Archaeological Institute in Tehran.

Iranian–German media seminar

A high-ranking delegation represented Germany at a joint seminar of the Iranian and German media held in Tehran in November 1995. The delegation met Iranian newspaper owners at the seminar, and also had meetings with President Rafsanjani, the Secretary of the National Security Council, and the Governor of the Central Bank. The seminar and the associated meetings were widely reported in the Iranian and the German press. *Kayhan* newspaper published the following report in anticipation of the event: "The joint seminar for the Iranian and German press, which is to take place in November of this year, will be an effective step for understanding between the people of the two countries. Peter Hausmann, a government spokesman and the head of the German media organization, in a meeting with our country's ambassador, Hossein Mousavian, drew attention to the question of dialogue with Iran as a theme for the conference, and emphasized the continuation of the German government's policy of dialogue." *Kayhan* went on to report Mr Hausmann's emphasis on the importance of the role of young journalists in creating understanding between the two countries, and also mentioned a statement from the present author in which he praised the part played by journalists in raising the level of understanding of Iran in Germany, and called for the two governments to encourage realistic media coverage of Iran.[36]

Seminar on Islam and Christianity in Nuremberg

At the official initiative of Iran and Germany, a seminar on Islam and Christianity was held in Nuremberg on February 24, 1996. Dr Mohammad Javad Larijani and Professor Falatouri participated in this seminar, together with the German

Deputy Minister of Justice, Mr Funke, in addition to numerous other Iranian and German personalities. On February 27, 1996, Dr Larijani, the Iranian Head of the Iranian–German Parliamentary Friendship Group and Deputy Head of the Parliament's Foreign Policy Committee, met Ms Ritha Süssmuth, Speaker of the German Federal Parliament. At this meeting, Ms Süssmuth announced that her country had rejected a request by the United States to sever ties with Iran, and would maintain its policy on relations with Iran.[37]

Dr Larijani also met Ms Leni Fischer, a member of the German Federal parliament, who had just been elected President of the Parliamentary Assembly of the Council of Europe and Head of the Parliamentary Assembly's Christian Democratic group. At this meeting Dr Larijani affirmed that, as he put it, "Iran has supported cooperation and peaceful coexistence between the world of Islam and Europe, and considers the only way to proceed to be the reaching of proper understanding and mutual respect through constructive dialogue."[38]

Visit to Tehran by the Managing Director of the Deutsche Press Agency

On June 27, 1996, the Managing Director of the Deutsche Press Agency (DPA), Dr Walter Richtberg, began a visit to Tehran, during which, on June 29, 1996, he and the Managing Director of the IRNA, Mr Verdinejad, signed an enhanced contract for cooperation between the DPA and the IRNA.[39] Mr Richtberg also met a number of political and cultural figures in Iran.

Visit to Germany by the Iranian Minister of Mines and Metals

In June 1991, the Iranian Minister of Mines and Metals, Mr Mahlouji, arrived in Germany at the head of a high-ranking delegation. In his weeklong visit, he met with the heads of major German companies such as Siemens, Krupp, Mannesmann, Salzgitter, Thyssen, Ferrostahl, K.H.D., Karl Meier, Klockner, and M.A.N., as well as with the German Economy Minister. On this trip he signed various memoranda of understanding with German companies for the promotion of joint enterprises in the field of mines and metals.

First joint Iran–Germany economic commission

In June 1991, the German Economy Minister, Jürgen Möllemann, arrived in Tehran at the head of a high-ranking delegation, including senior representatives of German companies, for the inaugural meeting of a joint German–Iranian economic commission. Mr Möllemann announced after his initial talks that Iran would sign billion mark contracts with German companies. During talks with Iranian officials he gave assurances that in the future the limitations that had hitherto applied to government guarantees for foreign trade would be removed in respect of exports to Iran. Both Iran and Germany desired the raising of the ceiling for Hermes government credit insurance, and Mr Möllemann confirmed that the availability of this insurance would be raised for exports to Iran.[40] He said exports to Iran in 1991 had already showed a 65 percent increase over the previous year, and exports in the first three months of the year had been double those of the same period the previous year. It was on this account that for the first time since 1975, the decision had been taken to set up a joint German–Iranian economic commission. Reports of the visit mentioned that it seemed likely to result in contracts amounting to over DM 10 billion. Bearing in mind the recent decline in Germany's export trade, the deals made with Iran came at a very appropriate moment. German television's Channel 1 reported that the formation of a renewed joint German–Iranian economic commission after a lapse of 15 years was an indication that the two countries had taken a firm decision to expand their economic relations. Germany was not only Iran's biggest trading partner, but for traditional reasons, Iran, in its economic relations, has preferred Germany above other Western countries. Mr Möllemann announced that it was very probable that Chancellor Helmut Kohl would visit Iran before the end of 1991.

Among Mr Möllemann's meetings was one with President Hashemi Rafsanjani, during which the issue of completing the construction of the Bushehr nuclear power plant, begun in 1975 by German companies, was high on the agenda. However, because of US political pressure, the German Economy Minister said Germany would continue to oppose the completion of the project. However, he confirmed that Germany would be active in other key fields: "Iran requires telecommunications equipment and German companies will be successful in this area. In addition, the country needs modern automobiles from its own car factories, and the construction of conventional [non-nuclear] power plants."[40] The construction of the Bushehr power plant, in which DM 8 billion had thus far been invested, and whose construction activity came to a stop in 1979, had become virtually the only topic of contention in economic relations between Iran and Germany. Obstacles to its completion were not removed, even after Iran announced that it would allow international organizations access to the plant and gave guarantees not to use the nuclear facilities for the manufacture of weapons.[41]

Visit to Germany by Iran's Vice President

Vice President Manafi, who was also the Head of Iran's Department of the Environment, arrived in Germany at the head of a delegation on August 19, 1991. In a meeting with his German counterpart, Dr Manafi signed the first memorandum of understanding concerning cooperation between the two countries in the field of environment. In 1990, during the Iraqi invasion of Kuwait, in the course of his efforts to investigate the environmental effects of the seepage of Kuwaiti oil into the Persian Gulf, Germany's Minister of the Environment, Klaus Töpfer, had visited Dr Manafi in Tehran, when he agreed to establish relations between the two countries in regard to environmental issues. After Mr Manafi's visit to Bonn, Germany sent equipments for measuring air pollution as a gift to Iran.

Unprecedented extension of Hermes insurance coverage for Iran

During his meeting on January 16, 1992, with Dr Kashan, Vice President of the Central Bank of Iran, the Director General of the German Economy Ministry, Mr Schomerus, announced that in 1991, of all its trading partners in the world, Germany had allocated Iran the highest level of Hermes insurance cover. Hermes agreed to cover a total of DM 9.3 billion, although contracts totaling DM 5 billion had already been signed between the two parties.

Visit to Germany by Iran's Minister of Heavy Industries

On January 29, 1992, at the head of a high-ranking industrial delegation, Dr Nejad-Hosseinian, Iran's Minister for Heavy Industries, arrived in Germany. He met the German Minister of Economy and Minister of Research and Technology, as well as the heads of important companies such as Daimler-Benz, M.A.N., Ivco, and Krupp, and visited important German industrial installations. The visit led to the signing and implementation of a major contract for the purchase of 5,000 German Ivco lorries, which were to be assembled in Iran.

Memorandum of understanding on road transportation

After months of negotiations, the draft of the first memorandum of understanding concerning road transportation between Iran and Germany was signed in Bonn on March 17, 1992, by the deputy ministers for roads and transportation of the two countries, and was prepared for signature by the two ministers.

Visit to Germany by the Iranian Minister for Industry

On May 27, 1992, at the head of a high-ranking delegation, the Iranian Minister for Industry, Mr Nemat-zadeh, arrived in Bonn, where he met the German Economy Minister and German industrialists, taking the opportunity to make a number of significant agreements for the expansion of industrial cooperation.

Billion mark credit agreed

During the visit of the Deputy of the Central Bank of Iran, Dr Kashan, on August 5, 1992, an agreement was signed between the Central Bank of Iran and the Dresdner Bank of Germany, in which the Dresdner Bank agreed to grant a credit of DM 4.5 billion to Iran. This was the highest credit to be granted to Iran since the revolution. A few days prior to this agreement, the media had widely reported the extent of Iran's debts and the postponement of its letters of credit. On September 10, 1992, in Cologne, the author gave the inaugural address at a seminar for those interested in investing in Iran at which 60 prominent German companies, together with officials from the Central Bank of Iran and the Ministry of Economy, participated. At the seminar, speakers discussed the practicalities of investment in Iran, the country's foreign exchange mechanism, and the present economic condition of the Islamic Republic. In his opening speech the author commented that "the attainment of a stable and long-term industrial and economic relationship between Iran and Germany requires extensive technological cooperation and joint investments, for the achievement of which relations between the two countries must be strengthened and expanded in the economic, cultural and parliamentary dimensions." The author went on to comment that it was fortunate, that during the past year, for the first time since the Islamic revolution, links between Iran and Germany had grown closer, with the holding of joint cultural seminars, and the establishment of parliamentary friendship groups, a joint economic commission, the Iran–Germany Friendship Association, and a technological cooperation group. The speech also noted the increase of political visits and the establishment of direct relations between the two countries, which had led to the holding of 13 meetings at the ministerial level between Iran and Germany in less than two years and to a significant expansion of relations between Iran and Germany in all dimensions.

The author's ambassadorial address also made the point that Iran had become the most stable country in the region. With the world's highest energy reserves, the Persian Gulf region and Central Asia hold a unique strategic significance, and in the interests of cooperation with Europe, Iran is prepared to help in establishing peace, stability, and security in the area. As a connecting bridge between the Asian countries of the former Soviet Union and the free waterways of the world, Iran has attained a special position from a geographic and strategic point of view and provides the possibility of rapid access to the region's markets.

The author also provided detailed information about steps that had already been taken to promote private investment in Iran: "With the aim of expanding private sector investment in Iran, major achievements have been made through the examination of the removal of the ceiling of 49 per cent which currently applies to foreign investment in an enterprise, as well as through tax exemptions and the subsidization of customs tariffs, and by lifting the obstructive regulations relating to the entry and exit from the country of foreign capital and the repatriation of profits, as well as by fixing an advantageous exchange rate for the entry of foreign investment capital." The author also pointed out the scale of foreign investment at the period in question, when the total German investments in Iran stood at approximately DM 160 million, and Iran's total investments in Germany were around DM 650 million; while the Iranian private sector had purchased shares to the value of some DM 100 million in companies located in the former East Germany, including an Iranian investment in the Leuna refinery, in Man Takraf Fördertechnik, and in the Pneumant tyre manufacturing plant. Meanwhile, joint investments by Siemens and Iran had been reviewed and approved in recent talks with Mr von Pierer the chairman of Germany's Siemens company in Tehran.[42]

Visit to Tehran by the German Environment Minister

On October 2, 1992, the German Minister of the Environment, Klaus Töpfer, began a visit to Tehran, where he met Dr Manafi, Vice President and Head of the

Department of the Environment, and the Foreign Minister. Mr Töpfer also represented Germany at the Tehran International Trade Fair and signed a protocol concerning cooperation between the two countries.

Visit to Germany by the Governor of the Central Bank of Iran

On December 10, 1992, Dr Adeli, Governor of the Central Bank of Iran, began a visit to Germany, where he engaged in preliminary discussions with Mr Möllemann, the German Minister of Economy, the head of Germany's Central Bank, and the heads of Deutsche Bank, Dresdner Bank, Commerz Bank, B.H.F., and B.V., with regard to the deferment of Iran's loan payments and the granting of about DM 3 billion in credit.

Meeting of Iranian businessmen resident in Germany

A large gathering of Iranian businessmen residing in Germany was held in Bonn in the presence of the Iranian Minister of Commerce, Mr Abdolhossein Vahaji, who announced a strategy for the advertisement and marketing of handwoven Iranian carpets worldwide and for being approved by the Cabinet. This issue had been among a list of proposals sent to President Rafsanjani by the Iranian embassy in Bonn. In 1992, the embassy organized in Bonn the first and biggest conference on Iranian carpets with 200 participants from all over the world, and the conclusions of the conference were conveyed to the President.[43]

The first stage of rescheduling Iran's debts

In April 1993, the first agreement for the deferment of Iran's debts to the German private sector was signed with the Siemens company. DM 430 million of Iran's debt, acquired from 1990 to 1993, was deferred under this agreement.

The resolution of clashes arising out of the so-called "Parchin 6" agreement

On October 14, 1993, the Head of the Iranian Defence Industries Organization, Dr Bazargan, traveled to Germany to sign an agreement for the peaceful resolution of the conflict between his organization and the Fritz Werner company, under which Fritz Werner agreed to pay DM 75 million to the Defence Industries Organization. The dispute related to an arms sale agreement known as Parchin 6, for which the contract had been signed under the previous Iranian regime. After the revolution, the deal was cancelled, resulting in 15 years of mutual litigation in international courts.

Definitive rescheduling of Iran's debts to Germany

At a meeting on Wednesday, February 2, 1994, with Mr Schomerus, the Director General of Foreign Relations of the German Economy Ministry, Iranian officials, including the author, were able to reach a general agreement with regard to the deferment of all of Iran's debts. A date was set for a visit to Germany on February 16, 1994 by Mr Navab, the Iranian Deputy Economy Minister, and a further visit by Mr Vaezi, the Iranian Deputy Foreign Minister, was arranged for February 21, 1994. The technical details of the plan were to be finalized by Mr Navab in a meeting with the German Deputy Economy Minister, Mr von Würtzen. Any remaining difficulties would be reviewed and resolved during Mr Vaezi's political talks. The plan was in due course implemented, and an agreement for the deferment of all Iran's debts to the German government was signed, with Hermes state insurance cover amounting to DM 4.2 billion. This agreement set the scene for the drafting of similar agreements for the deferment of DM 4 billion of Iran's private sector debts, which were not covered by Hermes. A few days after the agreement with Germany, Japan followed suit and rescheduled the repayment of its loans to Iran. Within a few months Iran was able to reach an agreement with most countries for the deferment of its debts, on the model of the agreement with Germany. This resolved the biggest financial and political difficulty facing President Hashemi Rafsanjani's government, which, thanks to American policies, had been facing apparently insuperable difficulties.

The Iranian newspaper *Hamshahri* reported an interview with the author after the debt rescheduling had been agreed, as follows: "Happily, agreements in principle have been finalized between delegations representing the two countries for the repayment of Iran's overdue debts to Germany. Based on this agreement, German commercial banks will place the necessary credit for the repayment of Iran's overdue debts to Germany at the disposal of one of the Iranian commercial banks, with the guarantee of our country's Central Bank. It has been arranged for talks soon to begin on organizing the necessary banking agreements between the union of German banks and the Central Bank of the Islamic Republic of Iran."

In addition, the author made comments on the political context of the agreement, which were quoted by *Hamshahri*: "With respect to Washington's serious opposition to the settlement of financial difficulties between Iran and Germany, Hossein Mousavian said, 'In the course of the past few months, the United States has attempted to prevent the resolution of the financial problems between Iran and Germany; however, in light of the good relations that exist between Iran and countries such as Germany and Japan, and the political will shown by these countries, American efforts have been in vain.' In reply to the question, 'What effect would the agreement have on our country's foreign economy?', Mr Mousavian said that the lateness of Iran's debt repayments in the recent past had entailed difficulties with Iran's trading partners, which could have impeded the success of Iran's Second Economic Reconstruction Plan, but added that the agreement reached between Iran and Germany would now remove this obstacle from Iran's path; while, following this agreement, similar agreements with Japan and other European countries seemed likely to follow." The paper also reported comments made by Germany's Chancellor Kohl at his meeting with Mr Vaezi: "While mutually welcoming the expansion of relations between Iran and Germany and expressing satisfaction over the existing situation, Helmut Kohl expressed his interest in the improvement and expansion of relations between Iran and the European community. Noting the agreements which have been reached, Helmut Kohl said, 'We are prepared to use all our strength and amenities so that the financial difficulties will be finally resolved as soon as possible.'"[44]

Rheinische Merkur, a political weekly published in Bonn and popular among Bonn politicians in general, wrote as follows about the general issue of relations between Iran and Germany: "Now that fifteen years have passed since Iran's Islamic revolution, and five years since the decease of Ayatollah Khomeini, the Islamic Republic of Iran is more than ever attempting to break out of its international isolation. Iran's relationship with the Federal Republic of Germany is important to its efforts in this direction. It is for this reason that high-ranking Iranian officials make regular official trips to Germany, to the extent that in the past year alone the following senior Iranian officials have visited Germany: Mr Hassan Rowhani, vice speaker of Parliament; Mr Ali Fallahian, minister of information; Dr Mohammad Javad Larijani, head of the Parliament's Foreign Policy Committee and a member of the National Security Council; Mr Mohammad Hashemi Rafsanjani, the brother of the Iranian president and the head of Sedava-Seema (the Iranian Radio and Television organization); and Mr Mahmoud Vaezi, deputy foreign minister of Iran." The paper went on to comment that the important nature of Germany's own interests in Iran have meant that Iranian guests are generally received at the highest level, either by the foreign minister or by Chancellor Kohl himself.

Noting that Iran has recently experienced difficulties in making debt payments, *Rheinische Merkur* offered an interesting analysis. This was because Iran's economic relations with the United States have also expanded, but rather than offering credit to Tehran, the United States wants all transactions with Iran to be paid in cash: "For this reason, Iran's hard currency reserves have been exhausted so that the country is unable to make payments to German companies. It is said that in the current year the United States is to replace Germany as Iran's largest trading partner." The paper continued: "But these changes are astonishing. For it is the United States which never tires of accusing Iran of terrorism; and it is the United States, which, along with Britain, has repeatedly criticized Germany on the grounds that its relations with Iran have led it to breach the political isolation of Iran which Washington would like to impose. On the other hand, from Tehran's point of view, the United States is the land of Satan, and is considered Iran's prime enemy."

Rheinische Merkur also looked at the role of humanitarian issues in the relationship between Bonn and Tehran, noting that Bernd Schmidbauer, the Minister of State responsible for the German Federal Intelligence Service, invariably seeks to justify his dealings with Iran on philanthropic as well as political grounds. The paper looked back at the release of the German hostages, Strübig and Kemptner, as a success for Germany's humanitarian policy, but took a more skeptical stand on other cases, noting that Bonn's efforts to obtain a pardon for the German national Helmut Szimkus, condemned to death for alleged espionage, had so far not borne fruit. The paper also noted that only limited progress had been made in the field of cultural relations, commenting that the prospects for reopening a Goethe Institute in Tehran were not good.

The article also reported comments recently made by the author about the Salman Rushdie case, and the continuing controversy over the *fatwa* pronounced by the late Ayatollah Khomeini, which in effect sentenced Rushdie to death. "In a recent press conference, the Iranian ambassador in Bonn, Hossein Mousavian, presented the matter in another light. As a former editor in chief of the *Tehran Times*, he considered the support of the Western countries for Salman Rushdie to be itself a violation of human rights, adding that this individual had insulted Islam and, along with it, had hurt the feelings of millions of devout Muslims. The Iranian ambassador accused Western countries of judging Iran's human rights records by different standards than those by which other countries such as Kuwait and Saudi Arabia are judged." The paper commented that Iran's religious leaders were refusing to recognize the centrality of the Rushdie case to the issue of whether or not Iran will successfully emerge from its isolation, and viewed skeptically Iran's claim to be observant of international law while the reward for the death of Mr Rushdie offered by a religious foundation in Iran is still on offer. The Iranian government's claim that the reward was not offered by the government but by a private foundation was not convincing, said the paper, since, "in the Islamic Republic of Iran, religion and politics have been totally blended; a private foundation cannot exist."

Rheinische Merkur accepted, however, the validity of the author's claim that Iran is misrepresented or disregarded by the Western press. Iran is accused, the paper said, of supporting terrorism, producing nuclear weapons, or claiming to be superior to neighboring countries. But positive stories about Iran tend not to be brought to the public's attention. For example, concedes *Rheinische Merkur*, Iran had admitted 2.5 million Afghan refugees; it had mediated in the tension between Azerbaijan and Armenia; and Iran was the first country in the region to sign the chemical weapons convention. Meanwhile, the number of secondary school students in Iran in 1994 had almost doubled since the Islamic revolution in 1979, with an increase from 47,000 to 85,000, and the number of university students had increased from 175,000 to 650,000, with a particularly large increase in the number of female students. But, commented the paper, "the presentation of such positive statistics cannot cover the fact that Iran after Khomeini has remained the same as before. Inflation, economic difficulties, the alarming increase in population, a lack of tranquility in certain cities, and the suspicion that Iran has a hand in the killing of figures associated with opposition groups outside the country persists in Germany. If Iran can succeed in better controlling its difficulties, in that case it can expect Germany's aid to Iran to increase. But it appears that the time for this has not yet arrived."[45]

Contract between Iran and Germany concerning maritime transportation

On September 18, 1994, after some months of negotiation, the Deputy Head of the Iranian Council for Ports and Shipping Organization, Dr Hosseini, traveled to

Bonn at the head of a delegation. After talks, a contract relating to maritime transportation between Iran and Germany was finalized by Dr Hosseini and his German counterpart.

Visit to Iran by the German Deputy Minister of Posts and Telegraphs

In October 1995, the German Deputy Minister of Post and Telecommunications, Mr Gerhard Pfeffermann, attended Tehran's International Trade Fair. In meetings with his Iranian counterpart, he held talks on cooperation between the two countries in the field of postal affairs and telecommunications. It should be noted that after 1990, German delegations, in comparison with those of other Western countries, participated at a higher level at the Tehran International Trade Fair.

Further credit from Germany for Iran's Second Economic Development Plan

The author held a meeting in March 1995 with the Iranian Minister of Economy and Finances, Mr Mohammad Khan, and briefed him about recent developments and agreements with major German companies such as Siemens, Höchst, and S.E.L., as well as with German banks and the German government, related to the provision of fresh credit for the country's Second Economic Development Plan. It was possible to inform the minister that DM 5 billion in credit had been made available for Iran's economic reconstruction, which would sustain a number of economic plans and projects.

Visit to Germany by the Minister for Mining and Metals and the Minister for "Construction Jihad"

In a period of relative tranquility in relations, it was possible for the Iranian embassy in Bonn to implement plans previously made during a visit by Mr Hossein Mahlouji, the Minister of Mines and Metals, and Mr Forouzesh, the Minister for Construction Jihad. Mr Mahlouji discussed with Mr Höpner, the Prime Minister of the state of Sachsenanhalt, the purchase by Iran of the machine manufacturing equipment SKET, the largest machine manufacturing plant in eastern Germany, situated in the city of Magdeburg. Talks were held with the Sachsenanhalt Ministry of Economy also. Mr Mahlouji also held talks in Bonn with the German Economy Minister Mr Rexroth.[46]

Mr Forouzesh, Minister of Construction Jihad, arrived in Germany on January 12, 1996. At a meeting with the German Minister of Agriculture, he signed a memorandum of understanding between the Iranian Dairy Industries Organization and the German GEA company relating to the construction of a dairy produce processing plant. However, the problems engendered by the Berlin trial, with the accompanying crisis in German–Iranian relations, continued from later in the year until April 10, 1997, when the court in Berlin gave its final verdict. This was a fatal blow to relations between Iran and Germany. The crisis will be covered separately later, but it should be said here that its effect was to semiparalyze relations between Iran and Germany during the whole of 1997. Finally, it should be emphasized that the developments in Iran–Germany relations, which took place in the early 1990s, were not limited to those mentioned in this chapter. Dozens of political, economic, cultural, and parliamentary delegations were exchanged between the two countries at various levels. In this discussion, only a sample of the exchanges that took place have been referred to, sufficient to clarify the general trend in relations.

Conclusions

This review of developments in Iran–Germany relations after German reunification serves as an indication of the enormous changes that took place after the 1979 Islamic revolution. From 1990, mutual relations improved and further developed in a multitude of spheres. Relations between the two countries' foreign ministries were unbroken and at a high level, with more than 20 visits during 1990–6 at different levels, including the ministerial, deputy ministerial, and official levels. During this period, relations were at a particularly critical stage, which brought about the participation of the political leaders of both countries. A foreign minister who visits Germany would normally be unlikely to meet the Federal Chancellor. It is therefore notable that Iranian foreign ministers, on every occasion without exception, have met the Chancellor during their visits to Germany. Furthermore, a meeting between a deputy foreign minister and the German Chancellor is an even rarer event and happens only in exceptional cases. So it is of real significance that Chancellor Kohl also chose to receive personally the Iranian Deputy Foreign Minister, Mr Vaezi. Very few other deputy foreign ministers and certainly none from Middle Eastern and Persian Gulf countries had ever received such a treatment. Relations between the parliaments of the two countries also underwent significant development. Between 1990 and 1996, some 15 reciprocal parliamentary visits took place between Germany and Iran. Meetings between parliamentary officials at various levels, such as the vice chairmen of the Bundestag and the Iranian parliament and the heads of various parliamentary committees, as well as the formation of parliamentary friendship groups, were evidence of an active evolution of relations between the two parliaments, which were nonexistent in the immediate aftermath of Iran's Islamic revolution in 1979.

But the event that is most significant and deserves particular attention is the development of close collaboration between the security services of the two countries. The three separate visits to Iran by the Minister of State Bernd Schmidbauer, the effective Head of Germany's Intelligence and Security Services who reported directly to Chancellor Kohl, was an indication of the closeness of relations in the intelligence field. It is noteworthy that the visit to Germany in 1993 by the Information Minister Mr Fallahian was extremely controversial. Germany was the only Western nation, and certainly the only NATO member country, to have such a close relationship with Iran in the fields of security and intelligence. Mutual collaboration and close relations between Iran and Germany even extended to situations involving third countries, such as the prisoner exchange between Lebanon and Israel, in which both Germany and Iran played significant roles. A further indication of the level of mutual collaboration between Iran and Germany was the release with Iranian mediation of the German citizens held hostage in Lebanon and the release from prison in Germany of the Lebanese citizen Abbas Hamadi.

The presence of hundreds of German soldiers in Iran during the 1991 Gulf War in order to give assistance to Iraqi Kurdish refugees was an exceptional indication of regional cooperation between the two nations. The refugee assistance operation by the German military contingent cost over DM 300 million. Dialogue on the issue of human rights was another aspect of the relations between the two countries in the period after 1990. The joint seminars that were held on the subject of human rights in Islamic and Western culture, Islam and Christianity, and the several meetings between the human rights committees of the two countries' parliaments constituted a unique development and were unparalleled in Iran's contacts with other Western countries and the EU member states.

Economic relations between the two nations underwent considerable change and development after 1990. One example of this was the agreement by the German insurance giant Hermes to lift its restrictions on cover relating to exports to Iran in 1991, the first such move by any European financial institution in the period after Iran's Islamic revolution. During the ensuing three years, Hermes covered some DM 14 billion in German exports to Iran. This was an extraordinary instance of the close relations between Germany and Iran, since in 1994 only Brazil, of all Germany's export partners, outranked Iran in the use of the credit facilities provided by Hermes.

The rescheduling of Iran's outstanding debts was another issue that was crucial to Iran's economy. In light of the pressure exerted by the United States, no state had been willing to reschedule Iran's arrears. The country's first economic development plan had been completed, but Iran's foreign debt situation had to be resolved before the second five-year plan could be inaugurated. The credit facilities of foreign banks were entirely closed to Iran, and the need to reschedule the debt was probably the most complex and challenging economic dilemma faced by President Hashemi Rafsanjani during his tenure of office. The German Ministry of Finance was the first foreign institution to agree on rescheduling Iran's debts, with the deferment of DM 4.2 billion of Iran's loans under the protection of Hermes, after which the German private sector debt of DM 4 billion was also rescheduled. As a consequence of Germany's decision to reschedule Iran's debt of DM 8.2 billion, other countries began to follow suit, and Iran's entire loan and debt issue was in due course resolved. All this was facilitated by the activities of the first post-revolution Iran–Germany joint economic commission, which held its inaugural session in Tehran in 1991.

Other indications that Iran's relationship with Germany was much more highly developed than Iran's relations with other countries include the establishment of the various joint commissions on subjects such as transportation, environment, culture, and so on, and the interchange of more than 200 separate economic delegations, as well as the continuing credit facilities provided to Iran by German banks. An indication of close relations in yet another field lay in the reciprocal visits of the Deputy German Justice Minister to Iran and the Deputy Iranian Judiciary Chief to Germany, which resulted in agreements on cooperation in the judicial sphere. The holding in Dusseldorf of the largest Iranian arts and culture festival seen in Germany either before or after the revolution, as well as the convening of joint cultural meetings, media and press seminars, and the conclusion of agreements between the two countries' news agencies (DPA & IRNA) were—as were all the developments in question—indications of the uniquely significant and positive tendency in the relations of the two countries.

Germany's political structure and decision-making process are primarily centered around the federal chancellor, the foreign ministry, the finance ministry, the parliament (Bundestag), and the security services. It is significant that all of these institutions were involved in the development of Germany's relationship with Iran. The chancellor and the foreign and finance ministries all played determining roles in improving relations with Iran, and the security services acted as mediator. Before 1990, relations with Iran were handled by the foreign and finance ministries, but after the chancellor became personally involved, the relationship became more dynamic. The Chancellor's personal involvement, incidentally, resulted in some sensitivity and even jealousy on the part of the German Foreign Ministry. The release of the German hostages, the exchange of Israeli and Hezbollah prisoners, and the question of the German national held in Iran, were all personally handled by the Chancellor, while the foreign ministry claimed they fell within its jurisdiction. In fact, while Hans-Dietrich Genscher was foreign minister, the principal foreign policy body within the German government remained the foreign ministry; but after Genscher's departure, Chancellor Kohl took direct control of certain foreign policy matters, while the foreign ministry was relegated to a subordinate role. This applied particularly to relations with Iran. When the Mujahedin Khalq leader Maryam Rajavi was refused entry into Germany and the German government became the first European country to say it regarded the MKO as a terrorist organization, this took place on the initiative of Chancellor Kohl as well as that of the foreign ministry. Even the significant contribution made by the German finance ministry in developing the two countries' relations during the 1990s would unquestionably not have been possible without the consent and approval of the chancellor and the foreign minister.

The two countries cooperated even on wider international issues. An official letter sent by Chancellor Kohl to President Rafsanjani urging Iran to sign the chemical weapons convention (CTBT) had a determining effect in persuading Iran eventually to sign the CTBT treaty. During the regular G7, EU, and NATO gatherings at which Western nations met, Germany played a very important role in countering and opposing American policies, which were aimed at the isolation of Iran. In conclusion, it is quite evident that relations between Germany and Iran saw a significant improvement and growth in various areas—political, economic, cultural, parliamentary, security, and others—after German reunification in 1990; and that this was a unique development not comparable to anything that took place in Iran's relations with any other European or Western country in the period after Iran's 1979 Islamic revolution.

3 Challenges to Iran–Germany relations

External actors and foreign policy constraints: The United States, United Kingdom, and Israel

Priorities in German foreign policy

Many politicians believe that united Germany is in a position to take a more assertive stance in world affairs than was possible in the Cold War era, when the foreign policies of the two truncated states, which made up the former divided Germany, were largely occupied by the contest of political and security issues that the two great alliance systems North Atlantic Treaty Organization (NATO) and the Warsaw Pact played out on their soil. After the Second World War, West Germany placed its faith in NATO in the field of military security, and firmly rooted its economy in the European Community. German statesmen continued to assert that the state's external policies would be expressed through and in line with the collective policies of international institutions, a move in part meant to reassure those concerned about a Germany of increasing power and influence. At the same time Germany is not without influence in governing the direction taken by those institutions, since its restored sovereignty, its vigorous economy, and its crucial geographic position all conspire to give it an influential voice. Indeed, some observers criticize Germany for continuing to take a relatively low profile in international politics, particularly in the area of peace-keeping operations, though it must be remembered that others are already uneasy over the level of assertiveness Germany has chosen to exercise in the international arena.

Germany's diplomacy on Iran has been singled out by analysts as an example of the country's readiness to conduct a foreign policy of its own, distinct from any line dictated by the United States. This however may not be justified, and the author's experience of seven years at the head of Iran's diplomatic mission in the united Germany has led him to the conclusion that foreign policy priorities in Germany are still generally based on the fundamental principle that a strong and stable link between Germany and the United States outweighs other considerations, though European considerations are beginning to take a higher profile in German thinking. The foreign policies of all German chancellors after Chancellor Konrad Adenauer have been based on the maintenance of close ties with the United States in combination with two other principles: the fostering of

European unity, with concern for the policies of Germany's European partners, especially France; and the need for special care in Germany's relations with Israel. These three approaches still appear to be the main axes of German foreign policy.

Germany's geographic position, its economic strength, the large size of its conventional forces, and its influence in the European Union (EU), coupled with the end of superpower rivalry and the impetus of national unification, are all factors that give Germany the opportunity to play a central role in international affairs. Germany, now comprising 16 states, boasts a population of about 80 million, approximately one-third of that of the United States, which makes it substantially larger than any other European state. Germany is also relatively densely populated, with an area equivalent to the single American state of Montana and eight times more inhabitants to the square kilometer than in America. In addition, Germany is prosperous, with a per capita GDP roughly the same as that of the United States, so that its GDP in absolute terms is around one-third of the American figure. Germany is a leading trade partner of the United States and remains its close political ally.

The history of Germany's relationship with the United States, both before and after the collapse of the Berlin Wall, has been a determining factor in its present position. In the past, Germany, as a major power in the European region and as a world decisive economic power, always adjusted its relations with the United States as its strategic partner and a close ally.[1] After the Second World War, the United States used its economic strength to assist in rebuilding Western Europe, and also led the effort to establish the NATO alliance to counter the Soviet threat on the continent. American leaders believe that the security of Western Europe is closely tied to the security of the United States. A strong United States role in European affairs has therefore been deemed to be in America's interest by a succession of Washington administrations. During the Cold War, West Germany saw the US military presence and US political leadership as vital to German security.

Today, however, the unified Germany in post–Cold-War Europe is much less directly dependent on the United States and positions itself in a less subservient relation to American power. German economic policies, and increasingly its security policies, are being determined within and in consultation with the European institutions rather than in primary consultation with the United States. Nevertheless many observers believed in the 1990s that the continuation of long-term transatlantic cooperation will be shaped in part by relations between Germany and the United States. On May 23, 1996, the Chancellor visited President Clinton, which was his twenty-third visit to the United States since becoming chancellor in 1982.[2]

During the period under consideration, the United States and Germany were bound by economic ties: Trade between the two countries consistently stood during the 1990s at an annual figure of over DM 100 billion. The United States has taken the leading role quantitatively in foreign investment in Eastern Germany and thus makes a considerable contribution to Germany's economic growth. There were also substantial political links: The German authorities believed that Europe and the United States share responsibilities and should play a joint role in the maintenance of the world's new order. Germans are of the opinion that in the uncertain world of the future, with its possible dangers, including the proliferation of nuclear weapons and weapons of mass destruction (WMD), the possibility of racial violence, and continuing threat from Russia, the United States will be the main partner and supporter of the Europeans in the preservation of the security and stability of the continent. From the point of view of the Germans, although the power of the United States may not be ideal as a means to preserve world security, the world without America's involvement would undoubtedly be excessively dangerous.[2]

On the other hand, the creation of a united Europe, and in particular of a stable relationship between Germany and France, is of special importance for Germany, which pursues this goal through a European emphasis in its foreign policy running in parallel to the American track. Germany views the EU as the institution central to its political and economic future and to the future of Europe as a whole. EU member states represent Germany's most important trading partners, with France, Italy, and the Netherlands heading the list, and almost 47 percent of Germany's foreign trade is with EU states. Many Europeans, including the Germans themselves, view the strengthening of the EU's economic and political structures as a way of anchoring a reunified Germany in the West and of ensuring the emergence of a Germany rooted in Europe, while avoiding the appearance of a German domination, which Germany's European partners would not wish to see.

Nevertheless, as the EU's largest and economically strongest state, Germany undoubtedly has considerable influence over EU policy. The other European states are well aware that few important policy initiatives in Europe are able to survive without German support. However, Germany cannot control outcomes. Berlin must act in concert with other member states on important policy initiatives. On crucial issues, such as the enlargement of the EU or modifying the EU's areas of responsibility, approval by all the EU countries is necessary. A weighted majority voting system in the Council of Ministers determines the outcome of less critical legislation. Germany therefore needs to look for allies to advance its policies in EU councils. German foreign policy lays stress on the necessity of the development of European convergence, and identifies as crucial the process of strengthening of the bond between Germany and France.[3]

Germany gives its unequivocal support to key EU policies, including the European Monetary Union (EMU) and the planned Common Foreign and Security Policy (CFSP). Germany also plays its part in the European parliament and supports other European institutions, such as the Council of Europe, the Western European Union (WEU), Organization of Security Cooperation of Europe (OSCE), and the NATO. In particular, Germany is supportive of NATO's policy of enlargement toward the east, which will be advantageous to Germany in relation to its interests in Eastern and Central Europe.[4] Naturally, the Federal Republic also gives a special weight to its relations with Russia, and maintains active relations with Russia in the cultural, military, and economic fields, which it hopes to preserve despite Russia's reactions against American policies and the eastward development of NATO.

The other element in the determination of German foreign policy, especially as it concerns the Middle East, is the special relationship between Germany and Israel, which has its roots in the events of the Second World War. The slaughter of the Jews during the war by the German Nazi regime, and the emphasis placed upon this by the Jewish communities of the world, as well as the constant pressure and continued influence of the world Jewish community, have meant that Germany's Middle East policy has been heavily influenced by the relationship between Germany and Israel; indeed it could perhaps be said that Germany's policy toward the Middle East is directly under the influence of its ties with Israel. Meanwhile there exists a widespread self-censorship in Germany concerning Israel's aggressive, expansionist behavior and violation of human rights, and its policy on the development of WMD.

On the basis of all these considerations, the three axes in question, the United States, Europe, and Israel, are all able to affect Germany's relation with Iran. Despite the tendency on the part of Berlin following the reunification of the country toward the expansion of ties with Tehran, Germany has always been obliged to bear in mind what would be the likely attitudes and reactions of the United States, Germany's European partners, and Israel with regard to German ties with Islamic Iran. On the other side, after the Iranian revolution of 1979, Iran's foreign policy was based on the principle "Neither East—Nor West."

One factor was the transformation of Iran–US relations soon after the Islamic revolution. Slogans such as "Death to America" became popular. But it was not until after the crisis over the American hostages held in Tehran that relations with all the Western countries became critical. Iran severed its diplomatic relations with Israel and made statements denying the right of Israel to exist. The principle of exporting the revolution was considered a threat by all the member states of the Gulf Cooperation Council (GCC). In consequence Washington tended to view revolutionary Iran as a geostrategic threat, because of American perceptions of Tehran's efforts to undermine the position of America's allies in the Persian Gulf and its threats to the existence of Israel. However, postrevolutionary Iran and postreunification Germany never ceased to seek the revival of their traditional good relations, even though each of the two states faced great contradictions within their foreign policies as a result. At the same time, Germany viewed Iran as a traditional partner who would help to achieve German objectives in the Middle East and the Persian Gulf. Before taking up his post as the first Iranian Ambassador to reunited Germany, the author met President Rafsanjani who explained the importance of Iran's relations with Germany as Iran's door to Europe and its foreign policy objective of the improvement of relations with what the president called "The West minus America."

Political pressures from the United States, Britain, and Israel

Political pressures applied by the American, British, and Israeli governments had a detrimental effect on the development of relations between Iran and Germany after German reunification. These pressures revealed themselves on two levels:

overt and covert. In the course of the author's seven-year mission in Germany, scarcely any meeting with German officials can be recalled during which the issue of the United States and joint US–Israeli pressures did not arise. A number of German officials privately commented that probably no German delegation had ever traveled to Washington or Tel Aviv without the issue of Tehran–Bonn relations being at the top of the agenda. Similarly, they explained, every delegation that visited Germany from Israel or the United States would give the highest priority to Tehran–Bonn relations. In this section are the details of some examples of overt and covert pressures.

On October 10, 1991, the Political Director General of the German Foreign Ministry, Mr Schlagenweit, explained to the author in his capacity as ambassador that the United States had issued a warning to Germany regarding what were said to be Iran's terrorist activities. The German official explained that in a classified document the US department for combating terrorism had warned the German Foreign Ministry that Iran continued to be involved in terrorist activities as a means of achieving its foreign policy objectives. According to the document, the murder of the former Shah of Iran's last Prime Minister, Shahpour Bakhtiar, after he had been granted political asylum in Paris, was an act authorized by the Iranian government. The Americans also claimed to have information indicating the likelihood of complicity between Iran and the organization headed by Ahmad Jebril, Hamas, and Hezbollah to engage in joint terrorist activities aimed at disrupting the Arab–Israeli peace process. Tehran forcefully denied these allegations, and it was also the case that no terrorist action was carried out against the participants in the Arab–Israeli peace talks.

On March 13, 1991, the author met Mr Hirschmann, the Managing Director of KWU, a subsidiary of the Siemens Corporation. Since the beginning of the author's diplomatic mission in Germany, the completion of the Bushehr nuclear power plant had been an objective of the Iranian embassy's operations in Germany, and as ambassador the author had pursued the matter in more than 200 meetings with German political, economic, and security officials. KWU was a signatory to the contract for the Bushehr power plant, and in this context Mr Hirschmann spoke as follows: "I will say it directly and in a friendly manner: The main obstacle preventing the implementation of the contract for the Bushehr Power Plant is the United States. Furthermore, behind the scene the Israelis also exert pressure; and these pressures are so great that they have prevented the possibility of any action on the part of German Foreign Ministry."

The completion of the Bushehr plant has been consistently among the most important topics of disagreement between Iran and Germany. The German Economy Minister Jürgen Möllemann during his visit to Tehran in 1991 proposed a gas project to Iran as an alternative.[5] But when Iran's President Rafsanjani pressed his case for the completion of the Bushehr nuclear power plant, the German Minister made it clear that the German government would not allow the German companies concerned to undertake any further work on the project.[6]

At a meeting on July 13, 1992, Chancellor Helmut Kohl's Minister of State, Bernd Schmidbauer, informed the author unambiguously that the United States and

Israel were determined to bring about a cooling of relations between Iran and Germany.

At a meeting on November 30, 1992, Mr Schlagenweit, in reference to an American proposal to censure Tehran put forward at the G7 meeting held in Germany on November 20, explained that in Germany's view the American plan was in essence intended to lead to the imposition of sanctions on Iran. However, the German official added that Germany had refused to endorse Washington's proposal, which had resulted in a sharp verbal disagreement. The Director General also discussed a British draft of a proposed human rights resolution against Iran, which contained highly critical language, and which also, he stated, the German government dissented.

In a meeting held on March 23, 1993, Mr Schmidbauer, the Minister of State in the German Chancellor's office, informed the author that during the course of a visit to the United States to prepare for the Chancellor's forthcoming visit he had held a number of meetings at the White House with regard to relations between Iran and Germany, in which the principal issues were nuclear weapons, terrorism, and the Middle East peace process. Mr Schmidbauer commented that he had never before seen the Americans so serious in their antagonism toward Iran and their hostility to the continuation of warm relations between Germany and Iran.

On December 1, 1993, a meeting of the NATO was held in Brussels. The United States and Germany disagreed at the meeting over Bonn's determination to elevate its political and economic ties with Tehran, with the consequent dilution of Washington's efforts to isolate Tehran. In a news conference at the NATO Headquarters in Brussels, the American Secretary of State Warren Christopher said that he had held discussions with Germany on the issue, but his efforts had resulted in failure. Christopher added that the United States was of the opinion that Iran was, in his words, an "outlaw state." He went on to allege that Iran acted against the interests of the Middle East peace process, and that it sponsored terrorism throughout the world. For this reason, Mr Christopher said, Germany's policy of maintaining relations with Tehran had become an obstacle to those who wished to limit Western trade and investment in Iran. In a meeting with the German Foreign Minister Klaus Kinkel, Mr Christopher also issued a firm warning to the effect that the continuation of meetings between high-ranking Iranian and German officials had further aroused Washington's ire.[7]

On the night of March 29, 1995, Israel's Prime Minister Yitzhak Rabin arrived in Bonn on an unscheduled visit. After a long meeting with Chancellor Kohl he left Germany the same night. The German media were uncertain about the purpose of the visit until March 31, when the media disclosed that it had been to discuss the differences between Bonn and Tel Aviv on the issue of Bonn–Tehran relations. A spokesman for the German government confirmed that, in addition to Iran, the Middle East peace process had been discussed. However, when the author followed up the matter by contacting friendly German government officials, it was revealed that a few days earlier a telephone conversation between Chancellor Kohl and Mr Rabin concerning relations between Iran and Germany had culminated in a sharp exchange between the two heads of state, whereupon the Israeli Prime

Minister had hung up the telephone without saying goodbye. Chancellor Kohl then immediately notified Israeli authorities that his forthcoming visit to Tel Aviv was cancelled. It was clear that Rabin's behavior had threatened relations between the German and Israeli governments, and Rabin's special visit was aimed to appease the German Chancellor.

The author met Peter Hartmann, the German Deputy Foreign Minister, at his request, on November 17, 1995, and was told that President Clinton had sent a letter with supporting documents that claimed to show that the intelligence services of Iran and Sudan had conspired to carry out acts of terrorism against prominent American officials, with immediate effect. The German official said that the German government held no opinion on the accuracy of the charges. Tehran denied the allegations, and the fact that no such events occurred was a demonstration of the inaccuracy of the American claim.

With the visit to Germany of Ali Fallahian, the Iranian Information Minister and the effective Head of the Iranian Intelligence Services, tensions between Washington, London, Tel-Aviv, and Bonn reached their peak.[8] Bernd Schmidbauer, the Minister of State at the German Chancellor's office, took the view that his contacts with Mr Fallahian were proper and defended them, affirming that the discussions that had taken place were held on a political and humanitarian basis. Mr Schmidbauer confirmed that bilateral relations on intelligence matters had begun in 1992, and as a result were able to win the freedom of two German hostages in Lebanon, Thomas Kemptner and Heinrich Strübig. However, Mr Schmidbauer's most recent contacts with Iran aroused the ire of the United Kingdom and the United States, while the German opposition Social Democratic Party (SPD) asked the German government to explain the reason for the contacts.[9] The British Foreign Secretary Douglas Hurd expressed his concern in writing to German Foreign Minister Klaus Kinkel. With regard to the world's hostile reaction to his meetings with Mr Fallahian, Mr Schmidbauer said: "They are lying. They are not facing reality. They engage in fraud and deception. They too have held talks. When I hear certain calls from abroad, I ask myself: What have they themselves done in the past few years? They, too, have held their own ample dialogues and discussions."[9]

When the German government agreed in 1994 to reschedule Iran's debt payment, it opened credit coverage of DM 150 million with the government-owned Hermes insurance company, which prompted other European insurance companies to follow suit. This special cover for new transactions between German companies and Iran prompted severe criticism from Israel. The Chairman of the Committee for Foreign Relations and Defence in the Israeli parliament, Ori Orr, said Israel believed that the secret talks held in Bonn between Iran and Israel aimed at freeing the missing Israeli pilot Ron Arad, as described in *Frankfurter Allgemeine*, had been arranged by the German government to justify the rescheduling of Iran's debt repayments to Germany and the normalization of relations between Germany and Iran.[10] However, the German Economics Ministry announced that there had been no change in Germany's trade policy toward Iran, and that to date no permit had been granted for the delivery of weapons or other sensitive merchandise to Iran. The ministry added that the German government monitored exports very carefully and was especially sensitive with respect to Iran. Although Israeli Radio reported billion-dollar transactions and the drafting of weapons contracts between Iran and Germany, Bonn's exports to Tehran in 1993 actually decreased by 50 percent compared with those in 1992, amounting to DM 4 billion.[10]

In answer to the rhetorical question, "Should the West be horrified by Islamic fundamentalism, or should it find a way of peaceful coexistence with it?," an American analyst Justine Berg wrote in the *Christian Science Monitor* in February 1995 that "the likelihood of the appearance of a nuclear Iran forces the West to take a comprehensive look at the phenomenon of Islamic fundamentalism. Although most Western governments agree that Islamic fundamentalism, as it is known in Iran, is a threat to their security interests, the strategies of these governments differ from one another in facing the problem."[11] She went on to say that one school of thought, followed at the time by the United States, supported the policy of isolating Iran so as to prevent the propagation of Islamic fundamentalism; however, Germany's approach was founded on the belief that allowing Iran to play a role on the global economic and political scene would result in the modification of its behavior.

The Head of the Institute for Oriental Studies in Germany, Udo Steinbach, was quoted as commenting that if the West were to help the economies of the Islamic countries, support for Islamic fundamentalism among their communities would be reduced. According to the *Christian Science Monitor*, this German stance had aggravated Germany's differences with the United States over Iran. A number of American officials, discussing the impact on Israel's security, were quoted as expressing concern that Germany's attitude raised the question whether giving priority to economic over security interests can lead to dangers.

In the same article Rabbi Andrew Baker, Head of the Commission for American Jews in Europe, was quoted as saying that Iran was "a major supporter of international terrorism and a sworn enemy of the Middle East peace process," and added that despite this fact, Germany had continued to defend its maintenance of relations with Tehran.[11] Officials of the Commission for American Jews had held a meeting with Chancellor Kohl and other German officials in order to discuss their differences over Iran. On the other hand, German experts and officials at this time reacted to the American accusations by accusing the United States of duplicity. They believed, the article said, that Washington was encouraging other countries to sever ties with Iran, while the United States itself would continue its own profitable trade relationship.[11]

The Israeli Foreign Minister Shimon Peres, who visited Bonn in August 1994, questioned Germany's policy and its commitment to continued friendly relations with Tehran. In an interview, Peres said, "Israel supports the 'dual containment policy' of the United States, which aims to isolate the two outlaw states, Iran and Iraq."[12] Peres, who during his visit to Germany met Chancellor Kohl, Foreign Minister Kinkel, and a number of high-ranking industrial leaders, said: "Washington has clearly understood that the Iranians do not reciprocate any political favour they receive. Iran must be made to understand that it cannot continue its present policy, which is based on intimidation, destruction, murder, and bombings." Peres went on to say that "in comparison with Germany's position, which was allegedly intended to offer encouragement to the moderates in Iran, Israel's policy was more in harmony with the American policy of the 'dual containment' of both Iran and Iraq."[12]

Addressing the Israeli parliament (the Knesset) in October 1994, the Israeli Deputy Foreign Minister Yossi Beilin expressed his government's concern over the widening cooperation between Germany and Iran. In reply to a question from a member of the Knesset, he said that the expansion of business between German companies and Iran, and Bonn's position with regard to this increase of activity, was one of the most complicated issues facing the Israeli Foreign Ministry. He added: "The Israeli government follows with intense concern the cooperation between the security organizations of Germany and the Islamic Republic of Iran."[13]

Chancellor Kohl's second visit to occupied Palestine, 11 years after his first such visit, was widely covered in the German media, though foreign visits by German officials to other countries have commonly been treated as run-of-the-mill news stories. For the most part, the media have tended to view the existence of good relations between Germany and Iran as the only bone of contention between Germany and Israel. This took place at a time when Germany was Europe's largest provider of financial assistance to Israel. The case of Ron Arad, the Israeli Army officer whose plane disappeared over Lebanon in 1986, came up for discussion during Chancellor Kohl's visit to Israel, when he met Mr Arad's family. After this meeting, the German Chancellor announced that he had made a personal telephone call to President Hashemi Rafsanjani on the subject of Ron Arad.[14]

One must remember that on the eve of Kohl's 1995 visit, hope had sprung up in Israel that Ron Arad might still have been alive and could soon be freed. However, indications soon emerged that the missing Israeli was in fact no longer alive. Some reports claiming this proved that the German Minister of State in the Chancellor's office, Bernd Schmidbauer, had been deceived by Iranian officials. However, the author had made clear to Mr Schmidbauer, during all the meetings he held with him in his capacity as ambassador in the period from 1993 to 1995, that Iran had no access to information about Arad's fate. Meanwhile, behind closed doors, Yitzhak Rabin continued unequivocally to express his dissatisfaction over Germany's links with Iran. In addition, it appeared that at this period Israel came to the conclusion that the Arab countries also took a negative view of Germany's policy on Iran.[14]

The Head of the Society of German Jews, in the course of anniversary ceremonies in various parts of Germany honoring victims of the Nazi Holocaust during the Second World War, criticized Western relations with Iran and China, especially those of Germany. Referring to a planned conference on closer ties between the West and the Islamic World, which had been cancelled only due to Iranian Foreign Minister Velayati's inability to attend, the Head of the Society of German Jews severely criticized the German government, condemning Germany's relations with the government of Iran.[15]

When Chancellor Kohl visited the United States in May 1996, the issue of relations between Iran and Germany and wider links between Iran and Europe once more attracted the attention of political circles in Bonn. Political analysts in the German capital as well as the German media announced that the relationship between Iran and Germany would be one of the most important issues for discussion between the American and German leaders. Criticism was leveled at the American Secretary of State, who appeared to have acted deliberately to create a difficult atmosphere for the talks when, two days before President Clinton was due to meet Chancellor Kohl, he brought up once more America's concern over Iran and again criticized German policy, insisting that the policy of dialogue with Iran favored by Germany had failed to bring any tangible results.[16]

In a letter addressed to party leaders in the US Congress, the EU representative in the United States, Hugo Pearlman, replied to American criticism directed at Europe. "Certainly, differences of opinion exist," he said. "However, one must be open to a variety of opinions, and each individual must be able to express his opinion on the manner of facing intricate problems." The EU representative warned the United States of the potential emergence of serious problems in commercial relations between the United States and Europe, adding his view that "by approving laws which impose sanctions on other countries, the United States cannot impose its will on the rest of the world."[16]

In March 1996, a German official confidentially informed the Iranian embassy about the expulsion from Germany of an American spy accused of espionage against Iran. The CIA bureau in Germany had been collecting information on German companies that exported merchandise to Iran, and in particular the Americans were attempting to discover the names of German companies that were engaged in exporting advanced technology to Iran. In 1994, two staff members of the US embassy in Bonn approached the head of one of the sections of the German Economy Ministry concerned with Iran, who then informed the German internal security agency BVS.[17] The expulsion of the spy, who was working as a diplomat at the US embassy, and was told to leave Germany by May 30, 1996, was announced by Peter Frisch, Head of the German Constitutional Court.[17]

Conclusions

Undoubtedly, after German reunification in 1990, the efforts made to intensify relations between Bonn and Tehran were observed with great concern by the United States, the United Kingdom, and Israel. These countries did their utmost to undermine the developing relationship between Iran and Germany, which was as much the revitalization of an old established relationship as the creation of a new one. Good relations have traditionally existed between Iran and Germany since the middle of the last century, involving both political and economic interests, and both sides have benefited from these links.[18] However, during the 1990s, continuous pressure was exerted on Germany, especially by the United States, not only to curtail commercial relations between Germany and Iran, but, as far as possible to halt them entirely. The United States adopted the tone of a crusader against Iran, and attempted to persuade the EU countries fall in line with its position, with the aim of using the pressure of economic sanctions on Iran to weaken the country, to isolate it, and ultimately to bring it to its knees. But dissent was voiced in Germany, and in a comment on the reasoning behind the policy of the United States toward Iran, Dr Johannes Reisner, a specialist in Islam, took a skeptical view, commenting that, "the extent of unproven claims by information agencies regarding terrorism or nuclear weapons is alarming!"[18]

Tehran's potential regional power is a prime cause of American concern. Iran is on its way to exercising substantial power in the region, and is keenly aware of the potential to exploit its crucial position between Central Asia and the Persian Gulf, in a way that could thwart American objectives in the region and could also impede the policies of other states with interests in the region. One concern for the United States and other powers with regional interests is the growth of the influence of an avowedly Islamic state. However, the antagonism displayed toward Iran by the United States, Britain, and Israel also has its roots in the complex history of relations between the West and the Gulf. The three countries share traditional and historical common interests in the Middle East and the Gulf region, but in recent years policy has increasingly been set by Washington rather than by London. Israel's influence has also increased, because of its ability to use the Israeli lobby in the United States to affect the direction of Washington's policies.

During the Second World War, relations between Germany and Iran had alarmed the United States and Britain. After the war, the allied forces occupied Iran, because of its close cooperation with Germany in the war, and in due course, a leadership favorable to the United States and Britain took power in Tehran. Now, after a half century of division and weakness, Germany has regained its unity and is once more able to take its place as a power in the world, while Iran also acquired a new regime. The revitalization and intensification of the relationship between Germany and Iran's Islamic government, which have taken place after German reunification, and the resumption by Germany of an important role in the world, have aroused intense suspicion in Washington, London, and Tel Aviv.

Interference and pressure from these quarters fall into two categories: first, their general effort to influence bilateral relations between Germany and Iran, and second, their particular attempt to interfere in the outcome of the so-called Mykonos trial. With respect to the phenomenon of the general attempt to hamper the development of bilateral ties, it must be conceded that this has been effective, and caused a number of difficulties for the German government in the 1990s. However, there is evidence that outside influences were unable in the end to disrupt relations between Bonn and Tehran. First, the expansion of the relationship between Iran and Germany continued regardless of American pressure. Second, though Germany bore the brunt of the pressure exerted by the United States, the attempt to undermine the concept of "critical dialogue" was intended to apply to the whole EU. The EU, however, did not succumb to Washington's efforts, and even took a collective stand against the measure specifically directed against Iran passed by the US Congress, the so-called D'Amato bill, which it rejected just as it had already rejected the similar American measure against Cuba, the Helms–Burton law. Ultimately, the EU opted to maintain its relations with Iran in the form of the critical dialogue, while the United States refrained from executing the sanctions outlined in the D'Amato bill against European companies. These were factors that gave some comfort to Germany in its own particular effort to maintain its good relations with Iran.

In the European parliament, in fact, certain groups strongly condemned the laws that have been passed by the US Congress, detailing regulations with respect to trade with Iran and Libya. A German spokesman for the Christian Democratic Group in the European parliament, Peter Kittelmann, announced his decision to raise in the appropriate committee of the parliament the increasingly negative impact of US legislation of this kind. He said the European parliament would attempt in this matter to enlist the support of the other major European institutions, the European Commission and the Council of Ministers. In the course of a formal dialogue with American officials, the spokesman continued, the European institutions would attempt to negate the effects of the legislation in the US Congress relating to trade with Iran and Libya.[19] Mr Kittelmann criticized some officials of the EU for failing to stand up to American pressure, and said the European parliament needed to apply pressure on the other institutions of the EU to prevent the worsening of the situation, adding that, as he put it, "day by day, the United States plays the role of policeman for world trade, and this is not acceptable to Europe."

Mr Kittelmann went on to say that the EU had an objection in principle to the proposed American laws limiting trade with Iran and Libya as well as with Cuba, which threatened that any European company that trades with one of these countries would be subject to retaliatory measures in the shape of limits placed on its exports to the United States. Such an American law, which purported to extend American jurisdiction to foreign soil, would be strongly rejected by the EU. The European Commission and the Council of Ministers were already, he said, most regretful that such American legislation had begun to undermine the regulations of the World Trade Organization (WTO), and had placed transatlantic relations under pressure.[19] It began to be suggested in EU circles in Brussels that in the event that talks in Washington on the planned American legislation were to fail, the EU must be prepared to take retaliatory measures against the United States. According to Mr Kittelmann, the American proposals constituted a blatant disregard of international law, which went beyond the breach of WTO rules, and could result in a loss to Europe of billions of dollars in investments.

In conclusion, however, it must be conceded that the extent of US pressure against Iran was never comparable with that which had historically been exerted on Cuba. At the same time, German policy took strength from the fact that it was broadly in line with European policy. The result was that American pressure, while distinctly weakening relations between Iran and Germany, failed in the end to bring their relationship to a halt. Nevertheless, the particular interference exerted by the United States, Britain, and Israel with respect to the Mykonos trial was effective. This topic will be considered in a separate chapter.

Outstanding issues in Iran–Germany relations

Weapons of mass destruction and conventional weapons

Iran and NATO: Mutual threats and interests

The nuclear status quo in the Middle East may soon be a thing of the past.[20] Israel is still the only state that is definitely known to possess nuclear weapons, though it has not so far explicitly avowed its nuclear status. However, Iraq is now assumed to have sufficient nuclear expertise to build weapons if the necessary material were by some means to be obtained, and could perhaps produce active nuclear weapons in a matter of months. On the fringe of the region, Pakistan has also declared its possession of nuclear weapons, and has therefore become a more acute threat to the national security of Iran. In addition to these states, and perhaps because of their actual or potential capacity, the consensus of international observers is that Iran itself is also seeking nuclear weapons. Iran's declared intent remains only to acquire a nuclear capability for civilian purposes, and Tehran has joined in calls for the creation of a nuclear-free zone in the Middle East. Iran has also signed international conventions related to WMD such as the Non-Proliferation Treaty (NPT) and the Comprehensive Test Ban Treaty (CTBT). However, in spite of these gestures, there were suspicions that Iran was already trying in the 1990s to acquire the capacity to make and use nuclear weapons. Observers drew this conclusion from the nature of Iran's nuclear power plant at Bushehr, as well as from the details of some of the technology Iran attempted to acquire in the 1990s, in addition to Iran's efforts to build long-range missiles that could be employed as delivery vehicles.

Analysts contend that Iran has its rationale for its nuclear ambitions, the logic of which seems compelling when viewed from Tehran. Under the Shah, Iran was armed by the West, an option that is not available to the Islamic Republic. Following the 1979 revolution, Iran was left to face Baghdad virtually alone during the war with Iraq from 1980 to 1989, while the Western powers, at the instigation of the United States, whose analysts saw Iran as the greater threat to the West, offered tacit support to Iraq. For this reason, post-revolutionary Iran has placed a strong emphasis on military self-reliance, and since 1988, Iran has been at pains to develop its own military industries and to reduce its dependence on foreign arms suppliers, in order to minimize the potential impact of future embargoes, and to create the foundation for a modern military, capable of dealing with a range of potential threats. At various times, revolutionary Iran has actually or potentially seen itself threatened by the Soviet Union, the United States, and Israel, as well as by other regional neighbors, including Afghanistan, Azerbaijan, Turkey, and Iraq. On the other hand, the defeat of Iraq in the 1991 Gulf War and the subsequent international sanctions against it, have taken much pressure off Iran.

Iran has also characterized the logic of the acquisition of nuclear weapons by Pakistan as part of a general effort by the Muslim countries to counter Israel's capabilities and to redress the relative weakness of the Muslim world. Senior Iranian officials have made explicit statements to the effect that an Islamic bomb would counter Israel's nuclear capability. On the other hand, Iran's peaceful nuclear efforts themselves invite a further threat from Israel. The destruction of Iraq's Osiraq nuclear reactor by Israel in 1981, by a long-range air strike, is an object lesson still remembered in Tehran, and Iran has been alarmed by statements from senior Israelis making it clear that they reserve the option of attacking Iranian nuclear facilities in a similar way. As the result of Israel's expanding military cooperation with Turkey, Israel could now more easily strike into Iranian territory. Iran was acutely conscious in the 1990s that its nuclear power plant at Bushehr could become a target of attacks, which could nevertheless, paradoxically, be deterred were Iran to succeed in its effort to acquire nuclear weapons.

It must also be conceded that Iran's motivation to raise its military capacity to a higher level may be seen as logical, even if it is not entirely defensive. Iran sees itself as a significant regional power and is determined to be a power in the Persian Gulf, for geopolitical and economic reasons. For this reason, Iran needs to be able to wield effective military power, and it remains the case that nuclear weapons are a cheaper option than the conventional arms buildup, which could be highly expensive, and which Iran is less able to achieve while it continues to suffer from the financial problems arising out of restrictions on its economic activities. The American sanctions on the Iranian economy may therefore be seen as having, during the 1990s, actually encouraged Iran to develop peaceful nuclear technology, as a more rapid and less expensive route toward its goal of securing its position in the region. In fact, nuclear technology may be the only means for Iran to become a major military power without exhausting its economy in the process. It has been estimated that while a nuclear technology program could cost Iran billions of dollars, rebuilding its conventional military would cost tens of billions. For reasons like these, Iranian strategic thinkers may have concluded that only the possibility of a nuclear threat would in the last resort give it the ability to deter an American aggression in the Persian Gulf, if Washington were to opt for such a course of action.

As to the details of the threats against Iran, Tehran was concerned during the 1990s about instability across its northern frontiers. Even though the demise of the former Soviet Union eliminated the only major threat from the north and east, Iranian policy makers continued to fear that instability in the Caucasus and Central Asia could destabilize the country, or at least its border regions. But the Persian Gulf remains the region about which Iran feels least comfortable. Throughout the 1990s, the Americans were highly active in the Persian Gulf, and Tehran disliked the presence of American naval power in what it regards as its home waters. These two challenges also to some extent coalesced, with Iran's suspicion that the United States and its NATO ally Turkey were keen to create an anti-Iranian alliance to the north and east. Tehran even took the view that Washington was looking for a Taleban victory in Afghanistan, eliminating the power of the Shiite minority in the north of the country sympathetic to Iran. In addition, a Taleban victory could hamper Iran in its struggle against the worldwide efforts of the Iranian opposition group, the Mujahedin Khalq Organization. Meanwhile the concern over Azerbaijan sprang largely from Iran's determination to maintain its hold over the southern section of ethnic Azerbaijan, which lies within Iran's frontiers, a concern whose onset coincided with increasing American interest in Azerbaijan. Tehran's fears could be summarized as a concern about American efforts at geopolitical encirclement, the effect of which was to cause a further deterioration in Iran's situation. Iran at this time faced six specific threats: the nuclear capacity of Pakistan, combined with its support for the Taleban in Afghanistan; India's nuclear capability and the tension between India and Pakistan; India's capability in the general field of WMD; the presence of American bases in territories surrounding Iran; US assistance in the military buildup of countries neighboring Iran; and Israel's capability in WMD.

US and EU policies directed against Iran

The Western powers and the Western blocs and alliances, for their part, put great stress on the need to prevent Iran from reaching the rank of a nuclear power. NATO, for example, saw the acquisition of weapons by Iran as a potentially catastrophic revision of the regional balance of power. The United States and its allies in the region, especially the EU and the GCC, have for most of the past 20 years concurred in their suspicion of Iran, though they have taken differing views of the gravity of the perceived threat and the appropriate response. From the GCC's standpoint, given its proximity, Iran was seen as representing a potentially fundamental threat to the stability and territorial integrity of the Arab states of the Persian Gulf. The EU member states fear Iranian disruption of regional stability, and the potential for terrorism on their own soil. The United States, however, has tended to view Iran, perhaps exaggeratedly, as a profound geostrategic threat. Washington has taken the view that Islamic Iran has never shrunk from efforts to overthrow or undermine governments friendly to the United States, and that Iran's geographical position and regional interests imply the continuation of its efforts, exercised through various intermediaries, to obstruct the Middle East peace process. The United States also sees a global threat implicit in Iran's ongoing strategy aims, which combine the development of long-range missiles with the acquisition of nuclear technology and other WMD.

While the measures employed by the United States, the EU, and the GCC to achieve their particular objectives have differed, a broad distinction can be drawn between Washington's approach and that of Europe, within which German policy has been formulated. American policy in the 1990s toward Iran relied largely on threats. Washington sought to counter Iran's strategy by denying it the access to arms and technology it wanted, and by the imposition of economic sanctions with the twin aims of curtailing Iran's ability to make arms purchases and of putting it under an economic strain that might induce Tehran to abandon policies the United States regarded as undesirable. The Americans made substantial efforts to recruit other countries to this pattern of engagement with Iran, but with less success in the case of Germany than with other EU member states.

By contrast, the EU's own approach to Iran has concentrated on incentives. The EU policy of "critical dialogue," which characterized the period from 1992 to 1997, was intended to boost the position of moderates in Tehran and to bring about changes in Iranian policy. The countries of Europe in general, and Germany in particular, were reluctant to forego a major slice of foreign trade by imposing sanctions on Iran. Critics of the European approach, and especially of German policy, saw it as to some extent hypocritical: A means by which Europe could express its disapproval of those of Iran's positions, which it did not accept, without losing the benefits of a commercial relationship. The maintenance of links with Tehran was also seen, according to critics, as cynical: Functioning more as a way of sheltering Europe from Iranian-government-sponsored terrorist activities than as a principled policy. Of course, Germany's position, and the European policy as a whole, received a major setback in 1997 when the German court, which was hearing evidence concerning the Mykonos murders of 1992, accused the most senior members of Iran's leadership of responsibility. The critical dialogue was temporarily broken off. However, after a year, links between the EU and Iran were resumed, with the aim of strengthening the position of the country's new president, Mohammed Khatami.

American policy toward Iran appeared in the 1990s to have succeeded in impeding Iran's efforts to modernize its armed forces, by preventing Tehran from successfully concluding arms deals with other countries. Iran has been denied access to sophisticated Western arms and technology, and has been obliged to rely on suppliers such as North Korea, China, and Russia. Washington's efforts have also had an impact on Iran's development of civilian nuclear technology. It was largely as the result of American pressure that Germany repeatedly refused Iran's requests to German companies that had entered into contracts with prerevolutionary Iran to fulfill their contractual undertakings to complete the Bushehr nuclear power plant begun under the regime of the Shah. Iran also had specific setbacks, many of which were traceable to American efforts behind the scenes. In 1987, Argentina refused to supply Iran with nuclear-fuel fabrication and reprocessing technology and a 20–30 MW research reactor. In 1990, China denied Iran a 30 MW research reactor, and in 1998 it refused to conclude a contract to build a uranium hexafluoride conversion plant. India rejected in 1991 a request to supply Iran with a 10 MW research reactor. Finally, in 1995, Russia refused to transfer either a gas centrifuge-enrichment facility or a 330 MW research reactor, both of which it had promised to Iran.[21]

Meanwhile, American economic pressure has also taken its toll. Iran cut its military expenditure by more than half from 1989 to 1999. Following the Iran–Iraq War, Iran planned to spend $2 billion per year on weapons purchases over five years. Actual spending and the level of arms acquisitions, however, fell far short of their projected target.[22] Iran expanded its naval force and artillery as planned, but in other areas it was less successful. While Iran had hoped to obtain some 1,000–1,500 tanks, in practice it acquired only some 225. Of a planned acquisition of 250 to 500 infantry vehicles, it bought only 80; and of a projected purchase of 100–200 aircraft, it acquired only about 65.[23]

The Middle East peace process

The EU and the Middle East peace process

Germany was involved in the Middle East peace process throughout the 1990s, both through its own efforts and as part of the wider EU initiatives. The EU has many reasons for its interest in the stability of the Middle East. Europe has substantial economic interests in the region. Oil and gas from the Middle East are crucial to the European economy, and the Middle East provides a lucrative market for European industrial goods. Europe also sees the Middle East, and in particular the Gulf, as a major market for military hardware and technology. On the other hand, Germany is not centrally concerned with the particular issue that attracts the attention of the southern European states, and in particular France, Spain, Italy, and Portugal, namely the impact on their own territory of potential instability in the Arab states of North Africa. However, the EU as a whole believes Europe should play a major role in the Middle East peace process, balancing what some European strategists see as American hegemony in the region, especially after the demise of the Soviet Union and the erasure of Russian influence in the region. A major role in Middle East peacemaking is seen in Europe as a desirable symbol of Europe's view of itself as a major power broker, in conformity with the size of its population and its economic weight, and would also arise naturally from Europe's substantial financial investment in Middle East peace. The Middle East also appears to be an area of primary interest and involvement in the first stages of the development of the EU's CFSP.[24]

The Euro-Mediterranean Partnership launched at the Barcelona conference in November 1995 marked the onset of a new phase in the EU's Middle East policy. The aim of the European and other states that met at Barcelona was to set up a Mediterranean free trade area, and to promote the long-term goal of a wide regional security within which peace between Israel and the Arab states would be one element. The Euro-Mediterranean process was intended, according to European Commissioner Manuel Marin, to create an area of political stability and economic prosperity in the region through the establishment of a long-lasting and well-founded political, economic, and social partnership. Though the Barcelona process was intended to be independent from but parallel to the Middle East peace process, it was meant to underpin it and facilitate it by setting up the real conditions for long-term stability and economic development in the region.[25]

The EU, according to Commissioner Marin, has contributed over half of the cash that has been spent on promoting the Middle East peace process and the EU's view is that as the basic shareholder, Europe should also be a key coordinator of the process, and that in particular the international economic effort should be coordinated by the EU. The European economic input to the Middle East, where Europe's payments provided the basic support for the Palestinian authority, also implies a major role for Germany, which is the largest contributor to the budget of the European community. Germany's share of Europe's budget is over 25 percent of the total, with the implication that Germany also sustains a quarter of the

European payments made to the Palestinians. Germany also willingly takes on its role in the Middle East for quite other reasons. Since the establishment of Israel in 1948, Germany has taken responsibility for Nazi Germany's treatment of the Jews before and during the Second World War, and has made payments to the Israeli state. Germany takes the view that it must atone for its past treatment of the Jews.

There arises a paradox, however, when Germany's relationship with Iran is considered. Since the Islamic revolution of 1979 in Iran, Tehran has denied Israel's legitimacy and its right to exist as a state. Iran has also opposed the Middle East peace process, which it regards as a way of perpetuating Israeli domination in the region whose effect will be to deny justice to the Palestinians, and has offered support both to the Palestinian groups opposed to the peace process and to the Hezbollah of Lebanon, groups that oppose the imposition of a two-state solution. Tehran consistently backs groups that take the view that the Palestinians have the right to the whole of the territory of pre-1948 Palestine. When the United States, following the Gulf War, convened the Madrid Conference in October 1991 to initiate the process of political negotiation between Israel, its Arab neighbors, and the Palestinians, Iran immediately convened a parallel conference in Tehran, which brought together all those groups and organizations hostile to any negotiation with Israel, which were ready to continue the struggle against it in a common Islamic front.[26] This presented a problem for bilateral relations between Iran and Germany, which was continuously present in the period from 1990 to 1997, despite the willingness of both sides to seek an understanding.

Sensitivities in German internal politics concerning Israel and the peace process

During the period from German reunification in 1990 until 1997, the German parliament repeatedly subjected Bonn–Tehran relations to public scrutiny, and the German opposition parties repeatedly attacked the coalition government over the issue of Germany's relations with Iran. The main issues of debate were Tehran's objections to the Middle East peace process, its alleged support for terrorism, and disregard in Iran for Western standards of human rights. The Social Democratic and Green parties displayed particular discontent, and it is certainly the case that relations with no other country were the subject of debate and difficulty in the German Federal parliament as much as those with Iran.

A debate held in the Federal parliament in November 1995, following the assassination of the Israeli Prime Minister Yitzhak Rabin, serves as an example of the extent of opposition party activity. After Rabin's death, Iran's President Hashemi Rafsanjani made a statement interpreting the event as divine punishment, and, though no other Western parliament subjected it to such scrutiny, this statement led to a debate in the German parliament on Germany's relations with Iran, which had very serious political consequences. At the time, Iran's Foreign Minister Ali Akbar Velayati had been due to travel to Bonn at the invitation of the German Foreign Minister Klaus Kinkel to deliver the opening address at a conference on Islam and Europe. After the parliamentary session, prominent government officials held a two-hour emergency meeting on the crisis in Iran–Germany relations. The issue was no longer whether the planned conference could go ahead, or if the invitation to Dr Velayati should be withdrawn; it was rather the survival of Mr Kinkel as Foreign Minister, and even the fate of the coalition government itself.

The coalition government faced the prospect of its worst defeat in that parliamentary session. The Green Party Leader Joschka Fischer, who ironically was later to become foreign minister, planned to criticize severely Klaus Kinkel's projected conference on Islam, and to ask parliament to withdraw the invitation to Dr Velayati, on the grounds that since Iran had apparently officially adopted the view that Rabin's assassination was a proper and justified act, it would no longer be acceptable for him to be met by the German Foreign Minister. He submitted his petition to parliament with the support of the SPD, and many members of the governing CDU and CSU joined him when the issue was put to a vote. The result was a political crisis, when more than 50 members of the coalition government voted with the opposition, which led to the defeat of the government, and to the postponement of the conference, much to Mr Kinkel's anger. Following the debate, Chancellor Kohl held an emergency debate of the coalition leaders behind closed doors, after which rumors spread that Klaus Kinkel was ready to resign from the post of foreign minister, on the grounds that he was not willing to see what he regarded as the government's carefully planned long-term policy on Iran destroyed by parliament. In the event, however, Mr Kinkel evidently withdrew his decision to resign: In a brief statement he announced that while he had no intention of quitting his post, the conference that Dr Velayati had been due to attend would in fact be postponed.[27]

In an editorial comment the newspaper *Suddeutsche Zeitung* gave an account of how Klaus Kinkel justified his position, which indicated the level of importance he placed on the relationship he had built up with Iran: "After the emergency Cabinet meeting, Kinkel repeated that although he stood firm on his views, he would respect the Parliamentary vote. He said that dialogue with Islam was important, but could only be useful in the absence of circumstances such as those currently prevailing, after the assassination of Rabin and the resulting anger over Iran's reaction, which had introduced tension into the situation. 'I understand that in such an emotional situation,' he said, 'parliament may take a different opinion.'"[28]

In this case, the crisis in relations between Bonn and Tehran was seen as sufficiently important to have led the opposition parties in the Federal parliament to inflict the first parliamentary defeat of the session on the Chancellor and his government. This was the first time since the Second World War that a German government had undergone such a parliamentary defeat, with members of the ruling parties voting against their own government, an event of such significance that it led the German Foreign Minister to the brink of resignation. In retrospect, the German government and ruling parties referred to the day as "Black Friday."

Conclusions

The issues concerning Iran, namely its apparent efforts to acquire WMD, its alleged interference in the Middle East peace process, and its supposed support for terrorism, together with the reaction to them from the opposition parties in the German parliament, were factors that put mounting pressure on the relationship between Iran and Germany. For the coalition government, the bitterest incident was its defeat in the Federal parliament, which had no precedent during Chancellor Kohl's term in office, or indeed in the postwar history of parliament. On account of the government's relationship with Iran, the German Foreign Minister was brought to the brink of resignation.

Undoubtedly, these developments had a negative impact on the development of Bonn–Tehran relations. However, they failed to bring the relationship to an irrevocable halt. This was because, in the last resort, though the opposition parties had objected to a particular development in relation to Iran in the immediate circumstances following the death of Yitzhak Rabin, the opposition nevertheless collectively held to a basic belief in the principle of maintaining relations with Iran and in the policy of a critical dialogue. In the last resort, no party sought the severing of ties with Iran. At most, some were prepared to use relations with Iran as a lever against the coalition government. The factional struggle for power was the underlying impulse behind this outbreak of political turmoil.

After the parliamentary debate, Karsten Vogt, the SPD Spokesman on Foreign Policy and Security, made it clear to the author that the majority of Germans sought good relations with Iran, and all the major parties in the Federal parliament essentially took the same positive opinion with respect to relations and dialogue with Iran. However, he went on to say that while on some international issues, such as Bosnia and the Caucasus, there is undisputed common ground between Iran and Germany, on other issues, such as the Middle East peace process, that common ground does not exist. Nevertheless, he took the view that continued dialogue could eliminate these problems.[29] The author also met the Deputy Leader of the Parliamentary SPD, Günther Verheugen, who said that the German SDP was totally against isolating Iran, and that the recent debate had demonstrated that there should be no hiatus in relations or dialogue, which should on the other hand continue in greater depth.[29]

Thus, it can be concluded that though the issue of the acquisition of WMD and the peace process were major factors, exerting pressure, which weakened Bonn–Tehran relations, they nevertheless did not halt the critical dialogue. The key question left outstanding was, what could be the framework of compromise between the EU and Iran over the peace process? The following agenda could be seen as an appropriate solution. First, the EU member states should accept the reality that Iranian policy is not a principal factor determining the success or failure of the peace process, and that external pressure, from Iran or elsewhere, will not make that much difference to the state of Israeli–Palestinian relations.[30] Second, Iran has in fact frequently reiterated that it would not act to upset the balance of the peace process. A working group could be established by Iran and the EU as a confidence-building measure to remove suspicion about the provision of financial and military assistance by Iran to the militant opposition Palestinian groups. Third, the EU should exercise tolerance toward the political views of Iran about the peace process, which are sincerely held. Iran believes that the agreements made between the Palestinians and the Israeli leadership do not constitute "justice" and would not lead to a "long-lasting peace" in the region. Fourth, and finally, a regional system for cooperation, security, and stability should be created. This regional cooperation system should initially involve Iran and the GCC member states; and in due course, in a post–Saddam Hussein era, Iraq could be invited to join, to create a comprehensive cooperation system for the Persian Gulf.

In the long term, such a system should be expanded to the Middle East as a whole, in order to bring about comprehensive cooperation between all the Middle East countries in the field of security, and particularly in the removal of nuclear weapons, the struggle against terrorism, and the control of conventional arms purchases by all the Middle East countries. For the moment, Iran's strategy is to continue to build up its civilian nuclear infrastructure while avoiding activities that would clearly violate its NPT commitments. However, Iran also needs modern conventional weapons in order to enjoy minimum security in the face of the prevalent threats in the region. The current policy of the United States, which is based on isolating Iran and weakening the Iranian economy, will only encourage Iran to go for the cheaper and faster solutions to its security problems, which basically means the acquisition of nuclear weapons as the only short-term means of ensuring that potential threats can be countered.

To avoid Iran crossing the nuclear threshold, a number of factors would serve as the framework for a solution. These are: first, Iran's full commitment to international WMD conventions; second, Iran's security concerns should be addressed by means of security assurances from the major powers; third, the creation of a regional security system as a means of reducing tensions, enhancing stability, and creating regional confidence; and fourth, an end to the American policy of containment, together with the opening of cooperation between the EU and Iran in the transfer of peaceful technologies in the nuclear, biological, and chemical fields within the framework of the existing international WMD conventions.

Terrorism as a challenge in Iran–Germany relations

Report by the Verfassungsschutz

In its annual report for 1993, the Verfassungsschutz (the Department for the Protection of the Constitution, or in other words the German Internal Security Service) accused the Iranian embassy in Germany of espionage and the illegal pursuit of opposition groups on German soil. The report claimed that Iran had continued its policy of exporting the Islamic revolution, had striven to prevent the progress of the Middle East peace process, and was continuing to act in any way it could against Iranian opposition groups. Attacks had taken place, according to the report, which were aimed at the opposition to Iran outside the country—for example in Turkey, Italy, and Pakistan—and it was said to be probable that the Iranian Security Service was involved in most of these attacks.

In addition, the report noted that the *fatwa*, or religious decree, declaring it to be legitimate under Islamic law to kill Salman Rushdie, the author of the book, *The Satanic Verses*, was still in place, and the Iranian leadership's stated view of its legitimacy was little changed. Some Islamic authorities in Iran had even confirmed it. Western experts believe that the attempt on the life of the publisher of the Norwegian translation of *Satanic Verses* was linked to the *fatwa*.

However, the report also touched on the opening of the so-called Mykonos case in October 1993, which has been mentioned elsewhere and will be separately treated later. The accused in the Myknonos trial were four Lebanese citizens and one Iranian accused of murdering the leaders of the Iranian Democratic Kurdistan Party on September 17, 1992, in Berlin, an affair in which the German Prosecutor-General took the view that the Iranian Security Service bore the responsibility for the killings. According to the report, an Iranian residing in Germany, who in the opinion of the prosecutor was a spy for the Iranian Security Service, had taken the lead in these activities.

The report also commented on the activities of the only recognized Iranian organization in Europe, the Union of Islamic Student Associations in Europe, which it said shared the same aims as the Islamic revolution. However, the report conceded that the Union of Islamic Student Associations in Europe had not under-taken any substantial propaganda activity in the previous year. On the occasion of Jerusalem Day, on March 20, 1993, along with other radical Islamic organizations, this group had demonstrated in Bonn in favor of unity among the oppressed peoples and nations of the world and other similar demands.[31]

The publication of the contents of this report in the German, European, and American newspapers introduced a degree of strain in relations between Iran and Germany, and in his role as ambassador it was the author's duty to convey to the German authorities the Iranian government's objections to what were seen as base-less allegations. At a meeting with Kurt Schulter, the German Deputy Minister of the Interior, the author conveyed Iran's complete rejection of the contents of the report, and informed him that Iran was ready to present any documentary evidence that might be required for its rebuttal. The German Deputy Minister of the Interior expressed satisfaction at Iran's readiness to cooperate in the removal of any obsta-cles to good relations between the two countries. The author also mentioned Iran's willingness to cooperate with Germany in action against the illegal trade in narcotics and reminded the German Deputy Minister that the United Nations had repeatedly expressed its appreciation of Iran's activities in this field.[32]

This had not been the first hostile intelligence report concerning Iran. In 1992, Germany's Verfassungsschutz had already prepared a report in which it claimed that certain Iranian organizations and companies in Germany were engaged in espionage activities and had participated in the identification and pursuit of those opposed to the Iranian government, as well as helping to facilitate Iran's weapon purchases.[32]

Arms discovery on board an Iranian ship

On March 11, 1996, the Belgian media reported the confiscation by Belgian security forces of a cargo of mortar shells hidden inside food containers whose destination was the German city of Munich, after its discovery in the course of an inspection of a state-owned Iranian ship, the *Iran Kolahdooz* at the Belgian port of Antwerp. The author was summoned to the German Chancellor's office by the Minister of State, Bernd Schmidbauer, who conveyed the German government's displeasure. However, after leaving Antwerp, the *Iran Kolahdooz* was given a further thorough inspection at the port of Hamburg, and on this occasion the chief of the criminal section of the German Police Department announced that no indication of the presence of explosives was found.[33] Nevertheless, the Belgium and German media published numerous reports alleging the existence of mortar shells and other explosive materials and mortar shells aboard the vessel.

The murder of Reza Mazlooman in Paris and accusations against the Iranian embassy in Bonn

An Iranian suspect was arrested in Bonn immediately after the murder in Paris of Reza Mazlooman, the former deputy minister of education in the Shah's government, and the German and European media accused the Iranian embassy in Bonn of implication in the incident. *Der Spiegel* magazine wrote as follows: "The German prosecutor general has once again pointed the finger of suspicion at Iranian circles in Europe, who have in all probability murdered a member of an opposition group. Last week, the German prosecutor general in Karlsruhe opened a judicial investigation of an Iranian named Ahmad Jayhouni, a resident of Bad Godesberg." According to the magazine, the charges against Jayhouni were that during the latter part of May 1996, by order of the Iranian Intelligence Service, he participated in the murder of Reza Mazlooman, a former Iranian deputy minister, who lived in a Paris suburb, and a judicial file on him had been opened in France, pending his extradition. Others were thought to have been involved in the incident, while the suspect was alleged, in the report's words, to have "received his orders for the perpetration of this act from the Iranian Embassy in Bonn."[34] *Der Spiegel* also published a photograph of the Iranian embassy in Germany.

Iran accused of kidnappings in Germany

In February 1996, there were extensive reports in the German media after a kidnapping incident in Henf, near Bonn. An Iranian resident of Henf was kidnapped on February 2, and allegedly subjected to severe torture, but escaped after two days and put himself under the protection of the police while his captors were attempting to transfer him to another location. The police did not exclude a political motivation for the incident. The Mujahedin Khalq Organization (MKO) claimed that the Iranian government was responsible, but the Iranian embassy in Bonn categorically denied this accusation.

On February 16, 1996, Ibrahim Zakeri, a member of the Council of Resistance of Iran, and a spokesman for the Mujahedin, alleged at a press conference in Bonn that the kidnapped individual, aged 28, had been given terrorist training in Iran but had defected and asked for political asylum in Germany, where he had lived since the beginning of the year. Zakeri added: "Seyed Hossein Mousavian, the Iranian ambassador in Germany, has been aware of this matter, for this individual has fled Iran and has published information on Iran's domestic problems."[35] Zakeri added that Iran had sent up to five intelligence agents between January 18 and February 1, to silence the fugitive, in an operation organized by a counselor at the Iranian embassy who is responsible for intelligence services in Western Europe.

Meanwhile, the Bonn prosecutor confirmed that because of the kidnapping and the physical injury to the person concerned, the case was under investigation, but was not prepared to comment on its political implications. The Iranian embassy in Bonn rejected all imputations of guilt, and said that in its view the affair was a matter of rivalries between competing opposition groups. The Iranian embassy also asked the government of the Federal Republic to take appropriate measures to protect Iranian citizens against what it called terrorist attacks.[35]

Actions detrimental to Iran–Germany relations by the Mujahedin Khalq Organization and other Iranian opposition groups

The Mujahedin Khalq Organization (MKO), the principal Iranian opposition group active abroad, had apparently made extensive plans to take violent action with the intention of causing disruption in relations between Iran and Germany. The MKO's campaign of violence began in protest against the visit of the then Minister of Culture and Islamic Guidance, Mr Khatami, to the Iranian Art and Culture Festival in Düsseldorf in 1991. The MKO planned demonstrations at the site of the festival. After the end of the inaugural ceremonies, while Mr Khatami and his entourage were leaving the hall, they threw eggs at him while chanting insulting slogans.

A more significant development took place in early April 1992, when the MKO attacked 13 Iranian missions throughout the world. The most serious attacks were carried out in Germany against the representative offices of Iran in Bonn, Hamburg, and Munich. The attacks almost totally destroyed the Iranian embassy in Bonn, leaving nothing undamaged except the walls and ceilings. Assailants also set on fire the Iranian Consulate in Hamburg and did much damage to the Iranian Consulate in Munich. As ambassador, the author blamed the German government and police for showing excessive lenience in the face of the MKO's assault on the Iranian political mission in Germany, since the MKO demonstrators were allowed more than 90 minutes to destroy the embassy building before the incident was halted by the police, even though police officers arrived at the scene a few minutes after the initial assault. The German police did not allow Iranian employees and diplomats to act in defense of Iranian property in the embassy, which is agreed by diplomatic convention to be on Iranian soil. On the other hand, some embassy employees were injured and arrested by the police.

As ambassador, the author demanded the implementation of the Vienna Convention with respect to the preservation and protection of diplomatic premises and diplomatic personnel in Germany. The Iranian embassy invoked the United Nations Security Council resolution on the withholding by third countries of support for Iraq, in order to ask the German government to clarify its position with respect to actions carried out by terrorists based in Iraq.[36] Because of the total destruction of the embassy, the author was obliged to carry out his ambassadorial duties from the embassy residence for a period of six months. However, during the reconstruction of the embassy building, the author was able as ambassador, together with his diplomatic colleagues, to avert any further deterioration in relations with Germany, to the extent that a number of visits by high-ranking delegations were exchanged between the two countries within this period. The German government paid DM 5 million in reparations for damages incurred at this time by Iranian missions in Germany.

In June 1992, groups opposed to the Iranian government organized demonstrations against the impending visit by the Iranian Foreign Minister Dr Velayati to Germany. Hundreds of Iranians in exile demonstrated in many German cities against Dr Velayati's visit, while Iranian opposition organizations made it clear that they were opposed to any kind of rapprochement between Bonn and Tehran.[37] Nevertheless, Dr Velayati came to Germany as planned in July 1992, when he met Chancellor Helmut Kohl, Economy Minister Günter Rexroth, and Foreign Minister Klaus Kinkel, as well as members of the German parliament's Foreign Policy Committee.

However, in an incident that marred the visit, a number of people threw eggs at Dr Velayati's car as his motorcade passed a park adjacent to Cecilienhof Castle in Potsdam. Immediately after the attack, three Iranians were arrested. The material damage inflicted in this incident was very slight, no one was injured, and Dr Velayati himself said that "it was nothing." However, the Iranian Foreign Minister decided as a result to bring his visit to Germany to an end sooner than had been anticipated. An unidentified woman contacted the offices of *Suddeutsche Zeitung* in Munich by telephone, and claimed responsibility for the attack on behalf of the MKO, whose aim, she said, was to protest against the increase in cooperation between Iran and Germany. During the attack, the demonstrators shouted slogans, including "Velayati is a terrorist" and "Do not trade with Iran." The following day the Bonn police arrested 13 Iranians, who were released after being held for five hours. The German Foreign Minister Mr Kinkel expressed his regret at the incident and the curtailment of Dr Velayati's visit, asking for an inquiry to be held.[38]

The MKO had also organized a large-scale hostile propaganda campaign ahead of Iranian Foreign Minister Velayati's trip, claiming that Dr Velayati's intention in visiting Germany was to bring influence to bear on the course of the Mykonos trial. Before the beginning of the trial, the Iranian Foreign Minister had indeed approached the German government in an attempt to prevent it from proceeding.[39] Violent activities on the part of the terrorist organization Mujahedin Khalq continued in this manner. Every stage of Iran's efforts to maintain and improve its relationship with Germany was accompanied by violent demonstrations by the MKO against successive Iranian delegations.

Another example of MKO violence was their coordinated attack on Dr Rowhani, the Deputy Speaker of Iran's parliament and the Head of the Parliamentary Foreign Policy Committee, during his visit to Germany in April 1993. This meeting represented a significant improvement in Iran–Germany relations, and the Head of the German Parliament's Foreign Policy Committee, Mr Strecken, made an encouraging statement regarding Germany's view of Iran's weapons acquisition policy when he said: "Iran is fully prepared for the inspection of its chemical and atomic plants, which should answer accusations made by the United States and other Western countries that Germany is providing Iran with nuclear, chemical and biological weapons." In addition, the commutation of the death sentence of Helmut Szimkus, a German citizen, who had been sentenced to death in Iran for spying for Iraq, was first proposed during this visit. However, the Mujahedin Khalq protested against Dr Rowhani's presence in Germany, claiming that as a member of Iran's National Security Council, he was responsible for exporting terrorism.[40] MKO demonstrators attempted to attack Dr Rowhani in his hotel after an official dinner but were arrested by the police. Dr Rowhani expressed his anger at the fact that the Mujahedin Khalq, a group known to be opposed to the Iranian government and regarded in Iran as terrorists, were apparently at liberty to move about in Germany.[41]

Debates in the German parliament

A major debate took place in the German parliament on November 30, 1996, after the German Prosecutor-General, in his closing speech at the Mykonos trial, accused high-ranking members of the Iranian government of responsibility for the deaths of Kurdish leaders, alleging that these officials had ordered the murders of the victims. Following this statement, widespread protests were held on the streets of Tehran and other Iranian cities against Germany and the German Prosecutor-General. The German parliamentary debate, held before the court in Berlin issued its final verdict on the defendants, took place in the presence of the Chancellor, Cabinet members, and party leaders.

In the course of the debate, the Christian Parties CDU, CSU, and the Free Democrats put forward a draft resolution, the text of which read as follows:

"The Federal Parliament has observed with concern recent developments in Iran–Germany relations. This matter has been particularly the case regarding the demonstrations held last week in front of the German Embassy in Tehran and, with respect to the Mykonos trial, the threats made against representatives of the German judiciary.

1. The German Parliament emphatically supports the Federal Government and categorically defends the German judiciary. It confirms the judiciary's independence and rejects Iran's charges that the prosecution in the Mykonos trial has been political. In his letter to the Iranian president, the Chancellor has made Germany's position absolutely clear, as have the ministers of foreign affairs and of justice. The German Parliament welcomes the government of

Iran's efforts to prevent any worsening of the situation… and the fact that the government of Iran has promised to protect German citizens in Iran in accordance with its international legal commitments.

2. The German Parliament encourages the Federal Government to adopt an active and persuasive policy, together with other member states of the EU and in close harmony with the United States, to compel Iran to adopt a clear and positive posture toward the Middle East peace process, and to refrain from supporting terrorism, whether politically or logistically or financially; to support and abide by conventions on chemical weapons and their non-proliferation; to respect human rights in its own country and to refrain from any kind of activities against, or pursuit of, political dissidents living abroad."[42]

Meanwhile the opposition Green and Social Democratic Parties put forward their own draft resolution:

"The German Parliament emphatically and categorically rejects the accusations and threats by Iran against representatives of the German judiciary in the Mykonos trial. The parliament gives unqualified support to independence of the German judicial branch. In a case such as the Mykonos murders, all suspects must be subjected to investigation. This is a basic principle of our country, which accepts the rule of law, and applies it even if suspicion is directed at a foreign government. The German Parliament expects the governments of foreign countries to accept this principle of government based on law. Many Iranian exiles in Europe and Germany have been threatened and murdered, and this particular crime, which took place on German soil, must be more intensively investigated. An effort must be made to prevent the reoccurrence of incidents of a similar kind, all the more because of the suspicion that the Iranian intelligence was involved. The relationship between Iran and Germany is based on Germany's global security and economic interests, and on its international legal commitments regarding human rights. Diplomatic relations are necessary for the realization of such goals. However, the present behaviour of the Iranian government does not allow contacts and cooperation to develop beyond the level of normal political relations."

The opposition resolution went on to make the following specific provisions:

"The German Parliament expects the Federal Government's policy with respect to Iran to be based on the following principles: The extent and form of relations with Iran would depend upon the degree to which Iran takes into consideration German security interests, while Iran should also actively share in reducing tension in the Middle East and in the struggle against international terrorism. Germany's economic relationship with Iran should not involve the export of materials which could be used in the production of nuclear, biological and chemical weapons, and the export of weapons materials be halted.

Germany also expects Iran to abide by its international commitments including commitments with respect to the human rights of its own citizens whether in Iran or abroad. Above all this means that it would guarantee easy access to and permit investigations by independent human rights organizations such as Amnesty International in relevant cases. Iran should cease to persecute dissident writers and intellectuals, and must provide information with regard to the fate of the writer Faraj Sarkuhi, as well as eliminating from the judicial system sentences of execution, including those against members of the Bahai faith, on account of apostasy. Finally, as a condition for continued cooperation in the field of intelligence, Iran should also be in a position to rebut allegations that it has connived at the murder of exiled Iranian citizens."[42]

In addition to this debate censuring Iran, the German parliament also passed each year during the 1990s an annual resolution critical of Iran over the issue of the *fatwa* relating to Salman Rushdie pronounced by Ayatollah Khomeini, the only European parliament to take such a measure. In 1995, for example, a joint resolution by the Christian Democratic parties (CDU/CSU), Social Democrats (SPD), the Green Party, and the Free Democratic Party (FDP) called on the government of Iran to do all within its power to ensure that the call for the death of Salman Rushdie would be given no further publicity and would not be carried out. The German Federal parliament went on to say that it expected Iran to seek the revocation of the *fatwa* issued on February 14, 1989, by the late Ayatollah Ruhollah Khomeini. In the event that any attempt was to be made on Rushdie's life, the parliament would hold Iran responsible for the act, which could have grave consequences for Iran's political and economic interests. However, one SPD deputy, Gerhard Zwerenz, made a personal statement expressing his dissent from the resolution.[43]

Helmut Szimkus: Arrested in Iran

During the war between Iran and Iraq, Helmut Szimkus, a German citizen, was active in Iran as a spy for Iraq. In 1993, as a result of his own confession, he was sentenced to death. However, the Supreme Leader of Iran, Ayatollah Seyed Ali Khamenei, pardoned him on June 14, 1994 and allowed him, aged 59 after over five years of imprisonment, to be released from Evin prison and to return to Germany, after years of discussion between Iran and Germany, and pleas on his behalf by Klaus Kinkel, the former minister of justice and the present foreign minister, and by Bernd Schmidbauer. Immediately before the announcement, the Iranian Foreign Minister Ali Akbar Velayati had been in Germany for talks with Chancellor Helmut Kohl to discuss the issue. The German government made the following statement: "In 1989, Helmut Szimkus was arrested in Iran on charges of providing classified information to a belligerent power, Iraq. In 1993, he was sentenced to death. It is alleged that during the Iran–Iraq war, which lasted from 1980 until 1988, he informed Iraqis of the landing points of Iraqi missiles in Iran. During interrogation, Szimkus confessed to spying. Bernd Schmidtbauer, Minister of State at the Chancellor's office, is presently in the Iranian capital for negotiations with Iranian officials. Mr Schmidtbauer, who, along with other government officials, has been active in negotiating to free Szimkus, intends to thank the Iranian government for its actions. Mr Schmidbauer, along with Johannes Görster of the CDU and Bürchard Hirsch of the FDP, traveled to Iran for the release."⁴⁴

Jakob Petros: Arrested in Karlsruhe

In May 1992, the German Federal prosecutor's office issued an order for the arrest in Karlsruhe of Jakob Petros, aged 51, an employee of the Federal Press Office. According to the media, Petros had from the beginning of 1991 handed over classified documents, which were accessible to him through his official position, to an intelligence organization in Iran. These documents included telexes and faxes from and to German embassies in Middle and Near Eastern countries. Petros was arrested and imprisoned, and after a trial held in camera he was given a prison sentence.⁴⁵

Gerhard Bachmann: Arrested in Tehran

The day after the return of the Iranian Information Minister Mr Fallahian from his official visit to Germany in 1993, the arrest was announced in Iran of Gerhard Bachmann, the Director of the representative office of the German MAN lorry manufacturing company in Iran. Mr Bachmann was also a member of the administrative board of the Iran–Germany Chamber of Commerce. The author, in his capacity as ambassador, was summoned to the German Foreign Ministry and was requested to provide information concerning the detention of a German citizen. The Justice Department of the Iranian Armed Forces informed the embassy that a German national by the name of Gerhard Alfred Bachmann, had been arrested after being accused of unauthorized contact with army personnel involving the revelation of military secrets. Mr Bachmann's commercial position meant that he had an extensive network of commercial contacts with Iranian military personnel.⁴⁶

The author met Dieter Kastrup, the German Deputy Foreign Minister, and informed him of the accusations against Mr Bachmann, which included bribery, unauthorized contacts with military personnel, and the disclosure of military secrets concerning Iran. The embassy also reported to the minister that Mr Bachmann had been arrested under the terms of a judicial decree, and that according to Iranian law and international practice he was entitled to a defence lawyer, as well as explaining that Mr Bachmann's whereabouts were not secret, and that he had been informed of the charges against him. While expressing gratitude for the Iranian government's prompt response, the German Deputy Foreign Minister also conveyed his hope that the issue could soon be resolved and that it would not lead to any problem in relations between the two countries. At the request of the German Foreign Ministry, the Iranian judicial authorities agreed to allow a representative of the German embassy in Iran to visit Mr Bachmann in prison.⁴⁷

British press reports claim Germany has provided Iran with espionage equipment

In 1993, various London publications accused the German government of having provided Iran with advanced espionage equipment. These reports were widely followed up by the German press, and a German parliamentary committee ordered the issue to be investigated. According to the English newspaper *The Sunday Times*, the German government had agreed to make available to the Iranian government an elaborate computer system to aid it in tracking down members of opposition groups inside and outside the country, and to train Iranian security officials in its use. In return, the Iranian Security Service had agreed not to use the computer equipment for tracking down and attacking Iranian opposition groups in Germany. This agreement was allegedly made during Dr Ali Fallahian's 1993 visit to Germany, which took place three weeks before the opening of the trial of five Iranians accused of murdering Iranian opposition groups abroad. At the same time, the Supreme Court of Germany had announced its intention to indict Dr Fallahian on a charge of killing members of the Iranian opposition. However, on the orders of senior government officials, the Federal Court was prevented from pursuing the matter.[48]

Firsch and Schlags: Arrested and freed

In 1993, a German citizen by the name of Paul Dietrich Firsch was arrested, convicted, and imprisoned in Iran. Paul Dietrich Firsch owned a company in Nuremberg, but for 24 years had lived in Iran, where he became a property developer, building 326 apartments. His arrest caused tension between the two countries. In the end, he was freed for humanitarian reasons. Mr Schlags, a German citizen resident in Italy, was engaged in gunrunning to Bosnia. He had been arrested in Iran after financial difficulties with Iranian governmental agencies. He had received money from Iran to deliver arms to Bosnia but he failed to deliver part of what had been agreed. After some days of negotiation between Minister of State Bernd Schmidbauer and the Iranian embassy in Bonn, Mr Schlags was freed.[49]

Dr Javadi: Prosecuted in Germany

The prosecution in 1994 of an Iranian citizen named Dr Mehdi Javadi for his part in an alleged fraud perpetrated by Dr Jörgen Schneider, a German real estate tycoon, was an issue to which the German media paid considerable attention, and which created difficulties in relations between Germany and Iran. Dr Schneider's fraudulent activities, involving a sum of DM 6 billion, were seen in Germany as very serious and had undermined public trust in the business community. Dr Javadi was accused of arranging the transfer of huge sums of money out of the country on behalf of Dr Schneider. Dr Jörgen Schneider addressed a letter to Javadi, the owner of a large carpet store, apparently asking him to take rapid action to transfer money abroad ahead of impending bankruptcy proceedings. The criminal investigators regarded the letter as evidence of Javadi's involvement in the affair, and the police said they suspected him of helping Schneider to transfer a sum of between DM 200 million and 300 million to Swiss and other foreign banks. Witnesses said that Dr Javadi was innocent. In the end he was acquitted by the German courts.[50]

Two Iranian diplomats deported amid allegations of spying

The German and other European media gave wide coverage in August 1995 to a report alleging that Germany had expelled two Iranian diplomats, a story that emerged first in an American newspaper. Diplomatic circles on both sides were apparently anxious to play the story down. The German Foreign Ministry spokesman Martin Erdmann refused to make any comment on the report that two German diplomats might be expelled from Tehran in retaliation, while an Iranian embassy official denied that the two had been deported. The two Iranian diplomats, named Ali Osooli and Jalal Abbasi, were employed at the Iranian consulates in Bonn and Frankfurt.[51] In consultation with the German Deputy Foreign Minister Peter Hartman, the author, acting in his ambassadorial capacity, was able to agree on an announcement that the two diplomats had come to the end of their normal period of service.

German media allegations against the Iranian embassy in Germany

In 1996, there was substantial criticism in the German media of the activities of the Iranian embassy. In one such critical report, *Suddeutsche Zeitung* commented that it was widely assumed that the Iranian embassy in Bonn was the center from which Iranian intelligence activities in Europe were coordinated.[52] According to the paper, actions presumed to have been carried out with the knowledge of the embassy included the murders at the Mykonos restaurant on September 17, 1992. Similarly, the murder in Paris on May 28, 1996 of Reza Mazlouman, a former minister under the Shah's regime, was supposed to be traceable to this embassy. However, the paper added that officials of the German Internal Security Organization, the Verfassungsschutz, had been unable to confirm the alleged implication of the embassy. On the other hand, the paper said, it was an open secret that the Iranian embassy in Bonn was keeping under surveillance Germany's Iranian residents, who number approximately 100,000, and the report also alleged that Iran especially strove to persuade Iranian scientists and other experts to return to their country in order to participate in the reconstruction of the country.

The newspaper was particularly anxious to expose what it said was Iranian pressure on the opposition in exile: "Pressure is brought to bear especially on the opposition, and in this respect the messengers of the clergy have no qualms about intimidation and scare tactics. The Mujahedin Khalq recently published a document describing 3,000 such incidents, though German security officials will not confirm the figure, saying only that they are aware of such cases. According to Germany's Internal Security Agency, in addition to influencing

Iranians, Iran attempts to use religion to exercise influence on all Muslims and to persuade them to accept its own religious point of view." The paper also reported that Iran was attempting to improve its weapons capability and was attempting to purchase technological information, spare parts for weapons, and other related materials. As the paper commented: "Those who guide such illegal activities at embassies are protected by diplomatic immunity." In the case of the Iranian embassy in Germany, the special relationship that exists between Bonn and Tehran affords the opportunity for Iran's intelligence activities.

Discovery of bugging devices at the Iranian Consulate in Berlin

A number of elaborate bugging devices were discovered at the Iranian Consulate in Berlin while building repairs were being undertaken in November 1996, a development that occasioned serious anger in Tehran and was the subject of a strong protest delivered to the German Foreign Ministry by the author, in the course of his responsibilities as Iranian ambassador. Among the devices found was a tiny receiver installed in the wooden columns of the consulate so that dialogues, which took place inside the building, would be heard outside. The German Federal Office for Criminal Investigation immediately opened an inquiry into who had installed the devices, with the aim of defusing hostility between the two countries. By mid-November, the inquiry claimed to be in a position to exonerate the German Intelligence Service of responsibility for the incident. The question was then asked, had the bugging of the Iranian embassy been carried out by Israel, or the CIA? Or could Iran itself have installed the devices, with the aim of presenting itself as a victim of Western intelligence? It was reportedly even conjectured by the German Federal Office for Criminal Investigation that some Western intelligence service had informed Iranian officials of the existence of the bugging devices, in order to disrupt relations between Iran and Germany, knowing that the Islamic government in Iran would be enraged by the discovery.[53]

Developments in Iran

In July 1996, the Iranian security forces entered the home of a German diplomat serving in Iran, Jens Gust, the Cultural Counsellor at the German embassy in Tehran, and arrested six Iranian opposition writers, including Faraj Sarkuhi, whom Gust had invited to his home for dinner. Gust himself was accused of spying. The German Intelligence Service commented that the incident appeared to be some kind of retaliation for developments in the Myknonos trial, at that time proceeding in Berlin. Faraj Sarkuhi, a journalist and known dissident, had already been arrested on a previous occasion in Iran when, together with 133 other Iranian writers, he had signed an open letter to the Iranian President requesting a guarantee of freedom of speech. On that occasion, according to German press reports, he was held in prison under interrogation and allegedly tortured for 47 days, while Iranian officials spread the rumor that he had departed for Germany. In November 1996, the German diplomat Jens Gust was withdrawn from Tehran, for security reasons.

On December 20, 1996, Mr Sarkuhi suddenly appeared at Tehran airport, and at a turbulent press conference, he announced that he had been in Germany and, for personal reasons, had not contacted his wife. Mr Sarkuhi then again disappeared, and was presumed by his family to be held by Iranian intelligence. In early 1997, there was considerable tension between Germany and Iran over Sarkuhi's fate, and on two occasions, the German government summoned the Iranian ambassador to the German Foreign Ministry. The issue put relations between Iran and Germany under considerable tension for a prolonged period.[54]

Conclusions

The incidents detailed above were not the only sources of tension of this kind between Iran and Germany during the period from 1990 to 1997. There were many other similar incidents in the period after German reunification. Of course, the arrest and detention of foreign citizens is an everyday occurrence in any state: For example during the 1998 World Cup, a number of German and British citizens were arrested in France for public order offences and several were deported, without any resulting deterioration in relations between any of the countries involved. However, between 1990 and 1996 more than 80 percent of the Western citizens who were detained for whatever reason in Iran were Germans. This was a situation that was difficult to reconcile with Iran's general foreign policy of improvement of relations with Germany.

A separate factor, the violent activities of the terrorist organization Mujahedin Khalq, did create some difficulty in relations between Iran and Germany, but in the end had relatively little effect. There is substantial evidence for this. In spite of even the most extreme MKO activities, such as their attacks on Iranian diplomatic premises, the improvement of relations between Iran and Germany continued. The German government, indeed, denounced the MKO as a terrorist organization, which was acting in violation of international law, and prevented its leader Maryam Rajavi from entering Germany. Clearly, Germany was not disposed to regard the existence of an active opposition movement to the government of a country as a reason for loss of confidence in the government of the country concerned. In the similar case of the attacks by the Kurdish PKK against Turkish missions on German soil, the actions of the opposition had little effect on Bonn–Ankara relations, and the activities of the Mujahedin Khalq could not be compared with those of the PKK, with a Kurdish population of some 400,000 and at least 40,000 supporters on German soil. At one time, there was a serious PKK attack on some Turkish target in Germany virtually every week, but although attacks by the PKK were far more numerous than those of the MKO, Bonn–Ankara relations were not derailed from their path.

However, issues related to terrorism, and especially the Mykonos affair, did create real problems for Iran's relationship with Germany in particular and the EU in general. As has been stated earlier the Mykonos affair and its implications will be discussed in the next chapter.

4   Analyzing a crisis

Onset of reciprocal measures leading to a full-blown diplomatic crisis between Iran and Germany

The killings at the Mykonos restaurant

On September 17, 1992 at 11 p.m. two masked gunmen burst into the *Mykonos* Greek restaurant in the Wilmersdorf district of Berlin, spraying the back room of the restaurant with bullets from an Uzi automatic machine gun and a Lama-Spezial revolver, and killing four men, all Iranian Kurds, including Sadegh Sharafkandi, the exiled Secretary-General of the Kurdistan Democratic Party of Iran (KDPI), a political party officially dissolved in Iran.[1] The front room of the restaurant was full of ordinary customers. Although the Mykonos restaurant bore a Greek name, it was in fact an entirely Iranian restaurant, and had become the customary haunt of Iranian opposition figures identified with leftist organizations.[2] On this occasion the owner, Aziz Ghafouri, a former member of the Marxist–Leninist Organization *Fadaian Khalq*, had set aside a large table in the back room for a group of visitors, who, by the late hour of the attack, were relaxing round the table, debating and arguing about political issues concerning Iran.

Sadegh Sharafkandi, the principal target of the assassins, was visiting Germany along with representatives of his party at the invitation of the German Socialist Party (SPD), which in that year was hosting the *Tagung der Sozialistischen Internationale* (Conference on International Socialism).[2] Sharafkandi had succeeded Abdul Rahman Qassemlou, who had been assassinated in Vienna three years earlier in not dissimilar circumstances. The others who were killed were Fattah Abduli, a KDPI representative in Europe, Homayoun Ardalan, the KDPI representative in Germany, and Nuri Dehkurdi, a translator. Other members of the group were severely injured and the restaurant owner himself died later of his wounds. Sharafkandi had been sitting at the table, and fell to the ground after being hit. To ensure that he was dead, one of the murderers, before leaving the scene, fired a last bullet into his head.[2] After the incident, the mass media immediately leveled accusations against the Iranian authorities,[3] seeking to connect the event with the murder of Qassemlou, Sharafkandi's predecessor, and to incriminate Iran's intelligence services.[4]

Following the assassination, foreign intelligence services, including MI6, the British overseas intelligence organization, revealed that, according to reliable sources, two of the murderers of the Kurdish leaders were still at large in Germany. These were two Lebanese citizens, Abbas Rhayel, aged 26, and Youssef Amin, aged 25, who were revealed to be hiding in the home of Youssef's brother, Ahmad Amin, who lived in the state of Nordrhein-Westfalen. German agents stormed the house at night, arrested everyone and found a substantial amount of foreign currency. Youssef Amin was the first to confess. He revealed the location where the weapons had been hidden and the whereabouts of the car in which the assassins had made their escape. He also disclosed the address and personal details of another conspirator, an Iranian, Kazem Darabi, who was arrested three days later.

British intelligence, it emerged, had for as long as 20 years kept Kazem Darabi under surveillance, intercepting his telephone conversations.[5] He had been on the point of being deported from Germany in 1983, but the German government had interceded with the immigration authorities, enabling him to remain in Germany.[6] Darabi had previously been among the active leadership of the Islamic Student Union in Iran, and was a supporter of the Islamic revolution.[7] The German Intelligence Service and Criminal Department made the allegation, as soon as Darabi was implicated, that the killers had been working on behalf of the Iranian government and accused Darabi of responsibility for organizing the crime. The Federal Office for the Protection of the Constitution (Bundes Amt fur Verfassungsschutz) described him as an "Iranian spy."[8] Those who were finally accused in addition to Kazem Darabi were Youssef Amin, Abbas Rhayel, and two other Lebanese citizens, Attallah Ayyadh, aged 27, and Mohammed Idris. According to media reports, another member of the group who carried out the attack, Fazlollah Haidar (known as Abu Jafar), had been able to flee to Lebanon.[9] British newspapers also pointed the finger of accusation at the government of Iran and emphasized that the issue was larger than that of the fate of Darabi himself and the four Lebanese who were to be tried with him. The Iranian government itself was involved, the papers claimed, and this was a fact that politicians in Bonn found disagreeable.[10]

Iran's minister of information subpoenaed

On Friday March 16, 1996, the judge presiding over the court in Berlin that had for two and a half years been hearing the trial of the accused in the Mykonos case issued a subpoena to Mr Ali Fallahian, who had been Iran's minister of information since 1989, summoning him to appear before the court on suspicion of implication in the murders. The subpoena, which was confirmed by Germany's Federal Supreme Court, was requested by the German Prosecutor-General Kay Nehm, who claimed that there were concrete reasons to suppose that the murders had been perpetrated under the supervision of the Iranian Ministry of Information.[11] A few weeks before the murders in 1992, in a television interview in Iran, Ali Fallahian had identified the Kurdish organization to which the victims belonged as a target of his ministry's activities, and declared that he would pursue them both inside and outside the country. The German government had already emphasized in 1995 that it did not intend to interfere, either in the normal legal procedure of the case or over the issue of the subpoena.

The first serious threat to Iran–Germany relations

Bonn's policy of "critical dialogue" with Tehran was shaken by the issue of the subpoena, a new development that clouded the political atmosphere. After the German Prosecutor-General decreed the issue of the subpoena to Mr Fallahian, with the consequent implication that he would be arrested and brought to trial if he came to Germany, Tehran threatened to take reciprocal action. Meanwhile the German government continued to insist that the subpoena was an exclusively legal issue. It was however unclear why, some two and a half years after the opening of the Mykonos trial, the German legal authorities had begun to act as if they had apparently acquired new information. Though suspicions had been constantly voiced in Germany since the Mykonos incident that direct orders had been issued for the murders by the Iranian Ministry of Information, no proof or documentary evidence had hitherto been produced. It appeared to be significant that the sudden incrimination of Mr Fallahian and the issue of the subpoena had occurred after the international antiterrorist conference held in Sharm el-Sheikh.[12] In reality, of course, it must be remembered that the issue of an order to arrest an Iranian minister could have had no real effect, since Mr Fallahian was not due to visit Germany, while in any case the principle of diplomatic immunity would have shielded him from the implementation of the subpoena.

Up to this time, Germany and Iran had taken pride in their good relations. Since the signature of the first commercial contract and friendship agreement between Iran and the German state of Prussia as long ago as 1875, the exchange of goods and ideas between the two countries had continued almost uninterrupted. By 1995, German business and industry constituted the most important trading partner of present-day Iran, and German technical assistance was more needed by Iran than ever before. German politicians had been unstinting in their efforts to build up the good reputation of German merchandise, while Germany had in addition begun to draw benefit from its relationship with Iran, which enabled it to exercise influence in the region similar to that of other Western powers. After the Islamic revolution in Iran, the then German Foreign Minister Hans-Dietrich Genscher made no secret of his readiness to open discussions with Iran's new regime, in order to avert the total isolation of the new Islamic government from the West, which could have contributed to Iran's potentially destabilizing influence. While the United States constantly strove to bring about the isolation of Iran, the succeeding German Foreign Minister Klaus Kinkel developed the concept of the "critical dialogue" and, in a visible display of Bonn's intention to maintain its relationship with Tehran, German politicians were prominent among Western officials present at the first autumn exhibition in Tehran after the revolution.

However, there were indications in 1995 that German policy had its ambiguous aspects. Two years earlier, Bonn had signed a series of treaties with Tehran rescheduling the repayment of Iran's debts, in a move especially welcomed by German banks. In contrast, however, the state Hermes Insurance Company agreed to back business deals with Iran only up to an insignificant level. Apparently, there had been some tendency within Germany's policy toward the imposition at least of de facto sanctions on Iran, by restricting the level of business between the two countries. In this, Germany was following the lead of the United States, perhaps on a more significant level than the German government was openly prepared to admit. In November 1995, when the German Foreign Minister Kinkel faced severe parliamentary criticism, he was obliged to recognize that, in the context of Germany's domestic politics, his strategy toward Iran was facing difficulties, which were increasing from day to day. The German Federal parliament cancelled its invitation to Iranian Foreign Minister Velayati, and Bonn then suddenly cancelled the long-planned Islamic Conference. All this took place apparently because Tehran had indicated that it viewed the recent assassination of Yitzhak Rabin as a divine punishment, and even welcomed it. With the issue of the subpoena, the situation in relations between Germany and Iran took a turn very difficult for Mr Kinkel to control.

Iran's reaction to the subpoena

A spokesman for Iran's Ministry of Foreign Affairs, Dr Mohammadi, announced Iran's rejection of the issue of the subpoena to Mr Fallahian, describing it as contrary to the normal standards of international behavior and thus unacceptable. The spokesman asserted that no documentary evidence existed to support any suggestion of a connection between officials of Iran and the Mykonos case, and added that the determining factor behind the decision of the German public prosecutor to request the subpoena had been international propaganda, in addition to pressure on the part of various groups and parties who were opposed to the continuation of constructive relations between Iran and Germany based on the national interests of the two countries. These were groups, Dr Mohammadi said, which had striven continually to create difficulties in relations between Iran and Germany. Without doubt, he added, rapid progress in the fair and accurate investigation of the Mykonos case would serve to reveal the truth and to eliminate what he called falsehoods and baseless accusations against Iran.[13]

The subpoena withheld by the German government

In a letter to the presiding judge of the court in Berlin, Mr Kubsch, the German Minister of Justice, requested that the court should refrain from despatching the subpoena to the Iranian Minister of Information. Following his receipt of this letter, the judge announced that the court would waive the subpoena summoning Mr Fallahian as a witness. The German newspapers *Die Welt* and *Frankfurter Rundschau* reported that a letter sent by the German Ministry of Justice to the Head of the Berlin court had confirmed that the ministry did not intend to request legal cooperation from Tehran to issue the summons to Mr Fallahian. The reports added that the presiding judge had made a statement to the effect that in the circumstances he considered the summoning of Mr Fallahian to the court in Berlin not to be feasible.[14]

The appearance in court of Bani-Sadr and Witness "C"

In August 1996, the BBC World Service broadcast a report that the former President of Iran, Abolhassan Bani-Sadr, would appear in court in Berlin to testify against Iranian officials, who, as he claimed, had ordered the murder of the three Kurdish party officials at the Mykonos restaurant. Radio Liberty, a radio station established in Prague by the United States, reported the following week in its Tajik language service that Bani-Sadr had accused the leader of Iran, Ayatollah Khamenei, as well as President Rafsanjani, of issuing the order that the murder of the Kurdish dissidents in Germany be carried out. Mr Bani-Sadr said that he was in possession of documents, which would prove the accusations.[15]

In September 1996, Abolhassan Bani-Sadr appeared in court in Berlin and claimed that he had access to a witness formerly employed by the Iranian Ministry of Information who would testify anonymously. Bani-Sadr claimed that this witness was in possession of firsthand information regarding the involvement of the highest echelons of the Iranian leadership in the Mykonos affair. According to alleged documents in possession of the witness, decisions on terrorist actions outside the country were taken by a so-called "special committee" comprising Ayatollah Khamenei, President Rafsanjani, the Foreign Minister Dr Velayati, and the Minister of Information Mr Fallahian. Allegedly, terrorist actions would be carried out only with the approval of the supposed committee.[16]

In its mid-September session, the court decided to convene in closed session to hear the evidence of the individual named by Bani-Sadr, who was designated Witness "C". The presiding judge ruled that the court should sit in camera because of the danger to the life of the witness if his identity were to become known, adding that the Iranian authorities had already determined to kill the witness in order to silence him. The judge also issued an order binding all parties to the case to observe confidentiality to preserve the witness's anonymity.[17] In court, Witness "C", who fled the country after giving his evidence, claimed that Iran's political leaders were the instigators of the murders. He alleged in his testimony that the President of Iran, President Ali Akbar Hashemi Rafsanjani, together with the Iranian Foreign Minister Ali Akbar Velayati, was aware of plans to carry out the murders, and that the Head of Iran's Intelligence Service, Ali Fallahian, was charged with the responsibility of seeing that the murders were carried out. One of the prosecution attorneys, Axel Joschke, said afterwards that the witness had confirmed certain conjectures, which had hitherto been only a matter of suspicion. However, in an interview with *Der Spiegel*, President Rafsanjani dismissed the claims made in the Berlin court as baseless, stating "We are against any kind of terrorism."[18]

The prosecutor's closing address

On Tuesday, November 12, 1996, the Prosecutor-General delivered his closing address to the court. The trial had lasted for three years, and three days were set aside for the address, in which the prosecutor alluded to the political implications of the incident, while reiterating that the German government had not attempted to influence the court's proceedings. The prosecutor used the term *state terrorism*, while claiming that Ayatollah Khamenei, President Rafsanjani, the Foreign Minister Dr Velayati, and the Minister of Information Mr Fallahian had participated in the issue of the order for the Berlin murders, acting in their capacity as members of a so-called special committee formed to oversee the execution of terrorist acts abroad. The public prosecutor thus gave credence to the evidence that had been given to the court, to the effect that the Iranian authorities, acting clandestinely, had been responsible for the murders.

According to the prosecutor, it was Ayatollah Khamenei himself who took the initiative in ordering that the murders should be carried out, and the decision was endorsed by the alleged special committee, of which the Iranian President and Foreign Minister were supposedly members. It allegedly fell to the remaining member of the committee, Mr Fallahian, to put into practice the decision to execute the Kurdish leaders. The prosecutor also claimed that Kazem Darabi, the Iranian accused of complicity in the crime, was the leader of the group that actually carried out the killings. The public prosecutor detailed how the principal culprit and his supporters made preparations, including the provision of forged identity documents, and the preparation of an escape plan. During the prosecutor's address, one of the accused became ill as a result of stress, and as a result the trial was temporarily adjourned.[19]

The importance to the case of the evidence of Bani-Sadr and Witness "C"

The prosecutor's accusations were founded on the evidence given by Bani-Sadr and Witness "C", who decided at this stage to reveal his identity. He introduced himself as Abolghassem Mesbahi, aged 39 years, asserting that he had formerly held a position of high responsibility in the Iranian Intelligence Service. He claimed to have been in 1984 the Iranian Intelligence Service's operative at the Iranian embassy in Paris, until his deportation by the French authorities. In his evidence to the court, he referred to the freeing of a German hostage in Lebanon by the name of Rudolf Cordes, who was an executive for the German Höchst Company. Mesbahi said that during the period concerned he had conducted secret talks with German politicians with respect to Cordes's freedom, and that in exchange for Cordes, Tehran had asked for the freedom of the Hamadi brothers, two Lebanese sentenced to 13 years imprisonment in Germany in April 1988 for hijacking an aeroplane. Mesbahi added that he had held talks, among others, with Erhard Epler, Hans-Jochen Vogel, and Hans-Jürgen Wischnewski, parliamentary deputies for the German Social Democratic Party (SPD). Rudolf Cordes was held hostage in Lebanon, until September 1988, when he was freed after 600 days of captivity. In 1993, Abbas Hamadi was released from prison.

Mesbahi's evidence played an important role in the court proceedings, to the extent that his claim that the Iranian leadership was implicated in the murder of the four Kurdish opposition figures was what led the prosecutor to name for the first time the President of Iran as the instigator of the murders, in the course of his examination of the witness, the opinion that was also expressed in the prosecutor's closing speech. This development gave rise to a serious protest from Iran, and was the occasion of a demonstration by the Iranian clergy in the city of Qom when the German prosecutors were threatened by a *fatwa* calling for their death. However, Iranian sources continued to insist that "Witness C" was no more than a professional liar. During the second phase of the court's interrogation of Mesbahi, strict security measures were observed.[20]

The German ambassador in Tehran summoned to the foreign ministry

The German ambassador, Horst Bachmann, was summoned to the Iranian Foreign Ministry, where Morteza Sarmadi, the Deputy Minister for Communications, conveyed to him Iran's strong protest. The Iranian authorities objected strongly to what they regarded as the insults and false accusations of the German judicial authorities. Mr Sarmadi said that Iran took the view that the German judicial authorities and the judicial branch of government had embarked on what he called a dirty political campaign against Iran, allegedly under Zionist influence. Mr Sarmadi said in his statement to the German ambassador that "the repetition by the German public prosecutor of politically motivated insults and unfounded accusations, which have no part in the judicial process, against the highest-ranking religious and political authorities of the Islamic Republic of Iran indicates that by its politicization of the trial of the murder of a number of Kurdish Iranians, together with its subservience to Zionist interests, the German judiciary has damaged its credibility."

Sarmadi reminded the German ambassador that the accusations made against the highest Iranian officials were based on the testimony of witnesses who had themselves taken part in the hijackings of aeroplanes and other destructive and terrorist activities directed against the nation and system of Iran, and that these were crimes of which the Iranian courts had documentary proof derived from terrorist sources. While emphasizing that the government of Iran would under no circumstances tolerate such insults, the Deputy Foreign Minister added: "It is evident that such hostile actions will have an undesirable effect on relations between the two countries and the responsibility for their consequences will lie with the German Government." The German ambassador replied that he would immediately convey the views of Iran to his government.[21]

Demonstrations and marches in Iran against Germany

A wave of demonstrations and marches hostile to Germany took place in cities across Iran, in which the people expressed their condemnation of Israel, the United States, and the German judicial system. In Tehran, numerous demonstrations took place in front of the German embassy. At one major demonstration in the city of

Meshed, thousands of ordinary Iranians from all walks of society averred their disgust at the insults against the sanctities of Iran's Islamic system contained in the pronouncements of the German judiciary. Filling the streets of Meshed between Shohada Square to Imam Reza's Holy Shrine, the demonstrators chanted slogans against the United States and the Zionist regime in Israel, and displayed banners demanding an apology to Iran from the German authorities. Speaking to the demonstrators in Meshed, Iran's Foreign Minister Dr Velayati expressed his approbation of their action, endorsing it as an indication of the people's religious courage and their respect for Islamic beliefs. "So long as such sensitivities toward Islamic and religious sanctities exist in Iran's people," he added, "the country's system could not be harmed and others would not dare to interfere with it."

In a comment on the protests of the demonstrators against the German judiciary, Dr Velayati said, with reference to the German government's insistence on its lack of control over the judicial system, that the government of every country must occupy the predominant position regarding everything that takes place, especially in the matter of international relations, which are based on mutual respect, and that this need not be incompatible with the independence of the judicial branch. He added that Iran had repeatedly emphasized that relations between the Islamic world and the West must be based on mutual respect and understanding. Referring to the German government's reluctance to see its relations with Iran damaged, he reiterated that Iran's expectation was that the German authorities attempt to compensate Iran for the disrespect to which it had been subjected. The Foreign Minister added that Zionist influences undoubtedly lay behind the action of the German prosecutor in insulting high-ranking officials of the Islamic Republic. According to Dr Velayati, similar claims were made in a magazine known to be under Zionist control at the same time as the pronouncement of the German court, a circumstance that justifies the suspicion of a connection between Zionist influence and the action of the German judicial system.[22]

Letter to President Rafsanjani from Chancellor Kohl

In a bid to calm the atmosphere, the German Chancellor sent a letter to President Rafsanjani, the full text of which appears below:

"November 21, 1996

Bonn

The Honourable Hojjatoleslam Akbar Hashemi Rafsanjani

The President of the Islamic Republic of Iran

Tehran

Honourable President,

During the past few days I have observed with concern and dismay the trend of relations between our two countries, and especially its reflection in the media. Unfortunately, I fear that in this process the long-standing friendly relations between the two countries may be damaged.

Mr President, I am willing to assure you that, contrary to what has appeared in some of your country's declarations, the Mykonos trial, which is currently being held in Berlin, is not a 'political trial'. Rather, an independent German court, which does not receive political orders, is attempting on the basis of documents and evidence alone to discover the circumstances that led to the crime. The German courts are independent. This is true not only of the pronouncement of sentence, but also of the method of prosecution.

Our courts make a concerted effort in the struggle against terrorism. Under no circumstances would the government of the Federal Republic of Germany or the Ministry of Justice have any intention to inflict pain on the religious sensitivities of the Iranian people and their religious leaders.

As you know, I have always been committed to a trusting dialogue between the two world religions, and I have had an ample exchange of views with you on political issues such as the political changes which have taken place in Bosnia. This is equally true of our cooperation in the resolution of humanitarian problems in the Middle East in the course of which, most recently, we have achieved a constructive cooperation with Iran, which produced positive results for the people of this region.

It is in the interest of both nations to refrain from exacerbating the current deterioration in our relations. I earnestly request that you use all your influence so that further tension will not arise. I especially request that, in accordance with international law, you provide for the security of German citizens, German institutions and German interests in your country, in a manner similar to that in which the German Federal Government would itself naturally act.

I hope that in the days and weeks to come, we shall succeed in safeguarding the relationship between Iran and Germany from further injury.

With friendly regards,

Helmut Kohl"

President Rafsanjani's response

The Iranian president sent a strongly worded response to the German Chancellor. Immediately after the receipt of the letter, the author, in his role as Iranian ambassador in Germany, was contacted by the Chancellor's office and by Germany's Deputy Foreign Minister, Mr Hartmann, requesting that the contents of the letter not be made public. The request was conveyed to President Rafsanjani, who accepted it with great reluctance. The text of the President's response follows:

"In the Name of God

The Honourable Helmut Kohl, Chancellor of the Federal Republic of Germany

Your tactful and timely letter has been received; it was helpful in correcting the tendency of the incidents that have occurred between the two countries, which have gone astray as a result of unconsidered statements. I share with you a concern that the warm and substantial relations between our two countries may be damaged, and I am concerned lest those who are opposed to a constructive dialogue between Iran and the European Union (EU) succeed in their unholy attempts to prevent the two sides from arriving at constructive results through a critique of each other's views. Although after a week of agitation a degree of comprehension has developed in both countries, there remains room for concern over the future in view of what has occurred in the past.

When I see that an individual in a prosecutor's position, in a country such as Germany, in spite of the discernment of well-wishing authorities and our own benevolent warnings, is nevertheless able to cause such a disturbance with his irresponsible statements, how can we be sure that this kind of action will not be repeated? While we are aware that there exists a prosecutor whose hands are empty of reliable evidence and trustworthy proofs, who relies on statements of questionable witnesses and invites an aeroplane hijacker as witness, and who can unjustly accuse a revolutionary Islamic system and people, having no concern whatsoever for the ultimate consequences, we cannot have peace of mind. In view of the circumstances in your country, you are justified in speaking in your letter of the independence of the judicial branch of your government. However, I expect your Excellency to also give our people the right to be pessimistic about the outcome of this trial. This is especially the case since we have reliable information that these so-called witnesses have alternately been at the service of the intelligence Organizations of France, Britain and the United States, and it is through these connections that they have established a link with your public prosecutor.

Although it is possible that soon the same public disgrace which befell the United States in using a fleeing swindler, Manuchehr Mo'tamer, in the Argentine explosion and the Oklahoma bombing will also befall our friend, Germany, it may be too late. In any case, while relying on mutual trust, we have overcome one stage of the danger, and we hope that the accuracy and fairness of the court will end in a just verdict for the accused, far removed from political motives. We also hope that we shall not see your judicial system becoming a platform for Zionist and American propaganda and, without doubt, neutral observers would be pleased to see the preservation of the honour and validity of the German judicial system.

It is doubtful, unless the people are unaware of the facts, whether the German nation is satisfied to see its judicial system unjustly accuse a nation of terrorism, especially a nation which, more than any other, is itself a victim of the iniquity of known terrorists, some of whom have unfortunately taken refuge in the same state which is holding the trial in question and are allowed to continue their crimes. It is even harder to accept that the German authorities would approve the fact that the distorted thinking of one judicial official could be allowed to destroy the positive atmosphere of constructive co-operation between our two countries in political, economic, and cultural affairs, and in the sensitive regions of the Middle East, the Persian Gulf, Central Asia, the Caucasus and the Balkans, when an example could be set for judges in other countries to assist the leaders of nations. In conclusion, I wish for the prosperity and happiness of your Excellency and the people of Germany.

Akbar Hashemi Rafsanjani, President, Islamic Republic of Iran"

Relative calm after the exchange between political leaderships

After the German Chancellor's letter, the adoption of a conciliatory tone in Friday prayer sermons delivered by President Rafsanjani led to a diminution in the atmosphere of turmoil. The German government attempted to prevent relations between Germany and Iran from deteriorating any further and, in addition, to clarify the fact that the German judicial system was independent of political issues. German government officials believed that President Rafsanjani had given an indication that Iran had taken heed of Chancellor Kohl's concern that relations between the two countries should not be subjected to increased strain. It was also believed in Bonn that the Iranian government had welcomed Chancellor Kohl's letter for its potential influence on internal developments in Iran. The German government had intended to withhold the letter for 24 hours, while awaiting its evaluation by Iran, but when it became clear that Iran would prefer the contents of this message to be made public, Bonn decided to publish it at once. Of course, Chancellor Kohl refrained from explicitly using the word *apology*, but nevertheless the letter was seen as an attempt to counter the accusation that Germany had intended to insult Islamic values. However, another section of the letter indicates that Germany continued to be reluctant to concede that there was any shared responsibility for the strain on Germany–Iran relations. On the contrary, the letter reminds Iran that it bears the responsibility for preventing any further turmoil.

After Iran's initial strong statements and threats, at the next Friday prayers President Rafsanjani took a different line, and one which went some way toward assuaging Bonn's anxiety. The Iranian president said he wanted to see good relations maintained, adding: "There is no doubt that Iran and Germany are determined to continue their friendly relations, which began after the Second World War." After the Qom demonstrations and the death threats to German judges, Rafsanjani's tone had a calming effect. He said that the Iranian people must understand that Ayatollah Khamenei had in fact meant to say that the real enemies of Iran were the United States and the Zionists. Iranian officials had drawn the inference that the Berlin public prosecutor's incrimination of the Iranian leaders was meant to insult the religious leader of the Iranian Shiites—that is, Ayatollah Khamenei. President Rafsanjani, however, commented that Iran had no absolute or specific evidence to suppose that the German government bore any responsibility for the decisions or pronouncements of the German courts. On the other hand, he added, there was clear evidence that a large segment of the German government did not desire relations between the two countries to come under the kind of strain that had arisen as a result of the trial.[23]

Bonn officials took President Rafsanjani's statements at the Friday prayers as a reaction to Chancellor Kohl's letter. President Rafsanjani said that he would soon respond directly to the Chancellor's letter, adding that Germany must not allow itself to be provoked by what he called "satanic elements," or by circumstances beyond the control of the governments in Bonn and Tehran. The expression is used to refer to the United States and Israel. In his role as ambassador, the author issued a denial that a high-ranking Iranian official had threatened the murder of the German prosecutors, and in an interview with *Suddeutsche Zeitung*, the author lent his authority to the view that a non-Muslim German cannot be threatened by the issue of a *fatwa*, so that there was in fact no threat to any German citizen. The author added in the interview that the Iranian government was a respecter of international law, with the implication that it had made no threats of murder or terrorism. However, Iran expected Germany to offer a full and official explanation of what had occurred at the Mykonos trial, and Germany's stance with regard to Islam, to Iran's religious leader Ayatollah Khamenei, and to Iranian government in general, was expected to have been made entirely clear.[23]

After these developments Chancellor Kohl consulted Foreign Minister Klaus Kinkel, Defense Minister Volker Rühe, and Treasury Minister Theodor Waigel, who was also the Head of the CSU, in detailed talks on relations with Iran and the current situation. The opposition was critical of the government's attempt to maintain good relations with Iran apparently at all costs. In an interview with *Bild* magazine, a deputy for the SPD in the Federal Parliament, Wilfried Penner, said, "Should Iran's interference in the Mykonos murders be proven, political relations must end." Another SPD Deputy, Friedhold Bertel, said, "So long as it is not fully clear to what extent the Iranian leadership was involved in the Mykonos case, relations must remain stagnant." Dieter Scheuer, the representative of the Green Party, said the probability was that the German government was handling Iran carefully in order not to endanger Bonn's economic and intelligence relations with Tehran. She added: "No one wants the complete severance of diplomatic relations. However, the level of relations must be reduced to a minimum; this is necessary as a diplomatic gesture. In the long term, the German Government cannot maintain a high-level relationship with Iran, as it has had until the present, nor should there be cooperation between the two countries' intelligence services." Even some government supporters were less than keen on the government's anxiety to maintain good relations. A Christian Democrat Deputy Hans-Otto Wilhelm said, "We must quickly recall our diplomats from Iran, for one cannot trust national leaders who issue orders for murders to be carried out inside and outside their country and implement those orders."

The government quickly reacted to these criticisms and expressions of caution. A spokesman, Mr Hausmann, said: "The German Government is determined to carefully supervise the events in a cool-headed manner." He went on to say that there were claims by some judicial officials that there were elements in the government who were attempting to absolve the Iranian leadership of the accusations made against them in court at the Mykonos trial, but the German government, he added, had never attempted to influence the actions of the court. A senior official of the Foreign Ministry, Mr Heuer of the Free Democratic Party, denied reports claiming that Bonn's position was based on its economic interests, commenting that: "The volume of trade with Iran is currently DM 2.3 billion, which is not of great significance." In an interview with Radio Saarland, Mr Heuer said: "There is no evidence of any kind that the Iranian Government has supported threats against the lives of prosecutors. However, whoever threatens the independence of the German judicial system must be aware that this cannot be tolerated by Germany. Feelings in Iran are at the moment inflamed by anger and the situation remains confused. At the moment, Germany in particular and the European Union in general should attempt to behave in such a way as to influence Iranian officials in the direction of moderation."

The Chairman of the Foreign Policy Committee of the Federal Parliament, Karl-Heinz Hornhues of the CDU, as well as the Deputy Speaker of Parliament, Mr Hirsch, avowed that diplomatic relations with Iran should be fully preserved. Mr Hornhues said that there were indications that Iran was making great efforts to reduce the present level of tension, and that in such circumstances the severing of active diplomatic relations would be unhelpful. The Deputy Speaker of Parliament said: "It is very important that we continue our diplomatic relations with Iran, but of course on condition that Iran does not make it impossible. I do not believe that Iran would threaten murder and thus cross the boundaries of the possible."[23]

The Berlin court pronounces its verdict

The court in Berlin issued its verdict at 10 a.m. on April 10, 1997. The Berlin prosecutor's office made the following official announcement:

> "Today, Thursday, 10 April 1997, on the charge of four simultaneous murders, and because of the severity of the crime, the Court has sentenced Kazem Darabi and Abbas Rhayel to life imprisonment. On the charge of assisting in the four murders, the court sentenced Youssef Amin to 11 years in prison, on the charges arising out of the present case together with another crime, and sentenced Mohammed Idris to 5 years and 3 months. Attallah Ayyadh was acquitted of charges of assisting in the murders."[24]

The Berlin Prosecutor's Department also published a summary of the reasoning that lay behind its verdict, in which the Iranian state was implicitly accused of involvement in the Berlin assassinations, and named individuals in the Iranian government who were explicitly associated with the decisions that led to the killings (see Appendix 3).

Major disruption of relations

When the court in Berlin pronounced its verdict, there followed the most serious disruption, which had ever taken place in relations between Iran and Germany, and in consequence in relations between Iran and Europe as a whole. At noon on the day the verdict was promulgated, the author, in his role as ambassador, was instructed by the authorities in Tehran to request a meeting at the highest level at the German Foreign Ministry, to convey Iran's protest and to inform the Ministry that the ambassador had been recalled to Tehran. An hour later the German Foreign Ministry informed the author that he had been summoned by the Deputy Foreign Minister, Peter Hartmann. The meeting took place at 5 p.m. on April 10, 1997, when Mr Hartmann and the author informed each other of the particulars of their respective countries' protests. Mr Hartmann informed the author that Bonn had decided on the following steps:

1. The recall of the German ambassador from Tehran.
2. The suspension of the "critical dialogue" with Iran.
3. The expulsion of Iranian intelligence agents from German soil.
4. The cessation of exchanges at the ministerial level.

At 7 p.m., the Dutch presidency of the EU announced the EU's position, which comprised the same four measures taken by the German government. Thus, the dialogue between Iran and Germany was suspended, and the dialogue between Iran and the EU also came to a halt. In response, Iranian ambassadors were recalled from Europe to Tehran and, reciprocally, ambassadors from the EU were recalled from Tehran. Germany deported four Iranian diplomats as intelligence agents, and subsequently Iran deported four German diplomats.

The German Federal Prosecutor-General abandons the prosecution of the remaining members of the alleged special committee

Regarding the pursuit of the prosecution of the Iranian Intelligence Minister, Mr Fallahian, and the decision to abandon the case against the remaining members of the so-called special committee, a matter under his jurisdiction, the German Prosecutor-General made the following statement:

"The Federal prosecutor-general has placed under prosecution three members of the Iranian Intelligence Organization due to strong suspicion of their participation, on 17 September 1992, in the murders of members of the opposition group, and has issued an order for their arrest. The order of the Federal Court dated 14 March 1994 for the arrest of the Iranian Minister of Information and Security Ali Fallahian remains effective. The Federal prosecutor-general dispenses with the legal prosecution of the remaining members of the 'Committee for Special Affairs'. The particulars of the matter are as follows: In the verdict delivered on

April 10, 1997, in addition to the four individuals who were convicted, the Berlin Court named three employees of the Iranian Security Organization who participated in the commission of the crime." It is stated therein that the decision for the murder was "taken at a 'Committee for Special Affairs', of which the President of Iran, the 'Religious Leader', the Foreign Minister, the Minister of Information and Security, as well as representatives of the security organization and other organizations, were members." There is absolutely no truth to this claim and the alleged committee does not exist.

"In accordance with information obtained, the Federal prosecutor-general has begun legal prosecution against the Iranian nationals, Abdul-Rahman B. (alias Sharif), Asghar A., and Ali K. (alias Khalil), because of a strong suspicion of their having committed premeditated murder, or having assisted in its commitment. On 14 May 1997, the inquiring judge at the Federal Court issued an order for the arrest of the above-mentioned individuals. The place of residence of the accused is unknown. The order for arrest is based on the following facts. Two to three months before the murders, the accused, A. and K., travelled to Germany on a mission on behalf of the Iranian Security Organization to prepare for the perpetration of the crime. They investigated locations and ways of escape and obtained other information. After their return this information was used in the murder plan. The accused, B., was a staff member of the Iranian Security Organization, who, as the leader of 'The Strike Team', participated directly in the perpetration of the crime. With Abbas Rhayel, who has been sentenced to life imprisonment, the accused entered the Mykonos restaurant and fired at the four people who were targets of the attack. All four were killed. The owner of the restaurant was fatally injured. Abdul-Rahman B. escaped. The legal prosecution, whose responsibility lies with the Criminal Department, continues.

However, in accordance with the following considerations, the Federal prosecutor-general dispenses with the penal prosecution of other individuals who are believed to be members of the 'Special Committee'. The domain of immunity based on international law remains to a large extent unclear. The possibility of further investigation in order to determine the precise manner in which the decisions of the committee were reached and to establish the specific criminal responsibility of each Committee member does not exist other than in the case of the Minister of Information Ali Fallahian. Due to these circumstances, legal prosecution against members of the Committee is deemed to be against the common good."[25]

Iran's protest to Germany

In the course of the author's meeting in his ambassadorial capacity with Peter Hartmann, Deputy Foreign Minister of Germany, he conveyed to the German government the official protest of the Iranian government against what Iran regarded as the baseless accusations of the presiding judge at the Mykonos trial. At the meeting, the author categorically denied any Iranian government involvement in the Berlin incident, and made clear that it was Iran's view that the decision of the judge was, as it was officially phrased, "political and baseless." The author also reminded the German authorities that Iran had already officially informed the German government that Tehran was in possession of accurate information concerning the influence of foreign intelligence services and terrorist groups on the course of the trial and on the court's verdict. The author went on to present the German authorities with the Iranian view, that without forewarning the Iranian government, which was the object of the judge's criticism, or allowing Tehran the opportunity to defend itself, the presiding judge at the Mykonos trial had made a biased judgment, based purely on the statements of a group of armed terrorists and a criminal airplane hijacker and fugitive. Iran insisted that the information it had presented was accurate, and that the position it had taken was justifiable.[26]

The expulsion of the four German diplomats from Iran was also an immediate consequence of the Mykonos verdict. The Foreign Ministry of Iran summoned the German ambassador in Tehran, Horst Bachmann, in the afternoon of the day the verdict was pronounced, to inform him of the order to expel the four German diplomats. This followed the expulsion of four Iranian diplomats serving in Bonn.[27] Ambassador Bachmann, was also asked to explain the statements of the presiding judge, Mr Kubsch, and his allegation that the Myknonos murders were the responsibility of Iran.[28] Further diplomatic moves followed in rapid succession. The German government's decision immediately to terminate the process of "critical dialogue," which had been pursued by the EU with respect to Iran since 1992, and of which Germany was the principal supporter, was an early move. This brought some satisfaction to the United States, which had for a long time brought pressure on Europe to change its policy toward Iran.

Meanwhile, the unlimited joy of the Iranian opposition in exile, who celebrated the court's verdict with singing and dancing, was in itself an expression of the humiliation and disgrace suffered by Tehran as a result of this verdict. Alexander von Stahl, the former Federal prosecutor, said that he had been under heavy pressure from the German government not to name Iranian officials. Bonn, which had been unwillingly thrown into the center of this political upheaval, was pondering what statement it might be able to make so as to prevent further damage. German officials believed that it would be pointless to reopen the critical dialogue before the Iranian presidential election due in May 1997, but Bonn was nevertheless determined to prevent the further deterioration of the situation. The German Foreign Ministry, alarmed at the violent reaction in Tehran, advised German citizens to travel to Iran only in emergency.[29]

EU declaration on Iran

The Council of Ministers of the EU issued the following declaration on April 29, 1997:

"In the light of the Mykonos case, the Council of Ministers of the European Union has debated at length the European Union's relations with Iran. The Council has re-emphasized the Union's declaration of 10 April 1997, and reconfirms the position as set out in the declaration made at the 1992 Edinburgh Conference, that the European Union has continually sought constructive relations with Iran. However, progress will only be achieved if Iranian officials respect the international principles of human rights and, while refraining from terrorist acts, for example against Iranian nationals abroad, they also co-operate in preventing such acts. The Council requests Iran to abide by international agreements, which it has accepted, such as agreements on human rights and the non-proliferation of weapons of mass destruction, and to ratify the Chemical Weapons Convention. Determined to struggle against terrorism in all forms, regardless of who its perpetrators or what its motives may be, the Council has agreed upon the following actions:

- Confirmation that under the present circumstances there exists no basis for the continuation of 'Critical Dialogue' between the European Union and Iran.
- Suspension of official bilateral meetings with Iran on a ministerial level, while the present circumstances prevail.
- Reaffirmation of the present policy of member countries of the European Union, to refrain from sending weapons to Iran.
- Cooperation in ensuring the refusal of visas to Iranians engaged in intelligence and security activities.
- Concentration on the deportation of Iranian intelligence agents from member countries of the European Union. The Council is determined to keep under close scrutiny the European Union's relations with Iran, and has provided similar instructions to the Policy Committee. Member states of the European Union will instruct their ambassadors that, after their return to Tehran, they should cooperate on an ongoing basis in the evaluation of their relations with Iran."[30]

Iranian Foreign Ministry declaration

In response to the declaration of the Council of Ministers of the EU, the Iranian Ministry of Foreign Affairs issued a substantial and detailed declaration of which the following is the entire text:

"The Ministry of Foreign Affairs of the Islamic Republic of Iran considers that the declaration of the Council of Ministers of the European Union of 29 April 1997 has been influenced by Zionist propaganda and is redolent of colonialism. It regards the declaration as contradicting the principles of international human rights and international norms in relations between countries, and it thereby rejects it as lacking in validity. The ministry confirms the following points:

- The accusations of the regional Berlin court with regard to the interference of the Islamic Republic of Iran in the Berlin incident, which were falsely purported in the declaration dated 10 April 1997 made by the Presidency of the European Union to be supported by documents, in addition to the statements made by the above-mentioned declaration of the Council of Ministers, are not only purely false and totally baseless, but also constitute a direct violation of the international standards of human rights standards and the principles governing judicial procedures. They cannot be tolerated and are condemned by the international community.

- Any claim that there is a struggle against terrorism on the part of the European countries, where known terrorist elements have been freely active with the official and open support of those countries, from whose territories they organize, guide and provide financial support and armaments for terrorist acts against the Islamic Republic of Iran, is deceitful and unacceptable. While they make baseless accusations against the Islamic Republic of Iran, which is itself the biggest victim of terrorism, the member countries of the European Union are not in a position to avoid taking responsibility for their own official and open support for terrorism.
- The request of the European Union, that the Convention for Banning Chemical Weapons should be ratified by the Islamic Republic of Iran, which has itself been a victim of chemical weapons provided by members of the European Union to Iraq, and has acted as pioneer in the formation and signing of the convention, is viewed as a mere propaganda ploy.
- The Islamic Republic of Iran's acceptance of the request of the European Union, made at the 1992 Edinburgh Summit, for the opening of negotiations, was made with the aim of correcting and ameliorating the behavior of European countries in various respects, including:

  - Their insulting behavior toward the world of Islam.
  - Their support of terrorism and provision of asylum to terrorists.
  - Their double standards and human rights violations.
  - Their belligerence toward foreigners.
  - Their disregard of the rights of Muslim minorities.
  - Their support for the Zionist regime.
  - Their diffusion of conventional weapons and weapons of mass destruction.

Thus, as had earlier been officially announced, in view of the absence of goodwill on the part of the European Union, and its lack of political independence, the continuation of the 'critical dialogue' is considered in the present circumstances to be devoid of usefulness and effectiveness. At the same time, the Islamic Republic will refrain from any talks with the European Union and its member states in the frameworks of the related dialogues on the issues of human rights, terrorism, and conventional, nuclear, and chemical weapons.

- In accordance with its principles and fundamental values, the Islamic Republic of Iran does not accept any country's departure from international norms regarding the principles of mutual respect and the lack of interference in the internal affairs of other states. It will respond in kind and appropriately to any action.
- The Islamic Republic has carefully investigated and recorded the behaviour of governments during the recent propaganda exercises, and in planning its future relationships it will take this into account."[30]

The Iranian people's indignation toward the German court's verdict

Popular indignation in Iran was manifested through demonstrations against Germany held throughout Iran after the court verdict in Berlin. Slogans of "Death to America," "Death to Israel," and "Death to Germany" were chanted. The demonstrators, while protesting against the pronouncements of the presiding judge at the court in Berlin, marched after the Friday prayer sermons from the front of Tehran University toward the German embassy. However, effective security measures were taken to protect the embassy buildings, and the authorities also took steps to maintain discipline while monitoring closely the peaceful demonstrations. Nevertheless the popular demonstrations in front of the German embassy in Tehran were vast, and for the first time since the Second World War the German flag was burned. The marches and gatherings were widely covered by Iranian and German newspapers, as well as by the world's media.

The thousands who gathered to protest had a number of demands. They asked the Iranian government to sever its ties with Bonn, in the absence of a speedy apology from the German government, or at least its refusal to acknowledge the verdict of the Mykonos court, and they demanded that Tehran take the German government before the international courts on the charge of providing asylum to and supporting terrorists. In a six-part proclamation read in front of the German embassy in Tehran, the demonstrators demanded a direct apology by the German government to the political leadership of Iran, and asked the German government to condemn the court, the prosecutor, and especially the judge of the Mykonos trial for having admitted witnesses with a record of terrorism and aeroplane hijacking.

The demonstrators also demanded that the Iranian judiciary attend to the complaints of the thousands who had been injured by chemical weapons in the eight-year war imposed on Iran by Iraq, and that it should embark as soon as possible on legal proceedings against German officials and companies accused of having exported equipment, chemical materials, and biological germs to Iraq during that war. They also demanded that the Iranian judiciary should expeditiously begin the trial of Iranian terrorists who have fled abroad, especially to Germany, and issue orders for their extradition. In a speech at the protest march, Dr Tourani, who lost his sight in Iranian Kurdistan through the actions of the now dissolved KDPI, alleged that in providing asylum to members of this terrorist group the German government had committed a crime. Addressing his words to the German authorities, he said, "Under no circumstances would we accept insult and conspiracy against the Islamic Republic."[31]

Reciprocal measures between Iran and the EU

The recall of ambassadors

Initially, Germany recalled its ambassador from Tehran and immediately afterwards, in a declaration issued by the Presidency of the EU, held at that time by the Netherlands, the EU gave its support to the German decision. The recall of ambassadors had only one precedent in the history of relations between Iran and Europe, when in 1989 after Imam Khomeini issued the *fatwa* ordering the death of Salman Rushdie, the EU (then the European Community) recalled its ambassadors from Tehran, prompting reciprocal action from Tehran. However, that episode was short-lived, and the European Community expeditiously returned its ambassadors to Iran. However, after the Mykonos verdict, the ambassadors were withdrawn for a longer period, and did not return to their posts for six months.

The EU had specified in its declaration of April 29, 1997, that the European ambassadors could return to Tehran after 20 days. However, the Iranian Leader, Ayatollah Khamenei, insisted that the German ambassador must be the last to return, thus putting a condition on the resumption of their posts by the European ambassadors, which the member states of the EU rejected. During the resulting six-month absence of the ambassadors of the 13 European countries, the governments of the member states made diligent efforts for their return. However, because of the insistence of Iran that the German ambassador must be penalized, and that his return must be in accord with a special arrangement dictated by Tehran, which Europe refused to accept, the return of the ambassadors was delayed. Talks between the EU and Iran on the issue lasted some five months until, finally, the EU agreed on a compromise whereby the German ambassador would return to Tehran simultaneously with the French ambassador, after all the other ambassadors had gone back to their posts. The ambassadors of 11 of the European states went back to Tehran on November 14, while Iran agreed that it would satisfy its condition if the German ambassador could return simultaneously with the French ambassador ten days later. The Iranian mass media judged that the return of ambassadors from only 11 European countries was an embarrassment for the EU and a victory for Iran.[32]

The end of the "critical dialogue"

In their collective decision at the summit meeting held in 1992 in Edinburgh, Scotland, the EU had approved the policy of engagement in a so-called "critical dialogue" with Iran, regulating the various aspects of its relations with Iran within this general concept. The policy drew strong disapproval from Washington and Tel Aviv, to the extent that from 1990 to 1997, Iran was one of the principal sources of disagreement between the United States, Israel, and Europe. These policy clashes have been dealt with above. After the Mykonos affair, however, the decision taken by the EU in general, and Germany in particular, to terminate the policy of "critical dialogue" with Iran brought to an end an era of very positive dialogue between Europe and Iran, which it is no exaggeration to say had been in existence since the end of the Second World War. Even after the Islamic revolution in Iran, the European policy of dialogue was continued, at least at the ministerial level. The consequence of the Mykonos verdict was therefore grave: Namely that for the first time since the Second World War there was no dialogue between Europe and Iran.

Iranian intelligence agents deported from Europe

As the *Guardian* newspaper revealed: "The United States and the United Kingdom have applied pressure on the German Government to put an end to the close and questionable relations that exist between German and Iranian intelligence services. However, it is unlikely that Helmut Kohl would agree to this."[33] After the Mykonos verdict, the deportation of Iranian intelligence agents was among the decisions openly announced by Germany and the EU. The move had no precedent in relations between Iran and Europe since the Second World War.

Cancellation of ministerial visits

After the issue of the *fatwa* decreeing the death of Salman Rushdie, the exchange of visits at the ministerial level between Iran and the EU was terminated. For the EU, this was an unwritten and undeclared policy, and no formal decision to this effect was ever made, and the period during which this policy was operative was very short. But after the Mykonos verdict, the cancellation of visits at the ministerial level became the official policy of all the members of the EU, an entirely exceptional occurrence in relations between Iran and Europe in the period after the Second World War, which may be seen as the most major political upset in relations between Iran and Germany, and Iran and Europe, in the postwar period.

Analysis of the Berlin court's verdict and conclusions

The role of the United States, the United Kingdom, and Israel

The United States, United Kingdom, and Israel had already taken a conscious decision to attempt to vitiate the special relationship between Iran and Germany. However, prior to the Mykonos verdict, the efforts of these three governments had failed so far, in the period following German reunification, to achieve the desired effect. It was only natural therefore that they would attempt to capitalize on the Mykonos trial as a means to achieve their goals. An analysis presented in the *Guardian* newspaper on these issues, published two days before the Mykonos verdict, described the Berlin trial as a "dream opportunity" for London.

Referring to a high-level meeting of the EU member states in Brussels to plan Europe's strategy following the expected verdict, the article said: "Retaliatory action, which can include prohibition of the sale of European-made weapons to Iran, and the deportation of intelligence agents of the Iranian Government from European capitals, are in the planning, because this week a German court is expected to declare Iran guilty for issuing an order to kill three members of the opposition. Today in Brussels, high-ranking officials of member countries of the European Union met in order to plan appropriate action. The factional elements, at whose pinnacle are Britain and the Scandinavian countries, brought pressure on the Dutch president of the Union for concerted action. German prosecuting assistants consider Iran guilty for the gangster-like murder of three Kurdish opposition members and their translator in 1992, while they were dining at the Mykonos restaurant in Berlin. The long prosecution of four Lebanese and one Iranian is to come to an end on Thursday. This is while all countries throughout Europe are preparing themselves for facing difficulties, which might arise as a result of the revelation of the collective role played by high-ranking Iranian officials and Tehran's retaliatory actions. At today's meeting in Brussels, in spite of the existence of various commands and strong commercial interests among member countries of the European Union, there is still hope for dealing a heavy blow to Iranian intelligence activities throughout Europe....In order to sever the close and questionable ties between Iran's and Germany's intelligence services, the United States and Britain have brought pressure to bear on the German Government; however, it is not likely that Chancellor Helmut Kohl would agree to this. A British Government source said, 'We would like to see the end of it, but the Germans would resort to anything in order to reinstate it. Kohl views it as extremely important... He thinks that he should not take orders or injunctions from the Americans or petty judges.' Intending to terminate Iran's taking advantage of European soil as a springboard for destructive activity, terrorism, and the purchase of weapons, British officials consider the Mykonos prosecution to be a 'dream opportunity'.[33] The implication is clear: that the European Union states meeting in Brussels were looking forward to dealing a decisive blow to Iran's intelligence services, even before the Mykonos verdict was pronounced."

The *Guardian* also noted Britain's mistrust of Iran, but went on to explain that the Iranian position was different. "Germany, Iran's largest trading partner, explains its clandestine relations with Tehran by the fact that relations between Germany and Iran are a profitable and useful channel for a private and sensible mediation in the Middle East, which will bring about a connection between Israel and Lebanese groups such as the Hezbollah."[33] The lack of concern of the court for the effects of its deliberations on relations between Bonn and Tehran, said the *Guardian*, caused real concern to German officials, noting that the Minister of State at the Chancellor's office, Bernd Schmidbauer, was especially anxious after the issue of the subpoena to Ali Fallahian.[33]

The long-standing determination of the United States to bring about a change in German policy toward Iran may be judged from an article published the previous year by *Frankfurter Allgemeine*, quoting confidential German documents it claimed to have obtained in Washington from a member of the Mujahedin Khalq Organization, which purported to show that the German government was aware that Iran had condoned terrorist activities. The documents appeared to have been leaked by the American administration with the aim of discrediting Germany. As the paper said, "During the past week, Washington has repeatedly asked Germany to fall in line with American policy on Iran. On March 14, at the Sharm el-Sheikh anti-terrorist conference, President Clinton said, 'Any country in the world that has relations with Iran, when it wakes up in the morning it must stand in front of the mirror and decide whether it wishes to continue its policy, or change that policy; it should ask whether its policy be founded on principles, or be formulated in the light of other interests.' The U.S. Secretary of State Warren Christopher asked Europeans to terminate their 'critical dialogue' with Iran."[34]

On the same day *Frankfurter Allgemeine* published an editorial comment on the subject: "Naturally, the optimum outcome for Washington is that countries allied with it on this side of the Atlantic would completely sever their ties with Tehran and terminate the critical dialogue. On the other hand, the members of the European community ...do not wish to abandon hope that it may be possible to influence the moderate clergy in Tehran and to encourage them to demonstrate self-control in the Middle East, the Persian Gulf, and Central Asia. Also, Europe does not want to follow Washington's line without question. Though the fundamental friendship between the United States and Europe is not in question, Washington has accused the Europeans of maintaining relations with Iran for the sake of material gain, at the same time as Iran continues to preside over terrorist activity in the Middle East. It appears that the United States prefers to forget that until recently it was American companies that were the largest party to commercial negotiations with Iran."[34]

The politics of the subpoena issued to the Iranian Minister of Information

The subpoena summoning the Iranian Minister of Information to the court in Berlin was issued one day after Chancellor Kohl's return from the Sharm el-Sheikh Conference, convened in Egypt under the rubric "Struggle Against Terrorism" on March 13, 1996. Chancellor Kohl and Minister of State Schmidbauer participated at this conference. A number of related incidents concerning Germany–Iran relations took place at this period.

Three days before the conference, on March 9, 1996, the Iranian government vessel, *Iran Kolahdooz*, was impounded at the port of Antwerp, Belgium. The Belgian security forces alleged that a consignment of mortar shells was discovered in a food container destined for the German city of Munich and drew the matter to the attention of the German government. As Iranian ambassador to Bonn, it fell to the author to monitor the case on behalf of the Iranian government. A high-ranking German official in Bonn told the author that it was the United States that had informed the Belgian government and NATO, whose headquarters is in Brussels, of the presence of the mortar shells on board the ship. On the basis of the information given to the German government the ship was impounded on its arrival in Hamburg and, on a further inspection it was discovered that the consignment in question, whose crate number and container the Americans knew, had been removed from the vessel. This high-ranking German official said, "The Americans even knew the name of the individual who had transferred this cargo to the ship in the Iranian port of Bandar Abbas, and provided the information to the German Government."

Immediately after this incident, the author was summoned to Iran to report to President Rafsanjani. The President expressed his surprise at seeing such an incident reported by the Western media, and said he had raised the issue at the National Security Council. He added that Iranian intelligence and security officials were unaware of the matter, and that the Leader, Ayatollah Khamenei, had given orders that it should be investigated. The President said the German government should be asked to provide the relevant information to Iran so that the matter could be followed up internally within the country. The President stressed the significance of the incident for Iran's national security.

The incident did indeed indicate the existence of a conspiracy to disrupt the good relations between Iran and Germany. It is also highly relevant that only a few days after the discovery of the consignment of mortar shells, the Mujahedin Khalq Organization's newsletter published photographs and particulars of it. The question thus arises: How was it possible that a consignment of mortar shells could be discovered in an Iranian government vessel, without the knowledge of Iran's government and military commanders, and yet the United States government and the Mujahedin Khalq Organization appeared to know all about it? In addition, was it not significant that the details of the consignment were passed to the German government and to NATO just a few days prior to the Sharm el-Sheikh Conference?

Immediately after the Sharm el-Sheikh Conference, the subpoena to the Iranian Minister of Information was issued. The Berlin murders had occurred long before, on September 17, 1992. In his initial bill of indictment, which was delivered to the court in 1993 just a few months after the incident, the German prosecutor accused the Iranian Minister of Information of involvement in the murders. Acting on the basis of this bill of indictment, the judge of the court could have issued a subpoena to the Iranian Minister of Information as early as 1993. Since no such subpoena was issued, the conclusion must be that, on the basis of Article 153C of the criminal law,[35] the German government must have acted to prevent the judiciary from issuing the subpoena. In fact, after the issue of the prosecutor's initial bill of indictment in the Mykonos case, Mr Fallahian actually traveled to Germany for discussions, which led to the intensification of cooperation between Iran and Germany in the field of intelligence. An article in *Der Spiegel* commented as follows on the apparent invocation by the German government of Article 153C: "According to Article 153C of the law, in the event that there exists a danger that the prosecution of a criminal could have detrimental consequences for Germany, the government has the power to prevent the pursuit of such a case."[36]

However, in 1995, after the Sharm el-Sheikh Conference, the German government apparently decided to lift its prohibition and to allow the German Prosecutor-General to issue the subpoena, in contrast with its position in 1993, when following the naming of Mr Fallahian in the prosecutor's first bill of indictment, Germany seemingly regarded the maintenance of its good relations with Tehran to be in the national interest, using Article 153C to avert potential detrimental consequences for Germany. Between 1993 and 1996, nothing that had emerged at the trial seemed likely to be a reason for the German government's apparent change of mind. So the question arises, in what manner was the German national interest threatened after the Sharm el-Sheikh Conference, such that it led the German government to change its policy and forgo its legal right to use the provisions of

Article 153C? The apparent change of mind in Bonn appears to demonstrate that the issue of the subpoena to Mr Fallahian was more the result of a policy change than of the judicial process.

Frankfurter Allgemeine offered an analysis of this point: "A noteworthy point arising out of the suspicion [that the subpoena was political] is that after the anti-terrorism conference in Sharm el-Sheikh, the judiciary must have received new information – two and a half years after the opening of the Mykonos trial. Since the beginning it has been an issue whether orders for the murders were given directly by the Iranian Ministry of Information. However, up to now, no documentary evidence has been brought forward."[37]

The author took up with the German government, in his capacity as ambassador, the report in *Frankfurter Allgemeine* concerning the apparent theft by the Americans from Chancellor Kohl's office of confidential documents about the Berlin trial, and officials in Bonn confirmed that this had taken place. That this had taken place made it clear that the Americans were prepared to resort to extreme measures in order to obtain information substantiating the allegations that they wished to make against Iran. *Frankfurter Allgemeine* states frankly that the subpoena was issued as a consequence of American involvement: "Because of the dangerous situation which would result from this action, the German government had previously requested the German prosecutor-general not to issue a subpoena to Mr Fallahian, accusing him of having given the order to kill four Kurdish-Iranian politicians at the Mykonos restaurant in 1992. According to information provided to our newspaper, the subpoena was in the end issued as a result of testimony given by Americans, without any witness thus far being questioned by German officials."[37] Later, in an interview with German television networks, the well-known writer and reporter Peter Scholl-Latour said, "The prosecutors have based their investigations upon the testimony of people who cannot under any circumstances be examined or investigated. These spies who have appeared on the scene smell of the CIA. Bani-Sadr is not a neutral person. The United States intends to disrupt relations between Iran and Germany."[38]

The Berlin court's verdict was political

There are a number of reasons why it can be concluded that the verdict in the Mykonos trial was politically motivated.

Approximately two years after the beginning of the Mykonos trial, the author, as Iran's ambassador in Germany, sent a letter to the court in Berlin, as follows: "For a considerable time accusations implicating the Iranian government in the Berlin murders have been an issue both in the court and in the German media. The reason we have thus far been silent in court with respect to this matter was to not allow the slightest doubt to arise that the Iranian government might have been involved. Had our silence continued however, it might have given rise to the misapprehension that since Iran has shown no reaction, the accusations might be justified. Today, with this letter, I wish to clarify and confirm that the Iranian government was not implicated in the events under investigation by the court, and if the court entertains the smallest doubt, the embassy is prepared to co-operate in clarifying the truth." The court acknowledged its receipt of this letter, for which it expressed gratitude, but did not act on the offer it contained. It must be asked, what kind of court does not offer a defendant the chance to defend himself, and is it proper for a defendant to not even be informed of the evidence against him?

One high-ranking German official in Bonn informed me that the British intelligence service had provided Germany with the initial evidence against Kazem Darabi, alleging that he was a terrorist linked to Iran's Intelligence and Security Organization. In fact, Darabi's arrest and the action taken against him were prompted by the British intelligence service, who had taken a leading part in the hunt for him.

All the reasons given by the prosecutor for the issue of the subpoena, and all the justifications offered by the presiding judge concerning the allegations that high-ranking Iranian officials were involved are founded on Bani-Sadr's testimony, which in turn was based on the claims of "Witness C"—Mr Mesbahi. It must be asked, how reliable was Mr Mesbahi? He was a businessman in Iran who fled to Pakistan because of his debts and his fear of arrest. He spent one or two months in Pakistan, during which he applied unsuccessfully to European embassies for asylum, until he succeeded in obtaining a visa for France by convincing the French embassy that he was in possession of important information and documents with regard to the alleged Iranian terrorist network. A high-ranking Bonn official told me: "On his arrival in France, Mesbahi was put at the disposition of the French intelligence service, then spent some time in the United States with the CIA, then went to Belgium and ultimately passed a few weeks in London in consultation with MI6. He was finally sent under special protection from London to Berlin in order to testify."

So that the appearance of "Witness C" would have the maximum impact, it was arranged that Bani-Sadr, a well-known figure, would appear himself at the trial in Berlin and would announce that he had an important witness at his disposal. Later, in the most sensational manner possible, Mr Mesbahi was produced in court and testified that an alleged special committee, of which the Iranian leader, president, ministers of foreign affairs and information were members, and had given the order for the Mykonos murders. The presiding judge said he regarded the testimony of "Witness C" as reliable. With the pronouncement of the verdict, there began the most turbulent episode in the history of political relations between Iran and Germany and, by extension, in relations between Iran and Europe. However, shortly after the verdict Mr Mesbahi, in an apparent volte-face, denied in his own handwriting everything he had said before. In a letter written to *Frankfurter Allgemeine*, Mesbahi explained that no "special committee" had ever existed, and that the intention of his evidence had been to weaken the government of Iran, a move that had the effect of intensifying terrorist activities, as well as endangering world peace.

These matters were dealt with in detail by *Frankfurter Allgemeine*: "One of the important witnesses at the Mykonos trial, an Iranian by the name of Abolghassem Mesbahi, also known as 'Witness C', has retracted his own testimony. A few days after another witness, known as 'Witness B', withdrew his testimony, Mesbahi, also, in a letter filed at our newspaper office, has chosen to write as follows: 'Today, I know with certainty that a committee by the name of 'Special Duties' does not exist. The term was used with the aim of weakening the Government of the Islamic Republic of Iran, thus strengthening terrorist activities, as well as endangering world peace'. The Berlin Court had alleged that the 'Special Committee', whose members were Iran's President Rafsanjani, Ayatollah Khamenei, Foreign Minister Velayati, and Minister of Information Fallahian, had issued the order for the Berlin restaurant murders. Mesbahi had reaffirmed this matter in his evidence to the court. After the court's verdict all the European Union ambassadors were recalled from Iran. In reaction, a spokesman for the Karlsruhe prosecuting attorney, Ms. Schubel said: 'Even if Witness 'C' claims that the 'Special Duties Committee' did not exist, the Mykonos file need not be reopened, because the court in Berlin is in possession of other documents regarding this case.'" In his letter, according to the paper, Mesbahi went on to say that what he called the "true instigators of international terrorism" had taken advantage of his testimony. Mesbahi particularly attacked the Mujahedin Khalq Organization, whom he characterized as "mercenaries of the Baghdad Government," and whose international standing had increased after the Mykonos trial. Mesbahi referred to himself as a soldier for Imam Khomeini, and advised the Europeans to be aware of the virtue of Iran's religious leader, Ayatollah Khamenei. Mr Mesbahi, as *Franfurter Allgemeine* noted, "remained under the protection of the German Federal Criminal Affairs Department."[39]

In the main text of the Mykonos verdict only the conviction of the accused individuals facing the court was mentioned. No explicit mention was made of Iran or Iranian government officials. The judge rebutted reports in the press, which alleged that the Iranian government had also been in effect in the dock, emphasizing that the prosecution was directed exclusively against the five defendants. However, the positions taken by the Western media and the political attitudes of the European countries and the United States after the verdict indicate that as far as they were concerned the Iranian government had also been facing trial, and had been convicted. This was the reason for the curtailment by the Western states and organizations of their relations with Iran. Meanwhile a review of the address by the prosecutor clearly indicates that there was no convincing evidence for the existence of the so-called "special committee," and that the insistence on its existence was a political statement, on the same level as that made by Mr Mesbahi.

Mr Mesbahi's lack of credibility has been adverted to, and nothing could be more convincing in this connection than his retraction of his own testimony. However, with respect to Mr Bani-Sadr, the analysis published by the London-based newspaper *Al-Hayat* is revealing. The paper suggests that there is some evidence that the Iranian government at least welcomed the murders at the Mykonos restaurant: "There is convincing evidence that the Iranian regime – or an organ or organs within it – has resorted to political terrorism. From this point of view, the terrorist killings of a Kurdish–Iranian opposition leader and three of his followers in a Greek restaurant in Berlin is in complete harmony with the way in which the regime's enemies have been eliminated in Tehran. The fact that the perpetrators of the actions have been Iranian or Lebanese is also in harmony with current Iranian methods. One can perhaps add that attributing such actions to the Iranian security system, or a minister responsible for security affairs, is reasonable and understandable." But, argues *Al-Hayat*, this does not mean the entire Iranian government can reasonably be indicted: "What is absolutely not understandable or reasonable is that the leader of the revolution, Ayatollah Ali Khamenei, or President Ali Akbar Hashemi Rafsanjani are accused and convicted by relying upon the statements of a fleeing president and a former employee of the Information Ministry, who have taken asylum in the West. Ex-president Abolhassan Bani-Sadr has a record of activity against the system in Tehran and cannot be considered a just or reliable witness, and in addition, after the decade he has spent abroad, his information can no longer be regarded as first-hand. In spite of all this, the German court believed his accusations, perhaps because it wanted to believe them."[40]

The Federal Court's decision to dispense with the legal prosecution of the remaining members of the special committee was in itself significant. In his press statement of May 15, 1997, the German Federal Prosecutor-General said: "The order to arrest, issued by the investigator of the Federal Court, March 14, 1994, against Iranian Information and Security Minister Ali Fallahian stands on its own merits. The Federal Prosecutor-General dispenses with the legal prosecution of the remaining members of the 'Special Affairs Committee', on the basis of the following considerations. First, the degree of immunity, which is based on international law, is to a great extent unclear. The possibility of further investigation to determine the precise circumstances in which the committee made decisions, and the proof of its members' specific crimes, does not exist. Under such circumstances the opening of legal proceedings against members of the committee would be against the public interest."

Following the above statement, the Federal Prosecutor-General expanded a few points in his statement. As regards the diplomatic immunity of the remaining members of the special committee he said: "In this respect there exists no difference between Mr Fallahian and other members who are indicted, since the Iranian minister of information enjoys diplomatic immunity, as does the foreign minister. With respect to diplomatic immunity, they cannot be regarded differently". Concerning the impossibility of determining the precise circumstances of the committee's decision-making, and of obtaining proof of the members' crimes, he said: "There exist only two possibilities. Either the 'Special Committee' has made such decisions, or it has not. If the 'Special Committee' has made such decisions, the responsibility lies on the shoulders of *all* its members, not merely one. If it is not clear that the 'Special Committee' has taken such decisions, then none of its members can be accused. If the precise circumstances of the Special Committee's decisions have not been made clear to the prosecutor and the judge, and have not been subject to investigation, then how is it possible that in the subpoena, the prosecutor's final address, and the court's verdict it has been explicitly declared that the 'Special Committee' has issued the order for the murders?" He also pointed out that contradictions had indubitably emerged in the prosecutor's final address to the court, and in the statement in which the court announced that the remaining members of the special committee would not be prosecuted.

Finally, more than three years after the event, Mesbahi made a formal statement to the effect that he had been induced to speak out against Iran by the blandishments of foreign intelligence services. In November 2000, he told the office of the German Federal Prosecutor-General that he was now prepared to reveal facts concerning his relationship with the German Federal Criminal Department (Bundeskriminalesamt), the German Federal Prosecutor-General, and the Western intelligence services.[41]

There are also indications of political collusion and preparation by Germany and other European states before the pronouncement of the verdict in the Mykonos case. One day before the issuance of the subpoena to the minister of information, and approximately one year before the verdict of the Berlin court, the German government recalled its intelligence agents from Tehran, to which they never returned, a development that was reported, as we have noted above, in the *Guardian* newspaper.[42] In Paris, *Le Monde* reported the return to Bonn, out of fear of reprisals, of two German intelligence agents stationed in Tehran.[43] These are indications that, prior to the verdict of the court in Berlin, a political decision must have been made behind the scenes. Events on the day also took place with striking rapidity. The verdict of the court in Berlin was read at 1300 on April 10, 1997, while at 1700 on the same day, the German government announced its four-point action curtailing relations with Iran and, at 1900, the Presidency of the EU announced the EU's collective decision. The rapid sequence of events is a clear indication of the existence of political coordination before the verdict of the court.

Collusion between Europe and the United States over the Mykonos verdict

At a special meeting on April 17, 1997, the US Senate Subcommittee on the Middle East and South Asia, under the supervision of the Senate Foreign Relations Committee, examined issues relating to Iran, Europe, and the United States. At this meeting, Senator D'Amato made the following statement: "The results of the Berlin trial ought to be a good lesson for European countries and multinational corporations. Germany's experience has showed us how Iranians behave in order to export their revolution. The policy of sanctions on Iran must be viewed within the framework of US interests. From any point of view, economic sanctions are the strongest tools for fighting Iran, and it is hoped that America's European friends will also adopt such sanctions. The [United States] government has been able to arrive at an agreement with Europe with respect to bills relating to Cuba, Iran and Libya. However, this agreement does not mean that all European companies are exempt from U.S. sanctions, for in that case Iranians would laugh at us..."[44]

The next day, the *New York Times* wrote as follows: "This week, a US State Department delegation is visiting The Hague, Paris, Bonn and London so as to encourage the Europeans to take advantage of the newly-created opening, in the sense that we must once again devise a collective policy against Iran. One day after the announcement of the verdict of the Berlin court, Washington agreed to exempt European companies from inclusion under the D'Amato Act, for the reason that Europeans have shown a swift reaction to the German case. The US law penalizes foreign companies that invest in Iran and Libya, and this topic has become a critical issue in relations between Europeans and Americans."[45]

This statement from Senator D'Amato, together with the report in the *New York Times*, indicate that negotiations had taken place between Europe and the United States over a political deal in which the verdict of the Berlin court would go against Iran, in exchange for the exemption of European companies from the penalties of the D'Amato Law.

5   Analytical conclusions: Foreign policy-making and the management of bilateral relations

Internal and external factors shaping decision-making

Iran's foreign policy objectives after the Islamic revolution of 1979 fell under three main headings. These were, first, to secure the necessary conditions for Iran's economic growth and development, while safeguarding the country's national sovereignty and territorial integrity; second, to defend the rights of Muslims and of Muslim liberation movements, and to challenge the opposing positions of Israel and the Western countries, particularly the United States; and, third, to establish an Islamic society on the basis of the principles of the Shi'a sect of Islam.[1]

The first goal was scarcely controversial, since all nations aim to protect their sovereignty and territorial integrity. The second and third, however, were a different matter. The aim of defending the Muslims of the world and their liberation movements, while challenging the hegemony of the United States, Israel, and the West, in addition to the establishment of a Shiite Islamic polity in Iran, soon came to be seen as the two major causes of conflict between the Western world and revolutionary Islamic Iran. Iran's foreign policy in the post-revolution era was also conditioned by the state of the Islamic world, which had been subject to exploitation and colonization for nearly two centuries. Post-revolutionary Iran's declaration of its tripartite foreign policy aims was original and unique, deriving from the nature of its constitution, and no other state would have targeted similar aims.

The question arises, why were Iran's foreign policies a source of concern? In general, states that have transborder goals impose their own priorities, by the exercise of their regional and global power, in order to achieve them. The actions of Britain in the nineteenth century, or of Russia and the United States in the twentieth century, may be seen as evidence for this contention. In this context, Iran's first stated foreign policy objective was naturally uncontroversial from the points of view both of the Islamic world and of the West. However, its other two objectives soon aroused alarm. Iran's stated policy of support for liberation movements, for instance, was contrary to the interests of some governments, and gave rise to difficulties in Iran's relations with the governments of some Muslim countries, including Egypt, Iraq, and Saudi Arabia. Clearly it was impossible for Iran to cooperate both with the governments of those states and at the same time with opposition movements. In addition, Iranian attitudes toward the existing global order were different from those of the majority of regional and Islamic states.

The leaders of Iran regarded the current global order as contradictory to Muslim interests. They therefore directed their sharpest political attacks at the Soviet Union and the United States, the two superpowers of the Eastern and Western blocs, which had largely created and therefore enjoyed the principal benefits of such a world order. At the time, of course, most of the Islamic states fell within either the American or the Russian spheres, with the result that Iran failed to reach agreement with its neighboring states or even with other countries in the Islamic world. Meanwhile, there was also persistent tension in Iran's relations with the Western countries, and especially with the United States, while the attitudes of the majority of the Muslim countries toward the West in general and the United States in particular did not follow the model represented by post-revolutionary Iran.

Since the revolution, Islamic Iran has always taken a challenging attitude to Western policies, in contrast to many other Muslim countries, which have tended to maintain close diplomatic relations, and even strategic and military relationships with the West and particularly with the United States. In addition, the majority of the Islamic states, as their response to Israel's denial of Palestinian rights, were content to aim at a diminution of Israel's hold together with some form of recognition of the rights of the Palestinians. But postrevolutionary Iran totally refused to recognize Israel as a legal entity, and regarded its government as an illegitimate usurper of sovereignty. For these reasons, Iran's foreign policy after the Islamic revolution faced difficulties, and in the light of its second and third stated objectives, Iran found itself in special circumstances, in which it was impossible for it to reach an agreement, either with its neighboring states or with the wider Islamic world.

After the Islamic revolution, the conflict of interests between Iran and the United States led to an escalation of the political crisis which already existed in the Middle East and the Persian Gulf. The major interests of the United States in the region were its oil reserves, and its role as a market for the sale of arms and other goods. The significance of these was such that the United States was obliged to put all its efforts into the preservation of the regional status quo. In addition, the United States and its regional allies were fearful of Iran's policy of exporting the Islamic revolution, which led them to prioritize the protection of their own security interests. Among the measures taken for this purpose were the strengthening of the American military presence in the Persian Gulf, the conclusion of military contracts between the United States and the Persian Gulf littoral states, the formation of the Gulf Cooperation Council, and the escalation of the military presence of Israel and the United States in Turkey, Central Asia, and the Caucasus. Israel identified postrevolutionary Iran as the principal regional threat, which prompted the United States to put into operation its project to curb Iran.[1] The emerging situation also had an obvious impact on relations between Iran and Europe, including relations between Iran and Germany.

In its postreunification era, it was no longer possible for Germany to disregard the strategic potential it derived from the weight of its population, its economic strength, and its national interests, nor could it ignore its geopolitical position.

The main question for the new Germany was how it could exercise as wisely and responsibly as possible the power and influence it had gained after reunification. United Germany sought to focus its creative energies on a number of areas. First among these, and Germany's foremost concern, was the completion of European integration and the enlargement of the European Union (EU). Second, Germany was concerned to maintain the transatlantic partnership between the United States and the EU, which shared and was committed to similar values, including democracy, the market economy, human rights, and the securing of common interests after the end of the Cold War. Third, Germany had an ongoing commitment to the strategy of multilateral consultation and the strengthening of the role of the United Nations and the OSCE. Fourth, it aimed to promote the role of united Germany in international affairs with a focus on Europe's neighboring regions, especially East Europe, Russia, and the Middle East. There is no doubt that in the Middle East, Iran was Germany's focus.

Iran's relations with Germany after German reunification underwent enormous changes after Iran's 1979 Islamic revolution. After 1990, relations improved and underwent further development in many areas. Relations between the foreign ministries of the two countries were consistently highly active, with more than 20 visits during the period from 1990 to 1996 at different levels, ministerial, deputy ministerial, and official. At this juncture, relations in general were passing through a particularly active phase, as evidenced by the active participation of the political leaders of both countries. President Rafsanjani had regular phone contacts with Chancellor Helmut Kohl, indicating that the special relationship was more highly developed than the Iranian President's relations with the Persian Gulf and Middle East heads of state. The level of official correspondence between the two governments and the frequency of special envoys was an additional indication of the highly developed nature of the relationship.

Visiting Iranian dignitaries have always been received in Germany at a high level. Protocol does not normally indicate that a visiting foreign minister will meet the Federal Chancellor, so it is highly significant that all visits by Iranian foreign ministers, without exception, have included a meeting with the Chancellor. A meeting between a visiting deputy foreign minister and the German Chancellor is an even rarer event and happens only in exceptional cases, and so it is very significant that the German Chancellor chose personally to receive Iranian Deputy Foreign Minister, Mr Vaezi, an honor accorded to no other deputy minister from the Middle East to the Persian Gulf. Relations between the parliaments of the two countries were also assiduous. In the period from 1990 to 1996, some 15 reciprocal parliamentary visits took place between Germany and Iran. Meetings between parliamentary officials at various levels, including deputy speakers and the chairmen of various committees, together with such activities as the formation of parliamentary friendship groups, constituted an enhanced level of activity in relations between the two parliaments, which had not existed in the period immediately after the 1979 Islamic revolution.

But the development that was most significant and deserves particular attention was the close collaboration between the two countries' security services. Symbolic of the importance of these ties in the field of intelligence was the fact that the coordinator of the German intelligence and security services, Bernd Schmidbauer, who was also Minister of States at the Federal Chancellor's office and an adviser to Chancellor Kohl, paid three separate visits to Iran, while the Iranian Intelligence Minister Ali Fallahian paid a reciprocal visit to Germany. It should be pointed out that Mr Fallahian's visit to Germany in 1993 was extremely controversial. Germany was the only Western nation, and certainly the only NATO member country, to have such a close relationship in the field of security and intelligence with Iran. The mutual collaboration and close relationship of Iran and Germany extended even beyond the bilateral level. The major exchange of prisoners in the Middle East, mediated by Germany with Iran's assistance, which turned out to be the largest of its kind ever to take place in the region, was a case in point. The exchange included the dead bodies of two Israeli soldiers and 16 pro-Israeli Lebanese militiamen, who were exchanged with Israel for 20 Hezbollah fighters and a further 20 Lebanese army soldiers, together with the bodies of 120 martyred Lebanese.

It was also significant that a German military aircraft carried the bodies of the two Israeli soldiers back to Israel. This was the first German military aircraft to land on Israeli soil since the inception of the Israeli state, a reconciliation that Iran in effect helped to bring about. A further sign of mutual collaboration between Iran and Germany came when a number of German citizens taken hostage in Lebanon were freed with the help of Iranian mediation, in addition to the release of Abbas Hamadi, a Lebanese citizen imprisoned in Germany. Moreover, the presence of a sizeable force of some hundreds of German soldiers stationed in Iran in order to assist Iraqi refugees during the 1991 Gulf War, which followed Iraq's invasion of Kuwait, was an exceptional indication of regional cooperation between the two nations. This operation cost Germany over DM 300 million. Dialogue on human rights issues was another aspect of the relations between the two countries after 1990. The holding of joint seminars on the subject of human rights in Islamic and Western culture, as well as conferences on the relations between Islam and Christianity, and several meetings between the human rights committees of the two countries' parliaments, all constituted a unique and unrivalled level of cooperation in comparison with Iran's contacts with other Western and European countries.

Economic relations between the two nations also underwent substantial change and development after 1990. For example, the German insurance organization Hermes lifted its restrictions on covering exports to Iran in 1991, the first European financial institution to take such a step toward the promotion of trade with Iran after the Islamic revolution. During the ensuing three years from 1991, Hermes covered some DM 14 billion in exports to Iran, so that trade with Iran in 1994 ranked second in the world only to Germany's trade with Brazil as the beneficiary of Hermes credit guarantees. The rescheduling of Iran's outstanding debts was another development, which had a crucial and determining effect on the country's economy. In the face of coercion by the United States, no country had been willing to reschedule Iran's arrears. Meanwhile Iran's first economic development plan was already completed and, before the country's second five-year plan could be inaugurated, the foreign debt situation had to be resolved. All foreign bank credit facilities had been closed to Iran since the Islamic revolution, and the issue became the most complex and challenging economic dilemma faced by President Rafsanjani during his tenure of office. The German Finance Ministry became the first foreign institution to agree on rescheduling DM 4.2 billion of Iran's debt, which led private sector German banks to reschedule the remaining DM 4 billion of Iran's outstanding debt to Germany. As a consequence of Germany's decision to reschedule more than DM 8 billion of Iran's debt, other countries began to follow suit, with the result that Iran's entire loan and debt issue was resolved. All this took place in the context of the first postrevolutionary session of the joint German–Iranian economic commission, which was held in Tehran in 1991.

Further evidence of the existence of a relationship between Iran and Germany on a more highly developed level than that of Iran with other states is provided by the various joint commissions that were set up to cover subjects of mutual interest such as transportation, environment and culture, and the exchange of more than 200 different economic missions, in addition to the credit facilities for new trade provided by German banks. Another unique aspect of the relationship lay in the reciprocal visits made by the deputy German Justice Minister to Iran and the Deputy Iranian Judiciary Chief to Germany, which resulted in the signing of cooperation agreements in the judicial field. The holding in Dusseldorf of the largest ever Iranian arts and culture festival to be held in Germany or elsewhere in the world, before or after the revolution, together with joint cultural meetings, media and press seminars, and agreements between official state news agencies of the two countries, were also unique to relations between Iran and Germany, and a gauge of the significant positive movement in the relations of the two countries.

The German political structure and decision-making process center primarily around the federal chancellor, the foreign ministry, the finance ministry, the economics ministry, the federal parliament, and the security services. It is significant that all these key institutions were involved in the advancement of relations with Iran. The chancellor's office, together with the foreign and finance ministries, contributed decisively to the improvement of relations with Iran, while the security services played the role of mediator.

Before 1990, relations between Germany and Iran were basically handled by the foreign and finance ministries, but after Chancellor Kohl became personally involved, the relationship became more dynamic. Incidentally, the Chancellor's personal interest was a matter of some sensitivity within the foreign and economics ministries, and aroused a degree of jealousy among some officials. The release of the German hostages in Lebanon, the release and exchange of Israeli and Hezbollah prisoners, and the resolution of the further issue of the arrests of German citizens in Iran were personally handled by the Chancellor, though the foreign and economics ministries claimed they lay within their jurisdiction. In fact, prior to Hans-Dietrich Genscher's departure from the post of foreign minister, the principal decision-making body on foreign policy within the German government were the foreign and economics ministries, but afterwards, Chancellor Helmut

Kohl took personal control of foreign policy matters and, in particular, the foreign ministry came to play a secondary and subordinate role in the matter of Germany's relations with Iran.

Minister of State Bernd Schmidbauer also faced difficult problems in coordinating the attitude of the German security and intelligence services toward Iran. He kept a close control over the German foreign security service, the BND, which consequently took a more positive stance toward relations with Iran, in line with Federal policy. On the other hand, the German internal security service, the Verfassungschutz, maintained a more cautious and careful approach. It is significant that this latter organization played a negative role with respect to Iranian interests during the Mykonos trial in Berlin, and also that it was not willing to act effectively to control the activities of the Mujahedin Khalq Organization (MKO), which were detrimental to relations between Iran and Germany. The refusal to allow Maryam Rajavi, one of the leaders of the MKO, to enter Germany, and the reference to the MKO as a terrorist organization in a German government statement, the first time such a position had been taken by a European country, were both developments opposed by the German interior security service, but they took place nevertheless because of the efforts of the Foreign Ministry and Chancellor Kohl himself.

The German Economics Ministry also played a significantly positive role in developing the two countries' relations throughout the early 1990s but unquestionably this would not have been possible without the consent and approval of the Chancellor and the Foreign Minister. Meanwhile, in the German Federal parliament, the issue of Iran was the constant subject of political skirmishes and political maneuvers. The SPD and the Greens, then in opposition, frequently raised issues connected with Iran in order to challenge the government and the majority parties, the CDU, the CSU, and the FDP. Paradoxically, this meant that while the German Federal parliament had on the one hand, as an institution, embarked on an active and extensive relationship with the Iranian parliament, on the other hand, as a political body, it found itself frequently engaged in criticism of Iran.

Cooperation between the two countries extended even to international issues. An official letter sent by Chancellor Kohl to President Rafsanjani urging Iran to sign the chemical weapons convention (CTBT) had a determining effect in compelling Iran eventually to add its signature to the convention. During the regular meetings of international organizations, including G7, the various institutions of the EU, and NATO, Germany played a central role in countering and opposing American policies aimed broadly at isolating Iran. In conclusion, it is clear that after German reunification in 1990, relations between Germany and Iran saw a significant improvement and growth on various tracks—political, economic, cultural, parliamentary, and in the field of security—which was unique and not to be compared with relations between Iran and any other European or Western country after the 1979 Islamic revolution.

No one imagined that the 1992 Conference of the Socialist International, an organization headed by the veteran German socialist statesman and former Chancellor Willy Brandt, was to have such a fateful effect on the future of

Iran–Germany relations. Numerous political parties and groups from various countries were invited to participate at this gathering. Among the invitees was a Kurdish–Iranian political party, whose representatives took the opportunity to meet other Iranian figures in Berlin. Their rendezvous was the Mykonos café, where they were attacked by a number of individuals who fired on them and killed four Iranian Kurds. This incident took place in the autumn of 1992.

As was usual in such circumstances, the German judicial officials involved released little information and, pending further investigation, they were extremely cautious in their statements regarding the persons accused. By 1996, a number of German organizations began to accuse the Iranian leadership of having planned and participated in this incident. The German media initially referred to the case as the Café; since then, it has become known as "the Mykonos affair." When the court in Berlin hearing the case called upon the former Iranian president Abolhassan Bani-Sadr to appear as a witness, the media reaction reached a peak of sensationalism. Relying on apparently fictitious information, the source of which he did not reveal, Bani-Sadr confirmed that the Iranian leadership was involved in this act of terrorism. The German Prosecutor-General directly accused what he called "influential Iranian organizations" of having decreed that the terrorist acts should take place, and he accordingly issued a subpoena summoning to court the head of the Iranian intelligence organization, Ali Fallahian, even though Mr Fallahian had taken part in an exchange of visits with the head of Germany's intelligence organization, Minister of State Bernd Schmidbauer. Mr Fallahian had visited Germany after 1992, and had discussed with his German counterpart cooperation in various fields, including the exchanges of prisoners between the Lebanese Hizbollah organization and Israel in which Mr Schmidbauer took part, an event which political observers regarded as the beginning of Germany's contemporary involvement with the Middle East.

The order to arrest Ali Fallahian and the accusations leveled against the Iranian leadership by the German Prosecutor-General were the spark that ignited major demonstrations in Qom and Tehran at which Germany's apparently anti-Iranian policy was condemned. The opportunity was taken during the demonstrations to remind Germany that it had exported chemical weapons to Iraq, which had been used during the war with Iran, killing and injuring hundreds of Iranian soldiers and civilians. One thousand eight hundred Iraqi missiles constructed with the benefit of German technology killed thousands of Iranian civilians, and in contrast with Germany's agreement to pay DM 250 million to Israel in compensation for only one similar Iraqi missile attack on Israel, no recompense was offered. In another provocative incident, five Iranian dissident intellectuals were arrested at the home of the cultural counselor at the German Embassy in Tehran, one of whom was Faraj Sarkuhi, who was accused of spying on Germany's behalf. Meanwhile, press sources in Germany revealed the agreement on intelligence cooperation, made by Bernd Schmidbauer and Ali Fallahian, one of the provisions of which was that each country would permit three individuals involved in intelligence activities to be admitted to the other country as members of its diplomatic corps.

Following the storm resulting from the Mykonos trial, the German Foreign Minister Klaus Kinkel was to lose more than others. He had been leading a group in Germany, within the framework of the EU, which advocated a policy of conciliation with Iran. On numerous occasions he had expressed his dissatisfaction with the methods used by the United States in its relations with Iran. He had openly criticized the D'Amato Act, saying that he believed such a law would ultimately be to the detriment of Germany and inimical to the interests of the EU. The D'Amato Act stipulated that companies investing over $40 million in the fields of oil and energy in Iran would be subject to sanctions in the United States. The German Foreign Minister's policy of "critical dialogue" with Iran stood in contrast to the American approach. "Critical dialogue" was meant to imply continued contact and cooperation. Klaus Kinkel's view was that the Western nations had a common goal in their dealings with Iran, but differed in their methods.

Germany's strategy in relation to Iran was part of a broad attempt to raise the country's political profile in the international arena in general, and in particular in the Middle East, at a time when Germany's international influence was not proportional to its economic weight, a deficiency of which Germany's leadership was well aware and which led the German government to make efforts to redress the situation. Germany had three main aims. These were, first, a bid to make the case for a permanent seat for Germany at the United Nations Security Council. This drew support from the former UN Secretary-General Boutros Boutros Ghali, which was one reason why Germany supported his bid for reelection. However, after it became clear that the United States was determined to continue to dominate the United Nations and the Security Council, Germany scaled down its support. A second German aim was to play a larger role within the political councils of the EU, to match that of other major European states such as France, which, due to its worldwide political interests, combined with its significant role in the Persian Gulf region, and its evident influence in the Mediterranean and North Africa, appeared more influential than Germany.

The third German aim was the one which directly affected Iran, namely to preserve its historical relationships with a number of key non-European countries such as China, Malaysia, Indonesia, and Iran itself. The relationship between Iran and Germany, as has been explained above, is deeply rooted in history and has political, economic, and cultural dimensions. In addition, Iran's geopolitical situation has long attracted German strategists. This face was clearly reflected in German military planning during the Second World War, when Germany had an eye on the oil resources of the Middle East, and it wished to circumvent the positions of the Allied forces, and those of Britain in particular. For Germany's purposes, Iran's location in the Middle East was of crucial importance.

With its long borders with the Islamic republics of the former Soviet Union, and its shared history with a region much of which fell under Iranian rule until as late as 1828, Iran's position endowed it, from Germany's point of view, with great geopolitical significance, since the acquisition of influence in Iran would enable Germany to complete the strategic encirclement of Russia. Germany had long sought to prepare the way for its return to a position of influence in its former hinterland in Eastern Europe, where it had long seen itself as being in competition with Moscow. Germany had long planned to oust the influence of the Soviet Union from East Germany, was an early advocate of bringing the former socialist countries such as Poland, Hungary, and the Baltic republics into NATO, and saw the opportunity to extend its influence in the former Yugoslavia. Iran was also part of Germany's broader strategy of containment of its eastern rival.

However, the Gulf War of 1991 illustrated the limitations at that time of Germany's political role beyond its borders, and especially in the Middle East. Though Germany paid its share of the cost of this war, a significant contribution of some $11 billion, it was effectively excluded from both military and political decision-making, and took little part in the postwar diplomacy. This experience helped to convince Germany that a developed relationship with Iran would assist it to gain more influence in the region. In addition to the importance of Iran's position to the south of the former Soviet Union, its extensive Persian Gulf littoral, bordering on the site of the world's largest oil reserves, was also of high strategic significance. Iran's own oil reserves and the size of its population in proportion to other regional states were also factors that led the German Foreign Minister to declare in 1997 that "Iran is a bridge toward countries of the Islamic world and Asia."[2]

In addition, Iran has a significant role not only in the Persian Gulf but also in the Middle East itself. Iran's relations with the Arab states, and in particular its ties with Syria and the Lebanese Hezbollah, give it influence in the Middle East peace process. German cooperation with Iran in the exchange of hostages was a way for Germany to make its mark in Middle East politics. However, the German leadership was well aware of the difficulties that might stand in the way of this objective. Israel has always been opposed to a European role in the Middle East peace process, contending that the authority of the United States as the sole arbiter of the process must not be diluted. In addition, the United States itself regarded it important to exclude mediation by any other power, even Russia, which was given in theory an equal role at the Madrid Conference.

All the factors that have tended to create a bond between Iran and Germany are linked with the historically strong economic relations between the two countries that have been described earlier. Germany is Iran's principal economic partner on an international level, and the economic relations between the two countries that prevailed in the 1990s had their roots in the 1960s and 1970s. Iran continued to be a significant shareholder in Krupp-Thyssen. There were major economic contracts between the two countries, especially in transportation, infrastructure, and energy. The nuclear plant at Bushehr is still remembered as an example of economic cooperation, which failed under international pressure, when, after the Islamic revolution, the United States insisted that the contract signed by the Siemens company to complete the plant could not be honored. The possibility of extending German penetration of the Iranian market still exists, and many German economic experts believe that what has been achieved so far in the field of economic cooperation with Iran could in more favorable future circumstances lead to a higher level of economic interchange between the two countries, while Iran could be a bridge for Germany to reach other significant markets.

Iranian decision-makers were well aware in the 1990s of Germany's significant role in breaking the economic chains with which the United States had surrounded Iran. The elements of the American strategy ranged from the D'Amato legislation, to diplomatic lobbying against Iran, both openly and through secret channels, and to the allocation of a special budget for the CIA to develop schemes for the overthrow of the Iranian political system. In this context, Iran viewed its dialogue and relations with Germany as an important means toward the circumvention of the anti-Iranian policies of the United States. Iran also saw the potential acquisition of German technology, in the context of the impositions of sanctions by the United States, as vital to the development of the Iranian economy, which had been to a great extent dependent under the previous regime on American technological assistance. The prospect that the EU might become an economic world power on the level of the United States and Japan was also seen in Tehran as an opportunity which Iran could not ignore. In 1990, Iran's national strategy was to regard Germany as "the door to the European Union."

At the time of the worst vicissitudes in relations between the two countries, the political leaders remained conscious of the importance of their relationship. In his message to President Rafsanjani about the Mykonos trial, Chancellor Helmut Kohl emphasized that Germany placed importance on bilateral relations between the two countries, and added that Germany had no intention of insulting either the Iranian nation or its spiritual leader. President Rafsanjani, speaking to a huge crowd gathered for Friday prayers at Tehran University, said in response that, "Iran, too, has no inclination toward the disruption of bilateral relations, and it differentiates between the irresponsible words of a few German officials and the German leadership; while, in addition, it has no evidence of the involvement of the German leadership in the current assault against Iran."[2] While some German opposition political parties viewed the Mykonos trial as a victory for "the values of justice and human rights," in Iran it was viewed as a problem that had arisen out of what was regarded by some as global arrogance on the part of the West and by others as a particular attitude adopted by some Germans. It is impossible to separate the emphasis placed in Western circles on the Mykonos verdict, four years after the incident, which gave rise to the trial, from the attempt by the United States to prevent the German leadership from halting the deterioration in bilateral relations between Iran and Germany, and from the other aims of the United States, the reinforcement of the American-imposed encirclement of Iran, and the curtailment of Germany's ambition for a major role in the international arena, especially in the Middle East and the Persian Gulf.

Summary of conclusions

1. After 1990, bilateral relations between Iran and Germany underwent some major changes. Iran, after the Islamic revolution of 1979, was no longer under American domination, so that by the end of the Iran–Iraq War in 1989,

it was able to lay down entirely new lines for its foreign policy. In addition, Germany was also able, following the reunification of the country in October 1990 and its emergence from the hegemony of the Second World War Allies, to put on its agenda a review of its own foreign policy.

2.   The leaders of the two countries prioritized the renewal of the traditional and historical ties between Iran and Germany. Iranian statesmen also viewed France as a significant European country with which to develop bilateral relations. Germany, however, was strongly interested in the renewal of its relations with Iran, which offered a major opportunity to strengthen Germany's influence in the Middle East region.

3.   The gradual improvement in the relationship between Iran and Germany led to the development of links in the political, economic, cultural, and security fields, as well as parliamentary ties, to a level not previously seen in Iran's foreign relations with any other Western state (see Chapter 3).

4.   Despite their well-developed relations, Iran and Germany nevertheless faced serious difficulties in avoiding friction. These problems fell into two groups. First, there were Iran's general differences with the West. These included disputes over the issues of human rights, terrorism, weapons of mass destruction, and the Middle East peace process, all of which affected the relationship between Iran and Germany (see Chapter 5). Second, there were problems specific to the relations between Iran and Germany, due on one hand to interference by the United States, Britain, and Israel, and on the other hand to security issues, including the arrests and trial of each other's nationals, and mutual accusations of espionage (see Chapters 4 and 6).

5.   Germany and the other EU states established the policy of "critical dialogue" in 1992 in order to preserve their relations with Iran as well as to protest against the American policy of isolation. The policy served as a vehicle for discussion and criticism of Iran in relation to the four major issues of human rights, terrorism, weapons of mass destruction, and the Middle East peace process, though the principal focus of both Germany and the other European states was the human rights issue.

6.   Iran also took the opportunity of the policy of "critical dialogue" to criticize Europe's behavior. Criticism focused on eight issues: the insulting behavior of Europe toward the Islamic world; the support given to terrorism by EU member states, particularly through their provision of asylum to terrorists; their double standards in relation to their own human rights violations; their antagonism toward foreigners; their disregard of the rights of Muslim minorities; their support for the Zionist regime; their dissemination of both conventional weapons and weapons of mass destruction; and the EU's lack of political independence.

7.   Germany took a major part in the creation of the policy of "critical dialogue," thus putting a major obstacle in the way of the American policy of isolating Iran in the international arena. Germany's special relationship with Iran later became virtually the sole issue on which there was disagreement between

Germany and the Untied States as well as between Germany and Israel. Germany's high profile opposition to American proposals for sanctions on Iran made at the meetings of G7, NATO, and the Organisation of Economic Co-operation and Development (OECD) drew the attention of politicians round the world and was widely reported.

8. The relationship between Iran and Germany in the field of security angered the United States, Britain, and Israel more than the other aspects of the relationship. These three states made serious attempts to limit and degrade the relationship between Iran and Germany in this sphere, of which the most spectacular result had been the humanitarian exchange of prisoners in the Middle East.

9. The problems faced by a number of German nationals in Iran were an unusual occurrence.[3] Citizens of no other Western nation had experienced difficulties with the authorities in Iran on such a scale. At the same time, most of the assassination attempts against Iranian nationals abroad took place in either Germany or France, which seemed unlikely to be a chance occurrence. In addition, the discovery of mortar bombs in an Iranian ship *Iran Kolahdooz* bound for Germany just a few days before the Sharm el-Sheikh international summit on terrorism, and the level of information possessed by the United States concerning the case, aggravated the suspicion that there were deliberate attempts by outsiders to damage the relationship between Germany and Iran.[4]

In 1998, a maverick group within the Iranian Intelligence Ministry was identified and its members arrested. The Iranian state media attributed to the activities of this group many of the assassinations, as well as a number of murders inside Iran,[5,6] in reports that were never denied by the intelligence service. Later, however, an official announcement was made by the Islamic revolution's Leader Ali Khamenei that the group was controlled by Israeli agents, by whom its activities were planned and directed.[7-9] The Prosecutor-General of Iran's Military Court reaffirmed this assessment, adding that the maverick group was conducting espionage on behalf of Israel and the United States.[10-12] A film recording the confessions of those accused of the murders inside Iran was shown to 100 members of Iran's parliament, in which allegations were made against an Intelligence Ministry official, Saeed Emami, and his wife, of spying for the Israeli intelligence agency Mossad and for the United States Federal Bureau of Investigation, the FBI.[13]

10. Terrorism became the most crucial issue for the EU's member states, including Germany, leading to increased anxiety on their part over matters that could have possible repercussions on their own internal security. The verdict of the Berlin Court in the Mykonos trial, which accused Iran of what was described as state terrorism, led to the most serious crisis since the end of the Second World War in relations between Iran and Germany, and in relations

between Iran and the EU in general. Both the EU and Germany had been able to tolerate the differences that existed between themselves and Iran on the issues of human rights, weapons of mass destruction, and the Middle East peace process, but the verdict of the court in Berlin was the issue that caused them to abandon the policy of "critical dialogue."

11. The Berlin Court verdict, meanwhile, also undermined Iran's earlier stated policy of creating a relationship with the West minus the United States. Following the victory of Mr Mohammad Khatami in the 1997 presidential elections, and the West's consequently increased hopes for better relations between Iran and the United States, together with the enactment of Western-oriented reforms in Iran, relations between Iran and Europe were restored. Nevertheless, the relationship remained conditional on the West's assessment of the performance of President Khatami.

12. Within Germany, the opposition parties and the media played a considerable role in hindering the positive trend of relations between Iran and Germany. The Berlin Court verdict provided those who opposed the improvement of relations with further leverage against the government, of which they took full advantage. In Iran, the government, parliament, and public opinion were all in agreement on the desirability of the enhancement of the relationship between Iran and Germany. However, in the security sector of the Iranian government, there were differences of opinion on the issue. The action taken against some German nationals resident in Iran, and the case of Faraj Sarkuhi, and the raid mounted on the house of the German cultural attaché in Tehran, all had their origins in these factional differences. It must be concluded that the security establishment in Iran was out of harmony with other sections of the government, as well as with the parliament, public opinion, and the media.

13. The independence exercised by the German Judiciary and the Courts can be viewed as worthy of respect, but it does seem that the verdict of the court in Berlin appeared to reflect a will to undermine the relationship between Germany and Iran. The involvement of Abulhassan Bani-Sadr, the appearance of Witness "C," and the arguments developed concerning the earlier case are all factors that support the conclusion that the outcome of the case was influenced by forces hostile to Iran (see Chapter 7). It must be mentioned here, however, that all the evidence presented to the Berlin Court was harmonized and prearranged in such a way that the court would unavoidably come to the precise conclusion, which served the interests of the United States, Britain, and Israel. The political and propagandist exploitation that took place after the court's verdict, however, was beyond the powers of the court to control, and even beyond the control of the German government. In consequence, the incident was able to result in the precise effect on relations between Germany and Iran desired by the United States, Israel, and Britain.

14. In addition to the above arguments, a crucial feature of the evidence was that all the accusations in the court's verdict concerning the involvement of

Iranian officials were founded on the statements made by Mr Mesbahi, the alleged eyewitness. Mesbahi himself, however, in a letter published by *Frankfurter Allgemeine*, later retracted his evidence, claiming that all he had said in court was totally untrue. He later said he had been persuaded to lie in court by the blandishments of certain Western intelligence agencies, including in particular that of the United States, which promised him substantial inducements; but that when the United States refused to allow him even to enter the country, he had come to his senses and decided to make a public confession.[14]

15. In the context of its relationship with Iran, Germany, despite its will to build better relations, must come to terms with a number of facts. First, it is not yet wholly free from the hegemony of the Allies; second, its relations with the EU, Israel, and the United States are more important for it than its ties with Iran; third, its membership and obligations to the EU and NATO require it not to pursue an individualistic line in its relations with Iran; and, fourth, Britain, Israel, and the United States will not tolerate a coalition between Germany and Iran in the Middle East, and will not allow Germany to play a serious role in the Middle East and the Persian Gulf. The United States, which has so far determined policy in the region, also opposes such a role for the EU.

16. Meanwhile, Iran, in spite of its will for better relations with Germany, also has facts to face. First, that Germany is obliged to act within the framework of the EU; and second, that Germany has fundamental strategic interests in common with the United States and Israel. In the case where Germany faces a choice between its relationship with Iran, and its relationship with the United States and Israel, it must for the sake of its own national interests put its relationship with the United States and Israel first. The third fact that Iran must accept is that the United States, backed by Britain, continues to play the determining role in the Middle East, and will continue to refuse to allow the EU or its individual member states any scope for action.

17. For the establishment and maintenance of secure, stable, and unchallenged relations between Iran and Germany, and between Iran and the EU, the requirements to be met are as follows. First, the level of tension between Iran and the United States must be reduced. In other words, it is not possible for Iran to enjoy a warm relationship with Europe at a time of continuing hostility between Iran and the United States. Second, a consensus between Iran and Europe can and should be reached in a number of fields, including the promotion of human rights, both regionally and globally, the institution of a joint campaign against terrorism, a joint effort against the spread of weapons of mass destruction, and the creation of a regional cooperation mechanism for the promotion of peace and stability in the Persian Gulf, Central Asia, and Middle East regions, with the participation of all the regional states. This level of cooperation would be effective in paving the way for a stable and improved relationship between Iran and the West. Finally, the ground should also be prepared for an improved mutual understanding between Iran and

the United States in all fields involving the common interests of the two countries, including security and bilateral cooperation in particular fields of mutual interest and concern.

18. Meanwhile, it should be recognized that given the existence of a religious government in Iran, and the dedication of the Islamic Republic to the Islamic faith and its Shi'a interpretation, together with the allegiance of the West to its own culture, the forging of profound strategic ties between the two sides is hardly to be expected. The parties involved should therefore work toward the establishment of some more modest form of relationship between Iran and Germany, and Iran and the EU as a whole.

19. The relationship that sprang up between Iran and Germany in the period from 1990 to 1996 may be viewed as among the more remarkable political developments that followed the end of the Cold War. Nevertheless, the need to strengthen cooperation between the United States and Europe, in response to the new political conditions arising from the collapse of the Soviet Union, was an important political consideration that led to the prioritization of the relationship between Germany and the United States, and could not have failed to affect relations between Iran and Germany.

20. After the Islamic revolution and the liberation of Iran from the hegemony of the United States, Iran was and is still not fully immune from the conspiracies of the Israeli and American intelligence services, which, in order to protect their interests in the Middle East and the Persian Gulf, continue to employ their regional agents to influence Iran's foreign relations in the ways that serve their purposes.

Finally, NATO would not tolerate a high-level relationship in the field of security ties between one of its member states and Iran, unless the existing misunderstandings between the West and Iran on a global scale were removed.

Part II

Outstanding issues in Iran–Europe relations

6 The Middle East as a weapon of mass destruction-free zone

Much has been said and written about nuclear weapon free zones (NWFZs) throughout the world, their particularities, their structures, advantages and disadvantages, and above all, their function as a mechanism for nonproliferation of nuclear weapons. Latin America, the South Pacific, Southeast Asia, Africa, and Antarctica are cited as regions where NWFZs have been successfully established. I will not deal with the technical issues of NWFZs already established. Rather, I will present two basic propositions on the virtues and utilities of NWFZs in general, and two propositions, I hope new and perhaps controversial, specific to NWFZ or weapon of mass destruction-free zone (WMDFZ) in the Middle East.

Establishment of NWFZs in different parts of the world is considered to make our world safer on two grounds. First, NWFZs strengthen the nonproliferation system in a particular region, with a possible spillover effect in terms of building confidence between states. Second, they are designed, by definition, to limit nuclear-weapon states' freedom to project, station, and move unnoticed their nuclear capability and armed vessels into NWFZs, and also to encourage them to heed their obligation under the NPT for a phased, general, and complete nuclear disarmament.

The establishment of NWFZs is a much-needed boost in the arm of the NPT, and particularly its pillars of nonproliferation and nuclear disarmament.

The rationale for devising the Nuclear Non-Proliferation Treaty is as valid today, if not more, as it was in 1968. Nuclear weapons remain the most obvious symptom of humanity's continued immaturity, incivility, and our continued need for moral and ethical growth. We face many challenges globally today. AIDS, poverty, conflicts, and terrorism are only some of these challenges. The challenge of nuclear weapons, 36,000 of them, primarily in the United States and Russia, is qualitatively different and thus not comparable with other challenges we must encounter. The challenge of nuclear weapons is different because they can obliterate all human life and other forms of life on our planet in an instant and several times over. Albert Einstein is reported to have said that if there is going to be a Fourth World War, it will likely be fought with stick and stone. His response supposes that after a Third World War, in which nuclear weapons are used, the remaining human beings will only have the option of fighting with sticks and stones. David Krieger[1] of the Project of the Nuclear Age Peace Foundation regards Einstein's response to be overly optimistic.

Therefore, the general public, civil society groups, policy establishments and governments need constant education, reminders, and creative steps to promote the existential need for nuclear disarmament and nonproliferation.

Challenges of WMDFZ in the Middle East

Despite the first and the second propositions, when it comes to the Middle East, the complexities of the issue and the degree of the idealism in the effort for establishing an NWFZ or an WMDFZ in the Middle East becomes starkly obvious to the point of laughter. But laughter or not, perhaps no region in the world could have more dividends for international peace and security than does the Middle East by establishing a WMDFZ. Support for establishing a zone in the Middle East free from weapons of mass destruction seems abundant. However, practical progress to that end is far less than encouraging.

The most exciting progress on this arduous path came in the 1995 NPT Extension and Review Conference, where state parties also adopted unanimously, as an integral part of the outcome of the conference, to establish a zone free of weapons of mass destruction in the Middle East. This was the peak of progress, by then, 21 years of efforts in the United Nations General Assembly to establish an NWFZ in the Middle East. This effort had started in 1974 by Iran and had later been pursued jointly with Egypt in the UN General Assembly.

The adoption of the resolution on WMDFZ in the Middle East in the 1995 NPT Extension and Review Conference, which was an exciting progress on the subject, seems at the same time, to have exerted the greatest pressure not only on that initiative, but also on the actual indefinite extension of the NPT altogether. Furthermore, those members of the League of Arab States who acceded to the NPT between 1995 and 2000, as a result of the outcome of the 1995 Extension Conference, particularly the Middle East resolution, which was then considered positive by them and many developing states such as Iran, now believe that they had been misled and that their interlocutors did not keep their end of the bargain.[2]

In 1995, state parties to the NPT agreed to extend the Treaty indefinitely in a package deal consisting of three decisions and a resolution. The decisions related to undertaking to strengthen the NPT, achieving its universality, and to adopting principles and objectives to address the implementation of the Treaty. The resolution was about establishing the Middle East as a WMDFZ. More than 11 years since that conference, many developing states, including all Arab states and Iran, hold that no genuine action has been taken, neither is there any indication of intent or plan to implement any of the decisions or the Middle East resolution of the 1995 conference by states in a position to do so.

As a result, and in the context of the 1995 Middle East resolution, the league of Arab States has technically questioned the legality of the indefinite extension of the NPT.[2] By the same token, the foreign ministers of the states forming the New Agenda Coalition (Brazil, Egypt, Ireland, Mexico, New Zealand, South Africa, and Sweden) were on the record criticizing the nuclear-weapon states for failing to comply with their obligations for disarmament under the NPT. They openly reiterated in 2005 that they are concerned about the unsatisfactory progress of the nuclear-weapon states to implement the NPT and achieve complete nuclear disarmament. "At the review conference five years ago, the nuclear-weapon states made an 'unequivocal undertaking to accomplish the total elimination of their nuclear arsenals.'... Indeed, the nuclear-weapon states should acknowledge that disarmament and nonproliferation are mutually reinforcing processes: What does not exist cannot proliferate."[3]

These contentions may be evaluated by exploring the deliberations and documents of the 2005 NPT Review Conference—the conference that failed to agree on an outcome document partly because of these reasons.

The perception in the Arab world is that the indefinite extension of the NPT in 1995 was technically flawed. As a result, mistrusting the nuclear-weapon states and the West in general, and the United States and Israel in particular, on regional and global security issues have further widened.

They believe, as the position of the Arab League in the deliberation of the 2005 Review Conference amply illustrates,[2] that the big powers with influence over Israel, particularly the United States and also other nuclear-weapon states, tricked them into agreeing to the indefinite extension of the Treaty and to persuading the Arab states that had not acceded to the NPT by 1995 to do so as a result of the resolution on establishing a WMDFZ in the Middle East in the 1995 Extension and Review Conference of the NPT. They argue that the United States and others with influence had no intention or plan to exert any meaningful pressure on Israel to give up its nuclear arsenals, join the NPT, and put its nuclear facilities under the full safeguard system of the IAEA. There is sympathy in Iran for this Arab view.

As a result of the Middle East resolution and the commitments declared by the 1995 Review and Extension Conference, the remaining members of the Arab League nonparties to the NPT acceded to the Treaty by 2000. Israel is, therefore, the only state in the Middle East that has not yet acceded to the NPT and continues to defy the will of the international community, manifested in the 1995 Middle East resolution of the Extension and Review Conference, as well as about 26 resolutions of the General Assembly and UN Security Council resolution 687, calling for establishment in the Middle East of a zone free from all weapons of mass destruction. Israel continues to refuse, with impunity, to give up its nuclear arsenals and to place its nuclear facilities under the safeguard system of the IAEA.

Israel ostensibly supports an NWFZ in the Middle East

It is interesting to note that the annual UN General Assembly resolutions on establishing a WMDFZ in the Middle East have for years been adopted unanimously. In other words, this resolution is, unlike many other resolutions, relative to the Middle East in the UN General Assembly, which passes with mostly negative votes, or sometimes abstentions, of only the United States and Israel. Israel abstained in 1974 when Iran first presented the idea of establishing an NWFZ in the Middle East in the form of a resolution to the United Nations General Assembly.

As this resolution was adopted year after year in the UN General Assembly, Israel saw some tactical utility in supporting, or at least not objecting to, it. Popular perception in the Middle East seems to indicate that Israel, the United States, and perhaps other international players and well-wisher states have regarded the resolutions on WMDFZ in the Middle East as a possible bait to secure the much-needed commodity of legitimacy and recognition for Israel in the Middle East. This, Israelis and others thought, could be done through the lure of a continuing bilateral and multilateral negotiation between Israel and states in the Middle East, perhaps under some kind of international mechanism, and ostensibly for nuclear disarmament of Israel and establishing an NWFZ in the Middle East. Under such a scheme, if acted upon, the dividends for Israel would have been years of association, negotiations, and gradually even partnership with some states in the Middle East, resulting in securing recognition for Israel and perpetuating occupation of land, which Arabs would have otherwise regarded as illegal and unjust. I recognize that perhaps few in the mainstream politics in the West would consider this analysis tenable.

I would venture to say that considering Iran's political orientation under the Shah, the thinking behind Iran's first resolution on NWFZ in the Middle East to the UN General Assembly in 1974 could have hardly been far from an attempt to launder and legitimize Israel in Middle East politics.

Notwithstanding the above, and irrespective of the original thinking by Iran, the United States, Israel or whoever else, behind the initial phases of the idea of establishing an NWFZ in the Middle East, it can plausibly be argued that now after more than 30 years, establishing a WMDFZ in the Middle East has gained a logic and an intellectual momentum of its own. According to some analysts,[4] with whom I agree totally, the process of establishing a WMDFZ in the Middle East can potentially facilitate a security arrangement and help find a just peace to the Arab–Israeli conflict in the Middle East.

Israel is said to have between 100 and 200 nuclear weapons in its arsenal. This is argued to have accorded Israel a false confidence and the audacity to reject any peace plan that is just and fair without any hesitation and impunity. Establishment of a WMDFZ in the Middle East can theoretically remove this Israeli arrogance and make it more receptive to a genuine and just peace process. The Israeli argument that its nuclear weapon is the final deterrent against the Arabs and the Iranians should find no receptive ear because the balance of conventional power, as shown in the previous wars, is in Israel's favor. Additionally, the bipartisan policy of the United States, as the only superpower, is to ensure a strategic edge for Israel, that is, to ensure Israel's military superiority in the Middle East. It would be hard to think that the United States is unable to ensure that security edge for Israel without it having a nuclear arsenal of its own.

The establishment of a weapons of mass destruction-free zone in the Middle East has direct bearing on a just peace process in the Arab–Israeli conflict and could potentially encourage Israel to abandon its intransigence and become more receptive to such a process.

Prospects for establishing an NWFZ in the Middle East

Most analysts agree that implementing a WMDFZ or NWFZ in the Middle East is far-fetched. It needs incremental measures, change of heart and mind, confidence-building measures, and a courageous resolve to save succeeding generations from the scourge of wars, to borrow from the UN Charter. Here is a nonexhaustive, interrelated, and mutually reinforcing list of steps to facilitate establishment of an NWFZ in the Middle East.

General steps

- Measures to promote respect for and implementation of the NPT.
- Measures to strengthen the nonproliferation system.
- Measures to strengthen nuclear disarmament and compliance by nuclear-weapon states to their obligations.

Specific steps

1. Bear in mind that progress on NWFZ or WMDFZ in the Middle East is possible when there is a reasonable degree of assurance for long-term peace.
2. Be creative, but not ambitious, in devising confidence-building measures on security issues in the Middle East.
3. Arrange for mid-level, regional governmental expert meetings to discuss and try to agree on political and security requirements of a situation in the future when negotiations for NWFZ in the Middle East could be constructive.

This step could be problematic. For this to be useful, participation of all states, in the region that do not recognize Israel (including Iran and Arab states) must somehow be secured. To jump start this process, creativity and flexibility ought to lead the way. Perhaps the easiest way out, procedurally of course, is to have the United Nations to hold such meetings, in which Arabs and Iranians usually participate.

4. Develop a political concept in those governmental expert meetings for a cooperative nonintrusive monitoring as a confidence-building measure toward an NWFZ or WMDFZ in the framework of a regional security arrangement in the Middle East.[5] This governmental expert group may be mandated to come up with an agreed text for nonintrusive verification of a possible NWFZ in the Middle East. The subject is appealing to the Arab states and Iran, and since consensus is necessary, enough assurance is present that all views, including those of Israel, will be taken on board.

Membership of the zone, states that need to ratify the zone before it becomes enforceable, and the extent and scope of peaceful uses of nuclear technology within the context of the current international debate on fuel-cycle facilities and technology could also be subjects of discussion within the governmental group.

This process will be purely exploratory and should not be regarded as negotiations. However, the literature produced in such deliberation and the possible consensus outcome document on nonintrusive verification of a possible WMDFZ could certainly be useful for future negotiations.

5.   As the only state in the region with nuclear weapon, Israel may initially take some steps that are strategically low-risk but symbolically high impact, in order to help begin the process. "Israel should consider shutting down its Dimona nuclear reactor and the associated facilities that make up the core of Israel's nuclear program. Israel must already possess more than enough nuclear material for a sizable deterrent, and the reactor and its periphery must be close to the end of their useful life."[6]

Before I conclude, I wish to make a brief reference to the Iranian Nuclear program now being considered in the Security Council. The issue is seen in Iran as the United States twisting Iran's arms for close to 30 years of rocky relations between the two countries, which the United States regarded as largely unbecoming to its status as the only superpower. The question of the Iraq debacle, and the Hezbollah and Israeli conflict, may have added insult to injury and thus rendered the United States more intent and emotional about exerting pressure on the IAEA, Europeans, Russians, and the Chinese, to make a negotiated resolution of the issue all the more difficult. To some NeoCons, the Iranians must learn and recognize who the boss is. But, things are not that simple. The United States ought to acknowledge that it should practise what it preaches, that its effort to halt proliferation must be even-handed or its efforts will not be taken seriously. The practice of threatening one state like Iran with international sanctions or even military action, while being in noncompliance with nuclear disarmament obligation under the NPT itself, or tolerating the proliferation of nuclear weapons by other states, cannot but be regarded as power politics and lack of interest in nonproliferation. The United States' double standards are not limited only to Israel. Its announced intention for nuclear cooperation agreement with India is another example of rewarding a state that has refused to sign the NPT and has developed nuclear weapons. This agreement is in violation of US obligation under the NPT and also in violation of Security Council resolution 1172, which calls on both India and Pakistan to eliminate their nuclear weapons programs.

As far as the NWFZ in the Middle East is concerned, I wish to point out that now, because of the United States' undue pressure on and the abuse of the international machinery of the United Nations, Iran is being considered guilty. Until proven innocent, Iran may see a more active and forthcoming stance in the process of establishing an NWFZ or an WMDFZ in the Middle East as at least a circumstantial way of substantiating its innocence and of the peacefulness of its nuclear energy program.

In conclusion, it is very clear that there is a window of opportunity to advance the seemingly utopian idea of NWFZ or WMDFZ in the Middle East in the midst of a heightening situation of Iranian nuclear program and the lack of any meaningful initiative on the Arab–Israeli conflict.

7   Iran's nuclear dossier

Iran's nuclear dossier is the subject of a dispute that has drawn much international attention. The power void resulting from disintegration of the former bipolar world order; prevalence of a security-based discourse in international interactions after September 11, 2001; the transatlantic divide resulting from the crisis in Iraq; security-based doctrine of the United States and the strategy adopted by neoconservatives in 2005; efforts made by the Eastern countries to regain their lost power; concerns about the rise of new regional hegemonic powers; new developments in Central Asia and the Middle East; and a multitude of other indicators, especially international concerns about the potential threat of Iran's nuclear capability to Israel's security, are factors that have increased the sensitivity of Iran's nuclear crisis. This existing situation has made the nuclear dossier the most complicated and even the most fateful political and international issue for Iran, following the imposed eight-year war with Iraq. Regardless of the end results of this crisis, it will directly affect the interests and national security of Iran and will impact all fields of activity in the country, including political, security, economic, international, and even social areas. Therefore, Iran's nuclear dispute is among a few international issues that will directly affect the security and interests of Iran and those of big international and regional powers, both inside the country and at a global level.

On August 14, 2002, a spokesperson for the Mujahideen Khalq Organization (MKO), claimed at a press conference at Willard Hotel in Washington that Iran was engaged in covert nuclear activities at three nuclear sites in Isfahan, Natanz, and Arak. About four months later, on December 13, 2002, CNN aired a documentary on the Institute for Science and International Security (ISIS), which included satellite pictures of the three sites. Both the spokesperson of the MKO and the CNN report claimed that Iran was pursuing secret nuclear activities for military purposes aimed at building an atomic bomb. During the same year, three huge nuclear complexes were under construction in Isfahan, Natanz, and Arak. The International Atomic Energy Agency (IAEA) was not informed about the construction of the Natanz facilities.[1] At that time, Tehran had not accepted the 93 + 2 additional protocol as well as "subsidiary arrangements." Subsidiary arrangements went beyond the safeguards, including the requirement that the country under subsidiary arrangements should report any activity, even construction activities related to atomic facilities, to IAEA six months before those activities begin. At that time, in view of the obligations of the Non-Proliferation Treaty (NPT), Tehran was not obliged to inform the United Nations' nuclear watchdog about the construction of the Natanz and Arak facilities. However, Isfahan's Uranium Conversion Facility (UCF) and the heavy water project at Arak were under the direct supervision of IAEA from the very beginning and no covert activities were conducted there. Anyway, claims made by MKO and the ensuing propaganda campaign launched by the United States and other international media paved the way for intensification of suspicions against Iran's nuclear activities.

However, the anti-Iran wave following the December report of CNN was practically marginalized after the US decision to attack Iraq, which focused White House's diplomacy on opening a wide front to topple Saddam. Therefore, Iran's nuclear crisis was in an embryonic stage in 2002. On February 22, 2002, the Director General of IAEA visited Iran to follow his negotiations with the officials. During that trip, Mohamed ElBaradei toured nuclear installations in Natanz. The Director General presented his report on Iran to the Board of Governors of IAEA in early March, in which he welcomed Tehran's cooperation with IAEA. The report insisted that Iran should sign in to the additional protocol.

In 2003, however, the sudden triumph of the US military in Iraq and the prevalence of military and security-based discourse of the American neoconservatives provided good grounds for the creation of a full-blown crisis against Iran. Since early April 2003, increasing pressure on Iran was put on the agenda of the US government. The meeting of the American–Israel Public Affairs Committee (AIPAC), which was held in early April, was the first venue for exertion of those pressures. During that meeting, Colin Powell, the then US secretary of state; Condoleezza Rice, US national security advisor; and John Bolton, US undersecretary of state, issued harsh remarks against the nuclear activities of Iran.

Mohamed ElBaradei presented the IAEA's report on the implementation of Safeguards Agreement in Iran to members of the Board of Governors on June 6, 2003, which was the main topic for discussion in IAEA's session in June. Legal and technical analysis of the report revealed that despite some positive points, general points related to the Board of Governors established a grave atmosphere against Iran. The eight-page report of the Director General had referred to failures and breaches of safeguards by Iran without any ambiguity, while commenting on Iran's corrective measures was made conditional on future treatment of the Agency by Iran, more inspections, and examining the results of subsequent tests. In that report,[2] the nuclear watchdog of the United Nations announced that Iran had failed to observe the content of the Safeguards Agreement and the NPT, at least with regard to the following five issues:

1. Failure to declare the import of natural uranium in 1991, and its subsequent transfer for further processing.
2. Failure to declare the activities involving the subsequent processing and use of the imported natural uranium, including the production and loss of nuclear material, where appropriate, and the production and transfer of waste resulting therefrom.

3. Failure to declare the facilities where such material (including the waste) was received, stored, and processed.
4. Failure to provide in a timely manner updated design information for the MIX Facility and for TRR (Tehran Research Reactor).
5. Failure to provide on-time information on the waste storage at Isfahan and at Arak.

The June 2003 report included such concepts as Iran's failures and breaches of the Safeguards Agreement, lack of complete trust in corrective measures, concern about the possibility of diversion, possible military use of nuclear facilities, and existence of many technical ambiguities. The Director General had also empha-sized in his report to the Board of Governors that Iran's acceptance of the 93 + 2 additional protocol was a necessary step to prove the truth of Iran's claims.

The meeting of the Board of Governors in June 2003 finally ended in a state-ment that contained reconciliatory terms,[3] but also very important demands. The Board of Governors on June 19, 2003, issued its statement, which was read out by the rotational head of the board,[4] and called on Tehran to make up for the declared failures and accept the 93 + 2 additional protocol without any conditions. The statement also encouraged Tehran to suspend introduction of nuclear material into centrifuges and cooperate with IAEA inspectors for environmental sampling.

As international pressures mounted on Iran, France, UK, and Germany sent a joint letter to the Iranian Foreign Minister on August 6, 2003. A day later, that is on August 7, 2003, the Russian Foreign Minister, Igor Ivanov, wrote a separate letter to Dr Kharrazi and explained Moscow's viewpoints. In this way, two trans-regional powers, that is, Russia and the European Union (EU), showed that despite convergence with the United States in June, they pursued their own inter-ests in a relatively independent manner and planned to open a new front in the face of the second Middle East crisis. The most urgent demand of that front was signing and implementation of the 93 + 2 additional protocol by Iran. Two letters written by the EU and Russia included another important point, which was described by some experts as a short-term solution by Moscow and Brussels to confront US plans. Both Russia and the EU had clearly asked Iran in their letters to stop its nuclear program.

The September meeting of the Board of Governors of IAEA was forthcoming. According to White House diplomacy, the meeting was considered a venue to reach a decision on Iran.[5] At the same time, Iran had not declared its official and final position on the requests of IAEA and other international parties. Under those circumstances, Iran's international standing and IAEA's requests were discussed at the highest decision-making levels of Iran. Tehran decided to send positive signals about negotiations on the 93 + 2 additional protocol and its acceptance and to start negotiations with IAEA for the implementation of the protocol. In view of the forthcoming meeting of the Board of Governors, this was considered a strategic and relatively effective measure on the part of Iran. Immediately after this decision by senior officials of Iran, major diplomatic activities were put on Iran's agenda. Iran's declaration of readiness to negotiate with IAEA on the additional protocol on August 25, 2003, was communicated to the Director General by Iran's representative at IAEA.

The resolution adopted by the Board of Governors after that meeting included austere requirements for Tehran. The requirements were so unexpected that the head of Iran's Atomic Energy Organization, as the official in charge of the nuclear dossier, described them as being totally impractical, saying, "It seems that the resolution has been engineered in such a manner as to guarantee its non-implementation."[6] The first reactions from Tehran were anger and surprise, which totally rejected obedience to the resolution. Regardless of Iran's anger and surprise, the resolution contained requirements and demands that made the previous policy of supervision and silence totally ineffective. Iran's situation was very critical during IAEA's meeting in September 2003 and the resolution issued by the Board of Governors turned Iran's case into a special subject. The resolution had referred to cases of low and high contamination in Iran's centrifuges, significant and material changes in Iran's statements, increased ambiguities, introducing nuclear material into centrifuges, and Tehran's avoidance of declaring all activities. It had expressed regret and concern over these points. The Board of Governors also gave Iran a 50-day deadline, while imposing further requirements. That is, the board asked Iran officially "to promptly and unconditionally sign, ratify and fully implement the additional protocol" and "to suspend all further uranium enrichment-related activities." The Board of Governors also gave Iran 50 days to take "essential and urgent" steps toward confidence building and to take "corrective measures." The measures included "providing a full declaration of all imported material and components relevant to the enrichment program," as well as "granting unrestricted access, including environmental sampling, for the Agency to whatever locations the Agency deems necessary for the purposes of verification of the correctness and completeness of Iran's declarations." The September resolution also noted that Iran had breached its commitments. This meant that needed legal grounds were provided for reporting Iran's nuclear dossier to the United Nations Security Council (if the country totally rejected the said resolution).

The September 2003 resolution was issued at a time when Iran's official assessments in the summer of 2003 had not expected predicted such a crisis and such a broad consensus.[7] The situation at that time could be summarized as follows:

1. Iran was suddenly on the verge of being referred to the United Nations Security Council. Lack of compliance with the resolution would have made Iran subject to articles 18 and 19 of the Agency's statute with the direct result of being reported to New York.
2. At that time, neoconservatives held great power at the White House and while beside themselves with joy due to the victories in Afghanistan and Iraq, they were mulling whether to attack Iran or Syria. Threats of reporting Iran's dossier to the Security Council were not a political bluff, but the main aspiration of the United States.
3. Iran was in no way prepared to handle the possible consequences of reporting of its nuclear dossier to the Security Council.

4. Reporting Iran's dossier to the United Nations Security Council would have led to Iran's isolation and rapid evolution of the dispute into a "security" matter.
5. When the September resolution was issued, there was a general consensus among Western countries against Iran, which paved the way for international confrontation with Iran. The pessimism had not only spread to Russia and China, but it was also rife in political capitals of the Muslim countries as well as Iran's neighbors.
6. The IAEA meeting in June and the resolution that was issued in September indicated increasing convergence toward suspension of, at least, part of Iran's nuclear activities. The request had gone past the American block countries to include the EU and Russia. More dawdling by Iran could have led to the creation of a broad front against Iran's nuclear programs.
7. The situation of Iran, from the viewpoint of technical and legal interactions with IAEA, was critical.
8. International public opinion when the resolution was issued was such that it considerably limited Iran's latitude. Impressed by the calculated, professional, and far-reaching propaganda of the international media, world public opinion had been mobilized against Iran.
9. Public opinion was not satisfactory inside our own borders. Domestic public opinion had not been convinced that Iran's nuclear activities were a cause of "national pride."
10. The "September Shock" led to grave concerns in Iran. Since late July 2003, the issue of a possible US military attack on Iran was a common topic of discussion for Iranian families. The concern was made worse in view of Iraq's occupation and the aggressive rhetoric used by the Zionist regime and US government against Iran.
11. Intense dependence of the Iranian market on the society's psychological state was a major factor that turned the summer of 2003 into one of the most inactive periods of Iranian history in economic terms. The crisis in September 2003 brought about economic stagnation in Iran, which, combined with vague future perspectives and widespread rumors about possible military attack by the United States on Iran, created conditions that led to capital flight.
12. Iran's plans to attract international investments were also changed. Japan suspended investments in one of the biggest upstream oil projects of Iran and the country's economic risk was deteriorated to E grade with international insurance firms reducing their cooperation with Iran's economy to a minimum.
13. Domestic political differences were soaring so high that they worked as a big hurdle to finding a rational solution to the dispute. Contradictory signals sent by Tehran were a full-blown catastrophe for the decision-making system of the country. At that juncture, there were practically two main fronts in the political scene of the country, each incriminating the opposite front with treason, or misinformation and ignorance.
14. The September crisis brought about conditions that made the opposition quite ecstatic. The October deadline and Tehran's early reaction to it, which openly

rejected the resolution, were considered a turning point in the opposition's activities and political groups opposed to the Islamic system in Europe and the United States started the countdown to the collapse of Iran.[8]

Strategies available to Iran at the time of crisis

Iran was facing a complicated situation in choosing the best strategy to tackle the September 2003 crisis and part of that complexity was rooted in special domestic conditions at that juncture. In reality, there were wide divides in the country in relation to this issue. The divides became wider and wider despite efforts that were made by high-ranking officials to bridge the gaps and create national unity in the country.

Iranian leaders tried to depict a unified picture of the country to pave the way for increasing national capacities in order to counter threats and provide consensual support for the final decision.[9] In a general division, strategies facing Iran at the time of the crisis can be summarized as six major approaches.

The first approach: The first approach called for the discontinuation of cooperation with the IAEA and rejection of the Board of Governors' resolution. This approach recommended angry and revolutionary reactions on the part of Tehran. Proponents of that approach believed that the September resolution was merely the result of US pressures on the international community and considered it a prelude to military action on Iran.

The second approach: The second approach emphasized on the technical and legal aspects of Iran's nuclear dossier. From this viewpoint, any negotiation with global powers or international political organizations about the nuclear standoff was considered incorrect. Proponents of that approach believed that Tehran should continue to cooperate with IAEA while refraining from accepting the Board of Governors' resolution because it was politically motivated.

The third approach: This approach put much emphasis on the political nature of the September crisis. It believed that the standoff was merely the product of widespread pressures exerted by the Western block and considered it a component of US strategy for the Middle East region and maintained that the crisis would continue until a final solution was reached for problems between Tehran and Washington.

The fourth approach: This approach stressed on the political nature of the crisis and the necessity to cooperate with IAEA. However, its proponents believed that the only way to control the crisis was to create a powerful block to support Iran in the face of the West. The proponents recommended that instead of relying on Europe or the United States, Iran should try to create maximum convergence among developing countries, the Islamic world, and such powers as China, Russia, and India.

The fifth approach: This approach advocated the "Libya model" for dealing with the nuclear crises. Proponents of this approach called upon Tehran to dismantle its nuclear energy program since pursuing such a program would inevitably lead to the destruction of the country's infrastructure either through economic sanctions or limited military attach. While comments supporting this approach were limited, they would occasionally get media coverage in domestic papers.

The sixth approach: This approach was based on the arrangement of the world powers at the time of crisis and a realistic assessment of international equations. Proponents believed that the nuclear crisis was purely political. They said expelling IAEA's inspectors and withdrawing from the NPT in objection to the resolution would be a generic repetition of Iraq's experience. The advocates of the sixth approach maintained that Iran has only three options to choose from with regard to political interactions: direct talks with the United States, bargaining with the EU, and relying on an alternative block comprising the Non-Aligned Movement countries, China, and Russia. Since direct negotiations with the United States was considered a redline at that time, the best possible approach was to engage in negotiations with the EU as the main negotiating party, continuing talks with Non-Aligned Movement countries and the East Asian powers, and full cooperation with IAEA to solve the remaining problems and eliminating technical and legal ambiguities.

Approaches taken by major powers to Iran's nuclear dossier

The United States of America

What happened on September 11, 2001, provided the United States with an opportunity to generalize its military supremacy to other layers of its ruling system on the pretext of fighting terror and through introducing a security-based international atmosphere. Now, the American neoconservatives were taking advantage of all their might to remove all obstacles in the way of the progress of the superpower. Emergence of regional hegemonic powers is one of the most important obstacles to the realization of the expansion goals of the United States, which is quite important, especially in the Middle East. Therefore, the militarization of the international environment after September 11, 2001, was the main outcome of the terror attacks. That achievement has turned the Middle East into the focus of the "strategic deterrence" policy of the United States.

Analyzing US measures in the face of Iran's nuclear contention indicated the formulation of a trilateral strategy in the White House for containing Iran. That strategy was followed at domestic, regional, and international levels with full force. The United States was trying to introduce Iran, in line with its idea of "axis of evil," as the most important threat against international security. A direct result of the success of such a strategy would be total isolation of Iran in political and economic terms. Eliminating Iran from the security equations of the region and the world would greatly reduce the cost of encountering Tehran. It appears that US success at the current juncture depends on proving that Iran is trying to build nuclear weapons, as an instance of breaching NPT. Efforts made to prove this have assumed technical (IAEA), political (Board of Governors), propaganda, and security (United Nations Security Council) aspects. The main goal of the United States was to bring Iran's nuclear program to complete cessation and even bar the country from building its nuclear power plant.

The European Union

In reality, Europe's success in solving Iran's nuclear crisis will, once more, bring up the old continent as the main defender of the diplomatic and nonmilitary approach to solving international crises. This will weaken US standing in the face of future crises in the Middle East. Therefore, the United States will have to pay renewed attention to the framework of the transatlantic interactions of 2000, which had been aborted after the military invasion of Iraq. Europe's failure to contain Iran's crisis will mean an end to traditional transatlantic cooperation and the beginning of a new era.[10] Marginalization of the EU in major international crises will be the first consequence of that development. Such an attitude to negotiations between Iran and three European countries will mean that Europe has to do its best to reach a final agreement on the said crisis.

In conclusion, it seems that there is undeniable convergence between the EU and the United States about Iran's nuclear activities. This convergence reaches common ground in the form of opposition to the establishment of complete fuel cycle in Iran. Despite the existence of these common grounds, there are still fundamental differences regarding how to interact with Tehran, application of peaceful nuclear energy, as well as perspectives for nuclear and even strategic cooperation with Iran.

Russia

Russia's approach to Iran's atomic programs is a contradictory and mixed approach, which has made accurate prediction of Moscow's behavior at critical junctures, quite impossible. In reality, nuclear cooperation between Iran and Russia has always been a direct function of Russia's relations with the Western world (especially the United States). Russia is the only big power that considers itself a friend and supporter of Iran's interests.

1. From an economic viewpoint, nuclear cooperation with Iran is very lucrative for the Kremlin. This has prompted Russia to pursue the policy of preventing Iran's access to complete fuel cycle as its main policy. Moscow's decision in this field is quite attuned to that of the United States and the EU.
2. From geopolitical viewpoints, Tehran is considered a very valuable portal for the expansion of Russia's influence in the Middle East.
3. Good relations between Tehran and Moscow are considered an important factor in bolstering Russia's position in Central Asia, especially after Iran proved during conflicts in Chechnya and Tajikistan that it is a committed and responsible partner for Russia.
4. Despite these facts, Russia's unwavering policy for opposing Iran's access to nuclear capability is undeniable.

5.   Continued nuclear cooperation with Tehran is one of the main mechanisms to prevent the full collapse of the nuclear industry that has been handed down by the former Soviet Union.
6.   By transferring nuclear technology to Tehran under international pressures, Russia will turn into the sole player in Iran's nuclear industry.
7.   Command over some aspects of Iran's nuclear program will be a good bargaining chip during negotiations with the United States to ask for more concessions.

Experts have taken three approaches to nuclear cooperation between Tehran Iran and Moscow.

1.   The first approach believes that the American part of the Kremlin will do its best to control transfer of nuclear technology and material to Iran, but will finally fail.
2.   The second approach has it that Russia considers continued nuclear cooperation with Iran to be in line with its large-scale interests and, therefore, will put up with US pressures.
3.   The third approach maintains that Russia is killing time in dealing with Iran. That is, while meeting some of Iran's needs, it also has an eye on bargaining with the United States on important points.

It seems that Russia is practically following a combination of these three approaches. The combined policy explained above was more evident in recent standoffs between Iran and the West. As the existing evidence shows, sudden convergence between Moscow and the American and European blocks has always been a possibility when pressures heighten.

China

1.   Relations between Tehran and Beijing lack lasting strategic bonds and strengthening components. Although cooperation between the two countries has been on the rise over the past few years, especially in the field of energy, bilateral relations have remained at an embryonic stage.
2.   China is a security-based and security-oriented country that seeks to boost its economic growth. When having to choose between security and growth, China will undoubtedly choose security.
3.   Unlike Russia, China enjoys fewer bargaining chips when dealing with the United States. Evidence shown by Beijing proves that in case of escalating tension between Iran and the United States and when faced with the final choice, the country will choose for "impartiality" in the most optimistic case, and will support Washington's approach in the worst possible case.
4.   Strategic cooperation between Iran and China, more than ensuring security approaches, aims to guarantee the economic interests of Beijing, with an eye on the temporary requirements of Iran.
5.   To keep its bargaining power when dealing with Washington about Taiwan, China has expanded arms cooperation with some adversaries of the United

States, including Iran. However, that cooperation has always been limited, conditional, and under full control.

6.   It seems that the interest of Chinese officials in expanding their relations with the United States will finally overcome existing ties between Tehran and Beijing.

Framework of Iran's new nuclear diplomacy (2003–5)

When Dr Hassan Rowhani took charge as Iran's chief nuclear negotiator, Tehran outlined the framework of a new strategy as its main approach to the nuclear case. The new strategy was drawn up by the nuclear negotiating team headed by Dr Rowhani, who had been appointed Iran's chief negotiator through consensus among all high-ranking officials.

Tehran's new approach was based on several "basic premises," which stemmed from realistic and comprehensive assessments and included the following:

1.   Reporting Iran's case to New York would have dire consequences in view of the domestic conditions and lack of necessary planning.
2.   If Iran's dossier was taken out of Vienna and into New York, it would be a triumph for the United States.
3.   Pressures put by the United States, destructive anti-Iran propaganda and some failures on the part of Iran provided good grounds for widespread global consensus against Iran.
4.   The nuclear case should be assessed as an issue far beyond ordinary disputes and should be considered within large-scale US strategy for the future of the Middle East.
5.   Sentimental and angry reactions to the September resolution would merely make the case more complicated and intensify existing disputes.

For formulating a crisis settlement strategy, Iran had to resort to certain measures to achieve the following results at tminimum cost and in the shortest possible time:

1.   Do away with the threat of reporting Iran's nuclear case to the United Nations Security Council.
2.   Diminish the risk of opposition by the international community to generalities of Iran's nuclear programs.
3.   Dispel real concerns of various countries about the nature of Iran's nuclear activities.
4.   Greatly increase the cost of a possible US military attack on Iran's nuclear installations and destruction of Iran's nuclear facilities.[11]
5.   Change the tense relations between Iran and IAEA and replace them with logical interactions.
6.   Depict a perspective for the resolution of all technical and legal ambiguities that were enumerated by IAEA.

7. Provide good grounds for transfer of nuclear technology to the country and continuation of nuclear cooperation with diverse partners other than Russia.
8. Manage existing political and psychological pressures against the Islamic system.
9. Reduce concerns in world public opinion and correct their misunderstanding about the nuclear activities of Iran.
10. Eliminate domestic consequences of the crisis, especially in social and economic fields.
11. Bring coherence to domestic public opinion.
12. Reduce domestic political rifts and differences about Iran's interaction with IAEA and the international community to a minimum.
13. Pursue the long-term strategy of "turning threats into opportunities" and, in this way, resolve some long-lasting problems facing Iran, especially with regard to economic and technological cooperation with the West.

After approving the major strategy in the face of crisis during a meeting of Iranian leaders and determining a framework for bargaining by Tehran, plans were made to initiate talks with Brussels and invite foreign ministers of the European troika. The maneuvering room for Iran's diplomatic delegation and even subsequent measures in the face of the September resolution had been pinpointed in the meeting of the Iranian leaders.[12] Therefore, obtaining maximum concessions from international sides in return for cooperation was the most important responsibility of the Iranian negotiators.

Iran's invitation to foreign ministers of three European countries (EU3) was immediately welcomed by the said countries. The European troika, however, insisted that simultaneous visit to Iran by French, British, and German diplomats was a working prerequisite for high-ranking negotiations. The request was granted by Iran and preparations were made for the upcoming visit by three Directors General to Iran.

Meanwhile, Mohamed ElBaradei, Director General of the IAEA, arrived in Tehran on October 16, 2003. His visit came at a time when Tehran had not yet revealed its final reaction vis-à-vis the September resolution. Along with the additional protocol, the most important issues that were discussed with ElBaradei included entry of centrifuges to Iran and secret aspects of Tehran's peaceful nuclear program. The IAEA had announced a long time ago that Iran's remarkable progress regarding fuel cycle would not be possible without testing centrifuges and introducing hexafluoride uranium (UF6). That comment had led to an important technical dispute between Iran's Atomic Energy Organization and the IAEA.

During his subsequent talks with Dr Hassan Rowhani and Gholamreza Aqazadeh, ElBaradei called for the suspension of Iran's fuel cycle activities. The main topic discussed by Dr Rowhani and Dr ElBaradei was the range of suspensions. Dr ElBaradei assured Dr Rowhani that if Iran avoided introducing gas into centrifuges, suspension requirements would have been met. The definition was much more limited than what the September resolution had asked for and it could be construed as a triumph for Iran in its bargaining with IAEA. That definition could have convinced the leaders of Iran to accept suspension of fuel cycle.

Tehran Statement: October 21, 2003

As the IAEA Director General was leaving Iran, Directors General of foreign ministries of the European troika arrived in Tehran. The concurrence led to short talks between the European diplomats and Dr ElBaradei at the VIP pavilion of Tehran's Mehrabad Airport. The next day, intense quadripartite talks were conducted between Iranian diplomats and representatives of EU3 foreign ministers.

It should be noted that during those talks, the European troika urged Iran to stop nuclear activities, not to "suspend" them. The expert delegation representing Iran categorically rejected their request and clearly noted that no talks would be held on that matter. Finally, the European side agreed to follow negotiations with Iran on the basis of short-term "suspension" and not "complete cessation" of Iran's peaceful nuclear activities. During those talks, the negotiating parties agreed to replace "mutual commitments of both sides," that is, Iran and the EU, for unilateral requests contained in the IAEA resolution. Acceptance of that principle, which was achieved through heavy pressuring and bargaining on the part of the Iranian diplomats, considerably changed the political equations resulting from the September resolution in Iran's favor.

Inside the country, the possibility of the arrival of foreign ministers of the European troika was powerful enough to provoke sensitivities and cause resistance in some quarters. There were various reasons and approaches in this regard:

1. The first group comprised those who believed, on the basis of revolutionary concerns but through inexpert analyses, that negotiations with Europeans was against the national interests.
2. The second group included those who considered achievement in nuclear crisis is a major factor that would affect parliamentary and presidential elections. Factional tendencies in this front had, unfortunately, turned a national interest to be viewed within the framework of short-term political disputes.
3. The third group included those who saw more tension and serious confrontation between Iran and the West to serve their interests best. That tendency was observed both in the opposition, which sought to topple the Islamic system, and among a few political activists inside the country.
4. The last group consisted of those who, due to personal problems with negotiating diplomats, were willing for them to fail in containing the crisis.

Immediately after diplomatic delegations from European countries arrived in Tehran, quadrilateral talks among Iran, France, Britain, and Germany started at the level of Directors General. The meeting aimed at solving the remaining problems, achieving a final agreement, and clearing the way for high-ranking quadrilateral negotiations. Anyway, insistence of Iran's representatives on their positions and persistence of the European sides on their own positions, led to relative failure of preliminary negotiations. About 09:30, Iran's delegation, which was led by the author and included Mohammad Javad Zarif, Reza Alborzi, Sirous Nasseri, Amir Zamani-Nia, and Mohammad Saeedi, left the negotiating table. Despite rudimentary agreements among the diplomats of the four countries on the Tehran draft statement, one of the most important issues, that is, "suspension," was left to high-ranking negotiations between the foreign ministers of the European troika and the Iranian authorities.

Of course, some political behaviors of Tehran in October 2003 reduced Iran's bargaining power during negotiations with the Europeans. The decision by some members of the sixth parliament (Majlis) to pass a triple urgency plan to force the government into accepting the additional protocol was one of them. The bill was never discussed on the Majlis floor, but it greatly reduced Iran's diplomatic maneuvering in negotiations with the West. Premature announcement of Iran's willingness to implement the 93 + 2 additional protocol and to "suspend part of its enrichment activities" were other steps that limited the ability of the Iranian diplomats in political dealings.

Before the Saadabad meeting between EU3 ministers and Dr Rowhani and before the Tehran Statement was released, high-ranking officials of Iran, including the President, had indicated Tehran's readiness to accept short-term and limited suspension of enrichment activities to build confidence with the world and reduce political as well as propaganda pressures. The request by Iran's strategic partners and the IAEA, in addition to the critical conditions of that time, were the most important reasons that convinced Tehran to take that decision. The Iranian side was trying to introduce partial suspension of enrichment as part of the political negotiation process with the international community.

However, during negotiations, two major differences emerged between Iran and the European troika:

1. First, the three European countries considered suspension of Iran's enrichment program as a legal obligation on the strength of the September resolution of the Board of Governors.
2. The second difference pertained to the dimensions of suspension. The European troika, relying on the September resolution, insisted that all activities related to enrichment in Iran should be suspended immediately.

Ministers and Directors General of foreign ministries of the three European countries arrived in Tehran on October 20, 2003. The last round of expert talks between the Iranian delegates and representatives of EU3 was held at 08:00 on October 21, at Saadabad Palace and an early draft agreement was finalized. During four-hour talks between EU3 ministers and Dr Hassan Rowhani, the two sides agreed on the "suspension of enrichment activities as defined by IAEA." Dr Rowhani accepted the suspension because Mohamed ElBaradei had assured him a week earlier that Iran's avoidance of "introducing gas into centrifuges" was the only thing that suspension was supposed to amount to. The Saadabad Statement was agreed upon and made public at 14:00 on October 21, 2003.

The Tehran negotiations entailed many achievements for Iran, including:

1. Agreement between Tehran and the European troika in opposition to reporting Iran's dossier to the United Nations Security Council was one of the most important achievements of the Saadabad conference, where Iran succeeded in obtaining a high-level assurance from the European negotiators. Emphasis put by the European foreign ministers on using their right of veto if the United States managed to take Iran's case to New York was construed as a major international breakthrough for Iran. The emphasis put by the final statement of the meeting on the necessity of solving all problems within the framework of IAEA was legal translation of the said agreement.

2. That political agreement at that juncture precluded possible military measures against Iran's nuclear installations by the United States and paved the way for the protection and development of Iran's technical structure.

3. The Board of Governors' request to Iran to offer a complete picture of its past nuclear activities was one of the most important technical and legal issues of the case. That is, both offering that report (due to some failures on the part of Iran) and refraining from producing that report (which would have been construed as noncompliance with the requests of the international community), would have taken Iran's case out of Vienna. Negotiations in Tehran provided good circumstances to get out of the deadlock and get the EU's support for Iran's corrective measures at IAEA. The emphasis put in the text of the agreement on the fact that "Iran...should clarify and compensate any possible failure within the framework of IAEA," was along the same lines. That emphasis showed that even if Iran's failures were proven, bilateral agreements would have been obligatory for both sides.

4. On the threshold of the Board of Governors' September meeting, the EU got closer to the US position and refrained from upholding Iran's right to pursue its nuclear programs. Faced with intense pressure from the Non-Aligned Movement countries and South Africa, the European countries finally agreed to include a general phrase in the resolution, without any direct reference to Iran. In reality, despite some superficial phrases, before the Saadabad meeting, the EU was not willing to accept Iran's right to achieve peaceful nuclear technology. This approach was quite evident in diplomatic negotiations as well as political signals that were sent by Brussels. From this viewpoint, the Tehran Statement was a very important turning point. The European troika had not only accepted Iran's basic right in the final statement of the meeting, but had stressed on peaceful nuclear cooperation with Iran to achieve nuclear technology.

5. In the resolution that was issued in September 2003, IAEA's Board of Governors called on Iran "to suspend all further uranium enrichment-related activities, including the further introduction of nuclear material into Natanz,

and, as a confidence-building measure, any reprocessing activities, pending provision by the director-general of the assurances required by member states." The EU and the United States had reached an agreement on suspension and even complete cessation of all activities related to uranium enrichment and processing in Iran on the basis of the September resolution. Iran's resistance during the Saadabad negotiations finally led to reduction of the request to stop nuclear activities (in line with the September resolution) to "suspension" of those activities on the basis of IAEA's definition. In view of Dr ElBaradei's statements in Tehran, that definition was a great victory for Iran in the technical and legal aspects of the case.

6. The suspension that had been specified in the September resolution was a consensual demand of the international community and, from one viewpoint, was obligatory. The Saadabad Statement caused Iran's measure to suspend part of its nuclear activities to be officially termed a voluntary act.

7. Foreign ministers of the EU stressed in the Saadabad Statement that the additional protocol will by no means hurt "sovereignty, credit, dignity, or national security" of Iran. That emphasis was, from various aspects, in line with Tehran's goals and interests.

8. The Tehran Agreement delineated a positive and new perspective for future security cooperation between Iran and the EU in the region. New security equations in the Middle East, based on Tehran–Brussels cooperation, could meet various interests of Iran.

9. The emphasis put on creating a region free from weapons of mass destruction in the Middle East was also a direct reference to the Zionist regime, which is considered the staunchest enemy of Iran.

10. According to the Tehran Statement, which was issued on October 21, 2003, the two sides had emphasized that "full implementation of Iran's decisions after being upheld by the director-general of the International Atomic Energy Agency should help the Board of Governors to improve the current situation." That clause increased Iran's power to pressure the international community to close the case as soon as possible and reduced the United States' ability to avail of nuclear standoff, which was a potential threat to Iran. Under normal conditions, that clause could have paved the way for a "political and security dispute" to turn into a "technical and legal dispute."

11. Negotiations in October were considered a first step in a long process of solving existing problems between Iran and the EU. The phrase, "easier access to modern technology and other items in various fields" depicted a positive outlook for bilateral strategic cooperation and was a sign of ineffectiveness of US sanctions. That outlook became more important in view of joint interests and motivations between Tehran and Brussels.

12. The simultaneous visits to Tehran by three European foreign ministers was a unique event. The visits showed that Iran, as a major power in the region and an important country in the future Middle East, enjoys a unique position. The Saadabad negotiations clearly showed that the allegations of Iran's enemies to the effect that the Iranian government had been weakened by the West were

nothing but empty and baseless claims. The trip was in itself good evidence to importance and credit of Iran within the international community.

13. In the Tehran Statement, both sides have stressed the need for legal ratification of the 93 + 2 additional protocol and Tehran has been asked to implement the protocol before it is ratified as a confidence-building measure. That approach was opposite to the imperative tone of the September resolution, and distanced from the resolution. Just as it was on the issue of uranium suspension.

14. The distance between the resolution and decisions made in Tehran is considered a major achievement for the October 21 negotiations. The Saadabad Statement opened a middle road between submission and confrontation.

15. The Tehran negotiations did away with a wide range of domestic problems at the time of crisis. Tehran has been offered suitable opportunities to make plans, bargain with other powers, and satisfy domestic and foreign public opinion, as well as to cope with economic outcomes of the crisis and reduce its social harm. Iran also managed to forge considerable convergence among political activists inside the country through the agreement it reached with the European countries on October 21. That convergence reached its climax after declaration of resolute support of the Supreme Leader for those measures (on November 3, 2003).

16. When analyzing the consequences of the Saadabad negotiations, it is necessary to pay attention to an important point. In reality, all issues that were included in the statement that was issued on October 21, 2003, had been approved by high-ranking officials of Iran a few days earlier. Iran was determined to accept the additional protocol (and had declared its readiness to implement it since August) and also to boost cooperation with the UN nuclear watchdog. Negotiations by Dr ElBaradei in Tehran and the explanation offered by him about the dimensions of enrichment suspension as defined by him also provided the necessary grounds for agreement of the Islamic system to "short-term" suspension of part of its fuel cycle. On this basis, various debates were carried out at different levels of the Iranian government about how to proclaim those decisions—either unilaterally or through negotiations with other powers. Iran finally managed to gain more concessions through the Tehran negotiations that were in line with the achievement of its long-term interests.

The agreement signed between Iran and the European troika in October 2003 (Tehran Statement) presented guarantees required by Tehran to prevent reporting of its nuclear dossier to the United Nations Security Council. The first outcome of that event was facilitation of cooperation between Iran and IAEA and the beginning of a trust-building process. As a consequence of the September 2003 resolution, Iran had been faced with a dilemma to choose from two options, both of which led to the United Nations Security Council. After getting out of this deadlock, Iran decided to respond immediately to one of the main requests of the Board of Governors, which was presenting a complete report on its nuclear programs.

The report was drawn up by Iran's Atomic Energy Organization and was completed by senior diplomats of the crisis management team. Delivering the report to the UN nuclear watchdog on October 21, 2003, was greatly welcomed by diplomatic circles as the first practical step taken by Iran in the face of the September resolution. Presenting a complete picture of Iran's nuclear activities was also a formal confession of the past failures to notify part of the nuclear activities to IAEA on time.

The November meeting of the IAEA's Board of Governors started on November 20, 2003. Iran, which had already taken the necessary guarantees about the opposition of the three European countries on "noncompliance" in the resolution as well as reporting the case to the Security Council, started negotiations with member countries of the Board of Governors on the phrasing of the resolution. The United States, accompanied by Canada, Australia, Japan, New Zealand, the Netherlands, South Korea, Italy, and even Spain, put enormous pressure on the meeting to report the case to New York. The US block also insisted that the word "noncompliance" should be mentioned in the resolution. On the other hand, three European countries, helped by Russia, China, and the Non-Aligned Movement countries, launched intensive efforts to appease Washington and reduce US demands.

What was finally passed in the form of the Board of Governors' resolution on November 26, 2003, as a result of strenuous efforts by Tehran and measures taken by the European troika, was to a large extent conformant with the demands of Iran. Tehran, which had taken part in an international meeting using its full range of diplomatic armada, succeeded in changing meeting's atmosphere to a large extent in its own favor. Intense negotiations between the Iranian diplomats and ambassadors of the European troika, Non-Aligned Movement, and other countries, as well as bargaining on every word and phrase used in the draft resolution by Brussels, led to many changes in the initial draft. The critical atmosphere of the meeting, which was guided by the US block, at times, even led to verbal scuffles between the Iranian delegation and representatives of some countries. However, the final output of the November meeting of the Board of Governors was much different from the September resolution and quite distant from demands by the US block, which called for announcement of Iran's "noncompliance" and reporting its nuclear dossier to the United Nations Security Council.

The November resolution adopted by the Board of Governors welcomed Iran's "offer of active cooperation and openness" with the international community. The resolution also noted with satisfaction "the decision of Iran to conclude an Additional Protocol to its Safeguards Agreement," and welcomed Iran's decision to suspend enrichment and reprocessing activities. The Board of Governors also called on Iran "to undertake and complete the taking of all necessary corrective measures on an urgent basis." The resolution also strongly deplored "Iran's past failures and breaches of its obligation to comply with the provisions of its Safeguards Agreement," and urged Iran "to adhere strictly to its obligations under its Safeguards Agreement in both letter and spirit." The Board of Governors also reiterated that "the urgent, full and close co-operation with the Agency of all third countries" was essential in the clarification of outstanding questions concerning Iran's nuclear program.

The resolution adopted by the Board of Governors in November 2003 also included two major salient points.

1. It officially announced that suspension of uranium enrichment by Tehran was a "voluntary" measure. The announcement, which was a result of extensive negotiations between Iran and all member countries of the Board of Governors and was an outcome of the Saadabad meeting, was considered a major break-through, because the Board of Governors had officially and legally, and in opposition to all conventional interpretations of the September resolution, reiterated that the suspension was voluntary.[13]
2. There was another important point in that resolution, which was refered to by the international media as the "trigger mechanism,"[14] although efforts made by the Iranian diplomats led to major changes in the early draft resolution, including Paragraph 8. However, pressures exerted by the United States and decisions made by the European countries led to the final inclusion of that paragraph. The said paragraph had noted that "should any further serious Iranian failures come to light, the Board of Governors would meet immediately to consider, in the light of the circumstances and of advice from the Director General, all options at its disposal, in accordance with the IAEA Statute and Iran's safeguards Agreement."

On the whole, the resolution adopted by the Board of Governors in November 2003 was much more satisfactory to Iran than was the situation in September 2003. Positive conditions that led to relative satisfaction of Tehran included the following:

1. Inability of the United States to report Iran's case to the Security Council.
2. Avoiding the use of "noncompliance" in the resolution with reference to Iran.
3. Preventing notification of the Security Council.
4. Emphasizing the voluntary nature of enrichment suspension by Iran; and
5. Watering down Paragraph 8 of the resolution.

Enhancement of Europe's suspicions of Iran

In the aftermath of the November resolution, Iran took the necessary steps to solve technical problems and bolster the outlook of strategic cooperation with the EU. Iranian representatives at the IAEA signed the 93 + 2 additional protocol on December 18, 2003. The measure, which was taken after go-ahead from high-ranking Iranian officials, was another step toward confidence building and finding a final solution to the crisis. That situation prompted the United States to propose direct talks with Iran as a step to prevent its further isolation. Colin Powell announced on December 30, 2003, that the United States was ready to engage in direct talks with Iran about its nuclear programs.[15]

Under those conditions, when the wall of distrust between Tehran and Brussels was falling apart, new technical crises as well as consequences of past technical problems popped up in the course of Iran's international interactions one after the other. Some of those crises were so extensive and important that they even temporarily caused tension in Tehran's relations with IAEA. The most important problems and technical crises faced by Tehran from the November 2003 meeting up to March 2004 were as follows:

Centrifuges crisis

Iran had announced in its declaration in October that it had informed the IAEA about all aspects of its past activities. However, when the IAEA was scrutinizing Iran's October claims about P-1 centrifuges, it was informed through Libya that Tehran had got its hands on drawings of more advanced centrifuges called P-2.

The IAEA and the European troika construed Iran's abstinence of mentioning the drawing in its October declaration as an effort for secrecy and the issue was aggrandized by the American media as evidence to the nonpeaceful nature of Iran's nuclear activities and continuation of the past secrecies.

Polonium crisis

In January 2004, Dr Hassan Rowhani and a group of senior Iranian diplomats set off to Vienna. During the trip, Dr ElBaradei told Iran's chief negotiator that IAEA had information about Iran's activities with regard to polonium.[16] The Director General then asked for Iran's explanation in view of the fact that plutonium had not been mentioned in Iran's October statement.

Polonium is a neutron source, which has many applications in military and nonmilitary industries. Use of plutonium in explosive charge of nuclear weapons had made IAEA quite sensitive about the matter. Iran's Atomic Energy Organization announced that experiments with polonium were aimed at using the substance in batteries and related research.

Contamination crisis

The results of a sampling by IAEA in the spring of 2003 showed that some atomic installations in Iran have shown signs of contamination with enriched uranium. After Tehran's declaration was issued in October, the results of an analysis of IAEA's samples proved the existence of 36 percent enriched uranium. The said uranium isotopes convinced IAEA that the contamination was different from other instances[17] and was the result of reprocessing Russian power plant fuel.[18] The IAEA considered the possibility that the uranium may have originated from nuclear installations and activities of the former Union of Soviet Socialist Republics.

Gas test crisis

As mentioned earlier, IAEA firmly believed in the summer of 2003 that Iran's progress with nuclear fuel cycle would not be possible without introducing UF6 gas into centrifuges. Iran had persistently rejected the nuclear watchdog's claims before issuance of the Tehran Statement. In the meantime, IAEA's inspectors noted during an audit of UF6 gas that its quantity had slightly reduced. In response to the IAEA question about the loss, Iran's Atomic Energy Organization announced that the loss was due to a leak from a UF6 cylinder.[19] The amount of lost gas was, in fact, used to test centrifuges. Anyway, rejection of Iran's claims by IAEA and some of the Agency's measures and comments in this regard further complicated the issue.

Plutonium crisis

Tehran owned up to plutonium tests in its statement in October 2003.[20] Samples taken by IAEA from plutonium solution, vessels containing irradiated UO_2, as well as containers showed that contradiction existed between the Tehran Statement and the results of the sampling. Although the contradiction was removed in later comments by Tehran, its revelation to IAEA at that juncture exacerbated the technical crisis that already existed. Early results obtained by IAEA showed that Iran had estimatedly produced less plutonium than the actual amount. IAEA also declared that the lifetime of solved plutonium samples was less than the 12–16 years that Iran claimed.

Brussels Agreement and expansion of suspension

Technical problems following the November meeting of the Board of Governors provided good grounds for increasing Europe's and IAEA's pessimism toward Iran and also cleared the way for the intensification of the United States' publicity and political activities against Iran. The Board of Governors' meeting was to be held in March 2003. The American and European media resorted to Paragraph 8 of the November resolution as well as the technical crisis to emphasize that Iran's dossier should be referred to the United Nations Security Council. At that time, IAEA asked Tehran to expand the range of nuclear suspension.

In early February 2004, Tehran enhanced its efforts to get the case back to the normal course. However, getting Iran's dossier on the right track was dependent on two different processes:

1. Finding a solution to the technical problems of the case and assuring the UN nuclear watchdog that Iran had not diverted from the Safeguards Agreement, but had fully implemented it.
2. Negotiations with members of the Board of Governors to undermine US claims and convince them to close Iran's nuclear case.

The Director General believed that in case of expanded suspension and Iran's full and transparent cooperation with IAEA inspectors, the necessary technical and legal grounds will be provided to get Iran's nuclear case on the normal path in June 2004. From a political viewpoint, Tehran decided that if Europe provided the necessary assurances to close the nuclear case at the June 2004 meeting, it would expand the range of nuclear suspension as asked by IAEA within the framework of the Board of Governors' resolutions.

The September 2003 resolution had asked Iran to suspend all uranium enrichment-related activities. Tehran managed through the Saadabad negotiations and by changing the legal contents of the resolution into voluntary and political measures, to limit the resolutions' demands to mere "introduction of gas into centrifuges." From this viewpoint, temporary expansion of suspension changed Tehran's situation and its measures were approved by the Board of Governors in August 2003. Iranian experts and officials believed that short-term expansion of suspension in return for closing Iran's case by the European troika in the June meeting was a beneficial deal for Tehran.

Iran's decision led to planning complicated and difficult negotiations with EU3. During the ensuing negotiations, Iran's diplomatic delegation was headed by Mohammad Javad Zarif, who joined diplomats in New York. The negotiations finally led to the conclusion of the second agreement between Tehran and the European troika on February 23, 2004, which was called the "Brussels Agreement." According to that agreement:

1. Iran agreed to suspend manufacture of parts and assembly of centrifuges.
2. The European troika promised to do its best to normalize Iran–IAEA relations and close the nuclear dossier in the June meeting.
3. Iran's reasons for deficiencies in its October statement were explained.
4. No direct relationship was established between the Director General's conclusions and reports and the three countries' commitment to closing the nuclear case in June.
5. A time schedule was partially agreed upon for quadrilateral negotiations on solutions that would guarantee continuation of Iran's nuclear program.

The content of the Brussels Agreement and the EU's obligations were so significant that they were immediately turned down by the United States. The main assessment of the agreement by US officials was that after the situation becomes normal, Iran would be able to give up "voluntary" suspension and restore the situation that existed before September. Meanwhile, the six-month calm would have paved the way for the completion of Iran's nuclear technology and increase the country's nuclear capacity to higher levels compared with September. From this viewpoint, the Brussels Agreement could have deprived the United States of its main tool to pressure Iran, that is, special investigation of Iran's case at the IAEA. Therefore, the agreement came under heavy fire from the White House as well as conservative American and European media.[21]

Situation in and resolution of March 2004

The release of the new Director General's report on the implementation of NPT Safeguards Agreement in Iran (February 24, 2004) caused major power blocks to prepare for the March meeting of the IAEA Board of Governors. Tehran was bracing for the March meeting at a time when technical crises, heavy propaganda campaign by international media about Iran's deceitful behavior, and the November resolution of Board of Governors had relatively paved the way for referring Iran's nuclear dossier to the Security Council. Under those conditions, the Brussels Agreement and explicit obligation of the three European countries to normalize the case by June 2004 gave Iran more bargaining power to start activities regarding the meeting and its possible resolution.

The European troika, which respected its obligations according to the Brussels Agreement, believed that the results of the March meeting would not affect future efforts to normalize Iran's case in June 2004. The assessment led the three European countries to conclude that they could take advantage of the March meeting and boost the sense of participation among the Board of Governors' member states to soften any possible resistance in the face of positions that were to be taken by the troika in June. Therefore, European countries decided to let the United States get more active in the meeting.

However, the beginning of the meeting on March 8, 2004, and presentation of the surprising draft resolution by the United States turned the Brussels meeting into a playground for the United States. Washington relied on some conflicts in Iran's October statement as well as IAEA's findings after the November meeting while aggrandizing such issues as P-2 centrifuge, polonium, and laser enrichment, to prepare a draft resolution that, if approved, would have been the harshest resolution on Iran's case. The resolution was rejected by Europe as lacking legal and technical aspects. The EU announced that it rejected the US-proposed resolution because it was "rash, non-technical, and non-legal," and believed that it needed some revision.[22]

Iran's multifaceted activities, impact of the three European countries, the statement issued by the pro-Iran block, including Non-Aligned Movement countries[23] and insistence of NAM on the continuation of Iran's cooperation with IAEA finally made many changes to the early draft. Of course, the final resolution was by no means satisfactory for Iran and led to Tehran's harsh criticism of the board of governors, especially the three European countries.

The European troika announced its determination during the closing address of the meeting to take the case to a normal course in the next meeting (June). Britain and France had considered three conditions for normalization:

1.   Iran should ratify the additional protocol immediacy.
2.   The Director General should declare in the next meeting that Iran's cooperation has been complete and good progress had been achieved on various issues.
3.   No more failure should be found on Iran's side.

The resolution, however, contained a diverse range of "concerns," "emphases," and "requests" facing Iran, the most important of which were as follows. The IAEA Board of Governors:

•   Notes with serious concern that the declarations made by Iran in October 2003 did not amount to the complete and final picture of Iran's past and present nuclear program, considered essential by the Board's November 2003 resolution.

- Noting with equal concern that Iran has not resolved all questions regarding the development of its enrichment technology to its current extent and that a number of other questions remain unresolved.
- Noting with concern that, although the timelines are different, Iran's and Libya's conversion and centrifuge programs share several common elements, including technology largely obtained from the same foreign sources.
- Calls on Iran to continue and intensify its cooperation, as Iran's cooperation so far has fallen short of what is required.
- Calls on Iran to extend the application of this commitment (voluntary suspension) to all such activities throughout Iran.
- Deplores that Iran omitted any reference to its possession of P-2 centrifuge design drawings and to associated research, manufacturing, and mechanical testing activities.
- Echoes the concern expressed by the Director General over the issue of the purpose of Iran's activities related to experiments on the production and intended use of polonium-210.
- Calls on Iran to be proactive in taking all necessary steps on an urgent basis to resolve all outstanding issues.

There was another paragraph in the March resolution, which was considered by some diplomats as the most important paragraph. The ninth paragraph of the resolution[24] was a purely political decision that was directly dictated by the United States. The paragraph was ensued with Iran's intense negotiations with various power blocks, which led to ratification of the NAM amendments to a consensual resolution. According to Paragraph 9, "consideration of progress in verifying Iranw's declarations and of how to respond to the above-mentioned omissions" had been postponed until the next meeting of the Board of Governors. Therefore, all issues mentioned in the resolution as well as conflicts between the October statement and the findings of the nuclear watchdog (as claimed by the Agency) could have been raised again in the next meeting to provide needed legal grounds for reporting Iran's case to the United Nations Security Council. The fact that protagonists of the resolution avoided emphasizing the necessity of adapting future decisions of the Board of Governors to the next report of the Director General was another ground that had paved the way for making purely political decisions by power blocks. Ratification of the said paragraph in the final resolution (despite changes made because of Tehran's efforts) directed Iran's harsh criticism toward the European troika.

Iran's decision to accept the resolution was faced with two conflicting types of pressures and resistance both inside and outside the country.

1. Inside the country, some groups that were not aware of the course of events and framework of the February Agreement charged Tehran with giving in to the West's demands and submitting to the EU's pressures.
2. Beyond the borders, the American neoconservatives and radical anti-Iranian media emphasized that Europe had granted a major concession to Iran through the Brussels Agreement, without getting anything in return. From their viewpoint,

normalization of Iran's nuclear case would deprive them of the most important pressure tool against Tehran. They also maintained that accepting suspension of centrifuge parts manufacture should have been done much earlier in line with the September resolution.

Despite various efforts by Tehran, signals sent by the capitals of the three European countries showed that Brussels lacked enough resolve to fulfill its obligations according to the February Agreement. The signals reached their peak in the middle of May 2004. There were a host of reasons behind Europe's unwillingness to close Iran's nuclear case in the June meeting:

1. The main reason behind the failure of the European troika to abide by the Brussels Agreement was the enormous pressures put on them by the United States.[25]
2. The psychological war launched by the Western media against Iran and the atmosphere created by the international media were other factors that reduced Europe's motivations to implement the Brussels Agreement.
3. The unconditional surrender of Libya in the face of US pressures was another factor that undermined Europe's strategy vis-à-vis the United States.
4. The remarks made by the nuclear watchdog on the conflict between Iran's statements and IAEA's findings increased the suspicions of European statesmen toward Iran.
5. Inauguration of UCF in Isfahan led to a new wave of international pressures against Iran.
6. Iran's round-the-clock activities before suspension of manufacturing and assembling centrifuges in April 2004 constituted another reason for Europe's pessimism toward Iran.

The new Director General's report on the implementation of the NPT Safeguards Agreement in Iran (June 2, 2004) triggered another political marathon among member countries of the IAEA's Board of Governors:

1. The Director General emphasized progress in Tehran–IAEA relations and commended Iran's cooperation.
2. Considered inauguration of Isfahan facilities to be in conflict with IAEA's interpretation of "the range of Iran's decision on suspension."
3. Dr ElBaradei had mentioned issues related to "origins of LEU and HEU contaminations" and Iran's efforts for importing, manufacturing, and operating P-1 and P-2 centrifuges as two key problems that remained to be solved.
4. In that report, Iran had also been charged with declaring "contradictory information" on some issues.

The report, along with the six points mentioned here and the political atmosphere governing the Board of Governors, was enough to give rise to a European draft resolution against the Brussels Agreement and Tehran's expectations.

The June meeting of the Board of Governors started on June 14, 2004, when the Iranian Foreign Minister had criticized the Brussels' draft resolution two days earlier. Seyed Mohammad Khatami wrote a letter to the leaders of France, Germany, and Britain on June 14, 2003, implying that Iran may end talks with the European countries if they failed to comply with their obligations. In a press conference on June 17, 2004, the President stipulated that Iran will end enrichment suspension if the European side ignored its commitments.[26]

Finally, the Board of Governors released its resolution on June 18, 2004. In that resolution, the Board of Governors reiterated "its appreciation that Iran has continued to act as if its Additional Protocol were in force" and also emphasized on "Iran's voluntary decisions to suspend all enrichment-related and reprocessing activities and to permit the Agency to verify that suspension" while "noting with concern" that the verification was delayed in some cases, and that the suspension was not comprehensive. The board, however, admitted that "there has been good progress on the actions agreed during the Director General's visit to Tehran in early April 2004."

The resolution also called on Iran "to take all necessary steps on an urgent basis to help resolve all outstanding questions, especially that of LEU and HEU contamination found at various locations in Iran, including by providing additional relevant information about the origin of the components in question and explanations about the presence of a cluster of 36% HEU particles; and also the question of the nature and scope of Iran's P-2 centrifuge program." While welcoming "Iran's submission of the declarations under Articles 2 and 3 of its Additional Protocol" the Board emphasized "the importance of Iran continuing to act in accordance with the provisions of the Additional Protocol to provide reassurance to the international community about the nature of its nuclear program."

Intense diplomatic negotiations between Iran and various power blocks and making the most of Non-Aligned Movement's potentials along with numerous rounds of talks with the three European countries toned down the resolution. However, Tehran firmly believed that Brussels' political obligations and Iran's cooperation with IAEA necessitated normalization of the nuclear case. Tehran's consternation led to important developments in the aftermath of the meeting.

Cancellation of the Brussels Agreement

Tehran reacted angrily when the three European countries breached their obligations according to the Brussels Agreement to normalize the course of Iran's nuclear dossier in the June meeting. Tehran highlighted two major facts:

1. Inability of Europe in getting the dossier back to its normal course as envisaged by the Brussels Agreement.
2. Content of the Board of Governors' June resolution and future prospects for cooperation between Iran and IAEA.

With regard to the first fact, Tehran's reaction was firm and decisive and ended the enrichment suspension that Iran had accepted on the basis of the Brussels Agreement.[27] With regard to the second fact, that is, contents of the June resolution, early remarks made by Iran's officials showed that Tehran would not give in to the requirements of the resolution. The most important requests, mentioned in Paragraphs 7 and 8 of the resolution, were expansion of suspension to Isfahan's UCF project and a review of Iran's decision as to the Arak project. Negotiations between Iranian diplomats and power blocks during the Board of Governors' meeting led to changes in the said two paragraphs. After ratification of the said paragraphs, Non-Aligned Movement member countries reacted to it through a statement.[28]

Less than a week later, Iran wrote a letter to the Director General of IAEA as well as the foreign ministers of Germany, Britain, and France, officially announcing that Tehran had cancelled its obligation as per the Brussels Agreement. Renewed manufacture of parts and assembly of centrifuges by Iran conveyed two clear political and legal messages to the world:

1. Iran will not accept any unilateral obligation.
2. Iran insists on the voluntary nature of suspension, not only in words, but also in deed.

Iran's decision to resume manufacturing parts and assembling centrifuges was immediately met with various reactions on the part of the world powers and countries. The first consequence of that development was initiation of a war of nerves by Israel against Iran. Increased media evidence showing possibility of Israel's attack on Iran's nuclear installations (similar to the Osiraq experience) was noted by analysts. Unconventional rhetoric raged on through remarks by US Secretary of State Condoleezza Rice and Defense Secretary Donald Rumsfeld about "testing all possible ways" of preventing Tehran's activities. The *Washington Times* carried a report on July 4, 2004, to outline a plan, which the paper claimed was formulated by the Israeli army to launch "limited surprise attacks" on Iran's nuclear installations. The plan was published in various languages by mass media, first in European countries and then in Persian Gulf littoral states.

Finally, the warning issued by British Prime Minister Tony Blair to Israeli Premier Ariel Sharon (August 21, 2004) about the consequences of Israel's attack on Iran's nuclear installations, the remarks made by the German Chancellor, and Jacques Chirac's opposition to any "undiplomatic treatment" of Tehran marginalized the said scenario. Ariel Sharon, finally, denied that Israel intended to attack Iran on September 15, 2004.

Review of developments leading to September 2004—Second crisis in Tehran–Brussels relations

Cancellation of suspension, heightened pressures by the European troika on Tehran, and dismay on the part of the Iranian authorities and political activists led to tension in Iran's relations with the three European countries. The tug of war between the two sides was made worse because of multilateral pressures on Tehran and the European capitals:

1. Because of suspension of centrifuge manufacture and assembly by Iran and under internal pressures, the EU requested Iran's return to the situation that existed before the June meeting.
2. Iran was also under heavy pressures from domestic political groups and media that proposed withdrawal from the NPT and expulsion of IAEA's inspectors.

In July 2004, limited meetings were held between the two sides' diplomats in the European capitals without any major agenda.

Revelations about Tehran's decision to convert 37 tons yellowcake to UF6 gas led to escalation of political and propaganda pressures on Iran. The pressures triggered media countdown for referral of Iran's nuclear dossier to New York during the September meeting.

On July 24, 2004, Tehran proposed a plan named "framework for mutual guarantees," according to which a large-scale strategy for crisis management, that is, changing threats into opportunities, had been formulated. The plan was forwarded to the European troika during a quadripartite meeting in Paris on July 29, 2004.

According to the plan, Tehran proposed to the European troika that:

1. It had not diverted from peaceful nuclear activities and will not leave the NPT.
2. By assuming full responsibility for controlling its advanced technology, Tehran guarantees cooperation with IAEA's inspectors according to additional protocol.
3. Giving assurances about accepting responsibility for using advanced technology was another commitment of Iran.

In return for the said commitments, the European troika should have assured Iran on the following points:

1. Iran's most urgent and important demand was realization of its basic rights as per the NPT and the right to develop fuel cycle.
2. The three European countries were also called upon to promote their ties with Tehran to the level of strategic relations.
3. Transfer of advanced technology, including technologies with dual application, expansion of economic cooperation, defense cooperation, and granting Iran security assurances were other obligations to be shouldered by the European countries.

Despite the positive consequences of Tehran's plan, political conditions and tensions made a return to conditions that existed before the September meeting, practically impossible. The United States insisted on reporting Iran's case to the Security Council in September 2004.

Under those circumstances, Tehran once again intensified its diplomatic efforts ahead of the Board of Governors' meeting. Iran focused on negotiations with other power blocks, especially the Non-Aligned Movement countries and the East Block and more importance was attached to negotiations with Malaysia, India, South Africa, Cuba, China, and Russia.

The Board of Governors' meeting on September 14, 2004, was held under a politically charged atmosphere.

The content of the Board of Governors' resolution in September 2004 contravened the NPT. However, Melissa Fleming, spokeswoman of the IAEA, announced that the request was binding. In the resolution passed by Board of Governors in September 2004:

1. The general trend of Iran's cooperation with IAEA had been confirmed.
2. The Board of Governors also emphasized on required cooperation on P-2 centrifuges as well as plutonium separation experiments, and expressed concern over Tehran's decision to introduce 37 tons of yellowcake into the Isfahan UCF.[29]
3. The September resolution also urged Iran to respond positively to the Director General's findings on the provision of access and information at any time.
4. The Board of Governors called on Tehran to suspend all activities related to enrichment in various sectors.
5. Tehran was also required to reconsider its decision to start construction of a research reactor in Arak moderated by heavy water.
6. The Board of Governors also urged Iran to ratify the additional protocol without delay.
7. The Board of Governers requested the Director General to submit in advance of the November Board a report on the implementation of that resolution and a recapitulation of the Agency's findings on the Iranian nuclear program since September 2002, as well as a full account of past and present Iranian cooperation with the Agency.[30]

Europe later offered a plan themed, "The Way Forward," which delineated a wide range of common mutual cooperation aimed at achieving a long-term strategic agreement. However, the contradiction between some paragraphs of the said plan and Iran's viewpoints and long-term interests caused Tehran to reject the plan. The main reasons for Tehran's rejection could be enumerated as follows:

1. The EU had threatened Iran that in case of opposition to suspension, it would support reporting of Iran's case to the Security Council.
2. The requested period of suspension was unlimited.
3. The said plan contained a wide definition of global nonproliferation policies and also referred to the United Nations Security Council resolution 1540, which paved the way for putting more pressures on Tehran with regard to missile activities.

4. Iran had been obliged to ratify the additional protocol by the end of 2005.
5. Iran had been requested to take necessary measures to ratify the Complete Test Ban Treaty (CTBT).
6. They had called for full transparency on the part of Iran. This could have amounted to more requests that could have transcended the limits of 93 + 2 additional protocol.
7. Finally, the "objective guarantees" requested by Europe to assure that Iran will not divert toward nuclear weapons had been taken to mean "stopping" the nuclear program. That request had been frequently mentioned by Iran as a red-line for negotiations.

Europe, which felt a threat to the results of a whole year of negotiations after the developments of September 2004, increased diplomatic contacts with Tehran immediately after "The Way Forward" was rejected. On October 21, 2004, high-ranking expert talks started among diplomats from the four countries in Vienna. Less than a week later, that is, on October 27, 2004, a new round of talks was held in Vienna, which was announced as fruitless by the spokesman of the Iranian delegation.

During those negotiations, the ambassadors of France, Germany, and Britain offered Iran a "draft agreement" the at 09:00 on Tuesday, November 2, 2004. Tehran rejected the plan and offered an alternative proposal to the three European ambassadors at 20:00 on Wednesday, November 3, 2004. Although the last European plan was less defective than "The Way Forward," it was still far from the viewpoints of Iran.

The necessity of reaching an agreement ahead of the November meeting of the Board of Governors to reduce the crisis led the four countries to meet again on November 5, 2004. Those talks evolved into one of the most complicated and lengthy rounds of quadrilateral negotiations since October 2003 and took about 23 hours. The goal of the negotiations was to compare Tehran's and Brussels' proposals paragraph by paragraph and bargain on both sides' demands. Diplomats of the four countries finally reached an agreement on a single text that covered the viewpoints of both Iran and the European countries as much as possible. The text was later known as the Paris Agreement.

Achievements of the Paris Agreement

The Paris Agreement called for temporary suspension of Iran's nuclear fuel cycle on the one side, and the EU's support for resumption of those activities after the period of suspension on the other side. However, Europe would undertake to grant other concessions to Tehran and provide grounds for long-term strategic cooperation with Iran.[31] The Paris Agreement showed that achieving an agreement in support of Iran's enrichment program was possible because:

1. The main goal of the Paris Agreement was negotiation in order to achieve a solution that would be favored by both sides.
2. Recognition of Iran's basic nuclear rights by the European troika showed that such a solution was achievable.

3. Emphasis put by the Paris Agreement on the necessity of presenting "objective guarantees" by Iran on the peaceful nature of its nuclear program was another sign of the above fact.

Tehran reaped many benefits through the Paris Agreement, the most important of which are as follows:

1. The Paris Agreement had reiterated Europe's commitment to prevent Iran's nuclear case from being reported to the Security Council.
2. Normalization of the nuclear case in the November meeting of the Board of Governors was a brilliant consequence of the Paris Agreement.
3. The Paris Agreement and Europe's emphasis on normalization of the case attested to the fact that they had recognized Iran's nuclear program as peaceful.
4. The Paris Agreement had emphasized Iran's basic rights according to NPT. A major outcome of the Paris Agreement was recognition of Iran's right, and more importantly exercise of that right with no discrimination, by the EU.
5. The Paris Agreement not only emphasized on voluntary nature of suspension as a confidence-building step, but also recognized that suspension of Iran's nuclear program was not a legal obligation and just for the "period of negotiations."[32]
6. Emphasis on the need for Iran to provide objective guarantees to prove no diversion from the peaceful program attested to Europe's relative readiness to support Iran's nuclear fuel cycle.
7. The Paris Agreement, and Europe's readiness to develop broad-based relations with Iran, was a political development that occurred for the first time after the victory of Iran. According to the Paris Agreement, Europe agreed to provide Iran with "firm guarantees" on the establishment of broad-based relations with Tehran. That is, Iran's obligation for providing "objective guarantees" about no diversion in its nuclear program was in return for Europe's obligation to provide "firm guarantees" on developing broad-based relations with Iran.

Also, the Paris Agreement led to the establishment of three working groups to pursue complete realization of its goals. The working groups included the political and security, cooperation and technology, and nuclear fields.

8. The Paris Agreement called on the whole the EU to get engaged in negotiations along with EU3, which was a sign of promotion of negotiations compared with October 2003.
9. The Paris Agreement enabled Tehran and then Europe to take the initiative and prevent unrivaled political maneuvering by the United States.
10. Emphasis on cooperation between Iran and Europe in Iraq's political process was a clear message to the United States, which made efforts to prevent Iran's proactive presence in Iraq very difficult.

11. The Paris Agreement had taken a similar approach to MKO and al Qaeda terrorist groups and had stressed on fighting them.
12. The Paris Agreement reemphasized on the need for Brussels to support Iran's accession to the World Trade Organization and integration into the global economy.
13. A major achievement of the Paris Agreement was providing grounds for coherent and purposeful negotiations between Iran and the EU and resumption of trade talks.
14. Initiation of technical negotiations under the aegis of the Paris Agreement would provide a big opportunity for Iran's industrial and scientific community as well as domestic economy.
15. The Paris Agreement greatly reduced anti-Iran propaganda by international media.
16. The international community was assured through the Paris Agreement that Iran would opt for negotiations in eventful junctures.
17. The Paris Agreement totally eliminated threats against Iran that ranged from limited military operations by the Zionist regime to widespread sanctions.
18. The Paris Agreement, like the Saadabad Agreement, rapidly dismissed concerns in Iran's economic and industrial community, assured the market, enhanced investment, and reduced capital flight.
19. Negotiations ending in the Paris Agreement attested to Iran's diplomatic finesse in bargaining with the world's biggest diplomatic apparatus (Europe).
20. Another achievement of the Agreement was taking Iran's case out of the provisional agenda of the Board of Governors.
21. One of the most important achievements of the Paris Agreement was Iran's membership in the committee on multilateral approaches to the nuclear fuel cycle. Also, Iran agreed, for the first time, to suspend its nuclear program as defined by the Board of Governors' resolutions. Therefore, after conclusion of the Paris Agreement, Isfahan's UCF and the Natanz facility stopped operating and this issue led to tremendous domestic pressure on the nuclear negotiating team.

The United States and Europe had proposed at the end of 2003 that the IAEA Board of Governors should establish a committee to devise a new mechanism for enrichment and production of nuclear fuel.

Dr ElBaradei was preparing a proposal according to which countries that had not achieved the full nuclear fuel cycle should have stopped all their activities for, at least, five years.

Evaluation done at that time showed that the joint goal of IAEA and the United States could be pursued within the framework of three international bodies, that is, the committee on multilateral approaches to the nuclear fuel cycle, 2005 NPT Review Conference, and finally, the Director General's report to the summit meeting of the UN General Assembly.

Tehran was determined to become a member of the committee on multilateral approaches to the nuclear fuel cycle and conducted many rounds of negotiations in

September 2004 (after the Paris Agreement) to get the backing of the European countries for its membership. The talks finally made the EU declare to the Director General that it was not opposed to Iran's membership in the committee.

Extensive negotiations by the Iranian diplomats and the outcomes of the Paris Agreement finally turned the November 2004 resolution of the IAEA's Board of Governors (November 29, 2004) into one of the best and most positive resolutions to be passed by Board of Governors on Iran's nuclear program. The following points are noteworthy:

1. Iran's compensatory measures with regard to some of the past breaches were confirmed.[33]
2. The Board of Governors announced that all nuclear materials of Iran had been declared and there was no diversion to forbidden activities.[34]
3. The November resolution confirmed the Paris Agreement while emphasizing on the voluntary nature of enrichment activities as a confidence-building measure, which was not legally binding.
4. Although the resolution had described continued suspension of all enrichment and reprocessing activities as "essential," emphasizing that the measure was "voluntary and not legally binding" indicated that the goals of Article 18 of the Safeguards Agreement had not been met.
5. The November resolution had stipulated that IAEA's activities in Iran would be within the framework of the 93 + 2 additional protocol.[35]
6. According to the resolution, Iran's case was taken out of the Board of Governors' provisional agenda. This was a consequence of the Paris Agreement.
7. The approach taken by the November 2004 resolution showed that Tehran had been largely successful in the management of the crisis.

Based on these facts, after 14 months of negotiations and diplomatic efforts, Tehran found itself in a new position in November 2004, which was quite different from the beginning:

1. In September 2003, Iran was on the verge of being referred to the United Nations Security Council while in November 2004 the course had been reversed.
2. In September 2003, Tehran had been requested to suspend all its nuclear activities, while in November 2004, the suspension was considered to be voluntary, for confidence building and not legally binding.
3. At that time, a host of evidence presented by some Western countries indicated diversion of Iran's nuclear activities to military goals. In November 2004, however, the Board of Governors emphasized that Iran's activities were peaceful and there was no diversion to military programs.
4. The IAEA in September 2003 emphasized Iran's secrecy while in November 2004 more emphasis was put on Iran's compensatory measures.
5. At the outset of the crisis, Tehran was facing a global consensus against it. In November 2004, not only had the transatlantic gap been widened, but some countries of the American block were also opposed to US interests.

6. Washington, which had prepared the grounds for a limited military attack on Iran at that time, now emphasized on direct talks with Iran and was ready to give concessions after Tehran's interactions with the international community and developments in Iraq.
7. The International community, which considered Iran's nuclear activities to be a threat to international peace in September 2003, recognized Iran's rights and agreed to their enforcement in November 2004, but only postponed that enforcement to a few months later.
8. Even Russia and the EU, which considered suspension of Iran's nuclear fuel cycle to be in line with their economic interests, were sending positive signals showing their nod to a gradual start of the cycle in Iran.

It should be noted that all concessions given by Iran to Europe were limited to the requirements of the September 2003 resolution. Through tactful performance, Tehran accepted part of those requirements in November 2004, but in return:

1. The EU and IAEA accepted suspension as being voluntary and not legally binding. Also, suspension had been limited to negotiations, which in turn depended on both sides' progress.
2. IAEA and the EU recognized Iran's right to develop nuclear fuel cycle.
3. IAEA and the international community emphasized that Iran's nuclear activities were peaceful and without diversion to military purposes.
4. IAEA's Board of Governors announced that Iran's nuclear dossier was a normal case and not a special security matter.
5. IAEA and the international community stipulated that inspections should be limited within the framework of the additional protocol.
6. IAEA and the international community admitted that Iran had corrected its past failures.
7. The EU agreed to grant concessions asked by Tehran to pave the way for the expansion of strategic relations with Iran.
8. The EU agreed to engage in nuclear cooperation with Iran and fulfill the duties undertaken by nuclear-weapon states as per the NPT.
9. Tehran was offered a good opportunity to complete technical know-how of its scientists under calm atmosphere.

Comprehensive negotiations: efforts by Iran and Europe to support the Paris Agreement

Taking Iran's case out of the Board of Governors' provisional agenda and suitable content of the November 2004 resolution were construed as the first signs of the EU's compliance with its commitments as per the Paris Agreement. Assertions by European officials about "the commencement of a new chapter in Iran–EU cooperation" and IAEA's official invitation to Iran to become a member of the fuel cycle group (December 6, 2004) provided necessary grounds for the resumption of long-term talks with the European troika.

The Paris Agreement had projected that long-term negotiations between Iran and the EU should be pursued simultaneously through three committees. The most difficult part was related to the "objective guarantees" required by the EU to assure that Iran's nuclear program will not divert to military applications. Many rounds of talks were held on "objective guarantees" and "firm guarantees." According to the Paris Agreement, Tehran had agreed to give objective guarantees about absence of any diversion of its nuclear fuel cycle. Europe had also pledged to provide Iran with firm guarantees for the development of political, economic, security, technological, and nuclear cooperation with Iran. European diplomats were seeking guarantees that would not be affected by changing political conditions. Therefore, the first guarantee that they sought was closedown of Iran's nuclear fuel cycle. However, Tehran believed that giving a guarantee about anything was only possible when it did really exist. Therefore, erasing the problem could not be expected as a guarantee.

The difference in Iran's and Europe's understandings of the said issue accounted for the lion's share of negotiations. Tehran maintained that NPT, Safeguards Agreement, the additional protocol, and cooperation with IAEA were the best objective guarantees on no diversion in Iran's peaceful nuclear program. However, the EU did not consider those guarantees as sufficient because the European diplomats believed that secrecy was possible in all three fields. For this reason, Tehran said the issue of fuel cycle was not negotiable and asked the opposite side to explain about required guarantees (excluding the fuel cycle).

As time went by and negotiations slowed down, Tehran increased pressures on the EU.

The Rowhani–Chirac Agreement

The meetings between the Iranian and French authorities were significant from various viewpoints.

Dr Rowhani and the French President Jacques Chirac agreed in Paris in March 2005 to call on IAEA to assist in solving the sole remaining problem, that is, "objective guarantees" by defining the mechanisms through which such guarantees could be provided. The French Foreign Minister and Director General of the French foreign ministry, who were present at the meeting, opposed Chirac. Chirac, however, noted that the IAEA was the sole international authority to guarantee the peaceful nature of the nuclear activities of member countries and was in the best position to define the said mechanisms. The opposition by the French Foreign Minister was a good reason for subsequent opposition by his counterparts in Berlin and London. Dr Rowhani then met with German Chancellor, Gerhard Schröder, in Berlin. During the meeting, Schroeder said that even if they accepted the proposal, the Americans would not accept it.

1. The main framework of proposals to France pertained to weaknesses in negotiations and their structural problems. From that angle, it seemed that

reducing bureaucracy and bargaining with more powers could promote talks. The Iranian side asked Chirac to elevate the level of negotiations on the European side to facilitate further talks.

2.   The emphasis put on how IAEA should arbitrate in matters of differences between the two sides, especially definition of mechanisms for providing "objective guarantees" by Iran, was another proposal of the Iranian negotiating team. The proposal on how to define the objective guarantees that Tehran was supposed to provide the IAEA to assure the Agency about no diversion in its nuclear activities was initially accepted by the French President.

The second session of Iran's nuclear negotiations steering committee was held on March 22, 2005.

Tehran took two important steps following the steering committee's session in March 2005 in Paris:

1.   Tehran announced that it would stop negotiations with political and economic working groups. At that time, evidence showed that Europe was willing to grant concessions within the framework of political and economic working groups to get Iran's agreement on long-term suspension of fuel cycle. By withdrawing from political and economic negotiations, Tehran proved that it had not forgotten the main goal of the Paris Agreement and was still pursuing its main goal, that is, enrichment and reprocessing.
2.   Iran's second step was to present an innovative plan to build confidence with Europe and restart enrichment. That plan was the fourth plan to be offered by Iran's negotiating team.

The Iranian side proposed that if the European troika was not ready to accept Iran's fourth plan, another trend should be followed temporarily:

1.   In the first step, Isfahan's UCF was to become operational and its product would have been sent to a third country in return for yellowcake.
2.   Some 3,000 centrifuges would come on-stream in Natanz.
3.   A whole year was to be considered for negotiations on how to carry out industrial enrichment in Iran.
4.   The timetable for "industrial production" was to be coordinated with the time of "Iran's need to fuel consumption."

The author held several rounds of unofficial negotiations with the Directors General of the foreign ministries of the three European countries in Berlin, London, and Paris. To my understanding, they were ready to accept operations at Isfahan's UCF. However, when it came to the pilot plant in Natanz, Berlin and Paris could accept a limited number, for example 500, centrifuges operating at the pilot while it was not acceptable to London. On the other hand, the EU3 was willing to postpone an agreement on Tehran's proposed formula (UCF project of Isfahan + a pilot plant in Natanz + a period of negotiations) until after the presidential election in Iran. The Iranian leadership, however, maintained that, first, the number of pilot centrifuges should not be less than 3,000; second, negotiations should not take longer than one year; and third, agreement on the formula should be reached before the presidential election.

Later, the new Iranian Foreign Minister, Dr Manouchehr Mottaki, announced in an interview with Japan's NHK television that Europe had been positive toward Iran's proposal.[36]

Presidential election and the fate of negotiations

The remarks made by negotiating sides and creditable media evidence showed that Europe was on the verge of agreement with Tehran's enrichment activities. However, between the meeting of the steering committee in Paris on March 22, 2005, and London on April 28, a new factor was introduced in Tehran's talks with the EU, which was rooted in Iran's domestic political atmosphere. Iran's nuclear dossier was a main topic for contestants in the presidential race.

In the London session of the steering committee (April 28, 2005), Tehran offered another plan due to domestic pressure and called for speedy inauguration of the Isfahan UCF and continuation of negotiations while Europe asked Iran to adjourn negotiations until after Iran's presidential polls.

Subsequent to Tehran's decision to launch the Isfahan UCF and widespread reactions in the West to Iran's decision, the troika sent a letter to Iran's nuclear negotiator calling for a high-ranking quadrilateral meeting.

At the same time, three important international meetings were underway or pending:

1.   The NPT Review Conference, which was closing in New York.
2.   The World Trade Organization meeting.
3.   The meeting of IAEA's Board of Governors in June.

During the Geneva meeting, the EU was ready to cooperate with Iran and provide guarantees on some key issues, including the following:

1.   Full support for Iran's right to enjoy a peaceful nuclear energy program.
2.   Assuring long-term fuel supply to power plants backed by IAEA and the United Nations.
3.   Guarantees related to Iran's territorial integrity, independence, and national sovereignty.
4.   Bolstering political and security relations between Tehran and Brussels.
5.   Recognizing Iran as the main source of energy, including oil and gas, for the EU.
6.   Gradual removal of obstacles to sending "dual-use" equipment, advanced technology, and technological cooperation to Tehran.

7.   Strengthening international cooperation between Iran and Europe to fight terror and illicit drugs.
8.   Rapid progress in finalization of Iran–Europe trade agreement and Iran's membership at the World Trade Organization.

During the Geneva meeting, Tehran announced its two-month deadline for the EU and emphasized that any proposal that excluded enrichment would be rejected in advance.

The two-month interval was a good opportunity for the nuclear team to boost its activities away from the election hustings in Tehran.

Iran's chief negotiator visited South Africa before reopening the Isfahan UCF and the trip's achievements could have led to major developments and settlement of the nuclear crisis. The South African President proposed that the product of the Isfahan UCF may be exported to his country in return for yellowcake from South Africa.

In the meantime, the ninth presidential election was held in Iran. As a result, Mr Mahmoud Ahmadinejad was elected president through a runoff election. The election of Ahmadinejad shocked the Western world and led to heavy propaganda war against Iran. The atmosphere that was created by the Western media and some positions taken by political activists provided good grounds for the West to increase pressures on Tehran. As a result, the international community's dialogue with Iran changed greatly. Tehran emphasized that nuclear policies were made at high levels and were not affected by transient developments. However, that argument went unheeded because of various reasons, including nitpicking by world powers.

It was then that the EU presented its comprehensive package of incentives for Iran on August 4, 2005. The presidential election result, which had taken the Western world by surprise, also influenced the content of the incentives package. When submitting the package, European diplomats stressed that the door was still open to negotiations and the EU was prepared to promote all-out cooperation with Iran.

The European package

The goal of the proposed European package was to develop relations and cooperation with Iran based on mutual respect and the establishment of international confidence in the exclusively peaceful nature of Iran's nuclear program.

The European countries noted that to create the right conditions for negotiations, they were ready to:

1.   Reaffirm Iran's right to develop nuclear energy for peaceful purposes in conformity with its NPT obligations, and in this context reaffirm their support for the development by Iran of a civil nuclear energy program.
2.   Commit to actively support the building of new light water reactors in Iran through international joint projects, in accordance with the IAEA Statute and the NPT.

3.   Agree to suspend discussion of Iran's nuclear program at the Security Council on resumption of negotiations.

Iran was expected to:

1.   Commit to addressing all the outstanding concerns of the IAEA through full cooperation with the IAEA.
2.   Suspend all enrichment-related and reprocessing activities to be verified by the IAEA, as requested by the IAEA Board of Governors and commit to continue this during these negotiations.
3.   Resume implementation of the Additional Protocol.

Areas of future cooperation to be covered in negotiations on a long-term agreement included the following:

- Reaffirm Iran's inalienable right to nuclear energy for peaceful purposes without discrimination and in conformity with Articles I and II of the NPT, and cooperate with Iran in the development by Iran of a civil nuclear power program.
- Actively support the building of new light water power reactors in Iran through international joint projects, in accordance with the IAEA Statute and the NPT, using state-of-the art technology, by authorizing the transfer of necessary goods and the provision of advanced technology to make its power reactors safe against earthquakes.
- Provide a substantive package of research and development cooperation, including possible provision of light water research reactors, notably in the fields of radioisotope production and basic research and nuclear applications in medicine and agriculture.
- Give legally binding, multilayered fuel assurances to Iran.
- Support for a new conference to promote dialogue and cooperation on regional security issues.
- Improve Iran's access to the international economy, markets and capital through practical support for full integration into international structures, including the WTO, and create the framework for increased direct investment in Iran and trade with Iran.
- Civil aviation cooperation, including the possible removal of restrictions on US and European manufacturers, from exporting civil aircraft to Iran, thereby widening the prospect of Iran renewing its fleet of civil airliners.
- Establishment of a long-term energy partnership between Iran and the EU and other willing partners, with concrete and practical applications.
- Support for the modernization of Iran's telecommunication infrastructure and advanced internet provision, including possible removal of relevant US and other export restrictions.
- Cooperation in fields of high technology and other areas to be agreed.
- Support for agricultural development in Iran, including possible access to US and European agricultural products, technology, and farm equipment.

The new Iranian government, however, was determined to resume enrichment activities at Isfahan's UCF. Since the Europeans initially proposed that Iran should accept total cessation of enrichment activities for a ten-year period, Tehran decided to withdraw from the Paris Agreement. In a press interview at Élysée Palace, Tony Blair and Jacques Chirac urged Iran to suspend enrichment. Also, Vladimir Putin, Jacques Chirac, and Gerhard Schröder reviewed Iran's nuclear case and new developments in Kaliningrad and called on Iran to suspend enrichment and continue negotiations. As a result of those developments, the United States, which had already shown signs of flexibility toward accepting at the very least the UCF project in Isfahan, was opposed to the construction of the Bushehr nuclear power plant.

A few days before the reopening of the Isfahan UCF, a representative of the South African President, Abdul Samad Minty, contacted Hossein Mousavian to relay Thabo Mbeki's message to him. In that message, which was later rejected by leaders of Iran, the South African President had noted that the leaders of three European countries were ready to accept his country's plan and were willing to negotiate with Iran. Abdul Samad Minty also asked the Iranian leaders to postpone inauguration of Isfahan's UCF for a couple of weeks, so that it could be done after an agreement with EU3.

Under those conditions, Tehran decided to leave the Paris Agreement and inaugurate the Isfahan UCF. On July 31, 2004, Iran's official letter on the resumption of activities at the Isfahan facility was submitted to the IAEA. One day earlier, the seal of the facility was removed in the presence of IAEA inspectors. Dr ElBaradei subsequently reported reopening of the Isfahan UCF by Iran to the Board of Governors and the Board met emergently on August 8, 2005. Two days later, a resolution was released calling on Iran to reinstate the suspension.

The second round of nuclear diplomacy

The second round of Iran's nuclear diplomacy started in August 2005 after the election of President Mahmoud Ahmadinejad. The President appointed Dr Ali Larijani as secretary of the Supreme National Security Council and Iran's chief nuclear negotiator. Therefore, Dr Rohani and his negotiating team were replaced by Dr Larijani and his team. Javad Vaeidi was appointed official in charge of expert negotiations of the nuclear team while other team members included Ali Monfared (deputy secretary of the Supreme National Security Council for foreign policy affairs), Hosseini-Tash (deputy secretary of the Supreme National Security Council for strategic affairs), Saeedi (deputy head of Iran Atomic Energy Organization), Eraqchi (deputy foreign minister), and at times, Nahavandian (deputy secretary of the Supreme National Security Council for economic affairs). Apart from the deputy foreign minister, who did not play a significant part in negotiations and policy-making, other members of the nuclear team were not foreign ministry diplomats. The new negotiating team started to work by looking to the East and paid more attention to cooperation with such countries as India, China, and Russia. As Isfahan's Uranium Conversion Utility (UCF) started operations, IAEA's Board of Governors met on September 24, 2005, and issued a resolution.

1. It found many failures and breaches of Iran's obligations to comply with the NPT Safeguards Agreement, which constituted noncompliance in the context of Article XII.C of the Agency's Statute. According to that article, the Board shall report the noncompliance of a member country to all members and to the Security Council and General Assembly of the United Nations.
2. By reference to Article III of the Statute, the Board of Governors concluded that Iran's nuclear program had given rise to questions that were within the competence of the Security Council, as the organ bearing the main responsibility for the maintenance of international peace and security.
3. The Board urged Iran to reestablish full and sustained suspension of all enrichment-related and reprocessing activities, even activities related to research and development.
4. The Board called on Iran to promptly ratify and implement in full the Additional Protocol.
5. By mentioning the possibility of diversion of Iran's nuclear activities toward military purposes, it called on Iran to allow inspections that would extend beyond the formal requirements of the Safeguards Agreement and Additional Protocol.
6. Iran's missile activities also came into focus.
7. Iran's nuclear case was, once more, put on the Board of Governors' agenda.[37]

The resolution only adjourned reporting Iran to the United Nations Security Council to a later time. Ratification of the said resolution through the positive votes of India, China, and Russia proved the failure of the "Look to the East" approach in Iran's nuclear diplomacy and Iran indicated its willingness to restart negotiations with the European countries.

Iran indicated its willingness to negotiate the following points with Europe:

1. Full cooperation with IAEA to settle remaining problems and remove ambiguities.
2. Commitment to NPT and the Safeguard Agreement.
3. Continued implementation of the Additional Protocol.
4. Negotiation and agreement on offering objective guarantees in order to build confidence regarding nondiversion in Iran's nuclear activities.
5. Agreement on activities that were carried out at Isfahan's UCF and a pilot plant in Natanz and continuation of negotiations on "objective guarantees."

At the same time, Iran was not ready to suspend all nuclear activities as a precondition for negotiations with Europe. Negotiations between Iran and Europe started subsequent to the September 2005 resolution and European negotiators emphasized that:

1. First of all, Iran should suspend all its nuclear activities.
2. Negotiations should start and agreement should be reached on all points.
3. Iran should comply with the Board of Governors' resolution.

Failure of negotiations as a result of President Ahmadinejad's hard-line stances on Israel, holocaust, and the leaders of Western countries further complicated the situation.

After Iran initiated research and development activities at the Natanz nuclear facility on January 3, 2006, the Board of Governors immediately adopted another resolution in which it reiterated the salient points of the resolution adopted on September 24, 2005. The latter resolution highlighted the possibility of diversion in Iran's nuclear program toward fabrication of nuclear weapons, and noted that the Agency was not in a position to clarify some important issues related to Iran's nuclear program. It further requested the Director General, Mohamed ElBaradei, "to report on the implementation of this and previous resolutions to the next regular session of the Board, for its consideration, and immediately ... convey ... that report to the Security Council."[38] In this way, Iran's nuclear dossier was, for the first time, discussed by the United Nations Security Council and the Security Council adopted a statement through consensus, urging Iran to immediately implement the Board of Governors' resolution.[39]

Negotiations between Iran and Europe continued while differences remained unsolved until the United Nations Security Council adopted Resolution 1696 on July 31, 2006, which included the following points[40]:

1. It announced Iran's nuclear case to be related to global peace and security under Chapter VII of the UN Charter.
2. It considered suspension of enrichment and reprocessing activities at the Natanz facility and Isfahan's UCF, R&D activities, as well as all construction activities as mandatory.
3. It called for prompt implementation of the Additional Protocol by Iran as well as full and sustained suspension of all enrichment-related and reprocessing activities, and suspension of construction of a heavy water reactor in Arak.
4. It emphasized on the necessity of robust inspections well beyond the Safeguard Agreement and the Additional Protocol.
5. It linked Iran's ballistic missile programs to nuclear activities as being a threat to global peace and security.

In fact, two articles of Chapter VII of the UN Charter had been applied to Iran according to the said resolution:

1. Article 39, which stipulates that the Security Council shall determine the existence of any threat to peace.[41]
2. Article 40, according to which the Security Council calls upon the parties concerned to comply with such provisional measures as it deems necessary or desirable in order to prevent an aggravation of the situation.[42]

The Security Council determined Iran's nuclear activities as a threat to global peace and security and specified that "obligatory suspension" was needed to prevent aggravation of the situation.

Although Iran was not ready to accept suspension as a precondition for negotiations, Larijani and Solana started their talks. Iran presented a plan comprising 11 articles and claimed that it had reached an agreement with Solana on the same. The EU, however, rejected the claim and noted that such an agreement had never been reached. Germany's ambassador to Tehran, whose country was rotational chairman of the EU, denied Iran's claim about Europe's agreement to the 11-article plan. The author believes that the two sides had agreed on a two-month period of suspension before further negotiations. However, the Iranian side was willing to restart enrichment after that period while Solana and the EU could not accept that request. The Holocaust conference, which was held around that time, mobilized the international political atmosphere against Iran, and the subsequent deadlock in the Larijani–Solana negotiations led to the adoption of the second Security Council resolution against Iran. According to Resolution 1737, which was adopted on December 23, 2006, the Security Council started acting under Article 41 of Chapter VII of the UN Charter.[43] Article 41 of the Charter pertains to political and economic sanctions, which can progress as far as complete severance of economic and political relations. According to the resolution, sanctions were imposed on Iran's nuclear and missile programs. The sanctions committee, which was established by the Security Council, was to oversee full implementation of the sanctions and their follow-up. A list of Iranian persons and institutions related to Iran's nuclear and missile programs was drawn up and it was decided that their foreign travels should be restricted and their accounts in foreign banks should be frozen. The resolution also called for suspension of Iran's heavy water activities. Iran rejected the resolution describing it as illegal and "a worthless piece of paper,"[44] and announced that it would rapidly operate 3,000 centrifuges and would start industrial fuel production within a year.[45]

It is evident that if Iran refrains from implementing the Security Council's resolution, the Council will extend political and economic sanctions by adopting the next resolutions under Article 41 of Chapter VII of the UN Charter. It should be noted that during the second round of Iran's nuclear diplomacy, EU3 was replaced with permanent members of the Security Council in addition to Germany (known as group 5 + 1). After the Security Council released its statement in March 2006, 5 + 1 met in Paris to propose a new package of incentives to Iran. The package offered by 5 + 1 in August 2006 was not essentially different from EU3's package offered in August 2005. Both packages called for the expansion of political, economic, and technological cooperation with Iran, recognized the country's right to operate its nuclear power plant, and guaranteed nuclear fuel supply. The August 2005 package had asked Iran to suspend its nuclear activities and the decision was to be reviewed after ten years.[46] The package that was offered in August 2006 considered three provisions for the suspension:

1. Iran should address all outstanding concerns of IAEA. This could have taken years to materialize.
2. IAEA should have confirmed that no undeclared nuclear material existed in Iran. This process took 25 years in Japan.
3. Iran should build confidence with the world.

The said conditions would have, in fact, amounted to "indefinite suspension," which could have lasted for more than ten years.

Advantages and disadvantages of policies pursued in the second round of nuclear diplomacy

1. Major advantages

    1.1. Iran ended suspension and the measure bolstered Iran's nuclear capability. Isfahan's UCF project had been made operational during the first round of diplomatic efforts and 37 tons of yellowcake had been introduced into the facility to produce UF6 (UF6 gas). However, Iran increased its UF6 stock in the second round. During the first round of nuclear diplomacy, Iran had launched about 20 pilot centrifuges at the Natanz facility and 1,000 centrifuges were fabricated. However, in the second round of nuclear diplomacy, some cascades, each comprising 164 centrifuges, were made operational. This development allowed Iran to implement the test pilot operation at Natanz and showed to the world that it had the capability to produce nuclear fuel. It also showed that it had achieved a point of no return.

2. Major disadvantages

    2.1. Iran's noncompliance with IAEA's regulations was established beyond doubt for the first time.

    2.2. The Security Council was recognized as the authority qualified to attend to Iran's nuclear dossier.

    2.3. Iran's missile program was also introduced as a threat to global peace and security.

    2.4. Suspension was extended to include the Arak heavy water plant in addition to the nuclear facilities of Isfahan and Natanz. Meanwhile, suspension was no longer voluntary, but was considered obligatory.

    2.5. Iran's case was considered under Chapter VII of the UN Charter and political as well as economic sanctions were imposed on the country pursuant to articles 39, 40, and 41 of that chapter. Subsequently, limitations were imposed on not only Iran's missile and nuclear industries, but also on the whole economy, including suspension of foreign direct investment and grant of credits by international banks.

    2.6. Iran's relations with other countries were considerably strained.

    2.7. Iran's inalienable right to avail of peaceful nuclear technology within the framework of Article IV of the NPT was made conditional on the realization of Article II of the Treaty, that is, after it is proved that Iran's nuclear activities are peaceful. However, the Paris Agreement[47] had already recognized Iran's right under the NPT without discrimination.

At the same time, it is obvious that, at present, neither of the two sides is in a win–win situation. If 5 + 1 aimed to restrict Iran's nuclear capability, the capability has been bolstered. On the other hand, if Iran was trying to lower the cost of enrichment, in practice, the costs have not decreased and even military action by the United States against Iran remains a possibility.

The way out

Peaceful settlement of the nuclear case requires a framework that would be face-saving for both sides. I believe that the framework should be as follows:

1. International treaties should form the basis of the agreement. The NPT, Safeguards Agreement, the Additional Protocol, and IAEA regulations are major treaties with regard to the nuclear issues. Therefore, 5 + 1 should drop all requests that go beyond those treaties and Iran should agree to fully comply with them.
2. All disarmament treaties include "rights" and "obligations." Iran should accept "obligations" in return for the recognition of its right by 5 + 1 within the framework of NPT. Enrichment within the framework of NPT is Iran's inalienable right.
3. Policies adopted by 5 + 1 should be implemented without discrimination. Iran should be subject to no discrimination with respect to its rights and obligations, compared with other state parties to NPT.
4. Using double standards in dealing with the nuclear issue and disarmament in the Middle East should be stopped. Israel has not accepted any disarmament treaties and is the sole country in the Middle East to have an arsenal of nuclear, chemical, and missile weapons. At the same time, it is fully supported by 5 + 1, G8, and other Western countries. Iran neither possesses a nuclear bomb, nor has any diversion been observed in its nuclear activities. The country also complies with all international treaties pertaining to nuclear, chemical, and biological weapons. However, the West is challenging Iran's legal right within the framework of NPT.
5. Confidence building and providing objective guarantees should aim at assuring the international community about nondiversion in Iran's nuclear program toward a nuclear arms program.
6. Iran should also build confidence with the world regarding the time, level, and extent of enrichment. At the same time, haggling about Iran's right to enrichment should be stopped.
7. The following formula seems to be the best way out of the current stalemate:

Isfahan's UCF project + a pilot plant in Natanz + negotiations aimed at confidence-building + attuning industrial production of nuclear fuel to the time that Iran would need to use it.

It is clear that the case of Iran's nuclear program has not been closed and that this will remain a very important issue in the development of relations between Iran and the West as a whole.

8   Human rights

Human rights and the European Union (EU) foreign policy

Over the last two decades, Western policy makers have striven to base their policies on principles such as human rights and democracy, and a greater emphasis on the promotion of these principles has been particularly noticeable since the end of the Cold War. In particular, the EU has tried to integrate a human rights policy into its diplomatic relations with Iran with the introduction of the process which it called the "critical dialogue."[1]

The foreign ministers of the EU alleged in 1992 that Iran had committed human rights violations, that it gave support to international terrorism, and that it was obstructing the peace process in the Middle East. The EU also disapproved very strongly of Iran's refusal to revoke the *fatwa*, or religious decree, against Salman Rushdie.[1] The European policy of "critical dialogue" was intended to demonstrate to Tehran that the EU did not tolerate Iran's human rights policy. However, the United States rejected the European policy and opted for a stronger "dual containment" policy directed both against Iran and Iraq.[2] Washington accused Iran of acquiring nuclear weapons, as well as of supporting international terrorism and of disrupting the Arab–Israeli peace process. From 1993 onwards, the American administration implemented sanctions with the aim of isolating Iran and thereby correcting its behavior.[3] Europe on the other hand distanced itself from the policy of sanctions designed to isolate Iran, and this resistance to sanctions resulted in an ongoing tension between the United States and the EU.[4] The principal question that arises now is Why did the EU place human rights standards at the heart of its Iran policy, and how was this policy implemented?

The significance of human rights in EU foreign policy

The Common Foreign and Security Policy (CFSP), the successor of the policy of European Political Cooperation (EPC), was intended by the EU as the framework for future European foreign policy. After the Maastricht Treaty, joint initiatives by EU member states multiplied and the CFSP became the second pillar of the EU's institutional framework.[5] Article J of the Maastricht Treaty includes the following four provisions that state the aims of the CFSP: "to preserve peace and strengthen international security...; to promote international cooperation...; to develop and consolidate democracy and the rule of law, and respect for human rights and fundamental freedoms."[6]

However, since the part played by Europe in the maintenance of the world's peace and security cannot be compared to the superpower role of the United States, the promotion of economic cooperation has become a major factor in European foreign policy. In the Middle East, the EU is very actively engaged in economic development, making use of regional economic treaties such as those designed to promote a free trade area in the Mediterranean[7] and the trade agreement made by the EU with the Gulf Cooperation Council (GCC) states.[8] Before 1980, the role of human rights in the external relations of the EU was limited. A coordinated human rights policy became apparent only from the early 1990s.[9]

The principle that human rights should be a major factor in the EU's external relations was proclaimed in the Foreign Ministers' Declaration of 1986:

> Respect for human rights is one of the cornerstones of European cooperation... The protection of human rights is the legitimate and continuous duty of the world community and of nations individually. Expressions of concern about violations of such rights cannot be considered interference in the domestic affairs of a state.[10]

Later, the EU's 1991 Declaration on Human Rights took the emphasis on human rights as an element of foreign policy a step further:

> Tensions and conflicts arising from flagrant and systematic violations of human rights and fundamental freedoms in one country... are often a threat to international peace and security.[11]

Meanwhile, in order to promote human rights, the EU has consistently included clauses on human rights in its economic and cooperation agreements with the Third World.[12]

In the Resolution on Human Rights Democracy and Development of November 1991, clear lines of action are laid down:

> The Community and its member states will explicitly introduce the consideration of human rights as an element of their relations with developing countries; human rights clauses will be inserted in future cooperation agreements.[13]

The declaration stressed that the EU would give high priority to a positive approach through what it called an "open and constructive dialogue" to promote human rights.[14] However, it makes no mention of economic sanctions as an instrument to improve or promote human rights and in this lies the main difference between the EU and the United States in their respective policies. The main objectives of the EU in the field of human rights are as follows: the promotion of human rights as a key element in EU policy; respect for human rights as an important element in EU relations with the Third World; the subordination of economic cooperation and development aid to human rights; and the promotion of human rights in helping international security and improvement of economic cooperation.

Therefore, it may be concluded that the "critical dialogue" with Iran is closely linked to the development of a general European foreign policy based on human rights.

European institutions, foreign policy, and human rights

The European institutions most significant in relation to the formation and implementation of foreign policy are the Council of Ministers, the European Parliament, and the European Commission. In comparison with the other European institutions, the European Parliament is the body that has shown the most consistent concern with human rights. Since 1979, when the European Parliament was first elected, the issue of human rights has figured largely in its reports, resolutions, questions, and activities. Since 1992, when the European Single Act came into force, the European Parliament has withheld its approval of a number of agreements made by the EU with countries including Turkey, Syria, Morocco, and Israel on the grounds of its human rights concerns.[14] It is also true that the European Parliament has played a crucial role in shaping European public opinion on relations with Iran through its resolutions and reports and through the questions that it puts to the European Commission.

The European Commission, which is responsible for EU relations with the United Nations and other international bodies concerned with human rights, has regularly sponsored a resolution at the UN Human Rights Commission condemning Iran's human rights record. The Council of Ministers, as the core decision-making institution for the EU's international relations, has also demonstrated increased activity in the field of human rights. The Council initiated the "critical dialogue" and gave a mandate to the Troika, composed of the three member states that hold the current, preceding, and succeeding presidencies of the EU, to negotiate on human rights with Iran. During the last decade, the Troika has convened official meetings to discuss the "critical dialogue" twice a year, and the human rights issue has been under constant scrutiny both at these meetings and at other times.

European identity and human rights

Since 1980, the principles of human rights and democracy have rapidly become the central strands both of European integration and of the affirmation of Europe's identity throughout the world.[15] This affects critically the formulation of the CFSP and the application of the policy of "critical dialogue" with Iran. The "critical dialogue" translates into practise the human rights component of the EU's Iran policy, and represents the positive approach of promotion of human rights through dialogue. Of course, this constructive approach has weaknesses, not least because its adoption depends on the consensus of the EU member states.[16] On the other hand, the will to reach a consensus on policy toward Iran is substantial. Though the EU member states have not, for example, succeeded in formulating a common policy with regard to countries like China and Saudi Arabia, a consensus on Iran has been maintained, though a factor may be that Iran's human rights record is much better than the countries mentioned above. Another weakness lies in the fact that although the "critical dialogue," formulated on the level of common European policy, has shaped the EU's human rights strategy toward Iran, the bilateral relations of individual EU member states with Iran continued still to play an important role in determining overall European policy.

The "Critical Dialogue" between Iran and the EU

The historical background

The development of the policy of "critical dialogue" toward Iran began with the accession to office of President Hashemi Rafsanjani after the death of Imam Khomeini in 1989. Rafsanjani was seen as a "pragmatic" president and the council of ministers of the EU hoped that Iran would "normalize" its relations with the West.[17] The death of Imam Khomeini and the accession of Rafsanjani as president were perceived as marking the end of the revolutionary period and the start of a "second republic" in Iran.[18] In 1990, Iranian neutrality in the military operation against the Iraqi occupation of Kuwait was interpreted as a major step toward the onset of a "pragmatic era" in Iran's foreign policy.[19] During the Iraqi invasion of Kuwait, the EU lifted economic sanctions from Iran in October 1990 and welcomed the normalization of relations with Tehran.[20]

Another factor was the holding of Western hostages in Lebanon during the 1980s, which was a major obstacle to good relations between Iran and the EU. President Rafsanjani made a major political effort to resolve this problem, and the Western hostages were freed in Lebanon. This was welcomed in the West and helped to remove a major impediment to rapprochement.[21] Another issue was that in the period since the Islamic revolution in Iran, the UN Special Representative for Human Rights had not been able to visit the country. President Rafsanjani granted permission to the Special Representative to visit Iran, in a move which was interpreted by EU as a step toward respecting international human rights.[22]

Because of these developments, the EU began to take a more positive attitude toward Iran, and the European Commission, with the aim of strengthening the pragmatic wing in Iran, made a proposal to assist in President Rafsanjani's economic rehabilitation plans for the country. This policy was conceived with the aim of raising the level of the political and economic integration of Iran into the international community.[23] In the context of the enhancement of security and stability in the Persian Gulf, the EU supported the idea of the creation of a new system of regional security in the Persian Gulf, with the participation of Iran,[24] in order to safeguard Western Europe's oil supply.[25] At the meeting of German Foreign Minister Hans-Dietrich Genscher with President Rafsanjani in 1992, the principal issue under discussion was a proposal from Mr Genscher for a new system to ensure the peace, stability, and security of the Persian Gulf with the participation of both Iran and the GCC countries. President Rafsanjani gave an immediate welcome to the proposal.[26] Unfortunately, the plan failed because of American opposition and the existence of bilateral agreements between the United States and the GCC states.[25]

The optimism of EU over the potential establishment of a new system in the Gulf in which both Iran and the Arab states of the Gulf would be involved did not continue after the adoption of the policy of "critical dialogue." There were a number of significant developments that led the EU to opt for the policy of "critical dialogue." A leading issue was dissatisfaction with Iran's domestic human rights record, including the reaffirmation of the *fatwa* against Salman Rushdie and the apparent inability of President Rafsanjani to countermand the $1 million bounty for Rushdie's murder, offered by the private organization 15 Khordad Bonyad.[27] The assassinations of Iranian opposition figures in Germany and France were also an issue and gave rise to pressure from both these countries to take firmer action against Iran.[28] A separate development was the dispute between Iran and the United Arab Emirates over Abu Musa and the Tunb islands in the Gulf.[29] A further factor was Iran's opposition to the Arab–Israeli peace process and its support for Hamas, the Palestinian Islamic resistance movement. Hamas opened an office in Tehran in 1992 and in October a Hamas delegation from Palestine visited Iran.[30] Finally there were security issues, including allegations concerning Iran's alleged efforts to obtain nuclear weapons. The CIA reported that Iran would be able to construct nuclear weapons by the year 2000 even though Iran had been under regular inspection by the IAEA, which had found no evidence for this claim.[31] From the EU's point of view, these developments were contrary to the principles of human rights and international security, which were the objectives set up for the CFSP. The EU therefore halted the process of normalizing relations with Iran and set up the policy of "critical dialogue" in its stead.[32]

The statement of the "critical dialogue" policy that issued from the Edinburgh summit of December 1992 is as follows: "Given Iran's importance in the region, the European Council reaffirms its belief that a dialogue should be maintained with the Iranian government. This should be a critical dialogue, which reflects concern about Iranian behaviour and calls for improvement in a number of areas, particularly human rights, the death sentence pronounced by a *fatwa* of Ayatollah Khomeini against the author Salman Rushdie, which is contrary to international law, and terrorism. Improvement in these areas will be important in determining the extent to which closer relations and confidence can be developed."[33] Concern about "Iran's arms procurement" and the wish for a "constructive approach by Iran to the peace process" were also mentioned in the EU declaration.[34] But it is clear that the EU placed human rights first in its list of priorities in its relations with Iran.[35]

The stated reason why the EU did not choose the more conventional expression "political dialogue" for its policy toward Iran was that Iran did not meet the EU's preconditions for the holding of such a dialogue. Therefore, the unprecedented expression "critical dialogue" was chosen. European diplomats have informed the author that the policy of "critical dialogue" was aimed at strengthening the moderate position in Iran. This could certainly have been one of the EU's aims, but it nevertheless appears that the principal objective was to bring about changes in Iranian behavior by communicating European concerns.[36] Since the United Nations had not judged it appropriate to apply sanctions or take military steps against Iran, the civil procedure of "critical dialogue" chosen by the EU seemed an appropriate instrument. Further reasons why the policy of "critical dialogue" was an appropriate level to deal with Iran were the lack of any evidence of nuclear armaments in Iran, despite regular inspection by the IAEA[37] and the fact that Iran was a signatory to both the Universal Declaration of Human Rights and to the Covenant of Civil and Political Rights.[38] The first round of the official dialogue between Iran and the EU's troika of foreign ministers was held in Dublin in 1987, at a meeting where the author headed the Iranian delegation in his capacity as the General Director of the Western Europe division of the Iranian foreign ministry.

"Critical dialogue" in action

Diplomatic approaches and public declarations, together with regular meetings of the EU Troika with Iranian officials, were the three major means by which the policy of "critical dialogue" with Iran was implemented.[39] At the same time, the European Parliament tabled numerous human rights resolutions condemning Iran. (A list of resolutions and written questions is given in the bibliography.) It is the author's belief that these pressures were instrumental in Iran's decision to permit the United Nations Special Representative to visit Iran. However, the EU kept up its pressure after 1993, leading Iran to refuse to receive the Special Representative thereafter. In the case of the *fatwa*, the EU kept the issue on the agenda of the "critical dialogue," and asked for a written assurance from Iran not to pursue any attempt to kill Rushdie. The EU was successful in internationalizing the issue of the *fatwa* and facilitated meetings between Rushdie and officials of various countries that were seeking to pressure Iran.[40] Iran did not give a written assurance, but the President, the Speaker of Parliament, and the Foreign Minister gave verbal confirmation that Iran would not send agents to kill Rushdie.

On the issue of terrorism, little was done publicly, as the EU admitted it had no concrete evidence to support allegations that Iran directly sponsored terrorist acts. Meanwhile, Tehran issued a declaration deploring acts of terrorism irrespective of their perpetrators, even if such acts were committed by Hamas.[41] However, after the Mykonos verdict, alleging that the Iranian authorities had been directly involved in the assassination of the four Kurds in Berlin, the EU openly condemned Iran in a declaration issued by the European Council of Ministers on April 10, 1997.[42] The EU took the stand that there could be no progress in constructive relations with Iran while Tehran, as the EU statement claimed, flouted international norms and indulged in acts of terrorism.[43] It should be mentioned that Denmark in August 1996 had already independently withdrawn its support from the policy of "critical dialogue" with Iran, claiming that this policy "had showed no results," becoming the only European member state to break ranks with the EU's collective policy toward Iran.[44]

Western policy toward Iran

Germany, France, and Great Britain have traditionally taken the major part in determining EU policy toward Iran. After the Islamic revolution, Great Britain and France each had their particular problems with Iran, especially during the Iraq–Iran War of 1980–8. Germany, with its traditionally and historically good relationship with Iran, took a neutral position over the war. At a critical juncture for US–Iran relations, the war in fact represented an opportunity for Germany, and for this reason between 1978 and 1987, Bonn increased its share of the Iranian market from 21.9 percent to 26.2 percent, while regaining its position as the leading source of Iranian imports.[45] "Critical dialogue" served both as a basis for Germany's policy in particular, and simultaneously as a useful way to focus a common European approach toward Iran.[46]

Klaus Kinkel, foreign minister of Germany, presented in the German Federal Parliament in May 1996 a very specific formulation of the policy of critical dialogue. Mr Kinkel's demands on Tehran fell under a number of headings. He asked the Iranian government to take a positive attitude toward the Middle East peace process, and to extend recognition to what he pointed out was the legitimate Palestinian administration, the democratically elected Palestinian National Authority, together with a pledge to give its backing to cooperative and peaceful solutions to the problems of the Near East. He also called for Iran's implementation of the commitment it had made to the EU to abstain from sponsoring terrorism in the Middle East, both financially and logistically, and to make a concrete contribution to a peaceful solution in Lebanon by exerting a moderating influence upon Hezbollah. He asked for improvements in the human rights situation within Iran, and especially for full freedom of the press, speech, and religious observance, and for Iran's effective compliance with the Chemical Weapons Convention. And finally he called for an end to all Iranian intelligence activities that might threaten Iranians living abroad.[47]

It is the author's belief, founded on his seven years experience of dialogue with German officials in the period from 1990 to 1997, that for Germany "critical dialogue" was always mainly concerned with two issues: the peace process on the hand, and human rights on the other. During the author's term as ambassador alone, three joint German–Iranian human rights seminars took place, with the German authorities urging the participants to move from their rather abstract deliberations to concrete judicial and legal questions, such as were discussed in the previous seminar, in November 1994.[48] The Rushdie issue also played its part. During Foreign Minister Velayati's trip to Germany in June 1992, the PEN Club of Germany made representations to the German government opposing closer economic and cultural cooperation between Iran and Germany, on the grounds of the *fatwa*, which embodied a sentence of death on the British writer. The PEN club statement said that "without the lifting of the *fatwa* passed by the Islamic funda-mentalists against Rushdie, no improvement in Bonn–Tehran relations should take place." Moreover, the central government must present its position regarding the *fatwa* in an unequivocal and direct manner. The statement went on to imply that were the German government to remain silent on the issue, there would be reason to question its commitment to the freedom of speech.[49]

After German reunification, Salman Rushdie paid a number of visits to Germany, and on each occasion his case in particular and the issue of human rights in relation to Iran in general were featured prominently in the German media. During a visit to Germany in December 1993, Rushdie said in Cologne, "The key to the revocation of my death sentence is in the hands of Germany."[50] He saw his meeting with the German Foreign Minister Klaus Kinkel on December 9, when he explained his case to the governments of the United States and Europe, as the culmination of a struggle on his part, which had begun two years before. The meeting was held in private, and the German police took care to ensure that it did not attract unwanted public attention. After the meeting, Rushdie said, "I hope to see what I have been promised at this meeting come to fruition. No government in the world, including the Islamic governments, has supported the *fatwa* on my life. As President Clinton has stated, we can compel Tehran to revoke the decree only through international economic sanctions. Mr. Clinton has referred to withholding credit and boycotting trade to Iran. But without the participation of Bonn, international action would have no effect. Germany must take the first step, since no country in the world has such a close relationship with Tehran."[50]

In a news conference arranged by the German writer Günther Walraf, who was Rushdie's host in Germany, Rushdie said his meeting with Kinkel was a positive sign. However, he remained very dissatisfied with the position taken up by Bonn. Kinkel commented that the issue had a bearing on the intractable mutual hostility between Iran and Israel. Rushdie commented that Chancellor Kohl had been informed that he was to meet Mr Kinkel, and for his part he expected the Chancellor to refrain from any dealings with what he referred to as "the crimi-nals." The author repeatedly heard the German government's protests against the *fatwa*, whenever he was summoned as ambassador by the German Foreign Ministry during this period, and responded by reminding the German authorities of Iran's criticism of the Western support for Salman Rushdie, regarded by Iran as an apostate, while pointing out that the insistence of the West on backing him was an insult to over one billion Muslims throughout the world. In a meeting in January 1992 with the Director General for political affairs of the German Foreign Ministry, Reiner Schlagenweit, the author laid the blame for the crisis on the European countries, which had fanned the flames of controversy by inviting Rushdie, by conducting interviews with him, and by offering him various expressions of sup-port. As Iran's ambassador in Germany, it was the author's duty to inform Mr Schlagenweit that so long as the West supports such an insult to Islam, to Muslims, and to those things that they regard as sacrosanct, it must expect direct and forceful antagonism in return from the leaders of the Islamic World. Nevertheless, the author constantly emphasized Iran's view that the government of the Islamic Republic considered itself obliged to abide by international laws and regulations and by the principle of noninterference in the internal affairs of other countries.[51]

To clarify the position of Iran on this issue, on the occasion of the Troika meeting with Rushdie while Germany held the rotating presidency of the EU in September 1994, the author wrote a letter to Klaus Kinkel, the foreign minister of Germany, expressing Iran's view as follows: "It is well known to the EU that in his book, Salman Rushdie subjected the sanctities of Islam and the Muslims of the world to the ugliest insults, and infringed the rights of more than one billion Muslims, regardless of the fact that respect for cultural and religious values and those things held sacred by nations are among the most vital principles of human rights in today's world. Rushdie's action is a blatant violation of the rights of hundreds of millions of world Muslims. The invitation extended to Rushdie by the foreign ministers of the EU is in reality not so much an expression of solidarity with Rushdie as an endorsement of his insult to Islam and a step by Europe in the direction of hostility towards the Muslim population of the world. The Organization of the Islamic Conference has supported Imam Khomeini's *fatwa*, while dozens of law-abiding Muslims in India and Pakistan have lost their lives on account of the publication of the book, 'The Satanic Verses.' It is a matter of utmost regret to us that we do not perceive any real signals from Europe that it seeks peaceful coexistence and a proper understanding between the worlds of Islam and Christianity. On the contrary, while in one European country, which claims to be civilized, a Muslim girl is deprived of the freedom to wear her religious attire of choice, and does not have the right to enter school; while in another country, during the night the homes of Muslims, who are considered to be aliens, are set on fire, and lives are lost; and while in the heart of Europe, tens of thousands of Muslims in Bosnia-Herzegovina are massacred and dragged through blood and dirt; at the same time Europe's repeated invitations to Rushdie and the lack of condemnation of his anti-Islamic act severely damage the image of Europe in Islamic countries."[52]

Further developments that had a notably negative effect on the progress of relations between Iran and Germany came when the ministers of culture of the individual German states expressed their opposition to the drafting of a cultural agreement between Germany and Iran. Legally, no such agreement could be made by the Federal Government without the approval of the country's 16 individual states, but at a conference of the culture ministers of Germany's 16 states in Munich in May 1994, the ministers expressed the opposition of Germany's state governments to the signature of the agreement, already postponed since 1988. The ministers gave as the reason for their veto of the proposed cultural agreement with Iran the continued violation of human rights in Iran and the failure to revoke of the *fatwa* on Rushdie.[53] Ms Helga Tropel, the minister of culture in the state of Bremen and a representative of the Green Party in the Bremen state parliament, criticized the plan for the establishment of a German language institute in Tehran and the reestablishment of the German Archaeological Institute, which had been approved by the German Foreign Ministry during Mr Vaezi's visit to Bonn the previous March. She complained that she and other state ministers of culture had heard the news of the agreement made by Bonn with Tehran through the media, without prior consultation, adding that, "in view of the government of Iran's support of 'cultural savagery' in that country, the state culture ministers of Germany are opposed to any kind of formal cultural relations between Bonn and Tehran."[53]

German politicians and the German media also displayed an exceptional sensitivity to the situation of writers in Iran. Whenever any Iranian writer or publication faced difficulties, the issue was taken up by politicians and publicized by the German media. For example, *Frankfurter Allgemeine* published the following report about the case of Abbas Ma'roofi: "The severe sentence issued against Abbas Ma'roofi in January has been confirmed without appeal. This Iranian writer has been sentenced to six months' imprisonment, 20 lashes, and has been banned from publishing for two years. Ma'roofi's publication *Gardoon* has been banned, for having in recent years published articles in which the values of the Islamic Revolution and its founder Imam Khomeini have been subjected to derision."[54] *Frankfurter Allgemeine* went on to say that though the verdict on Mr Ma'roofi, who was currently the holder of a scholarship from the German state of Nordrhein-Westfalen, and was living at a student residence in Cologne, had resulted in international protest, Ma'roofi had nevertheless been summoned to present himself to the Iranian authorities so that his sentence could be carried out. Mr Ma'roofi's lawyers, the paper said, had advised him under no circumstances to return to Iran and Ma'roofi himself drew attention to what he said was the arbitrary fashion in which the law was applied in Iran. The paper also claimed, "The government of Iran would resort to any measure in order to intimidate Ma'roofi and other intellectuals and to ostracize them from the country."

In another example of the German media concern with issues concerned with cultural freedom, the newspaper *Frankfurter Rundschau* commented on a prison sentence passed on an Iranian cartoonist Manouchehr Karimzadeh, sentenced to ten years imprisonment for having drawn a caricature of Imam Khomeini. The newspaper reported that *Farda*, the monthly journal that published the caricature, was shut down by the Iranian Ministry of Culture and the Islamic Guidance under the provisions of Article 27 of the Free Press Law, which stipulated the closure of any publication whose publishing material was hostile to high-ranking religious dignitaries.

I believe that "critical dialogue" was conceived as a way of reconciling German policy toward Iran with the concerns of the German public, and that the agenda of "critical dialogue" inaugurated by Foreign Minister Kinkel was enunciated to satisfy the opposition parties in the German Federal Parliament, and also to fend off the pressures from Washington, London, and Tel Aviv, which have been specified in detail in previous chapters. Meanwhile, the EU approach was concerned exclusively with the political relationship between Brussels and Tehran, and never affected Germany's economic relations with Iran.

In particular, Germany took the lead in rescheduling Iranian foreign debts after the United States blocked rescheduling arrangements within the Paris Club, thus safeguarding Iran from severe financial problems.[55] It is widely held that the principal reason for Germany opting for a more cooperative approach toward Iran was Bonn's own economic interest. But, in the author's view, the particular engagement of Germany had deeper institutional, ideological, and historical roots. It was true that after the Islamic revolution of 1979, due to American pressure, Germany had agreed to implement very tight controls on its exports to Iran, especially on items that could be used for the development and production of weapons of mass destruction or for other military purposes.[56] Nevertheless, Germany had drawn two major lessons from the end of the Cold War and German reunification. These were, first, that the end of that conflict was more a result of its Ostpolitik, a policy of contact and reconciliation, than of containment and hard-line policy; and second, that economic embargoes are not effective, in the end only bringing suffering to the civilian population of the country to which they are applied. Germany applied these lessons to its relations with Iran.

Meanwhile it can be argued that while economic interests certainly played an important role in Germany's relationship with Iran, they were not paramount, and cannot fully account for why Germany opted for a policy that attracted so much criticism from the United States. The figures tend to confirm this view. From DM 8 billion in 1992, German exports to Iran fell to 2.34 billion in 1995 and 2.2 billion in 1996.[57] Imports from Iran have been in general between DM 1 billion and 1.5 billion. In Germany's foreign trade, Iran ranks roughly forty-fifth in exports and forty-ninth in imports. About 15 percent of Iranian imports came from Germany. Iranian investment in Germany was about DM 1.2 billion, while German investment in Iran was less than DM 200 million.

It must also be pointed out that the consensus within Germany in favor of good relations with Iran did not cover the full spectrum of relations established by the German government, and in particular that the close relationship established with the Iranian Ministry of Information did not meet with universal approval. However, broadly speaking, the opposition parties, the SPD and the Greens, were in favor of maintaining relations with Iran, in spite of their differences with the ruling parties, the CDU, the CSU, and the FDP, over the version of the "critical dialogue" favored by the government. In the seven years during which the author was Iranian ambassador in Bonn, from 1990 to 1997, he held regular meetings with senior members of both opposition parties, and especially the SPD, who emphasized the importance of the relationship with Iran and expressed their opposition to breaking off diplomatic relations.[58]

Yet the debate in the German Federal Parliament on German policy toward Iran after the Mykonos verdict showed a broad bipartisan sentiment that critical dialogue had failed. A parliamentary majority supported a move to ask the government to review relations with Iran and to create a new policy in conjunction with other member states of the EU. The Federal parliament supported the maintenance of relations with Iran while keeping them at a minimum level in the absence of a change of behavior on the part of Iran (see Chapter 5). After the pronouncement of the verdict on April 10, 1997, Germany tried hard to maintain solidarity between all the member states of the EU, and to arrive at a common programme of action, with the result that on the same day as the German government announced its own measures against Iran, the EU presidency adopted the same measures as the common position of all EU member states (see Chapter 7).

The crisis seemed unlikely to last more than three months and the EU decided in favor of a rapid return to normal relations. However, Iran complicated the EU's position by making it clear that the German ambassador would not be welcomed to return to Tehran. The EU's policy of insisting that Iran must treat all its member states equally came under severe strain and was close to breaking down until France made a proposal to resolve the difficulty. This was that the German ambassador would return later than the other ambassadors, as Tehran wanted, but would be accompanied by his French colleague whose return would also be delayed so that the German ambassador would not be alone when he took up his post. This was a formula that Germany was obliged to accept in order to maintain EU solidarity. Even after the return of all the ambassadors, however, the EU had no new policy to replace the now defunct "critical dialogue." In Iran, the return of the European ambassadors was seen as a victory over the American policy of isolation, while the later return of the German ambassador was viewed as a demonstration to Germany of Tehran's disapproval of the Mykonos verdict.[59] This was widely publicized in Iran, and was also a point stressed by the Leader of Iran, Ayatollah Khamenei, in his private meetings with the Iranian ambassadors in Europe.[60]

After the return of the EU ambassadors to Tehran, however, Germany was henceforth relegated by the Iranians to the position of an ordinary country, rather than as one with which, as had hitherto been the case, Iran had a special relationship.[61] In the circumstances, France made a bid to derive benefit from the curtailment of relations between Tehran and Bonn, and attempted to expand its trade relations with Iran. The French Total company signed a $2 billion contract with Iran to exploit the South Pars Gas Field in the Persian Gulf, after the blocking by the American administration of a bid from Conoco.[62] The German government was obliged to maintain its silence on the French deal in order to avoid the situation in which Germany would be seen as favoring either Paris or Washington. Other European countries, such as Italy and Spain, also made efforts to upgrade their relations with Iran and thus to take advantage of the stormy situation between Tehran and Bonn.[63]

United States policy toward Iran

After the 1979 revolution in Iran, relations between Iran and the United States were completely transformed. Popular chants in Iran advocating "Death to America" came second only to the religious slogan "God is great."[64] The revolution itself and the hostage crisis that followed it were the determining factors in this new and antagonistic relationship.

The hostage crisis, which erupted in November 1979, was a decisive turning point. After the establishment of the Islamic government in Iran by Imam Khomeini, the US Embassy was seized by a group of student protesters, in retaliation for the decision by the administration of President Carter to allow the former Shah of Iran to enter the United States for medical treatment. The capture of the American hostages and the 444 days of their captivity set the tone for subsequent relations between Washington and Tehran. The United States initiated a comprehensive sanctions program against Iran, including an embargo against all oil imports from Iran, the freezing of all Iranian assets in American banks, and restrictions on the shipment of military spare parts. The population of each country came to perceive the other in a strongly negative way, partially at least because of the extensive television coverage of the plight of the captives and of street protests in Iran against the United States.

Another decisive moment came in September 1980, when the United States chose to support the Iraqi leader President Saddam Hussein in Iraq's aggression against Iran. The Lebanese conflict was a source of further antagonism, when after the bombing of the US Marine base in Beirut in October 1983 with substantial loss of life, the United States accused Iran of involvement. Even after the Iraqi chemical bombardment of Iranian soldiers, and of their own citizens in Iraqi Kurdistan, the American administration continued to tighten its sanctions on trade with Iran.

Three major issues led to the prolongation of the American embargo against Iran: first, the holding of American hostages in Lebanon, and perceptions in the United States regarding Iranian involvement; second, Tehran's position regarding the peace process between Israel and the Arabs; and third, American perceptions regarding Iranian efforts to "export" its revolutionary ideology to surrounding states. Imam Khomeini was the central figure in the dispute: he continued until his death in 1989 to be seen in Washington as the key adversary of the United States, and was the object of widespread popular adulation in Iran.

However, an opportunity for change in relations between Iran and the United States appeared when the US administration asked Iran to use its influence with the Shiite leaders in Lebanon to work for the release of the American and other Western hostages. Two successive American presidents, President Reagan and President Bush, at this point proposed an exchange of goodwill, in other words, Iran's help in obtaining the release of hostages would lead to the mitigation of Washington's hostility toward Tehran. During the period from 1987 to 1989, in which all the Western hostages in Lebanon were freed, Mr Vaezi, Deputy Foreign Minister for Europe and America, and the author, as General Director for Western Europe in the Iranian Foreign Ministry, were given the responsibility for managing the process under the supervision of Dr Velayati, the then Foreign Minister, and of President Rafsanjani, who took the crucial decisions. This group of Iranian officials received messages from the political leaders and foreign ministers of many countries conveying on behalf of the United States the message that Iran's help in obtaining the release of the American hostages would be reciprocated by substantial concessions on the part of the United States.

It was President Rafsanjani's intention to make use of this opportunity to improve relations between Iran and the United States, and in the author's frequent private discussions with him, there was no doubt that he was working toward the resumption of diplomatic relations between Tehran and Washington. In the event, however, though all the Americans and Westerners held in Beirut were released, the US administration showed no particular goodwill toward Iran; on the contrary, it engaged in further hostile actions. The treatment of Iran by the United States in connection with the Americans held in Lebanon was undoubtedly the most important contributing factor to President Rafsanjani's failure to restore relations. The author recalls that, in a meeting with President Rafsanjani in early 1990, he described the position that had arisen as follows: "any plan for the restoration of Iran–US relations in under a decade would fail, because of America's mishandling of the unique situation which arose from the freeing of the American hostages in Lebanon."

From 1989 to 1997, therefore, the relationship between the United States and Iran did not exhibit any significant change. Over the 1990s, the objectives of American sanctions varied. During the initial stages of the sanctions program, trade controls were imposed on Iran. In 1995, the American Congress passed new laws, further strengthening the sanctions against Iran. In addition, the Iran–Libya Sanctions Act, passed in 1996, targeted non-American companies wishing to do business in Iran. According to reports in the press, three features of Iranian policy were in particular responsible for the new measures taken against Iran. These were, first, Iran's efforts to derail the Israeli–Arab peace process; second, Iran's attempts to acquire weapons of mass destruction; and third, Iran's alleged support for state-sponsored extraterritorial "terrorist" activity.

President Khatami's landslide victory in the Iranian presidential election of 1997 encouraged Americans to believe that Iran was about to take a new direction in domestic and foreign policy. But after some four years of Khatami's presidency had passed, there was still no major change in the relationship between the United States and Iran. This has been enough to suggest that there will be very little change in relations between the United States and Iran in the near future. The two sides remain very far apart in their ideas regarding what constitutes appropriate political behavior in both the domestic and the international arenas. In the late 1990s, there was a certain amount of movement on both sides, but gestures that were made were not of sufficient significance to achieve results. Furthermore, any change on the part of Iran seemed to have been the result of internal factors rather than of any efforts by the United States. The economic sanctions on Iran imposed by the United States have in reality had very little effect on Iranian policy, and this situation appeared set to continue.

This statement reflected the balance of forces inside both countries. For political decision makers in Iran, the cost of the sanctions was seen to be insufficient to justify change, in view of the importance placed by Tehran on maintaining its own position, together with the role of the Islamic revolution in the wider Islamic sphere, and its prestige in the Third World. The American policy of sanctions on Iran was doomed to failure from the start, because the demands made on Iran by the United States were too great. The American demands struck at fundamental philosophical values and asked Iranians to behave in a manner contrary to their deeply held religious and ideological beliefs. Meanwhile, even though the sanctions were ineffective in bringing about changes in Iran, there was, at least during President Khatami's first term, insufficient opposition to the sanctions within the United States itself to result in their being lifted. Though the sanctions imposed substantial economic costs on American companies, political leaders in the United States continued to be unconcerned.

A decade after Iran's Islamic revolution, therefore, President Rafsanjani's efforts to release the American hostages in Lebanon came as the first real opportunity by which the United States could have taken advantage to improve relations, an opportunity that was lost. In the late 1990s, another decade later, the new administration in Iran offered a second opportunity to the United States. In addition, the new potential for oil production in the Caucasus had increased the economic incentive to remove sanctions. But sanctions can be removed only through a deft political strategy on the part of those who oppose them, the cornerstone of which must be the creative development of appropriate linkages, and at this stage, it was unclear that there was any faction within the Untied States that had the will or capacity to act. Issues that might be linked to a lightening of sanctions could include assistance with American policy toward Iraq, the fate of Iranian assets in the United States, and the enhanced production and export of oil from the Caucasus. But the more probable outcome at the turn of the millennium seemed to be the maintenance of the status quo, at least in the short term, and perhaps for longer.

America's critique of the policy of "Critical Dialogue"

The policy of the United States toward Iran, that of "dual containment," was founded on a theory of the balance of power in the Persian Gulf. Iran was considered by Washington as a country hostile to American interests in the region and the core objective of the policy was to secure American hegemony in the Gulf by balancing the power of other interested parties against each other. For the Americans, human rights played no major role in formulating their policy of the "active containment" of Iran. In the words of the American official Martin Indyk "When we assess Iranian attentions and capabilities, we see a dangerous combination for Western interests... It's the foremost state sponsor of terrorism and assassination across the globe... We will pursue the effort of active containment unilaterally, maintaining the counter-terrorism sanctions... to encourage a change in Iranian behaviour."[65]

From the standpoint of either Iran or the EU, the American position offered no alternative to the European policy of "critical dialogue." The US Secretary of State Warren Christopher attempted, in June 1993, to persuade the EU's foreign ministers of the wisdom of the American policy of containment, but his efforts were unsuccessful because the EU ministers rejected his proposals for a trade embargo.[66] After the European rejection, the United States implemented unilateral economic sanctions against Iran,[67] causing a slowdown in Iranian economy[68] and increasing the EU's fears about expanding its economic relations with Iran.[69]

Later, Senator Alfonso d'Amato proposed a bill to the US Senate to sanction non-American companies investing in the Iranian oil industry, which was implemented as the Iran and Libya Sanctions Act (ILSA) of 1996.[70] The bill claimed that investment by the West in the oil industry of a so-called "rogue state" like Iran would only facilitate what he called "Iran's continuing aggression," and would threaten the national security and foreign policy of the United States.[71] The EU very strongly opposed the bill, and in particular its arrogation of extraterritorial powers, as a contradiction of international law.[72] In the EU's view, such apparently "illegal"[73] sanctions against Iran provided no alternative to the "critical dialogue," especially since the approach favored by the EU took seriously Iran's domestic situation and rejected the logic of collectively punishing Iran as a state.[74]

Warren Christopher confirmed that the ultimate goal of America's policy was to weaken and destabilize the Iranian government until its final overthrow[75] when he stated in January 1995 that "we must isolate Iraq and Iran until there is a change in their government."[76] A year later, the US Congress passed a bill authorizing the CIA to implement a programme to "change the nature of the government of Iran" and allocated a fund of $18 million for the purpose.[77] On the other hand, authoritative American analysts like the former National Security Advisers Zbigniew Brzezinski, Brent Scowcroft, and ex-Ambassador Richard Murphy later launched a strong critique of White House policy, arguing that the dual containment policy had failed as it threatened real American interests in the Persian Gulf.[78] The main points of the critique were that the Iranian military threat had been exaggerated;[79] keeping military installations in the Persian Gulf to support the containment policy had been too expensive;[80] and that the economic sanctions had in any case not been successful.[81] These well-informed observers believed that the US government should enter into what they called a "productive dialogue" with Iran,[82] and should not hinder American companies wishing to trade with Iran.[83] Another analyst, Graham Fuller, proposed a multilateral policy with an emphasis on regional security cooperation, arms control, and human rights, and for an end to the policy of "balance of power."[84]

Among the EU's institutions, the European Parliament was the main source of criticism of Iran. From 1989 onwards, nine resolutions were tabled at the European Parliament condemning human rights violations in Iran, together with three resolutions condemning Iran's call for the death sentence on the author Salman Rushdie, and countless written questions criticizing the dialogue policy (see the resolutions given in the bibliography). The European Parliament also held many debates in which views critical of Iran were aired.[85] In the resolutions that were considered, the Parliament heard accusations against Iran, which specified a number of transgressions against international standards of human rights, including the gross and systematic violation of human rights; the perpetration of what was described as "state terrorism," especially in the form of assassinations of opposition figures abroad; the *fatwa* against Salman Rushdie; the repression of religious minorities such as the Bahai Community; discrimination against women; and disregard for freedom of religion and expression.[86]

In May 1989, the European Parliament called on all the member states of the European Community (as the EU was then designated) as well as the European Community itself, to suspend their relations with Iran until it had dissociated itself from the encouragement of international terrorism.[87] Yet five months later, the

European Council of Ministers took steps to normalize its relationship with Iran. This was an illustration of the discrepancy between the European Parliament's position and the consensus of the policies of the governments of member states as expressed through the Council of Ministers. After the "Mykonos trial," the European Parliament asked the Council to put a definitive end to the critical dialogue.[88]

Meanwhile the Iranian opposition in exile had generally rejected the critical dialogue, lobbying widely among American and European politicians for tough sanctions against Iran. The military organization Mujahedin-e Khalq (MKO) represented politically by the National Council of Resistance (NCR) was the most active among the opposition groups outside the country. Even other groups such as the Foundation for Democracy in Iran, which had distanced itself from the NCR, joined in the criticism of the EU for its inconsistent policy toward Iran, while demanding the imposition of sanctions.[89] However, the Danish Parliament was the only European legislature that offered any support to these groups, with a motion passed in 1996. The EU itself maintained its skepticism in its assessment of the value of the claims of the opposition groups, while the German government actually went as far as outlawing the NCR.[90] Clearly, for the EU and its member states, there was the problem of assessing the legitimacy of the various Iranian opposition groups outside Iran, which led to a cautious approach. In the absence of an opposition party within Iran, the EU was placed in the position of offering support to the alleged "moderates" inside Iran.[91] For all these reasons, the EU was able to resist for almost a decade the weighty objections against its policy of "critical dialogue."

An evaluation of the policy of "critical dialogue"

Though "critical dialogue" was in practise a matter of persuasive diplomacy, which could not have been expected to produce immediate or dramatic results, it can nevertheless be argued that against all the odds the policy did bring about some changes in Iran's behavior. The core issues of the dialogue were human rights, the *fatwa* against Salman Rushdie, terrorism, Iran's opposition to the peace process, and the acquisition of weapons of mass destruction. The first question must be whether or not the policy had any impact on Iran's domestic human rights situation. From 1992 to April 1996, Iran refused to let the United Nations Special Representative for Human rights (UNSR) visit Iran despite massive criticism from the EU. However, Iran began slowly to set up institutions reflecting at least awareness that the unremitting international criticism needed to be addressed. As a result, in May 1995, the "Islamic Human Rights Commission (IHRC)" was founded.[92] The Iranian Parliament, for its part, set up a "Committee on Human Rights," while the Foreign Ministry established a "department of human rights."[93] Both the UNSR and the German government welcomed the establishment of new human rights institutions as evidence of "tangible" progress.[94]

Iran finally allowed the UNSR, Professor Maurice Copthorne, to visit the country in February 1996, but refused to permit him a second visit in December the same year, arguing that his report had been abused by "certain countries" in order to "reinforce their prejudgment and predrawn conclusions" against Iran.[95] Despite this setback, Professor Copthorne's second report in February 1997 contained evidence of major changes in Iran on human rights issues, including the status of women, and welcome developments in the increasingly open and controversial political debates then taking place both among the general public and in the Iranian press.[96]

Observed improvements in the realm of human rights were, however, ambiguous. Some of the changes, like the establishment of new institutions, could be considered a direct consequence of the European policy of critical dialogue, but other changes, including most of the positive developments reflected in the UNSR's report of February 1997, were related more to the evolution of the internal situation within the country. On the other hand, changes in Iran's foreign policy have been more visible and significant. In the regional sphere, Iran showed a growing readiness for good relations and for regional cooperation with the Central Asian republics and with the Persian Gulf littoral states.[97] Iran played an active role in the UN-sponsored negotiations for a peace agreement in Afghanistan, and Iran's contribution was given official appreciation by the United Nations (UN Reports on Afghanistan).

During this period, Iran refrained from actions that might be interpreted as threatening security and stability in the Persian Gulf, and in contrast made a number of proposals seeking a rapprochement with the GCC states.[98] Even in the thorny case of the dispute concerning sovereignty over the island of Abu Musa, Iran took part in a number of efforts toward the negotiation of a peaceful settlement, although not much progress was made.[99] Nevertheless, while other countries including the GCC states appeared to perceive the threat from Iran as lessening, the United States continued to emphasize Iran's threatening military policy and its potential nuclear capabilities. Even though Iran signed the relevant conventions on chemical and nuclear weapons, it was regarded by the United States as a continuing threat to regional security.[100]

As regards the Middle East peace process, Iran moderated the inflexibility of its opposition to any peace agreement with Israel and scaled down its support for Palestinian resistance movements, issuing a formal statement that it would not take any action to hinder negotiations between Palestine and Israel.[101] As explained above, a notable problem did arise in relations between Iran and Germany when President Rafsanjani characterized the assassination of the late Israeli prime minister Yitzhak Rabin as "the realization of God's promise to take revenge,"[102] and in an unprecedented move the German Parliament passed a motion condemning these words while calling on the government to cancel an invitation to Iran's Foreign Minister Dr Velayati[103] who had been invited to an Islamic conference in Bonn. The outcome was, as has been explained, that the German Foreign Minister Klaus Kinkel, rather than humiliating Dr Velayati by withdrawing his invitation, called off the whole conference, which was also a major setback for relations between Germany and Iran.[104]

On the issue of terrorism, it can be argued that the greatest inconsistency with regard to the "critical dialogue" was the European reaction to the assassination of members of the Iranian opposition abroad. In France, legal proceedings arising from the murder of the former Iranian Prime Minister Shahpour Bakhtiar were dropped due to lack of evidence. In April 1997, on the other hand, the court in Berlin hearing the case of the men accused of the murder of the four Kurdish opposition leaders in the Mykonos Restaurant in Berlin in September 1991 ruled unexpectedly that Iran's spiritual leader, as well as the country's President, the Foreign Minister, and the Intelligence Minister, had directly ordered the killings.[105] Only with the upheaval resulting from the verdict in this case in 1997 was the "critical dialogue" finally suspended, with the recall of European ambassadors from Iran. This opened the door to internal and external critics of European policy who argued that the EU had previously failed to take the Iranian government's alleged terrorist activities sufficiently seriously.

A key question concerns the impact of the critical dialogue on trade relations between Iran and Europe. Germany was Iran's main trading partner over the two decades that followed the Islamic revolution. After the cease-fire between Iran and Iraq, France and Germany emerged as strong competitors for the newly reopened Iranian market. The EU–Iran trade record must be viewed not only in the light of American pressure against trade with Iran, but also in the light of measures taken by Tehran to curb imports in reaction to falling oil prices, and taking into account Iran's generally weak economic performance. To look at the German case, German exports to Iran were reduced by one-fourth between 1992 and 1996, while imports from Iran remained at a consistently low level.[106] A major factor was that European firms were not permitted to deliver any armaments to Iran, while American pressure also resulted in a reduction in the export to Iran of the so-called dual-use products, civilian goods that could be put to military use.[107] The German firm Siemens eventually yielded to American insistence and definitively cancelled its participation in the nuclear plant at Bushehr.[108]

In 1995, however, Germany offered DM 150 million in credit guarantees under the Hermes programme with the aim of revitalizing its economic relations with Iran.[109] Although these credit guarantees were relatively small in volume, they nevertheless came under serious criticism from the American administration and the Israeli government. The French firm Total signed an agreement with Iran after US President Clinton decided to veto an agreement by the American-based firm Conoco to invest $1 billion in oil and gas fields in the Persian Gulf.[110] In February 1997, the chief of Iran's Central Bank revealed that the European countries, led by Germany, had helped Iran to reschedule about $22 billion in debts, and that the EU and Japan had offered Iran more than $5 billion in credit.[111] Thus, it can be concluded that the critical dialogue policy and the human rights issue did not bring about a significant diminution in trade between the EU and Iran. Essentially, the reason for this was that the economic interests of France and Germany exercized a stronger influence than the much discussed concern over human rights, and that EU consistently opposed the imposition of actual embargoes except where these were explicitly endorsed by the United Nations.[112]

Period of comprehensive and constructive dialogues

The period of critical dialogues did not last long. The election of Mr Khatami as Iran's president, which was welcomed by the Western countries and the EU, in addition to Europe's opposition to the D'Amato Act and the extraterritorial impact of secondary sanctions, promoted Iran–Europe talks to the level of compressive dialogue. During those talks much emphasis was put on human rights. EU member states that previously paid special attention to such issues as energy, fighting illicit drugs, refugees, environment, disarmament, and terrorism, turned to human rights as one of the most determining axes of the Union's foreign policy. European countries also made expansion of relations with Iran conditional on the situation of human rights in the country and respect for democracy. President Khatami, also, put special emphasis on the issue of human rights throughout his presidential term.[113] Since Iran believed in dialogue as the most effective means of interaction with the world, it not only bolstered its democratic and human rights infrastructures, but also established effective communication with international organizations with regard to human rights. An example was the initiation of human rights dialogue with the EU, which was carried out through four roundtables.[114]

Early efforts to establish the EU–Iran human rights dialogue were made under Demark as rotational chairman of the EU. At that time, Iran's relations with the EU had greatly improved. The two sides decided to negotiate a political cooperation agreement. They also decided to establish an official human rights discourse as a major component of enhanced relations. At Denmark's initiative, the EU's expert delegation visited Iran from September 30, 2002 to October 2, 2002. As put by Lars Faaborg Andersen, head of the Danish Department for the Middle East, North Africa, and Latin America, the visit aimed at creating a human rights discourse between EU and Iran. His report also recommended that the talks should be directed by the government's representatives, but should also include representatives of the civil society, human rights institutions, courts, and university lecturers.[115]

In line with those recommendations, the EU's council of ministers decided on October 21–22, 2002, to initiate human rights discourse with Iran. The first round of Iran–EU talks started on Iran's invitation in Tehran on December 15–16, 2002. Both sides' delegations comprised 15 members, including experts, representatives of the civil society, and state officials.

The Iranian delegates included the foreign ministry's Director General for International Legal Affairs Mehdi Danesh Yazdi; as well as a high-ranking judge from the Supreme Court; head of the international studies department of Tehran University; professors of Tehran and Shahid Beheshti universities; head of judiciary's research department; head of Human Rights and Women Department of the Iranian foreign ministry; the president's advisor and the head of the Constitution Supervisory Board; secretary of the IHRC; director of international relations of the Organization for Defending Victims of Violence (ODVV), which is a nongovernmental organization; deputy interior minister; head of the Society for Supporting Women's Rights; and some other related figures.

The EU was represented by Mr Andersen from the Danish foreign ministry; the official in charge of Iran–EU human rights roundtable and executive director of the Danish Institute for Human Rights (DIHR), Morten Kjaerum; member of the Europe and Luxemburg committee for the prohibition of torture; Danish human rights dialogue coordinator; secretary of the Italian Human Rights Commission; representative of the International Rehabilitation Council for Torture Victims (IRCT); instructors from Britain's Bristol University, Lisbon University of Portugal, Athens University, Germany's Police Academy, and the French Rene University; the ambassadors of Denmark and Greece in Tehran; the deputy director of Copenhagen's Human Rights Institute; Brussels' human rights and democratization expert; the Dutch Human Rights Institute; the deputy chairman of the Human Rights Federation; the representative of International Human Rights Federation; and the representative of German Human Rights Institute.

The roundtable was held on two days. The first day's speeches were focused on discrimination while torture was the main topic of the second day. Major criticism of Iran by the EU's representatives included the following points.

1. Discrimination

    Most of EU's criticism was related to discrimination against women such as:

    a. The issue of female inheritance.
    b. Female testimony at court.
    c. Blood money for women.
    d. Judgment by women (women cannot become judges in Iran).
    e. Obligation of hijab for religious minorities.
    f. Discrimination against religious minorities, especially Bahaeis.

2. Torture

    a. Physical punishment in Iran.
    b. Public punishment.

Both sides discussed those issues and answered questions. Discussions led to the following conclusions:

1. Importance of education in promoting human rights.
2. Readiness of the European delegation to train Iran's prison officers.
3. Establish a working group to follow up the results of negotiations and coordinate further talks.
4. Request to Iran to join the Convention on the Elimination of All Forms of Discrimination against Women.
5. Lauding Iran's agreement to receive UN special envoys, including UN special envoy on violence against women, who would visit Iran in April 2003.
6. It was decided that the dialogue between Iran and the EU should continue in early 2003 after Greece took over rotational chairmanship of the EU from Denmark. The EU statement in Tehran (which was drawn up without

cooperation from nongovernmental organizations) noted that the Union would assess the progress made in negotiations with Iran according to solid criteria.

7. Amnesty International and Human Rights Watch were willing to send representatives to the meeting, but the Iranian officials did not issue their visas. The human rights watchdog, which is based in the United States, regretted Tehran's refusal to let its members and members of Amnesty International take part in the roundtable.

8. The EU called for direct supervision over the situation of human rights reforms in Iran.

9. Members of the EU appreciated the role played by nongovernmental organizations in the negotiations.[116]

The second round of talks was held when Greece was rotational chairman of the EU. At that time, the EU considered trade agreement and cooperation in fighting terrorism as a single package and expected expansion of economic ties with Iran to be accompanied with similar progress in other fields, including improvement of the human rights situation.[117]

The second roundtable was held in Brussels on March 15 and 16, 2003. Those negotiations were held at a time when the fifty-ninth session of the UN Human Rights Commission was forthcoming. Also, the issue of Iraq and other regional problems hastened negotiations. With regard to the first event (Human Rights Commission session), as new voting members of the commission had been introduced and the EU's previous resolution had been rejected in the fifty-eighth session, the EU indicated that it was not willing to present a new resolution because the first and second round of talks with Iran had been fruitful.

With regard to the second issue, that is the situation in Iraq and the region, because of differences between the United States and EU over Iraq, the European leaders tried to attune the international atmosphere to their policies. Participants in those talks included three Iranian MPs, three members of Iran's presidential office, four representatives from the Iranian foreign ministry, five members of Iran's embassy in Brussels, three members of the judiciary, six university lecturers, three members of nongovernmental organizations, and a member of Iran's bar association. On the European side, there were three members from Greece, one from Italy, one from the EU Council, four from the EU Commission, eight university lecturers, four members of nongovernmental organizations, and the coordinator of the Iran–EU secretariat, Ms Tina Johansson. In this way, changes had occurred on both sides of the negotiations. The first day of the roundtable was allocated to rule of law and the second day included discussions on Article 14 of the International Covenant of Civil and Political Rights. Salient points of the roundtable can be summarized as follows:

• Discussions on Article 14 of International Covenant of Civil and Political Rights.
• The right to open court hearings.
• Independence (impartiality) of the Judiciary.

- Religious laws.
- Membership of judges in political parties.
- Presumption of innocence of the accused before court hearing.
- Communication between president and parliament and the right to fair trial.
- Openness of court trials even in some political cases.
- Special courts such as court-martials.
- Establishment of courts intermediate between ordinary and special courts.
- International Declaration of Human Rights and fundaments of the Islamic human rights.
- Separation of powers.
- Principle of fair trial within the frame of international laws and elimination of discrimination.
- Agreement between offence and punishment.
- Procedure for criminal investigations.
- Iran's punitive code and its relation to the International Covenant of Civil and Political Rights.
- Treatment of the accused by the police and respect for their rights.
- Power of attorney.
- The right to representation by a lawyer and required guarantees.
- Standards included in Europe's criminal procedures and examples from Greek courts.

At the end of the negotiations, both sides declared them as constructive and positive and expressed hope that negotiations would further strengthen Iran–EU cooperation to promote human rights.[118]

The third roundtable under the EU–Iran human rights dialogue was held on October 8 and 9, 2003, in Brussels themed "The Right to Freedom of Expression and the Right to Development."

The Iranian delegation comprised representatives of organizations that had taken part in previous roundtables, which at times were the same persons. However, participation of the civil society representatives was more pronounced. Similar changes were seen on the European side. The Iranian delegation was headed by Mr Danesh Yazdi, foreign ministry's Director General for international legal affairs, while the European delegation was headed by Mr Alessandro Fallavollita, chairman of the human rights department of the Italian foreign ministry.

The main topics of discussion included the right to freedom of expression and the right to development. It was emphasized that democracy should not commit suicide. Both sides considered freedom of expression as a main pillar of democracy, without which democracy cannot be realized. With regard to freedom of expression, attention was paid to freedom of expression for parliamentarians and their immunity, and it was emphasized that the immunity is not a privilege for MPs, but a guarantee for freedom of expression, which cannot be taken as a guarantee against legal punishment.

The second topic was the right to development. In this part, both sides stressed that the government's responsibility for enabling people and the civil society is a prerequisite for the realization of the right to development and that right was considered as an evolving concept that is not well-defined yet. It was also noted that fighting poverty and establishment of security are the ultimate goals of that right. The civil society, through activation of nongovernmental organizations and the international community, can facilitate realization of that right for people.

Salient features of the third roundtable included a friendly atmosphere for negotiations, which provided a good ground for theoretical and applied discussions on both sides. It should be noted that the two-day roundtable was concluded behind closed doors.

The third roundtable's success paved the way for the fourth roundtable, which was held in Tehran in June 2004 on how to implement justice in the judicial system and how to bolster international cooperation and collaboration with regard to human rights.

Like the preceding roundtables, Tina Johansson from the Danish institute for human rights was the facilitator of the fourth round of talks. Unlike past roundtables in which the Iranian delegates were headed by Mr Danesh Yazdi, foreign ministry's Director General for international legal affairs, the delegation was headed by Mr Akhundzadeh in the fourth roundtable. The European side was headed by Mr John Picard, director of the human rights department of Ireland's foreign ministry.

During the ensuing discussions, a member of the seventh parliament explained the measures taken by the Iranian legislature to protect human dignity and the rights of Iranian citizens, including steps taken to pass laws on sustainable development and active supervision over performance of judicial and executive bodies, such as various cases of investigation by the Article 90 Commission, which aimed to ensure the rule of law and the implementation of the Constitution and ordinary laws. The MP mentioned the following as the main steps taken to promote sustainable development by the Iranian parliament:

1. The law for adding a note to Article 297 of the Islamic Punitive Code (on equality of blood money for Muslims and religious minorities and elimination of discrimination).
2. The law for the presence of a jury to guarantee fair judgment and protect recognized freedoms.
3. The law on legitimate freedoms and citizenship rights.
4. Articles 578 and 579 of the Islamic Punitive Code (prohibition of physical harassment by state agents and civil servants).
5. The law on detention and the rights of prisoners.
6. Press Act and the right to constructive criticism.
7. The law on the activities of political parties, political and guild associations, Islamic associations, or recognized religious minorities.

The following laws were also mentioned that were in line with the objectives and regulations of the International Convention for the Elimination of all Forms of Racial Discrimination.

1. Charter of Organization of the Islamic Conference.
2. The law for the Iranian government's accession to the International Convention on the Suppression and Punishment of the Crime of Apartheid.
3. The law for accession of Iran to the anti-Apartheid convention.
4. The law of Mutual Relations and Principles of Cooperation between Iran and the Russian Federation Treaty.
5. Single-article law for respecting the rights of non-Shiite Iranians.
6. The law for attending to lawsuits on personal affairs and religious teachings of the Iranian Zoroastrians, Jews, and Christians.
7. The law for punishment against promoting racial discrimination.
8. Establishment of the IHRC.
9. Launching human rights courses at Shahid Beheshti and Tehran universities.
10. Reforming the social education system and establishment of the Welfare Ministry to teach religious efforts and give equal opportunities to all Iranian citizens.
11. Attention to cost-free education system.
12. Amnesty and pardon for prisoners.
13. Supporting nongovernmental organizations.

On the whole, the major topics of discussion between the European and Iranian delegates on the first day of the roundtable were as follows:

1. Human dignity.
2. Interaction between police and people, and human rights education for the police.
3. Principle of innocence.
4. Prohibition of forced admittance to crime.
5. Supervising performance of Judiciary's bailiffs.
6. Short prison term and its effect on behavior and the life of prisoners.
7. Inspection of prisons.
8. The rights of the accused (the right to defense, the right to representation).
9. Alternative punishments for imprisonment.
10. Rule of law.
11. Independence of judges and the Judiciary.
12. Request to Iran to join the Convention on Prohibition of Torture.

On the second day of the roundtable, discussions were focused on bolstering international cooperation and collaboration on human rights as per Article 56 of the UN Charter and both sides expressed their viewpoints. Major topics of the second day included the following:

1. International cooperation to improve the status of women in the world and countries' commitments with regard to promoting women's rights.
2. Emphasis on the role of nongovernmental organizations in the process of reviewing governments' reports.

3.   The EU Council's mechanism to supervise human rights.
4.   Reporting by governments to specialized human rights committees of the United Nations.

However, one week before the end of the fourth roundtable under the EU–Iran human rights dialogue, the EU issued a statement that claimed that despite four rounds of talks with the Iranian officials, widespread breaches of human rights continued in the country. It was one of the most outspoken and harshest statements to be issued by the EU on human rights breaches in Iran. The statement alleged that the EU, after about two years of dialogue with Iran on human rights, had reached the conclusion that no progress was made in that regard.[119]

In fact, the fourth roundtable was held soon after the seventh Majlis election when print media were raising questions about the election. This issue overshadowed the EU–Iran dialogue. Also, IAEA's anti-Iran resolution in 2004 and subsequent stances taken by the European countries on Iran's nuclear dossier made the new parliament and government of Iran review their interaction with the European countries. Therefore, despite many requests from the EU, Iran discontinued the human rights dialogue with Europe. The EU tried (and is still trying) through diplomatic pressures as well as frequent statements and resolutions on the human rights situation in Iran, to get Iran back to negotiations. For example, in the annual report released by the EU on December 12, 2005, on the situation of human rights, EU foreign ministers regretted Iran's rejection of the EU's offer to continue the human rights dialogue. The EU also warned Iran that if the country could not prove that it was committed to the implementation of human rights, the European countries would try to get the United Nations to condemn Iran through a resolution.[120]

It should be noted that the Europeans usually use a language of diplomacy when dealing with Iran. However, their policy came under fire from human rights organizations. During the fourth roundtable, the Human Rights Watch opposed the EU's negotiations with Tehran as being wrong and asked the European countries to be more outspoken in condemning further breaches of human rights in Iran.

Regardless, the statement that charged Iran with "widespread breaches of human rights" as well as "ignoring people's right to elect their representatives" during the seventh Majlis election in addition to a resolution that was forwarded by the European countries to IAEA in June, which criticized Iran's nuclear activities, paved the way for disruption of the dialogue.[121]

After disruption of the EU–Iran human rights dialogue, approval of resolutions and release of statements by various European institutions and, at times EU members, against the situation of human rights in Iran started once again. The European parliament's resolution, dated January 13, 2004, which was approved through 104 positive votes against two negative votes and five abstentions, was the main trigger of that trend. The resolution was released at a time that the human rights issue was used as leverage to put more pressure on Iran as a result of webloggers' case, summoning Mrs Shirin Ebadi by the Revolutionary Court, and the subsequent positions taken by the US State Department.

The EU statement on human rights breaches in Iran, dated June 20, 2004; the EU statement on detentions in Iran (2004); the EU statement on freedom of expression in Iran (2005); the British government's annual human rights report on Iran (2005); the EU statement on Iran, dated November 10, 2005; the EU's annual report on the situation of human rights in Iran (December 2005); and more recently, the European parliament's resolution on human rights breaches in Iran, dated November 16, 2006, were major measures taken by the EU to mount pressure on Iran regarding the human rights issue.

In addition to the said policy, the EU has always lent its support to anti-Iran resolutions at international bodies, including the third committee of the UN General Assembly (social, humanitarian and cultural affairs committee) and the General Assembly itself. Finland's support, as rotational chairman of the EU, for Canada's resolution at the General Assembly's third committee session on November 21, 2006, is an example.

In view of the above facts, it seems that the state of affairs, at least in early 2007, carried no sign of improvement in the said trend or the two sides' resolve to resume talks. Perhaps it would not be an exaggeration to say that the two sides' differing viewpoints on the issue of human rights will continue to remain a major debate for the unpredictable future, unless a strong resolve is shown on both sides for continuation of negotiations and removal of ambiguities.

The experience gained through four rounds of talks is too valuable to be ignored by any party to negotiations. In fact, although negotiations did not apparently lead to a tangible result or evident change in conduct on either side, they created an opportunity for experts and concerned authorities to face each other and inform the opposite side about the viewpoints of their respective country. If continued, that trend could eliminate many misunderstandings resulting from political ploys and create a totally scientific and legal atmosphere on the most important issue of human rights, thus paving the way for mutual understanding and overall improvement in relations.

9 Terrorism

The issue of terrorism

Accusations of terrorism against Iran during the period in question were brought in connection with two separate forms of alleged activity. These were, first, Iranian support for armed opposition groups in various countries; and, second, the assassination of Iranian opposition members living abroad. It is certainly true that Iran has supported opposition groups in Afghanistan, Bosnia, Iraq, and Lebanon. Western states, however, not only showed no anger at these activities, but even displayed some sympathy for Iran's support for opposition groups in Afghanistan, Bosnia, and Iraq. Even as regards Iran's support for Hezbollah in Lebanon, the West has shown some understanding, since Hezbollah, which also enjoys the status of an official political party in Lebanon, with representatives in the Lebanese parliament, was fighting against the Israeli occupation of southern Lebanon, with the aim of bringing about an Israeli withdrawal. Western principal concern centers around Iran's support for opposition groups in Palestine, which are struggling against Zionism and against the peace process as it stands at present. However, though it is undisputed that Islamic Jihad and Hamas get their main support from Iran, Iranian support for these groups has perhaps been less significant than has been claimed.[1]

With regard to the accusations against Iran over the assassination of Iranian opposition figures abroad, the following is a list of incidents that has been compiled from public sources and includes only those terrorist attacks in respect of which the Iranian government has been the object of public accusations, whether by law enforcement officials or in the media:[2]

List of incidents

December 7, 1979, Paris (France)—Shahriar Moustapha Shafiq, monarchist, a nephew of the former Shah, was assassinated.

July 18, 1980, Paris (France)—Shahpour Bakhtiar, monarchist, former prime minister, escaped an assassination attempt in which a policeman and a neighbor were killed and a third person was wounded. A Lebanese Christian, Anis Naccache, led the hit team. Naccache was sentenced to life in prison on March 10, 1982, but freed on July 27, 1990, when he was pardoned by President Mitterrand.

July 22, 1981, Washington, DC (USA)—Ali Akbar Tabatabai, former press spokesman at the Iranian embassy in Washington, was killed.

1982 (exact date unknown), Manila (Philippines)—Shahrokh Missaghi was killed.

1982 (exact date unknown), Istanbul (Turkey)—Colonel Ahmad Hamed was killed. Possible confusion with Ahmad Hamed Monfared, killed in 1986.

April 4, 1982, Mainz (Germany)—A young German woman was killed, and 18 Iranian opposition students were wounded, during a clash between pro- and anti-Iranian government students.

June 6, 1982, India—Chahram Mirani was seriously wounded.

August 1982 (exact date unknown), Karachi (Pakistan)—Ahmad Zolanvar was killed.

September 1982, India (exact date unknown)—Abdol-Amir Rahdar was killed.

February 1983, Paris (France)—General Gholam Ali Oveissi, monarchist, the former military governor of Tehran, was gunned down on the sidewalk in front of his home on the Rue de Passy, along with his brother, Gholam Hossein Oveissi.

August 16, 1985, Istanbul (Turkey)—Colonel Behrouz Shahverdilou, member of National Movement of Resistance (NAMIR) and a former army officer close to Bakhtiar, was killed.

September 9, 1985, Karachi (Pakistan)—Mirmanoute Balouch, former member of parliament from Baluchistan, was assassinated.

December 23, 1985, Istanbul (Turkey)—Colonel Hadi Azizmoradi was killed.

January 16, 1986, Hamburg (West Germany)—Ali Akbar Mohammadi, the former personal pilot of Rafsanjani, who had fled Iran, was killed.

August 19, 1986, London (UK)—Bijan Fazeli was killed.

August 24, 1986, Istanbul (Turkey)—Ahmad Hamed Monfared, former body-guard to the Shah, was shot.

December 1986 (exact date unknown) (Pakistan)—Vali Mohammad Van was injured in an attack.

July 7, 1987, Pakistan—Faramarz Akai was assassinated.

July 7, 1987, Pakistan—Ali Reza Pourchafizadeh was killed when two separate attacks against Iranian refugees in Pakistan in July, left three persons dead and 23 others wounded. The other known fatality was Faramarz Akai (see above).

July 7, 1987, London (UK)—Amir Hossein Amir-Parviz, monarchist, former minister of the Shah, was seriously injured, but not killed, when a bomb exploded in his car.

July 12, 1987, Vienna (Austria)—Hamid Reza Chitgar, member of Iranian Labor Party, worked at University Louis Pasteur, Strasbourg, France; disappeared on May 19, 1987; his body was discovered in July in Vienna.

July 25, 1987, Istanbul (Turkey)—Mohammad-Hassan Mansouri was shot by two assassins.

August 2, 1987, London (UK)—Mohammad Ali Tavakoli-Nabavi, who lived in Britain since 1979 with refugee status, was killed with his youngest son, Noureddin.

August 10, 1987, Geneva (Switzerland)—Ahmad Moradi-Talebi, a colonel and former pilot in the Iranian Air Force, was shot.

August 10, 1987, Paris (France)—Behrouz Bagheri was killed when his shop was firebombed.

August 1987 (exact date unknown) (Pakistan)—A hotel where Iranian opposition members were staying was firebombed, killing one person and wounding another.

October 1987 (exact date unknown), Istanbul (Turkey)—Abdol Hassan Modjtahedzadeh was kidnapped; presumed dead.

December 1987 (exact date unknown), (Turkey)—Javad Haeri was killed.

October 11, 1988, Erzeroum (Turkey)—Abdol Hassan Mojtahedzadeh (aka Sadiq el Hassani), PMOI, was found by customs officials bound and gagged in the trunk of a car with diplomatic plates registered to the Iranian consulate in Istanbul.

December 12, 1988, Karachi (Pakistan)—Balouch was killed when an armed man opened fire on Iranian refugees waiting in line in front of the headquarters of the UN High Commissioner for Refugees in Karachi.

July 13, 1989, Vienna (Austria)—Abdel Rahman Ghassemlou (Qassemlou), KDPI, was killed along with his deputy, Abdallah Ghaderi Azar, and Fadel Mulla Mahmoud Rasoul (a Kurdish intellectual living in Vienna) during negotiations with Iranian government emissaries by a pistol equipped with a silencer. The presumed assassin took refuge in the Iranian embassy in Vienna. After briefly being questioned by the Austrian police, he was allowed to return to Tehran.

August 23, 1989, Cyprus—Bahman Djavadi was assassinated.

August 1989, Cyprus—Gholam Kechavarz died of wounds after a failed assassination attempt.

February 1990 (exact date unknown), Taftan (Pakistan)—Haj Baloutch-Khan was killed.

April 24, 1990, Geneva (Switzerland)—Kassem Radjavi, PMOI, was shot by a hit squad.

August 15, 1990, Istanbul (Turkey)—Ahmad Kashefpour, ex-member of KDPI, was assassinated.

September 6, 1990, Stockholm (Sweden)—Effat Ghazi-Mohamad was assassinated.

October (Turkey) (exact date and place of killing unknown)—Gholamreza Nakhai was injured in an accident.

October 23, 1990, Paris (France)—Cyrus Elahi of Organization of Freedom Flag was gunned down in the street before dawn.

April 18, 1991, Paris (France)—Abdel Rahman Boroumand, member of the National Resistance Movement (NAMIR), was knifed by an unidentified assailant.

May 5, 1991, Soleimanieh (Iraq)—Safiollah Soleimanpour was killed together with his brother.

July 1991 (exact date unknown), Milan (Italy)—Alberto Capriolo, Italian translator of Salman Rushdie, was wounded in an attack, but survived.

July 12, 1991, Tokyo (Japan)—Hitoshi Igarashi, Salman Rushdie's Japanese translator, was killed in Tokyo.

August 6, 1991, Suresnes (France)—Shahpour Bakhtiar, former prime minister of Iran, member of NAMIR, was found knifed to death at home. Katibeh Fallouch, his personal secretary, was killed with him. One of the assassins was later arrested in Switzerland and extradited to France, where he turned out to be an Iranian.

August 7, 1991, Paris (France)—Jawad Mehrani, Iranian arms dealer believed to have links to the Iranian government, in the process of negotiating large helicopter purchase from Aerospatiale, was killed within 24 hours of Bakhtiar. Some police sources speculate the same hit team may have eliminated him because he was aware of the details of the Bakhtiar murder.

June 4, 1992, Istanbul (Turkey)—Akbar Ghorbani (aka Mansour Amini), PMOI, was abducted on June 4; body found on June 16.

August 7, 1992, Bonn (Germany)—Fereidoun Farokhzad [Farouchsad], opposition activist exiled since 1979, worked as a singer, actor, and poet; knifed to death in his apartment in Bonn.

August 8, 1992, Frankfurt (Germany)—Homayoun Moghaddam, Iran National Party, was wounded in a knife attack by three Iranians.

September 17, 1992, Berlin (Germany)—Sadegh Sharaf-Kindi, PDKI, was gunned down along with three colleagues at the Mykonos, a Greek restaurant in Berlin. He succeeded Qassemlou as head of DPIK. The others were Fattah Abduli, a KDPI European representative, Homayoun Ardalan, the KDPI representative in Germany, and Nuri Dehkurdi, a translator. Weapons found by the police included an Israeli-made Uzi, a Spanish pistol, and a "Llama" pistol with silencer. In March 1996, the German Federal Prosecutor issued an international arrest warrant for Iranian Intelligence Minister Ali Fallahian for having ordered the killings.

December 26, 1992, Istanbul (Turkey)—Abbas Gholizadeh, former bodyguard of the Shah, was kidnapped and allegedly turned over to Iranian intelligence.

January 1993, Germany—Ayatollah Mehdi Haeri escaped an assassination attempt, for which an Iranian citizen, Fakhrodine Zalikhani, was later arrested.

March 16, 1993, Rome (Italy)—Mohammad Hussein Nagdi, PMOI member and local representative of the National Council of Resistance (a front organization for the Massud Radjavi's Mujahedin), served as military attaché to Rome for the Islamic Republic until 1982. He was gunned down in his car by assassins.

August 1993, Istanbul (Turkey)—Mohammad Ghaderi, KDPI, was kidnapped and found dead in Turkey.

August 28, 1993, Ankara (Turkey)—Mehran Bahram Azadfar, KDPI, was assassinated.

October 11, 1993, Oslo (Norway)—William Nygaard, Norwegian publisher of Salman Rushdie, was shot three times but survived.

January 1994 (exact date unknown), Sweden—Abubakr Hedayati, KDPI, was wounded by a letter bomb.

January 4, 1994, Corum (Turkey)—Taha Kirmench, Iranian Kurdish activist, was killed by assassins who were later arrested.

January 29, 1994, Syraee (Turkey)—Nasser Hadji Rashidi, Iranian Kurd, was injured in an attack together with his sister, Mahtab Hadji Rashidi.

June 24, 1994, Copenhagen (Denmark)—Mollah Osman Amini, Iranian Kurdish refugee, was found dead in his apartment.

November 12, 1994, Bucharest (Romania)—Mohammad Ali Assadi was killed in his apartment by three assailants.

May 17, 1995, Baghdad (Iraq)—Two senior PMOI officials were killed and one was wounded in an attack on a Mujahedin vehicle.

June 5, 1995, Sulaymaniyah (Iraq)—Two members of an Iranian Kurdish group (Komelah) were gunned down in Iraqi Kurdistan.

July 10, 1995, Baghdad (Iraq)—Hussein Adidi, PMOI, was gunned down with two other Mujahidin officials, Ibrahim Salimi and Yarali Karatbar.

September 17, 1995, Paris (France)—Davoud Abdollahi's son Hashem Abdollahi, NAMIR member and the chief witness in the Bakhtiar murder trial, was murdered by unknown assailants.

February 20, 1996, Istanbul (Turkey)—Zahra Rajabi, NCR (PMOI), senior member of the National Council of Resistance, was killed.

March 4, 1996, Karachi (Pakistan)—Molavi Abdul-Malek Mollahzadeh Balouch, 45-year-old son of Iran's most prominent Sunni cleric, was murdered by two gunmen in a taxi as he was leaving his house in Pakistan.

March 5, 1996, Karachi (Pakistan)—Abdol-Nasser Jamshid-Zahi Balouch and Molavi Abdul Malek, leading dissidents from the Balouchi community, were gunned down on a Karachi street.

1996, Paris (France)—Reza Mazlouman, former vice minister of education under the Shah, was assassinated. An Iranian was arrested in Bonn.

July 3, 1996, Baghdad (Iraq)—Hamed Rahmani, PMOI, was killed while driving to his office in central Baghdad. The Mujahedin blamed the Iranian government for the murder, which they said was the sixth assassination of a Mujahedin member in Baghdad since May 1995.

It is noteworthy and significant that more than 75% of the assassinations that occurred in the European Union (EU) countries were perpetrated in Germany and France. This took place at a time when Germany and France were playing a leading role in the "critical dialogue" between EU and Iran, and when these two countries were the most sympathetic and helpful to Iran's political, financial, and economic approaches, during a difficult period when the aim of American and Israeli policies was to isolate Iran. It cannot be sufficiently stressed, and is an important element of the argument presented by the author in this thesis, that these events could not have happened by chance.

The reactions of both the United States and the EU to these events must be examined.[3] At the July 1992 summit meeting in Munich of G7, the advanced industrial nations group, Washington condemned Iran's attempts to obtain nuclear weapons and the alleged abuse of human rights in Iran. But the principal target of American criticism was Iran's alleged support for international terrorism. The European G7 members, however, and in particular Germany, were less keen to censure Iran. This was the origin of the concept of "critical dialogue," a policy later formulated explicitly at the EU's Edinburgh summit of December 1992 and especially promoted by Germany and France. The European concept was that more subtle diplomatic pressure would persuade Iran to mold its attitudes toward something more acceptable to the West, particularly if this persuasion, which it was hoped would help the Iranian regime to strengthen its internal position against extremists, were to be accompanied with an implicit promise to Tehran of economic incentives. Having failed to get European agreement to a tough line in Iran at these meetings, Washington in due course developed its own policy toward the region, which it called *dual containment*. The aim of this approach was to impose sanctions simultaneously on both the Iranian government and the Iraqi regime of Saddam Hussein. In early 1995, the US administration strengthened its policy to a total trade embargo on Iran.

As time went on, the EU displayed its faith in the success of its own policy of "critical dialogue" by agreeing to a rescheduling of Iranian debt and by boosting the level of European trade and aid to Iran. However, at the G7 summit of June 1995, the meeting's final resolution for the first time called on Iran to eschew state terrorism, a clear indication of a toughening of European attitudes. The following year, the G7 states also raised the subject of Iran's obstruction of the Middle East peace process, demanding an end to Iranian support for such organizations as Hamas and Hezbollah, in addition to asking Tehran for a formal renunciation of the *fatwa* concerning Salman Rushdie.

There is no doubt that the terror attacks on September 11, 2001, changed many presumptions in international politics, including the EU's concept of threat. Different approaches taken by the EU after September 11 and in the new millennium were in line with the EU's new understanding of threat. After September 11, the EU took speedy steps to bolster the transatlantic alliance and NATO announced its readiness, according to Article 5 of its statute, to serve US interests. However, two years after that event, many differences had emerged between a large number of the EU member states and the United States. Those differences stemmed from US plans to attack Iraq, on the one side,[4] and disagreement on how to deal with Iran's nuclear program through International Atomic Energy Agency's Board of Governors, on the other side.[5] As a result, the United States divided the continent into New Europe and Old Europe and tried to create a deep gap between the two parts of Europe, which could cast serious doubts on the future outlook of the EU. The conflict between New Europe and Old Europe reached its peak in the case of resistance by the so-called New Europe against ratification of the draft European Constitution in 2004, which led to the relative triumph of those countries.[6]

Sinusoid movement of the EU in getting close to or away from the United States gave way to renewed convergence as a consequence of US invasion of Iraq, expansion of terrorist threats in the world, as well as Iran's nuclear dossier. Undoubtedly, the systemic effects of US policies on global trends could not be ignored. Domination of US institutions on international relations and security has led to the emergence of converging viewpoints in the United States and Europe.[7] Even France, in its new strategy to avert terrorist threats, has followed suit with the National Security Strategy of the United States,[8] by considering the possibility of preemptive strikes and even use of nuclear weapons.[9]

Threats that have concerned Europe most are those that challenge the unity and harmony of the EU. Under current conditions in Europe, any conflict around the EU and at an international level can influence convergence inside the EU or even reverse it. Europe's Security Strategy, which was presented for the first time in December 2003, encompasses the most important threats and challenges resulting from the geopolitical environment. The most important issue for the European countries is security of the continent, not expansionist tendencies. The European security strategy has determined five key threats as its basis: terrorism, proliferation of weapons of mass destruction, regional conflicts, governments in crisis, and organized crimes such as drug trafficking, illegal immigration, and human smuggling. A shared factor among those threats is the threat-based approach taken by Europe toward the Middle East. The EU maintains that the Middle East is a region infested with conflicts, where the risk of proliferation of weapons of mass destruction is higher than in any other part of the world.

On the whole, terrorism and proliferation of weapons of mass destruction are the most important security issues for the EU.

Although conditions prevailing after September 11 called for more cooperation on such issues as terrorism, the focus on Iran's nuclear dossier and the priority attached to it during the Iran–Europe dialogue, practically marginalized terrorism.

Developments inside the EU during that time, creation of new structures such as the European constitution, and efforts made to forge joint defense and security forces, in addition to assimilation of new members, have turned security into the foremost concern of the EU. The European countries maintain that international terrorism is an evident and immediate threat to the security of Europe. The EU document dated November 24, 2005, which is titled, "European Strategy to Fight Extremism and Terrorism" has mentioned terrorism as a threat to the whole human community and has noted that the EU and the European citizens are exposed to that threat. It has also called for the adoption of a comprehensive policy to face it.

Although Europe has faced many terrorist threats in its history, at present, the most serious terrorist threat to Europe comes from al Qaeda. European citizens are also open to other forms of terrorist threats. At the same time, part of Europe is concerned about extremist currents that, at times, set up international terrorist networks. Therefore, extremist religious minorities and support afforded to them by some governments are considered a major threat. The situation in Iraq and daily terrorist operations that have, thus far, claimed thousands of lives constitute a blatant case of growth of bigoted social currents that are engaged in ruthless terrorist operations under the cover of Islam and through financial support from some Arab countries.

Germany's Interior Minister said in an address in 2005 that his country believes that it is a target for terrorists. He added that Islamist terrorists pose a major threat, which should be addressed at regional and international levels parallel to the eradication of terrorism through pressure and prosecution.

Therefore, al Qaeda is a topic of discussion between Iran and Europe with regard to terrorism. Despite the fact that Iran has acted successfully with regard to apprehension and controlling transit of al Qaeda members through its soil some Western authorities have frequently charged Iran with cooperating with the terrorist group. That charge has surfaced often in connection with al-Tawhid group. This is a branch of al Qaeda in Germany. Hans Joseph Beth, head of the antiterrorism section of Germany's intelligence agency, incriminated Iran in 2004 as having provided good grounds for the empowerment of al-Tawhid (in Germany) by al Qaeda because of its inability to control al Qaeda activities.

On the contrary, Iran has always criticized the freedom of action enjoyed by anti-Iran terrorist groups such as Mujahideen Khalq Organization (MKO) and other opposition groups in Europe, especially Germany, and has called for restrictions to be imposed on their activities in negotiations with the European countries. As a result of those talks, Germany revoked refugee status of some MKO members in 2005 and the German prosecutor-general labeled them a criminal (and not terrorist) group in the said year, banning all their activities in Germany. This happened after the conclusion of the Paris Agreement between Iran and the EU3 (France, Britain, and Germany), when the EU agreed to officially put MKO on its list of terrorist groups. According to the Paris Agreement, both sides agreed to cooperate in fighting terrorism. The agreement has called for banning activities of all terrorist groups, including al Qaeda and all groups affiliated to it as well as such terrorist organizations as MKO.

However, after Merkel took over as the new German Chancellor and the country started to pay more attention to transnational security, the issue of terrorism came up as a serious topic in negotiations between Iran and Germany, on the one hand, and between Germany and other European counties and the United States, on the other hand. Because of the connection established between Islam and terrorism by Western theorists, the German defense minister announced during the forty-third Security Conference of Munich in 2007 that international terrorism, proliferation of weapons of mass destruction, and weak governments were the most important challenges facing the German government that should be handled through military as well as political, economic, social, and diplomatic approaches. This policy has been taken as the basis for interactions between Europe and Iran on how to confront threats posed by Iranian terrorist groups such as MKO, on the one hand, and by other extremist terrorist groups such as al-Tawhid and al Qaeda, on the other hand.

Today, there are shared grounds and great potential in Iran and the West to fight al Qaeda as well as terrorist groups that are active in Afghanistan. At the same time, Iran and the West have different viewpoints on the political currents that are fighting against Israel's aggression. They include such groups as Hamas and the Islamic Jihad which are fighting Israel in Palestine, or Hezbollah which is defending Lebanon against the Israeli aggression. Such groups have been designated as terrorist groups by the Western countries while Iran considers them freedom movements, which are fighting against the occupation of their country. Therefore, there is serious disagreement between Iran and the West with regard to Palestinian militant groups and Hezbollah.

Therefore, differences as well as commonalties between Iran and the West with regard to terrorism are undeniable. At the same time, it is in the interest of both Iran and the West to first start cooperation in such fields as confronting al Qaeda and MKO. Then they can take part in the war on terror within the framework of the United Nations' resolutions. It cannot be denied that Iran has been among the major victims of terrorism since the victory of the Islamic revolution of 1979 and tens of high-ranking Iranian officials, including the president, prime minister, ministers, and parliament deputies, have lost their lives as a result of terrorist attacks.

10 The Middle East peace process

Major developments in the Middle East peace process after 1997: Approaches taken by Iran and Europe

The emergence of leftist governments in major decision-making countries of the European Union (EU) after 1997 caused member states to focus more on the internal structure of the EU. The trend was accompanied with further development of the EU, assimilation of more members, formulation of a common constitution, and providing conditions for the realization of common defense and security forces. The main serious concern, however, was how to keep a stable environment around the EU because that environment was capable of spreading instability within the EU.

Meanwhile, the threat-based approach taken by Europe over the past few years has been more and more focused on the Middle East region. From the viewpoint of European countries, the Middle East is a region that teems with conflicts and serious threats, such as the proliferation of weapons of mass destruction. In the meantime, developments in the occupied lands have had the highest influence on individual and collective decision-making by member states of the EU.

As intifada has raged on in parallel to peace talks, European countries have shown more interest in contracts that are based on the "peace for land" formula. Therefore, any peace contract that has been drawn up according to that formula has been welcomed by the European countries and they have asked Arab countries to recognize Israel in return for peace.

Developments in occupied lands: 1998–2006

First Wye River Accord

After 18 months of stagnation in peace talks following the Dayton Peace Agreement, the Wye River Accord was signed after nine days of negotiations between the chairman of the Palestine Liberation Organization, Yasser Arafat, and the Israeli Prime Minister Benjamin Netanyahu under the auspices of the US President, Bill Clinton, in Maryland. Technically speaking, the contract contravened the past agreements. An earlier agreement that had been reached in Oslo and was to be implemented in five years had been practically mothballed after Netanyahu took charge as Prime Minister of Israel. Because of international pressures and the struggles of Palestinian militants against Israel's policy to legalize occupation, the Israeli regime had to go for another agreement. The Palestinian authority, on the other hand, had to do the same because it had lost the past leverage.[1]

Salient points of the Wye River Accord included the following:

- Withdrawal of Israel from 1–3 percent of Palestinian lands that were occupied in 1976. Both Israelis and Palestinians agreed to take all necessary steps to prevent terrorist acts and hostilities against each other and cooperate in other fields. The Palestinian police forces were supposed to fulfill their duties in line with the accord. Also, a Palestinian–Israeli committee was to take necessary measures to end terrorism.
- The accord further emphasized that "the Palestinian side will apprehend the specific individuals suspected of perpetrating acts of violence and terror for the purpose of further investigation, and prosecution and punishment of all persons involved in acts of violence and terror."
- According to the accord, the Palestinian authority did not enjoy sovereign rights and a number of Jewish settlements were to remain on the occupied lands, even after peace was established.

A major achievement of the Wye River Accord was changing the political equation from "land for peace" to "security for peace," and led to the presence of more of the Zionist regime's army in the West Bank. In this way, total lands under the rule of the Palestinian authority amounted to 27 percent of the West Bank, while Israel continued to control border crossings.

According to the Wye River Accord, some Jewish settlements would remain on Palestinian territories, and finding a solution to the problem of Jerusalem and Palestinian refugees was postponed to a later time. Also, no mention was made of the establishment of a Palestinian government. According to the accord, the Zionist regime continued to have full control of vital water resources and such infrastructures as roads, electricity, and telephone lines, as well as the security system of Gaza airport.

That accord was more strongly worded than other contracts and, by putting various obstacles in the way of the Palestinians, damaged future outlooks for sovereignty, independence, and right of self-determination of the Palestinians, which had already been recognized by international law. Also, Netanyahu did not comply with most of Israel's obligations to withdraw from the occupied lands, release Palestinian prisoners, establish safe passage between the West Bank and the Gaza Strip, and inaugurate Gaza Port.[2]

Netanyahu's proposed formula of "peace for security" would have assured the security of the Israelis against any form of resistance.

Second Camp David (August 12, 2000)

The new round of talks between the Palestinian authority and the Israeli regime started in Camp David on August 10, 2000, under the auspices of the US President,

Bill Clinton. The meeting caused the main crack in the peace process, which had started seven years earlier in Oslo. The United States intended the meeting to end in the conclusion of a semifinal, or at least, a transitional agreement. However, despite the policy of "intentional ambiguities," which governed the Oslo Agreement, the negotiations failed to reach a conclusion on who would govern Jerusalem. When the futility of the negotiations became evident, the United States decided to postpone them for a few days. However, US officials later admitted to the failure of negotiations.[3]

Preparations for Camp David meeting

The Camp David negotiations started on July 11, 2000, at a time when Arafat and Barak had already reached certain agreements on major issues of difference, including al-Aqsa Mosque, refugees, Jewish settlements, sovereignty, and border crossings through secret talks that began in Tel Aviv and continued in Stockholm and Tel Aviv. However, they had fallen short of an agreement on the old city of Jerusalem (that is, East Jerusalem). Both sides agreed to discuss the last issue at a later time. Since Clinton was aware of the importance of East Jerusalem, he decided to organize a meeting between Barak and Arafat to achieve a final agreement, even without a basic solution to the issue of Jerusalem. He said it was possible to postpone discussions on Jerusalem until after further negotiations and intended to put more pressure on Arafat in the meantime through the Arab countries. Clinton and his secretary of state contacted the leaders of Egypt, Saudi Arabia, Jordan, and Morocco, without any clear achievements. The important point is that Egypt did not agree to put more pressure on Arafat and called on him to insist on his position and give no concession on the issue of Jerusalem. Saudi Arabia also took a similar position. Israel, on the other hand, announced that it was not ready to give any concession to the Palestinians on Jerusalem. At that time, the coalition government of Barak had been weakened and he was under fire for lenience during negotiations, especially his readiness to withdraw from Palestinian lands in the northern and southern parts of Jerusalem in return for annexation of major Jewish settlements around it.[4]

Five articles introduced by Barak included the following:

1. Solutions to the religious and municipal problems of Jerusalem.
2. Payment of remuneration to refugees and settlement of about 100,000 refugees including their families. Accepting the return of so many refugees was, in fact, recognition of the 1948 agreement by Israel, which regularly refrains from accepting any civil or legal responsibility for the return of refugees.
3. Some 80 percent of Jewish settlements were to remain and be annexed to the Zionist regime in return for Israel ignoring small settlements.
4. If needed, Israel could beef up its military presence in the al-Ghour region of Jordan to protect its security by preventing the military presence of the Palestinian Authority in that area, cooperating with Arab countries, and preventing the entry of foreign military forces into that area.

5.   Annexing settlements established to the east of the Green Line to Israel and expanding the borders of Jerusalem, while granting 94 percent of the West Bank to the Palestinians, excluding Jerusalem. Israel was also supposed to retain the remaining 6 percent of the West Bank for 10 years, while renting part of it for 25 years.[5]

Failure of Camp David negotiations

As Israel refused to negotiate on Jerusalem, and its position was supported by the United States despite the insistence of Arafat, the plan failed in spite of all the proposed concessions. The meeting also failed in reaching a "semifinal" agreement because of the insistence of the Israeli delegation that the Palestinian and Arab side should admit the end of war. "Arafat certainly lacked such a power because he could not make the Palestinian people accept that the Israeli government would not shoulder legal responsibility for what had happened over the past 53 years."[6] Since Barak insisted on the conclusion of a final and firm agreement that would cover Jerusalem, refugees, sovereignty, and border issues, he declined from signing an agreement that would not address the issue of Jerusalem.

It should be noted that the issue of Jerusalem still remains a stumbling block in the way of peace in the Middle East and will remain to be so. Of course, this is not the sole issue. The issue of refugees, including millions of Palestinian refugees, is another obstacle. Limited powers of the Palestinian authority and its fragmentation have prevented it from bringing about suitable conditions for the establishment of a consolidated political and economic system on Palestinian lands. Because of the lack of solutions that would realize the national identity of Palestinians and restore their national rights, the issue of Palestine has remained unresolved yet.

Sharm el-Sheikh contract (Second Wye River Accord)

The Sharm el-Sheikh agreement was mediated by Egypt and aimed at reducing differences between the Islamic countries and Israel.

The meeting, which focused on cease-fire between Israel and Palestine and was attended by US president Bill Clinton, Yasser Arafat, Ehud Barak, King Abdullah, Hosni Mubarak, and Javier Solana (coordinator of the EU's foreign policy), was held in Sharm el-Sheikh in 1999. Despite differences between the two sides, the Israeli and Palestinian interlocutors reached an agreement after two days of talks and issued a joint statement as follows[7]:

1.   Both sides agreed to issue statements on stopping violence and taking expedient measures to eradicate it. The two sides also agreed to restoration of military, security, and communication conditions that existed before the crisis.
2.   The United States was to establish a fact-finding mission in cooperation with the Israeli and Palestinian authorities after consultations with the secretary-general of the United Nations to investigate developments that led to the agreement and prevent their repetition. The committee's report was to be drawn up by the US president in cooperation with the UN secretary-general

and after consultation with the belligerent parties. Before being released, the report should have been signed by the US president. Although the Sharm el-Sheikh meeting failed to get the two sides to agree on Jerusalem, the incomplete agreement on removing friction points between the Palestinians and Israelis, withdrawal of Israeli troops from the West Bank and Gaza Strip, establishment of a committee under the control of Palestinian self-rule, inauguration of Gaza airport, and establishment of a fact-finding committee to investigate recent events in occupied Palestine, were considered a relative triumph for the US president in his effort to prove the existence of common viewpoints on ending the Middle East crisis.[8]

On September 4, 1999, the agreement was signed by Yasser Arafat, chairman of the Palestine Liberation Organization, and Ehud Barak, the Israeli prime minister, in Sharm el-Sheikh in the presence of US Secretary of State, Madeleine Albright; Egyptian president, Hosni Mubarak; and King Abdullah II, the Jordan monarch.

The agreement reached in Sharm el-Sheikh (Second Wye River Accord) was in fact a schedule for the implementation of the First Wye River agreement, which had been suspended by Netanyahu on the pretext that the Palestinian authority, led by Arafat, had violated it. Ehud Barak also intended to suspend implementation of First Wye River agreement until final negotiations. However, because of opposition from the Palestinian authority as well as international pressures, he agreed to take part in the Sharm el-Sheikh negotiations.

The most important features of Second Wye River Accord included the following:

- On September 5, 1999, to transfer 7 percent from Area C to Area B.
- On November 15, 1999, to transfer 2 percent from Area B to Area A, and 3 percent from Area C to Area B.
- On January 20, 2000, to transfer 1 percent from Area C to Area A, and 5.1 percent from Area B to Area A.
- To release 350 Palestinian prisoners.
- Opening the Southern Route and Northern Route of the Safe Passage between Gaza Strip and the West Bank "in accordance with the details of operation, which will be provided for in the Safe Passage Protocol."
- "Forwarding of the list of Palestinian policemen to the Israeli Side."
- Apprehension of suspects and forwarding reports on people involved in terrorist operations against Israel.

The agreement had provided Israel with many loopholes that would pave the way for nonimplementation of the treaty, including the call for "continuation of the program for the collection of the illegal weapons, including reports," and apprehension of suspects.[9]

Taba negotiations

Peace talks between Israeli and Palestinian officials started in Taba, Egypt, on January 21, 2001. The negotiations were attended by Israeli ministers of foreign affairs, tourism, and justice as well as speaker of the Palestinian parliament, minister of information, and a number of officials of the Palestinian self-rule.[10]

The Palestinians referred to UN resolution 194 and stressed on the right of about 7.3 million Palestinian refugees, banished from Palestine in 1948, to return to their homeland.[11] As put by Nabil Shaath, a senior aide to Arafat, the Palestinian and Israeli negotiators were to focus first on land and security before focusing on such issues as Palestinian refugees and al-Aqsa Mosque.

After a few days of talks, the Taba negotiations ended with a statement, but without achieving any clear agreement. The Israeli daily, *Maariv*, later disclosed details of agreements reached by the negotiating delegations in Taba. The newspaper wrote[12] that during six days of intense negotiations in Taba, both sides managed to settle disputes related to the final stage of peace talks. *Maariv* also reported that an average of 94–96 percent of the West Bank would be given to the Palestinian authority for the establishment of an independent Palestinian government and Jewish settlements would remain on the remaining 5 percent of the West Bank, while sacred lands were to be controlled jointly by both sides for a period of five years. During those years, Israeli and Palestinian authorities were to negotiate on the governance of the sacred lands. With regard to security matters, the Palestinian delegation acceded to most of Israel's demands, including dispatching the Israeli army under emergencies as well as its deployment at the Plain of Aaron for a period of six years.[13]

Roadmap

The visit paid by the then US Secretary of State, Colin Powell, to Jerusalem on May 11, 2003, and his meetings with Ariel Sharon, the then Israeli prime minister and members of his cabinet, which preceded his meeting with the Palestinian president Mahmoud Abbas (Abu Mazen) in Jericho, aimed at presenting the so-called "roadmap" to the said authorities after the Middle East experienced serious anti-US and anti-British activities subsequent to the invasion of Iraq. The measure was the climax of a long program, which had started with an address by President George W. Bush on June 24, 2002. During his address, Bush delineated the general framework for the settlement of disputes between the Arabs and Israelis. He said that a major goal of the plan was to guarantee the security and political recognition of Israel, which would have ended in the establishment of a Palestinian government within borders defined by the Arab states.

At that time, it was decided that the three-stage plan should be implemented by 2005. The plan was approved at the same time by the EU, international quadripartite committee (in charge of solving the issue of Palestine), and the United Nations.

The three stages included the following[14]:

1. The first stage (from October 2000 to May 2003): The Palestinian authority was asked to stop Intifada immediately and put an end to the unrest against the occupiers and coordinate security measures taken by the Palestinian and

Israeli authorities. In addition, the Palestinian authority should have held presidential elections and paved the way for instating the prime minister, with Yasser Arafat as ceremonial president. In return, the Zionist regime was required to observe the human rights of the Palestinians and avoid damaging their lives and properties.

Withdrawal from areas that were occupied by Israel on September 28, 2000, was made dependent on security cooperation between the Palestinian authority and Israel.

2. The second stage (from June 2003 to December 2003): In this stage an international conference would be held to initiate negotiations on the economic reconstruction of Palestine and to start talks on the establishment of the Palestinian government within temporary borders.

3. The third stage (from 2004 to 2005): In this stage, the second international conference on negotiations between the Palestinian authority and the Zionist regime was to be held. In that conference, participants were to discuss a final agreement to be forged before the end of 2005, as well as issues related to borders, al-Aqsa Mosque, and relations between the Arabs and Israelis.

Different stances taken on the roadmap

The Palestinians took two different positions on the roadmap, which are as follows:

Palestinian authority

The Palestinian authority approved the general outlines of the plan when it was first announced, though it criticized some aspects of it, including vesting all powers with the prime minister in a possible Palestinian government because it would have seriously reduced Yasser Arafat's powers as president of the Palestinian authority. Although the plan contained many negative points, including the call to end intifada and lack of any obligation on the part of the Zionist government to implement the above stages, the Palestinian authority considered it the sole opportunity for a return to peace talks and accepted it. The Palestinian authority welcomed the plan through Yasser Arafat and his Prime Minister, Abu Mazen, who believed that the plan could reactivate the trend of political negotiations (the option that was supported by the Palestinian authority). They hoped that the Zionist regime would have to retreat behind unspecified borders when faced with pressure from public opinion.

Palestinian nation and militant groups

Most militant Palestinian groups, including Hamas, Islamic Jihad, Al-Quds Brigades, People's Front, and other militant groups, opposed the roadmap because it largely ignored the rights and aspirations of the Palestinian people, tried to stifle intifada, and aimed to do away with the national unity of the Palestinian nation. Their worst fears came true when the Palestinian authority and its security agents, under guidance from Israel and the United States, started to apprehend armed militants who struggled against the occupiers. This could have fanned the flames of unrest and more clashes among the Palestinians.

Therefore, most militant Palestinian groups supported by the majority of the Palestinian nation emphasized on the continuation of current struggles as long as Israel stuck its occupationist policies. An opinion poll conducted by the Palestine Information Center in Jerusalem in the middle of April 2003 showed that 75.3 percent of Palestinians supported continuation of intifada. Some 64.6 percent of Palestinians also agreed to various forms of military operations against occupation of their lands, including suicidal attacks against the occupiers and the so-called Israeli citizens. The Palestinian authority and Fatah Movement tried through negotiations with Hamas in Cairo in November 2002 to pave the way for the implementation of the roadmap because the Palestinian authority and other political sides were fully aware that stopping the resistance movement would not be possible without the agreement of Hamas. It is noteworthy that the US-engineered roadmap was rejected by most Palestinian groups.

Israel

After the introduction of the roadmap, Colin Powell, the then US secretary of state, paid a visit to Israel. During meetings with Israeli Prime Minister Ariel Sharon and cabinet members, Powell was told that 14 amendments should be made to the plan.

The Bush administration agreed to the request and the Israeli officials subsequently announced that if the plan contained their viewpoints and underwent the necessary changes, they would agree to it. On the other hand, Colin Powell issued a joint statement along with the then US president's national security advisor, Condoleezza Rice, trying to assure the Arab leaders that Washington would make no change to the plan.

Since the US Government was opposed to Sharon's request for the removal of two articles from the plan, which emphasized the right of the Palestinian refugees to go back to their homeland, as well as removal of the "Arabic peace" phrase, Sharon refrained from implementing the roadmap. Instead, he called on Palestinians to implement the articles related to the first phase of the plan, including complete reengineering of Palestine's political system, restructuring the security organizations of Palestine per Israel's demands, putting an immediate end to violence, and making tangible efforts to apprehend groups and persons who embarked on violent attacks on Israel at any place.[15]

At that time, the Israelis made agreement to the plan conditional on the termination of Palestinian struggles and disarmament of armed Palestinian groups and claimed that the security mechanisms of the plan were inefficient and inadequate. They also raised objections to the schedule of the plan and called for removal of the article on the timetable, asserting that the plan should be implemented in proportion to compliance on both sides. In addition, the Israelis demanded that representatives of the quadrilateral committee should decide about implementation of every stage of the plan before moving on to the next stage. In addition to the earlier-mentioned conditions, the Israelis announced that implementation of the first phase of the plan and relevant negotiations should be postponed until after the general elections in Palestine.

Iran's plan

The Supreme Leader, as the highest decision-making Iranian authority, stipulated that the only way to solve the problem of Palestine was to hold a referendum in the occupied lands and added, "Those people who consider the issue of the Middle East an international crisis and are trying to harness the crisis, should know that the best solution is for the Palestinian refugees in Lebanon and other places to go back to Palestine. Then a referendum should be held attended by Muslims, Christians, and Jews to decide what kind of government should rule their country. The majority of Palestinians are Muslims and there are also Jews and Christians who inhabit the mainland of Palestine and their ancestors had lived there. They should vote for the system of government which suits them best and that government should decide what to do with the people who have migrated there during the past 40, 45, or 50 years; whether to keep them or send them back; or settle them in a specific place. It is for the ruling system of Palestine to decide about them. This is the best solution to the crisis and as long as it has not been implemented, no other solution would be efficient."[16] The former Iranian president, Mohammad Khatami, also pointed to the issue of Palestine as the foremost concern of the Muslim world and presented a basic solution for the Middle East crisis and reestablishment of stability and tranquility in the region.[17] His proposed solution included the following components:

1. Return of all Palestinians to their occupied homeland.
2. Holding a referendum among genuine Palestinians, including Muslims, Jews, and Christians, to decide about their future system of government.
3. Establishment of a ruling system that would be supported by all Palestinians with Jerusalem as its capital.
4. The independent Palestinian government would have the right to decide about the fate of current inhabitants of the occupied lands.

The Iranian foreign minister also considered intifada as the natural and legal right of Palestinians in line with their basic right of self-determination and said, "Palestinians who are fed-up with unfair solutions have no other way but to keep fighting and achieve their natural and legal right of self-determination through intifada."

Renewal of Germany's role and activation of the EU

There is no doubt that Germany's role in pursuing the peace process was revived under the new chancellor, Angela Merkel, after a period of decline under her predecessor, Gerhard Schröder. Following her election as German Chancellor, Merkel paid an official visit to the Middle East to announce that the peace process should go on and Germany was determined to help its success both individually and within the framework of the EU. Germany laid stress on Saudi Arabia and Egypt. On December 12, 2006, Merkel met with Ehud Olmert, the Israeli prime minister, in Berlin and while emphasizing the high importance of Germany's relations with Israel, called for enhancement of those relations. She also noted that Germany, as rotational chair of the EU, will do its best to promote the peace process in the Middle East. After the meeting, Merkel paid a short visit to Washington on January 2, 2007, calling on President George Bush to help resume the Arab–Israeli peace process. During a meeting with US Secretary of State Condoleezza Rice, the German Chancellor placed emphasis on cooperation and common interests of the United States and Germany to end the Middle East conflict.

Although Germany's interests require the country to play an individual role in the Middle East developments, it has occasionally tried to attune its policies to those adopted by the EU. Of course, unlike the first half of the 1990s, Europe did not play an influential role in the Middle East during the concluding years of that decade. This could be due to three main reasons:

1. Europe's regional influence is mostly restricted to Lebanon. Of course, that influence has been fluctuating. Many European countries, especially France, have been traditionally influential in that country. Others like Germany lacked a well-defined position in the Middle East because of the special conditions that governed them following the Second World War and their presence has been more economic in nature than political. Therefore, the European countries have played their most active role in crises that were directly related to Lebanon.
2. The Arab–Israeli conflict still follows the rules of the Cold War and is mainly managed by Anglo-Saxon countries. Therefore, because of strong bonds with the United States and Britain, Israel has not been willing for other European countries to get become involved in this issue.
3. The stance taken by the European countries in favor of the establishment of a Palestinian government and withdrawal of Israeli troops from Golan Heights has added to Israel's reluctance to let other European countries influence the peace process and other regional developments. Also, in view of the historical influence of the European countries among regional Arab leaders, Israel has always tried to keep the European countries away from negotiations.

In its pursuit of the peace process, Europe is trying to achieve at least three major goals:

1. Accelerating peace talks in the region in view of the necessity of long-term regional cooperation. Security and stability in the Middle East as well as enhancement of regional cooperation is vital to Europe's security, especially border security in that continent.
2. Failure of the peace process will be a major security threat for regional economy. From the viewpoint of a country like Germany, which attaches the

highest significance to economic and social development, conflicts in the Middle East will cause the region to lag behind the global economy. Although it is difficult to implement a European model in the region, powerful tools are needed to alleviate conflicts, realize peace, and encourage peaceful coexistence in order to facilitate regional economic cooperation. This clearly shows the importance of a successful peace process in the region.

3. Issues related to human values such as refugees, water, energy, health, and environment have been considered imperative by Germany and the EU for the establishment of stability and security in the region.

Europe has emphasized on the "land for peace" formula (which has also been highlighted by the quadrilateral committee) in its declared and official policies, and has pursued the same goal within the framework of the EU. In her recent regional tour, Merkel highlighted the necessity of recognition of Israel by regional countries and supported a statement issued by the Arab League in March 2007, which indirectly meets Germany's demands. Therefore, Germany, in particular, and the EU, in general, have given their nod to any accord that calls for trading land for peace including the agreements of Gaza-Jericho, Taba, Maryland, and other similar agreements.

Europe's positions are, in general, at loggerheads with Iran's stances. The conflict between two countries' positions and interests, on the one side, and between Iran and the EU, on the other side, has been escalating over the past two years. The issue of Holocaust and the effort made by the Iranian president to review Holocaust was met with vehement opposition on the part of the German political parties and the government. The first angry reaction from Germany was reflected in an address by Chancellor Angela Merkel at the Munich Security Conference. She frankly announced that believing in Holocaust is a basis for Germany's relationship with other countries and Germany will not show lenience toward those who deny Holocaust. As a consequence, some research institutes of Germany cut their relations with the Institute for Political and International Studies, which is affiliated to the Iranian Foreign Ministry and played host to a conference on negation of Holocaust.

On the other side, Iran's policy toward the Middle East conflict is still based on supporting the people and the cause of Palestine and opposing Israel's expansionist and inhumane policies. While rejecting Israel's legitimacy, Iran is by no means ready to recognize Israel even in de facto mode. That policy is based on strategic and ideological principles. Even during the period of détente under the reformist president, Seyed Mohammad Khatami, those principles were upheld and relations with Israel were considered redline.

On the whole, Iran's policies on Israel and the Middle East conflict can be summarized as follows:

1. Israel poses direct and indirect threats to Iran's national security. Therefore, it should be treated as a security matter.
2. Iran insists on the implementation of UN resolutions by Israel and the necessity of its compliance with international regulations.

3. Iran considers defending the rights of Palestinians an obligation both from the viewpoint of Islamic and human considerations and in terms of international laws and regulations.
4. Iran maintains that continuation of Israel's occupationist and expansionist policies is a major reason for the continuation of the crisis, instability, and insecurity in the Middle East. Iranian officials believe that holding a referendum in Palestine in which Muslims, and non-Muslims, in addition to the current inhabitants of Palestine, Palestinian refugees, and immigrants would be entitled to vote, is a good way to end the existing crisis. Iran urges that Israel has acted in violation of the United Nations security council resolutions as well as international law and maintains that the best solution to the crisis is withdrawal of Israel from the occupied territories and establishment of a Palestinian government that would be accepted by the whole Palestinian nation.

These points were discussed by Iran and Europe during negotiations that took place in 1999, 2000, and 2001. However, because of the later focus on Iran's nuclear case and subsequent nuclear talks between Iran and the three European countries, negotiations on regional developments have been marginalized. They are currently pursued through bilateral negotiations and remain a cause for differences between Iran and Europe.

Europe's decision to support Israel, and refrain from recognition of a Palestinian government in which Hamas holds a majority, has frequently led to failure of peace agreements, demographic changes, and continuation of Israel's policy for building more Jewish settlements in the occupied lands. The EU even supported Israel's 33-day aggression in South Lebanon. On the other hand, listing Hamas as a terrorist group by the EU has cast serious doubts on Europe's interaction with the Palestinian government.

Part III

Strategic conclusions: The way forward for improving Iran–Europe relations

It is very clear that Iran and Europe have a complicated relationship with both common as well as opposing interests. The central focus of Iran–Europe relations over the last 29 years has been on differences and opposing interests. There needs to be a new political movement to enhance fields where there are mutual interests (such as oil and gas, security, the environment, and transportation). The development of ties in such fields will expand the areas of common interest and will enable a better understanding between both sides. This will also reduce the differences that exist in other areas and will lead to an environment of closer cooperation, which will surely benefit the interests of both parties. More needs to be done to promote better Iran–Europe relations, and the following strategic conclusions highlight the way forward to that end:

1. Cooperation in establishing peace and security in the Persian Gulf, the Middle East proper, Central Asia, and the Caucuses. Today, the crises in Iraq, Afghanistan, Palestine, and Lebanon are considered among the most important issues affecting the stability of the international system. Iran plays a pivotal role in each of these issues and can be an important strategic player in helping to bring about peace and stability to the region as a whole.
2. Holding the fourth largest reserves of oil and the second largest reserves of natural gas, Iran can fulfill Europe's energy needs, especially its natural gas needs. Nurturing a strategic relationship between Iran and Europe in the energy field will therefore be an important development for both parties.
3. Achieving mutual understanding in regard to weapons of mass destruction will remove one of the main barriers impeding the improvement of relations between Iran and the European Union (EU). The following framework can be a positive model for nurturing mutual understanding between the two sides:

    a. International agreements regarding weapons of mass destruction—including the Non-proliferation treaty, the Chemical Weapons Convention, and the Biological Weapons Convention—should form the basis of negotiations and understanding.
    b. All conditions that go beyond the accepted international norms and guidelines must be removed from the negotiations. The extra conditions

such as access beyond the NPT, Safeguards Agreement, and Protocol 93 + 2 that were imposed upon Iran by the UN security council resolutions are clear examples of such additional guidelines that go beyond accepted international norms.

c. Europe should agree that discriminating against Iran in allowing it to draw upon its international rights to benefit from peaceful nuclear, chemical, and biological technology should be removed from the discussions. Iran's rights in using advanced technologies within the framework of international nonproliferation norms should not only be acknowledged but Europe must also be committed to actively cooperate with Iran to remove all limitations.

4. Terrorism is one of the disasters facing the world community today, and Iran has itself been a victim of terrorism. Taliban and al Qaeda are among the most dangerous terrorist groups and the UN Security Council has clearly passed resolutions, calling the international community to cooperate in battling these extremist groups. Iran and Europe can design a mutual model for combating this threat and can place UN Security Council Resolution 1737 as the basis for this agreement. Such an agreement will be successful only when each side moves to alleviate the other's concerns and when both sides are brought into the agreement on an equal setting. Fighting al Qaeda and the terrorist Mujahedin Khalq Organization, a group singled out by the Paris Agreement of 2004 between Iran and the European troika, are steps that can be taken for establishing mutual goodwill and can start the process on a right footing.

5. The Middle East peace process is a clear example of an area where Iran and Europe can work together. It is also a very clear example of the differences that exist between the two parties. Recognizing the undeniable rights of the Palestinian people, including the right of Palestinian refugees to return and the status of Jerusalem by the Europeans, are steps that can be taken in order to achieve some sort of a settlement in this drawn-out conflict. Both parties can move to implement UN resolutions that have been for years derailed by Israeli actions. Iran and Europe can move to establish peace and security in the region, based on a fair and just settlement of the Palestinian issue and with UN resolutions forming the basis of such a settlement. Such a move will have a positive impact on the broader Middle East region.

6. Iran–Europe discussions regarding human rights issues must be reestablished and activated. Seminars, discussions, and similar events can play an important role in bringing the sides closer together and can allow greater understanding between them. The collective agreements between the EU and the Organization of Islamic Conference can be placed as the focus of such a move and can allow for a broader dialogue initiative between the Muslim world and the West.

7. Europe should support Iran's bid to join the World Trade Organization without considering internal political developments in Iran or differences between Iran and Europe in other fields. Such a move will help enhance a

free, competitive, and market-driven economy in Iran. Such a development in itself will create unbreakable industrial and business ties between Iran and Europe, which will not only help promote better understanding between the two sides, but will also ensure greater flexibility by Europe and Iran for solving outstanding issues in other areas of mutual concern.

8. Europe has made it more difficult for Iranians to obtain visas to travel to the continent. This is a mistake. Developing people-to-people relations between the two sides is essential for fostering a foundation of greater understanding and creating a long-standing, strategic relationship. Therefore, by amending current regulations and easing restrictions, more can be done to promote relations between the citizens of Europe and Iranian society, which will only serve mutual interests.

9. A useful and active mechanism is needed to bring about such positive changes in Iran–Europe relations and to create the necessary framework for it. Thus, creating a "permanent working group" within the structure of a Steering Committee is an unavoidable necessity.

10. The Steering Committee will then have to work to create common committees on energy security, technological cooperation, political cooperation, security cooperation, fighting terrorism and extremism, fighting the spread of weapons of mass destruction, promoting human rights, etc. The creation of these working committees will ensure the implementation of the previously mentioned ideas and will bring the two sides closer together on all fronts.

Appendices

Appendix 1: Details of Hans-Dietrich Genscher's 1989 visit to Tehran[1]

On his arrival at Tehran's Mehrabad International Airport, his Iranian counterpart welcomed Genscher. During a short interview at the airport, Genscher said Germany was very interested to make constructive improvement in its relations with Iran. "Following my talks with Dr Velayati in Bonn and at the U.N. Headquarters in New York, we are expected to hold positive talks about expansion of relations between Tehran and Bonn during this trip to Tehran. We are interested to discuss international issues with the officials of the Islamic Republic of Iran and this trip will facilitate such negotiations. I am pleased for a chance to talk with Iranians," he said. In reply to Dr Velayati, who had expected a positive dialogue between the two countries, Genscher said: "I expect the same for my part and hope that the result of this trip would be positive."

During the meeting of the German Foreign Minister with Iran's President Ali Khamenei, the President welcomed the expanded relations between the two states with the careful observation of mutual interests. He said, "Such an exchange of visit has much benefits for the both sides. It will help the two to get familiar with each other's points of view on global issues. We believe that big countries in the world must get acquainted with our revolution and the language and culture of this revolution, and I think no such an orientation has occurred in a satisfactory manner so far. The Islamic Revolution is in fact a popular desire by people to revolutionize their life and lead an wholly independent life."

Referring to the big mistake committed by global superpowers and this misunderstanding of the revolution, President Khamenei said: "Regretfully I must say that the superpowers and above all the U.S. have committed a historical mistake in their relations with us and our people—mistakes which cannot be perhaps compensated or corrected easily. Of course I must praise Germany's position in the West. However, I am pleased to express my satisfaction over Germany's friendly stance toward Iran during these years and its fair position concerning the use of chemical weapons by Iraq. Yet as a whole, the position assumed by Western governments against the Revolution has so far been a gross historical mistake. They are totally mistaken about our country and our nation and for that reason I feel that Western governments are not fully acquainted with the culture of our revolution and the language and devotion that prevails among the Iranian people." Underlining Iran's neither Western nor Eastern stance, Ayatollah Khamenei added: "During the last one and a half century the Iranian nation has always been oppressed and insulted by big powers and for that reason our 'Neither-East-Nor-West' motto is the sweetest for our people. In our international relations we give very much weight to our independence, national interests and national identity. In fact, without relying on our Islamic and national identity we could have not gained all our achievements."

In conclusion while underlining the need for broader and deeper communication between Iran and Germany, the President thanked the German Foreign Minister for inviting the Iranian Foreign Minister and Minister of Economy and Finance to travel to Germany.

During his trip, the German Foreign Minister met with Ayatollah Akbar Hashemi-Rafsanjani who at the time was the parliament's speaker. In that meeting, Genscher said: "We have mutual interests and differences with you. You are Muslims and we are Christians, yet, our mutual interests have always overcome our cultural difference. Such an understanding can serve as a good basis for direct and broader ties between the two states. We are interested in a sovereign Iran and hope that our governments will cooperate with each other. Our economic ties are at a satisfactory level and we hope to collaborate with Iran in cultural and educational fields as well. Meanwhile, due to the sincerity of our ties we are also willing to conduct our political talks at ministerial level. We are interested to understand your revolution and your revolutionary people and for that reason we call for political dialogue with Iranian officials. Undoubtedly such contacts will be fruitful for the two states."

In reply to the German Foreign Minister, Ayatollah Hashemi Rafsanjani said: "I thank you for traveling to Iran. I expect that this trip will serve as a prelude for better relations between the two states and can eliminate certain misunderstandings. In the past and at present, our country has had an unbalanced trade relation with the West. Naturally our revolutionary people are sensitive to such matters and look with misgiving to our relations with the West. We hope that such contacts will help us to achieve a balance in our relations in all fields. The most important framework for the beginning of such cooperation is the common points of interests between the two states."

In a meeting of the German and the Iranian foreign ministers, the two sides focused on the bilateral relations particularly in the fields of trade and economy, obstacles in the way and solution for the problems, as well as the political situation in the region. Referring to the 1980–8 Iraqi-imposed war against Iran, Velayati said: "From the beginning of the [Iraq's] occupation of our country, Iraq has been chanting peace slogans persuading its supporters who are feeding it with money and arms to believe that, even though it is ruining our country and is killing our people, it is a peace-lover."

Concerning the atrocities committed by Baghdad (invasion of residential areas and use of chemical weapons), the Iranian foreign minister thanked Germany for condemning the Iraqi regime for resorting to chemical weapons.

Focusing on Tehran's relations with neighboring countries, Velayati said: "We wish to live in an atmosphere of peaceful coexistence with our neighbors and contrary to Iraq which wishes to internationalize the war and involve other countries in the battle, we are trying to stop the war from spreading over neighboring countries."

Informing the German Foreign Minister that it was Baghdad that had commenced the war, Velayati said: "Like Germany we are against escalation and internationalization of this war and are aware of the dangers involved in such a flare up." During that meeting the two sides discussed bilateral cooperation in technical fields, transfer of technology and trade and industry, and called for an expansion of ties and a balance in trade. The two sides agreed that a balance in trade could guarantee and consolidate German–Iranian relations. At the meeting, Genscher officially invited his counterpart to visit Germany and Velayati welcomed and accepted the invitation.

After seeing off the German Foreign Minister at the airport, Velayati made the following comments about the outcome of his talks with his German counterpart: "We had lengthy discussions about bilateral trade and industrial, cultural and political relations between Tehran and Federal Republic of Germany. Because of possessing advanced technology in many industries, Germany can serve as an active trade partner for Iran particularly in nuclear, telecommunication and electrical industries, fabrication of heavy machinery as well as chemical industries, and it was necessary to hold these high-level talks in order to coordinate between the different ministries of the two countries and achieve a balance in trade and prevent Germany from being the sole benefiting party. Our oil and nonoil sales and our imports from Germany should be equalized. Iran has always been an importer of technology. We must try to import technology from such countries, which possess advanced technology and are not hostile toward Iran. But it does not mean that we must stop criticizing German foreign policy. To hold relations with another country does not mean that we agree with all the policies of the other party. If we think as such we cannot find any country in the world whose foreign policy and ideology matches ours. During our negotiations we asked Germany to train a number of our students as experts in our required specialized fields and also warned them of some difficulties, which they have created for some of our students in recent years. We also asked them not to support terrorists and at the same time claim to be an advocate of human rights. If human rights is not considered a political tool, we said, they should not support it in any form. We reached agreements on exchanges of culture and science. We also reached preliminary agreement with them and their government's future performance will prove how much they will abide by their promises. We warned them to comply with our rightful wishes if they seek an expansion of relations with Tehran."

As to his assessment of relations between the two countries and Genscher's trip to Tehran, the foreign minister said: "Considering Germany's advanced technology which we need to rebuild our country, this trip was a positive trip and as a strong and stable government with good commercial and economic potential Iran can serve as a reliable partner for Federal Republic of Germany. Such relations will expand and will be consolidated in the future and we hope that what we have agreed with Germany will be translated into action in the future."

Asked whether the two sides discussed the war, Velayati said: "Of course this item was not on our agenda but it was mentioned by Genscher and he agreed with our position. We underlined the fact that it was Baghdad that had imposed the war on us and the German foreign minister was convinced and accepted this explanation." Velayati added: "With regard to Israel and the Palestinian rights we explicitly expressed our opinion to the Germans."

During his trip to Tehran, the German Foreign Minister also met and conferred with the Iranian Minister of Economy and Finance. During that meeting, bilateral economic and trade ties between the two countries, lack of trade balance between the two sides, and the need for Germany to adjust the balance of trade were discussed. We called on Germany to invest in Iran, solve the present problems in the way of investment, increase technical assistance, and train our manpower in the industry. Moreover, an invitation from the German Minister of Economic Affairs was handed over to the Iranian Minister of Economy and Finance to travel to that country.

Appendix 2: The full text of Sarkuhi's letter as it appeared in German publications[2]

The peak of sensationalism in the German and European media came when Berlin's *Tages Zeitung* published a letter by Sarkuhi. This newspaper devoted its first three pages to the publication of a letter by Sarkuhi, a concise version of which follows:

"A few days ago, an unidentified person telephoned the family of Sarkuhi and informed them that their two children have been taken into custody. Sarkuhi's family says that this telephone call was from the intelligence service. Sarkuhi and his brother have been missing since Monday. American organisations have simultaneously confirmed the fact that they are missing. The Iranian government has arrested him. He intended to join his wife who lives in Germany. He was missing for 47 days until his appearance at the Tehran airport. He wrote a letter, which, shortly before his disappearance, he sent abroad. In this letter he writes: 'I pleaded with the Iranian Intelligence Service to kill me'. This letter shows the destructive methods of Iran's intelligence system. With torture and a death threat, they intended to force him to co-operate with the intelligence service in order to unleash a propaganda war against the Mykonos trial. In this case, many Iranians are accused of the murder of the Kurds. Sarkuhi has become a victim of intrigues by the Iranian Intelligence Service. His wife is worried about his life, and his mother has contracted a heart ailment. In his letter, Sarkuhi explains the forced interview in which he said he had been in Germany for 47 days. In the Tehran airport interview, Sarkuhi was unable to present the passport containing a stamp to prove his entry into Germany. He said that his friend in Turkmenistan had taken it from him so as to help him obtain a visa for Canada. He later said that intelligence official had used his passport to travel to Germany in his place so as to prove his trip to Germany, while he himself had been in prison in Tehran. According to our information, the German Foreign Ministry is in possession of a copy of Sarkuhi's passport, which carries an entry and exit permit for Germany. The Foreign Ministry states: 'Sarkuhi, however, didn't in fact come to Germany, for the computer records every journey. Of course, the Foreign Ministry has not taken a stance. Sarkuhi is among 134 Iranian dissident writers. Thus far, many of these writers have been detained. This letter dated Day 14 [January 3] is as follows:

I write this letter in haste in the hope that many will read it some day. I want especially Saeedeh, Arash, and Bahar to become aware of my terrible destiny. I hope that after my detention or death, some will become aware of the pain of this unfortunate victim. Every second, I expect my arrest or murder, which would be presented to the world as suicide. Torture, imprisonment and death await me. Imagine my situation: I was arrested on November 4, at the airport. Until December 21, I was in the prison cell of the Intelligence Service. The Intelligence Service planned this before other incidents, such as my trip to Armenia, the attack on Mansour Koushan's house on the night we signed the writers' articles of association, followed by a visit to the German diplomat, Gust. My second arrest was in September 1996, two days after the attack on Koushan's house.

Gust, the German Embassy's cultural counsellor, had invited some writers. A total of six people had been invited, including Golshiri, Behbahani, Mehrangeez, Sepanlou, Roshanak Dariush and myself. I had not known Gust before. Manuel, the cultural counsellor at the French Embassy, had invited us before that. Nothing political was discussed. We only talked about the translation of literary works. But we were attacked and filmed while having dinner. They took me to prison and for the first time I became familiar with a man named Hashemi from the Intelligence Service. He spoke with me, Golshiri and Sepanlou. They said that the anti-spying department had come to save us, because we were not spies. Later, when the issue of Mykonos became sensitive, I realised that that they wanted to use us as a balancing weight against the Mykonos affair. I wrote a confidential letter to my wife. Two days later, while attacking Koushan's house they arrested me. They blindfolded, handcuffed and beat me. They forced me to telephone some people and arrange a meeting with them on the street for Wednesday.

On the same day, they registered my car in another name so as to give the impression that I had intended to escape. On that day, no one came but Golshiri and Mohammad Ali. Posing as a high-ranking official, a man spoke to us. These were all pre-planned. A few days later, they released me. The man by the name of Hashemi said that I am banned from leaving the country. One week later, my wife told me, 'It is rumoured that you have had an interview but I know nothing about it'. In late October, Hashemi called me and said that the ban on my leaving the country has been lifted; and I believed him. In evaluating myself during this incident, I believe I made two mistakes. One is that I had imagined that the Ministry of Information does not belong to the country's extreme factions. Secondly, I thought that because I had not been engaged in politics, they would have nothing to do with me. This created optimism in me and I bought a plane ticket to Germany, for I was very eager to see my wife and children.

At night, Hashemi called me and said that before the flight he must meet with me outside the main hall of the airport. I went to the airport with a friend. They handcuffed and blindfolded me and took me to the Intelligence Service prison. I became aware that they had sent someone else in my place to Germany so as to stamp an entry and exit permit in my passport. They had informed my wife that my flight would be on Lufthansa, but that it would be delayed. On the second or third day, they told me that, officially, I was missing. They said, 'You will remain here until the interrogation, interview and following investigations are over. We will then kill you and bury your body right here, or somehow we will take it to Germany.' They played a forged tape carrying my brother's voice, in which my brother, Ismail, was saying to my wife that the airport had informed him that I had left Iran. I had been sentenced to death without a trial, and without hope. My interrogation had begun on the 4th of November and had continued until the last day. But they spoke of it as if it had taken place in September. They questioned me at all levels.

They forced me to say the things they wanted me to say. Their plan was to psychologically exhaust me and force me to utter words that would be billed as a television interview. It was strange that this interview was forged in prison. They had prepared the interview themselves. Its main element dealt with spying. That is, in exchange for providing classified information to the German and French embassies, I had been given money. They forced me to say things about Gust, things which they wanted to hear. They forced me to say that I had sexual relations with women, as my other colleagues. But the main issue was spying. The question was, 'Why had I done it? Why had I been prepared to co-operate with them?' The truth is that I wanted it all to end and have them kill me. I requested in writing that they kill me or provide me with the means to kill myself so that I may be free of all this. This time I realised that they had many goals. They wanted to act reciprocally against the Mykonos affair. Make me a spy for Germany. The aim of the Ministry of Information was to set a trap for Germany and drag it into this intrigue. The second goal was to initiate propaganda against the Mykonos verdict. The third goal was to apply pressure on all writers in general, especially to cause my extinction.

Let us assume they attained all their goals, except to drag Germany into this affair and derive a benefit from it. To accomplish this, a more intricate design was necessary. The plan was to create a lot of noise. Due to my being missing, the Iranian government would at first keep silent, but later they would announce that I had gone to Germany. As Germany would announce my entry into the country, they would broadcast my interview. The other goal was that in the interview, which was supposedly conducted in September, it would be revealed that Sarkuhi had confessed to spying and had promised to co-operate, but had fled to Germany. Now, Germany must answer for all this. Where have they hidden Sarkuhi who is wanted as a criminal in Iran? In other words, Germany must extradite this spy and fugitive. Germany would then owe Iran the delivery of one Sarkuhi, while the real Sarkuhi has been put to death in an Iranian prison. During the Shah's reign I was detained for eight years, but that whole period was not the equivalent of five minutes of these 47 days.

But a snag appeared in this plan: Germany did not confirm my arrival. At this point, the second phase of their plan began. On the 4th or 5th December, they forced me to write a letter to my wife and tell her that due to family problems I have remained in Germany. They enclosed one page (or a copy of a page) of my passport and asked her to show it to my brother Ismail. Later, I realised that they had forced my wife to inform everyone of the subject of my letter. The goal was to ensnare Germany. But Germany had not confirmed or announced my entry. The Iranian government faced difficulty in officially announcing the matter. Therefore, the subject of a forged letter came up so as to publicly reveal my entry into Germany. But this did not happen. Not abandoning this plan, they said that they were prepared to set me free on condition that I obey their orders. They told me that I must appear at the Tehran airport and hold an interview with reporters. I accepted that. But I didn't trust their word. They dictated the words of the interview to me. I told the BBC and Radio France whatever they had dictated to me. In appearance, they had released me, but I was constantly under surveillance. I don't know what they will do to me. I hope that my wife and children will read this letter and become aware of my dire situation. I know that they will take me to prison. They will kill me and claim that I have committed suicide. They will accuse me of something, which will be contradictory with my life. Whoever receives this letter must give it to my wife after my arrest. The truth is that I died on Nov 4."

Appendix 3: The text of the Berlin Prosecutor Department about the summary of the reasoning of the Berlin Court verdict, April 10, 1997[3]

"With this vote, the court brings to an end a prosecution which took approximately three and a half years. The subject of the prosecution was the armed murders on September 17, 1992 at the Mykonos Restaurant in Berlin. Dr Sadegh Sharafkandi, the leader of the Kurdistan Democratic Party; Fattah Abdeli, the party's representative in Europe; Homayoun Ardalan, the party's representative in Germany; and Nourollah Mohammad-pour Dehkurdi, his consultant and translator in Berlin, were killed as a result of this murder. The owner of the restaurant was severely injured.

Merely by clarifying the incident of the perpetration of the crime at the scene, the court is unable to determine whether the accused participated in it or not, and in what manner they participated. Without sufficient information on the causes and circumstances of the incident, any description of the incident would convey a flawed picture to the mind. In such a case, the determination of the perpetrators of the crime and their assistants, and the determination of the crime and its punishment are not possible. The legal meaning of the perpetration of the crime is much broader. This meaning entails the total history of the event, in whose framework the accused have been charged with murder. Therefore, during the court's investigation, it had to be made clear why the victims should have lost their lives, and who is responsible for this? In addition to that, it had to be clearly demonstrated that in the face of legal principles and the right of each individual to life, according to Article II of the Declaration of Human Rights, with the legal tools at its disposal, the legal system shoulders the responsibility not to allow the obstruction of the prosecution of such crimes, to bring the guilty to book, and to identify by name those who support them.

Sometimes in media reports they have used the expression, 'Iran seated on the trial bench'. But the main trial is limited to five defendants. The determination of the source and informers of the crime is only for clarifying the share each defendant has had in the perpetration of the crime. This incident originates in Iran's historical relations after the Islamic revolution. The efforts of Iranian Kurds for acquiring independence set this segment of their community and political organisations—of which the Kurdistan Democratic Party is one—against the ruling regime. The leaders of opposition groups, who claimed rights to autonomy, were pursued, compelled to leave the country, propagating their goals from abroad. Thus, such individuals abroad were surveyed and pursued by the Iranian intelligence service such that in an interview, dated 30th August 1992, with Minister of Information and Security Fallahian, it can be deduced that one of the important organs under surveillance by this organisation was the Kurdistan Democratic Party. In order to silence this voice, Iran's political leader decided not only to fight against the leadership of Iran's Democratic Party, but also to destroy it.

The murder of Dr Abdul-rahman Ghassemlou, the former leader of this party, and two of his closest aides, on July 13, 1989 in Vienna, and the crime, which is the subject of today's judgement, are of the consequences of this decision. One cannot overlook the thread, which connects the incidents in Vienna and Berlin. One cannot relate these crimes to internal conflicts among the Kurdish opposition. After viewing the documents and the evidence, one can clearly observe the decision-making at the pinnacle of the leadership of the Iranian Government, resulting in annihilating people abroad who are opposed to the regime. Arriving at decisions for such actions is under the control of a 'Committee for Special Affairs', which is confidential and above and beyond the Constitution. Its members are comprised of the president, minister of the security organisation, the head of foreign policy, representatives of the security organisation, other organisations, as well as the 'religious leader'.

For further clarification, it is necessary to confirm at this point that the 'religious leader' is not the spiritual leader of Muslims. As before, a religious and spiritual leader is under the authority of the great ayatollahs, which are not members of the 'Committee for Special Affairs'. The 'religious leader', who is a member of this committee and considered to be the 'Leader of the Revolution', is the title of a political office, which has come into existence after the revolution of 1979. If the goal of these actions is the murder of an individual abroad, as a political authority, the 'religious leader' must have confirmed the order to commit murder, which would impart apparent legality to the crime in question. Neither in fact, nor legally—even if blessed with a *fatwa*—an order to commit murder is not obligatory. Even Shiite Muslims ought not to be forced to obey it. Rather, it is an order to commit murder for which no governmental law has been passed.

The 'Committee for Special Affairs' continually turns over to its members the execution of actions for which a decision has been made and, bearing the goal in mind, and by considering the means under their control, they choose the most appropriate individuals for the above-mentioned goal. For their part, the members determine an individual as the 'leader of the team', whose duty it becomes to commit the murder. The 'leader of the team' is an experienced warrior, has many capabilities, and has undergone training. He chooses special individuals for his team known as 'The Strike Team'. At the same time he has absolute powers to give the necessary orders to those individuals who participate at the scene of the crime and, based precisely on this method, the murders of Dr Sharafkandi and his companions were committed.

After Mr Fallahian reported to the 'Committee for Special Affairs', and the committee decided on the assassination of Dr Sharafkandi, on behalf of that body he became responsible for executing the action. Thereafter, he provided for the necessary preliminaries for the execution of this assassination, code-named 'Bozorg Alavi'. For such actions, at the Ministry of Information, Mr Fallahian handed over the responsibilities to a Department of Consultation for Special Duties. In late June and early July, Asghar Arshad and Kamali travelled to Germany. The two individuals are members of a cover-up organisation of the Ministry of Information and it is their duty to draw plans for the execution of actions and deliver the relevant report to Mr Fallahian. For pursuing such a goal, they made use of the existence of Darabi, a connecting member of VEVAK.

A member of the Guardians Corps., Darabi has been in Germany since 1980. His intelligence activities demonstrate that he is very suitable for planning the action. In addition, he is connected to the Hizbollah, which has been financially supported and equipped by Iran and possesses training camps. This group has the duty to resist with military tools any entity opposed to the Islamic regime. It is infamous for numerous violent terrorist actions. According to the order, Darabi created a group for the execution of the plan, which included the Lebanese Amin, Rhayel, and Ali Sabra, a member of Lebanon's Hizbollah. From an ideological and militaristic point of view, Amin and Rhayel have undergone training in Iran. In 1989–90, along with three other members of the Hizbollah, such as Ali Sabra who has requested asylum in Germany, the two came to Germany. Edris, who lived in asylum in Berlin, had close connections with Amin and Rhayel. Ayyadh had also requested asylum in Germany; he is not connected to the Hizbollah. He lived in Lebanon, was a member of Amal, and is an experienced warrior. He is the son of the brother of Darabi's son-in-law, who is his trading partner.

In July 1992, Ayyadh had become familiar with the preliminaries of the action. At the latest, in late August 1992, Amin, Rhayel and Edris were aware of the plan of action and announced their preparedness for their co-operation. In order to prepare for the preliminaries, on Aug 25, 1992, Darabi purchased a mobile telephone, which made speedy contact with his team possible, without the possibility of being bugged. On Sept 7, 1992, the famous team, known as 'The Strike Team', travelled to Berlin. The helm of the team was in the hands of Sharif, whose real name, according to statements by Mesbahi ('Witness C') was Abdul-rahman

Hashemi. Well-trained in guerrilla warfare, the execution of the major operations was in his hands. In order to execute the action, he contacted Darabi. For unknown reasons, Sharif set aside Ayyadh, while another individual by the name of Fazlollah Haidar from Asnabrück, who had a close friendship with Kazem Darabi, was chosen. He was responsible as driver. In addition, he made contact with an unknown person by the name of Mohammad, who was most probably a member of 'The Strike Team'. On Sept 11, 1992, the last phase of the preliminaries was prepared. Amin was called to Berlin and, on Sept 12, 1992, in a two-man apartment shared with Darabi, he met with Rhayel and Haidar.

Darabi arrived on the next day; during this period he had obtained the key to the apartment of Senften Bergerin, which was used the team's residence. Darabi ordered all traces in the house to be destroyed and to always carry objects with them. Furthermore, he said that he would go to Cologne or Hamburg, adding that if the authorities in pursuit of the crime sought him, it should be said that during the incident he was in West [Germany]. On the night of Sept 13, 1992, Darabi took Sharif and Amin in a car to their team residence. He instructed Sharif to telephone him when all was over. According to the pre-arranged plan, Darabi went to Hamburg on that night and remained in West Germany until Sept 18, 1992. On Sept 13, 1992, with the money, which Darabi had given him, one of Darabi's close friends, Ali Sabra, purchased an automobile. What is most likely is that on the same day, Edris stole his brother's passport in order prepares it for a likely escape.

On the night of Sept 14, 1992, Dr Sharafkandi arrived in Berlin. The next day, it was agreed that Sharafkandi would meet with members of his party and other members of the opposition at the Mykonos restaurant on Sept 17, 1992. On Sept 16, 1992, a traitor who has not been identified by name communicated the location and time of the meeting to the group at Senften Bergerin. On the same day, Rhayel and Haidar brought the weapons, which included an Uzi machine gun and a waist-worn Lama weapon, each equipped with a silencer, to the Senften Bergerin apartment. Guided by Sharif, on the same night Amin, Rhayel and others went to the site of the crime to inspect it. The next night, armed with weapons, these men awaited the signal for action. Close to 21:00 hours, the telephone at the Senften Bergerin apartment rang. It had been agreed upon with the betrayer that he would send a signal to indicate when the targets of the crime are all present at the restaurant, and they can thus begin the action.

Moments later, the assailants appeared close to the scene. Close to 22:50 hours, Sharif and Rhayel entered the restaurant and situated themselves at the back of the restaurant's main room. Amin stood behind a door and held the site in his vision. Before Sharafkandi or others became aware of the situation, or showed any reaction, Sharif uttered a profanity in Farsi: 'No doubt, you sons of whores...' and immediately, drawing a machine gun from a sports bag, he fired at Dr Sharafkandi, Dehkurdi, Abdeli and Ardalan. In the course of two short bursts, he emptied 26 bullets. Subsequently, with the waist-worn weapon, Rhayel fired 4 bullets. He fired one bullet at the back of the head of Ardalan, who had doubled onto himself, causing his immediate death. From the right, he fired two bullets at Sharafkandi's head. He then situated himself behind Ardalan, where, from a distance of 5 centimetres, he fired a bullet at Sharafkandi's stomach. Pierced with numerous bullets, Dr Sharafkandi was dead on the spot. Abdeli also died on the spot. Dehkurdi, who was transferred to the Steglitz Clinic, was not saved. Severely wounded, Ghafari's doctor survived. Sharif and Rhayel then fled, met Amin in front of the restaurant and entered a car carrying Haidar and 'Mohammad', who had been waiting for them. Thus far, 'Mohammad' has not been identified. Sharif flew to Iran via Turkey. As a reward for his actions, he received a Mercedes Benz 230. However, based on gathered information, a little before their planned escape, Amin and Rhayel were arrested by the German Intelligence Service. After their arrest, Rhayel was identified as the one responsible for the crime. He had behaved criminally by taking advantage of the defencelessness of the victims. His motive had simply been the baseness of his nature. According to judicial sentences, Rhayel had committed this murder simply out of being base. This action had no religious motive; that is, religious beliefs had not been the cause of this crime.

The victims had been accused of acting against the Quran and Islamic principles. Their motives had only been to seek power. That is, the fact that a government, as it were a 'divine rule'—as Iran understands itself—had ordered this crime, made no difference to them. Religious issues could not prevent the ruling regime in Iran from annihilating the opposition group, which lived outside Iran. The answer to the question, What circumstances have led to the political motives of this crime?, is not entirely clear. Rather, the answer varies with every instance. Here, the issue is the fact that the political leader of Iran had issued the order for this action in order to preserve his own power.

Such murders indicate complete disrespect for human rights, for they recognise no right to life for political opponents. This was an impudent act. Therefore, it has not been behavior which is based on religious blindness; no religious reason existed for it. For the accused it was clear that their victims should have been murdered not on account of issues of belief, but rather because of their opposing stance against the ruling regime in Iran. They did not have the least doubt that this action was a political action; but an assailant who resorts to political action must oppose an order to kill handed down by a government official. Therefore, it is totally impossible and highly improbable that Rhayel was duty-bound to carry out the action. Even if a *fatwa* were issued, which would not be connected with this murder, every pious Muslim is not duty-bound to kill someone. If he did resort to such action, it would be based on his personal will. That such action was committed with a base motive is not contradictory with the fact that its originator and commander was a government official of Iran. Therefore, not only does it deserve the most severe condemnation, but also an assailant who has placed himself at the service of such a crime must be severely punished. Any other action would indicate weakness against government terrorism.

Therefore, Germany's High Court must decide on the question as to whether the crime of the accused must be dealt with according to Article 57H, Band 1, Sentence 1, No. 2, of the Book of General Punishment. The court shall act based upon all the reasons and the characters of the assailants. Based upon this, it is determined that Darabi is guilty of having acted criminally. He has lived in Germany for many years; he well understands Western thinking. He is especially experienced with regard to his previous sentencing on account of wrathful actions and attacking opposition students in the city of Mainz. He has understood to what extent Germany's legal system values human physical well-being. His acquiescence with the killing of a human being for reasons of political opposition does not arise from the fact that he hails from another culture and society. His motive for participating in the crime is that, from the point of view of thinking and action, Darabi is in agreement with the perpetrators of the crime, thereby placing himself at the service of the Iranian Government's command to kill. Whoever acts in this manner is not a criminal who has acted with a special motive or intention, rather, if one is completely subservient to the Islamic Revolution it does not necessarily mean that he should participate in such a crime. When the totality of the incident and the character of the assailant are taken into account, his crime is determined to be very serious.

Amin, who is guilty of assisting in four instances of murder as watchman at the door, has participated in a major way in this incident, portraying him as an accomplice. However, based on his responsibilities, ultimate causes indicate that Amin participated in the crime only as an assistant. The results of the investigation have shown that Amin was connected with this incident much earlier. The court must not consider it unlikely that unwillingly and solely due to family reasons, Amin refused to take any responsibility for firing bullets. Family responsibilities caused him to refuse this action. Personally, he has had no inclination for killing the victims. The main factor has been his connection with this group, leading him to accept some responsibility and, in terms of location; he stood at a distance from the action of the murder. His behaviour indicates that Amin has not had any desire to wield influence over these actions. He took responsibility for a role from which he believed he could not withdraw. But, nevertheless, his behaviour arises from base motives. Amin knew what these actions meant. He was aware that the assailants were acting consciously. As an accomplice in the crime, his punishment must be based on rules pertaining to the crime. However, as an assistant, his punishment ought to be moderate. Therefore, within the framework of established punishments—3 to 15 years—it appears that 11 years would be a reasonable punishment.

Edris is also accused of assisting in four instances of murder. His crime is similar to that of Amin's. His preparedness for the performance of actions and his escape are completely observable. He obtained information on flights outside the country and after the action he took Rhayel to Rhein. By stealing a passport, he protected his brother from being accused. From another point of view, his participation is far less than that of Amin's. Another individual accused by the name of Ayyadh has been set free. Because he neither participated in the action, nor did he perform any action pertaining to the crime, which was previously promised or agreed upon. Rather, toward the end of this judicial inquiry, certain investigations have demonstrated that 'The Strike Team' most likely did not offer him any role to play. He is therefore not responsible for assisting in the crime. He cannot be convicted based upon an agreement to cooperate in committing a crime, for it is not clear what assisting role had been considered for Ayyadh."

Notes

Introduction

1. "Velayati: A Shia Activist in the Service of the Politics of Opening," *Frankfurter Allgemeine Zeitung*, February 19, 1990.
2. Dr Manoochehr Mohammadi, *Review of Iranian Foreign Politics During the Pahlavi Period*, Tehran University Publication Institute, 1997.
3. Ali Rahmani, *Reunification of the Two Germanies*, Institute of Political and International Studies, Iranian Ministry of Foreign affairs, 1991.
4. "Iranian Foreign Minister Visit to Germany," Report from German TV Channel (ARD), *Bulletin of Daily Reports of IRI Embassy in Germany*, June 25, 1992.
5. "Relations between Iran and Germany," *Rheinischer Merkur*, May 3, 1993.
6. "Iranian Majlis Vice-Speaker Visits Germany," *Frankfurter Allgemeine Zeitung*, March 30, 1993.
7. "Iranian Intelligence Minister Fallahian Visits Germany," German Press Report, Bulletin of *Daily Reports of IRI Embassy in Germany*, October 9, 1993.
8. "Agreement between Iran and Germany to Reschedule Iranian Debts," *Deutsche Zeitung*, May 18, 1993.
9. "Warm relations between Iran and Germany," *Die Welt*, June 15, 1994.
10. "Tension in relations between Iran and Germany," *Guardian*, August 24, 1996.
11. "Negotiation between German and U.S. Leaders on Iran–Germany Ties," *Süddeutsche Zeitung*, June 14, 1995.
12. "Israel Protests against Warm Relations between Iran and Germany," *Die Welt*, June 7, 1995.
13. "Rushdie's Expectations from Germany," *Stuttgarter Nachrichten*, December 16, 1993.
14. "Purchase of Equipment for Manufacture of Weapons of Mass Destruction from Germany," *Frankfurter Rundschau*, December 16, 1994.
15. "Terrorism, Was It Ordered by the Embassy," *Spiegel*, September 29, 1996.
16. "Possibility of Link between Assassination of Bakhtiar and the Mykonos Affair in Berlin," *Franfurter Rundschau*, December 22, 1993.
17. "Qassemlu's Assassination by the Iranian Government," *Focus*, March 27, 1995.
18. "Espionage for Iraq," *Spiegel*, February 1, 1993.
19. "Interview with Fersch," *Focus*, Issue 41, October 11, 1993.
20. "Clerics, Mykonos, Hitchhiking," *General-Anzeiger*, February 7, 1997.
21. "Iranian Embassy Attacked," *Frankfurter Rundschau*, July 17, 1992.
22. "Iranian Foreign Minister's car attacked," *Frankfurter Allgemeine Zeitung*, January 19, 1996.
23. "Crisis in Relations between Iran and Germany," *Die Welt*, April 11, 1997.

Chapter 1 History of Iran–Germany relations

1. *Germany*, 1st edition, Institute of Trade Studies and Research (ITSR), May 1989.
2. *Kölnische Zeitung*, Issue 151, June 2, 1873.
3. "Genscher Signs a Cultural Contract in Tehran," *Frankfurter Allgemeine*, November 30, 1988.
4. Andreas Weiss, German *ARD* First TV Channel Report, 22:30, November 30, 1988 (Press Report in Tehran).
5. "Genscher in Tehran," *Die Welt*, Germany, November 29–30, 1988.
6. "Schimili," *Sueddeutsche Zeitung*, November 28, 1988.
7. "Bonn Helping Iran to Rebuild the Country," *Deutsche Zeitung*, December 6, 1988. (Schneider's Trip to Tehran.)

Chapter 2 Development of bilateral relations, 1990–7

1. "Iranian Foreign Minister Meets with Genscher-Kohl. Bonn and Tehran Hope Iraq Will Show Flexibility," *Suddeutsche Zeitung* daily, February 19, 1991.
2. "Iraq is Prepared to Withdraw Kuwait Unconditionally", *FAZ*, February 21, 1991.
3. "Genscher to Travel to Tehran for Reparations," *Suddeutsche Zeitung*, May 6, 1991.
4. "A Visit to Refugee Camps in Iran—Genscher Calls German Physicians to Help," *Suddeutsche Zeitung*, May 11, 1991.
5. Report on Genscher's visit to Tehran, *ZDF* television network, May 7, 1991, at 19 hrs.
6. Report on Iran's relations with the West, *ARD* television network, May 7, 1991, at 20 hrs.
7. "Germany Calls for Iraq to Pay Reparations for the War Imposed on Iran," *Kayhan* daily, January 16, 1991.
8. "Kinkel's Trip to Tehran," *Morgen*, January 31, 1991.
9. "Two German Hostages Likely to Be Freed Tomorrow or the Day After," *Ettela'at*, June 15, 1992.
10. "Dr Velayati's Three-Day Trip, a Humanitarian and Economic Visit," *Die Welt*, July 14, 1992.
11. Report on Velayati's visit to Bonn, *Deutschlandfunk* radio, July 15, 1992.
12. "Talks on Co-operation with Tehran," *Frankfurter Allgemeine*, April 28, 1993.
13. "Iran Desires the Completion of Bushehr Power Plant," *Frankfurter Rundschau*, April 30, 1993.
14. "Bonn Intends to Cooperate with the Iranian Intelligence Service," *Die Welt*, October 18, 1993.
15. "The Policies of Germany and Other Western Countries with Respect to Iran," *Frankfurter Allgemeine*, October 15, 1993.
16. Press announcement by the Office of Press and Information, Federal German Republic, No. 399, October 19, 1993.
17. "The Likelihood of Pardoning a German Citizen Sentenced to Be Executed," *Frankfurter Allgemeine*, January 14, 1994.
18. "The United States Is the Main Obstacle in the Attainment of Collective Cooperation in the Persian Gulf," *Jomhuri Islami*, February 5, 1994.
19. "Germany Announces Its Preparedness for the Transfer of Technology to Iran," *Hamshahri*, April 28, 1994.
20. Official Declaration of the German Foreign Ministry, June 13, 1995.
21. Report by *the Islamic Republic News Agency (IRNA)* on the visit of the Vice Speaker of the German Parliament to Tehran, October 18, 1995.
22. Report by *the Islamic Republic News Agency (IRNA)* on Willy Wiemer's trip to Tehran, January 15, 1995.

23. Report by *IRNA* on the trip of Iranian Deputy Foreign Minister to Germany, February 23, 1996.
24. Report by *IRNA* on the trip of Iranian Deputy Foreign Minister to Germany, April 21, 1996.
25. Report by *IRNA* on the trip of Iranian Deputy Foreign Minister to Germany, April 23, 1996.
26. "Secret Trip to Tehran," *Focus*, No. 23, June 3, 1996.
27. "Statements by Foreign Ministry Spokesman on the Exchange of Bodies of Martyrs and Captives between the Hizbollah and Israel," *IRNA*, July 23, 1996.
28. Report by *IRNA* on the trip of German Deputy Foreign Minister to Tehran, September 27, 1996.
29. Declaration of German Foreign Ministry, Press Office, German Federal Republic, Wednesday, November 6, 1996.
30. "Kohl's Letter to Rafsanjani for Calming the Situation," *General Anzeiger*, November 23, 1996.
31. "The Iranian President's Sermons on the Iran–Germany Crisis," *Jomhuri Islami*, November 24, 1996.
32. "Iranian Festival, the German Press, and the Frankfurt Exhibition," *Salam*, October 15, 1991.
33. "Siemens Company Provided Expenses for National Football Team Training Camp," *Resalat*, April 8, 1992.
34. "Seminar on the Expansion of the Persian Language and Scholarly and University Relations between Iran and Germany," *Jomhuri Islami*, November 30, 1993.
35. "Iranians Are to Learn German as the First Foreign Language," *Die Welt*, September 11, 1995.
36. "Joint Meetings between Iranian and German Journalists, an Effective Step for Understanding between the People of the Two Countries," *Kayhan*, October 25, 1995.
37. Report by *IRNA* on Dr Larijani's trip to Germany, February 27, 1996, 1:43 hrs.
38. Report by *IRNA* on Dr Larijani's trip to Germany, February 27, 1996, 2:37 hrs.
39. Report on Iran and Germany Signature of New Contract for Expansion of Cooperation, *IRNA*, June 29, 1996.
40. Report on Möllemann's trip to Tehran, *ZDF* television network, June 29, 1991.
41. Report on expansion of relations between Iran and Germany, *ARD* television network, June 29, 1991.
42. "New Facilities and Methods for Investors in Iran Examined," *Resalat*, September 12, 1992.
43. "Government Approves Utilization of 1% of Carpet Exports for Advertisements and Marketing," *Farshe Iran (Iranian Carpets)*, printed in Germany, January 1993.
44. "Iran and Germany Reach an Agreement over Financial Difficulties," *Hamshahri*, February 27, 1994.
45. Udo Hahn, "Iranian Political Officials' Trip to Germany and Relations between the Two Countries," *Rheinische Merkur*, March 4, 1994.
46. "Iran Has Decided to Purchase SKET Industries in Magdeburg," *Frankfurter Allgemeine*, December 7, 1996.

Chapter 3   Challenges to Iran–Germany relations

1. Amir Beig, Kamal, "Priorities in German Foreign Policy," *Monthly Bulletin of IPIS*, No. 140, pp. 15–18 (here p. 17).
2. Donfried, Karen, "German–American Relations in the New Europe," December 5, 1996, p. 3, available at internet: www.fas.org/man/crs/91–018.htm
3. Rubinstein, Alvin, "Germans on Their Future," *Orbis*, Winter 1999.
4. "Superpower Europe," *The Economist*, July 17, 1999.

5. Report by *AFP*, "On the Aims of the German Economy Minister's Visit to Iran," June 29, 1991.
6. Report by *BBC Radio* on Iran–German differences over the Bushehr nuclear power plant, July 5, 1991.
7. "U.S.–Germany Tug of War on Relations with Iran," *International Herald Tribune*, December 2, 1993.
8. "The West's Anger Regarding Cooperation Between Iran and Germany, Hypocritical," *Frankfurter Allgemeine*, October 15, 1993.
9. Interview with Bernd Schmidbauer, "Germany's Response to U.S. and British Objections to Relations with Iran," German *NTV* television network, October 17, 1993.
10. "Israel's Objections to Iran–Germany Economic Relations," *DPA*, February 24, 1995.
11. Berg, Justine, "Differences in Strategy Between the U.S. and Germany in Facing Iran," *Christian Science Monitor*, as reported by *DPA*, February 24, 1995.
12. "Shimon Peres: Germany's Stance on Iran Is Questionable," *Reuters*, Bonn, August 18, 1994.
13. "Israel's Concern Over Expansion of Iran–Germany Cooperation," *AFP*, Jerusalem, October 21, 1994.
14. "Germany's Policy on Iran Has Fooled Israel," *Die Welt*, June 7, 1995.
15. "Head of Society of German Jews' Stance Against Iran," *German Radio, English Service*, November 20, 1995.
16. "Iran, the Most Important Issue of German–American Negotiation," *IRNA*, May 23, 1996.
17. "US Gathers Information on German Companies Exporting Technology to Tehran," *Der Spiegel*, March 17, 1996.
18. Wagner, Hartmut, "Covert Reasons for Creating an Atmosphere Against Iran—Propaganda by Israel's Supporters Against Iran," *Deutsche Wochen Zeitung*, June 7, 1996.
19. "Europe's Attack Against U.S. Policy on Iran," *Frankfurter Allgemeine*, May 9, 1996.
20. Eisenstadt, Michael, "Living with a nuclear Iran," *Survival*, 41, No. 3, Autumn 1999, pp. 124–128.
21. *Ha'aretz*, Internet Edition, 18 February 1998, http://www3.haaretz.co.il/eng/scripts/; *Washington Times*, May 7, 1998.
22. Riedel, Bruce, "US Policy in the Persian Gulf: Five Years of Dual Containment," The Washington Institute for Near East Policy, *Policy Watch* No. 315, May 8, 1998, p. 2.
23. U.N. Register of Conventional Arms, 1992–1996.
24. Steinberg, Gerald, Jerusalem Centre for Current Affairs, "European interests in the Middle East," http://faculty.biu.ac.il~steing/election
25. "The Role of EU in the Peace Process," Communication made by Mr Manuel Marin, Vice President of European Commission, January 26, 1998, pp. 7–9.
26. Ely Karmon, "Iran's Policy on Terrorism in the 1990s," paper presented on May 10, 1998 at the International conference on Terror at the Department of Political Science, Haifa University.
27. "Coalition Parties Facing a Mound of Difficulties—Emergency Meetings Due to Kinkel's Policy on Iran," *Suddeutsche Zeitung*, November 11, 1995 [trans.].
28. Editorial entitled, "Defeat of Coalition Parties in the Federal Parliament—Conference on Islam with Participation of Mr Velayati, Cancelled," *Suddeutsche Zeitung*, November 11, 1995 [trans.].
29. "All Major German Parties Have a Positive View on Iran," *Kayhan Havai*, December 6, 1995 [trans.].
30. Halliday, Fred, "Iran and the United Kingdom," unpublished report to the Foreign Affairs Committee, House of Commons, September 2000.
31. "German Security Organisation: Iran Continues to Pursue the Opposition," *IRNA*, April 20, 1994.
32. "Iranian Ambassador in Bonn Raises Serious Objections to the German Government," *Jomhuri Islami* newspaper, April 8, 1995.

33. "German Police Do Not Discover Any Evidence of Explosives on Iranian Cargo Vessel," *IRNA*, March 27, 1996.
34. "Terrorism: was it ordered by the Embassy?," *Der Spiegel*, No. 31, July 29, 1996.
35. "The Kidnapping of an Iranian," *General Anzeiger*, February 17, 1996.
36. "German Government and Police Culpable in MKO's Attack on Iranian Embassy," *Abrar* newspaper, April 8, 1992.
37. Report of Mr Velayati's visit to Germany, *Suddeutsche Zeitung*, July 15, 1992.
38. "After a Notable Incident, Velayati Ends His Trip Prior to Schedule," *Suddeutsche Zeitung*, July 17, 1992.
39. "Iranian Foreign Minister's Trip to Germany," *Berliner Morgen Post*, July 14, 1992.
40. Report on Iran's deputy Parliament speaker's trip to Germany, *Frankfurter Rundschau*, April 28, 1993.
41. Report on Iran's deputy Parliament speaker's trip to Germany, *Frankfurter Allgemeine*, June 30, 1993.
42. Documents of the Embassy of Iran in Bonn.
43. "The Federal Parliament's Support of Salman Rushdie," *DPA*, December 16, 1995.
44. "After 5 Years' Imprisonment, Iran Allowed a Prisoner to Travel Abroad," *Hannoverische Allgemeine*, July 4, 1994.
45. "The Arrest of an Accused," *Frankfurter Rundschau*, May 19, 1992.
46. "Iranian Ambassador Summoned to German Foreign Ministry," *Kayhan* newspaper, October 12, 1993.
47. "Representative of the German Government to meet spy in Iran," *Jomhuri Islami* newspaper, October 16, 1993.
48. "Germany Has Agreed to Place a Computer at the Disposal of Iran for Tracking Down the Opposition," Persian broadcast, *BBC World Service*, November 14, 1993.
49. Interview with Paul Firsch by Wilhelm Dietel, *Focus* magazine, No. 41, October 11, 1993.
50. *Focus* magazine, No. 23, June 6, 1994.
51. "Expulsion of Two Iranian Diplomats from Germany," *Al-Hayat* newspaper, August 23, 1995.
52. "German Internal Security Organisation Is Aware That Pressure Is Applied by the Iranian Embassy in Bonn," *Suddeutsche Zeitung*, July 27, 1996.
53. "Serious Protest of the Ambassador of the Islamic Republic of Iran in Bonn Against Installment of Bugging Devices at the Iranian Mission in Berlin," *Focus* magazine, November 27, 1996.
54. "Diplomacy—Silence," *Der Spiegel*, February 3, 1997.

Chapter 4   Analyzing a crisis

1. *Guardian*, August 24, 1996.
2. *Al-Watan al-Arabi*, June 10, 1994.
3. *Der Spiegel*, June 14, 1993.
4. *Al-Hawadeth*, October 16, 1995.
5. *Al-Watan al-Arabi*, June 10, 1994.
6. *Der Spiegel*, March 18, 1996.
7. *Der Spiegel*, June 14, 1993.
8. *Der Spiegel*, March 18, 1996.
9. *Al-Watan al-Arabi*, June 10, 1994.
10. *Guardian*, August 24, 1996.
11. *Deuschland Funk* (German radio), March 16, 1995.
12. "The Future of Iran–Germany Relations," *Handelsblatt*, March 20, 1996.
13. Islamic Republic News Agency, March 17, 1995, at 23:13 hrs.
14. "The German Ministry of Justice Waives the Summoning of the Iranian Minister of Justice," *IRNA*, March 30, 1996.

15. "Bani-Sadr to Testify in a German Court Next Week Against Iranian Officials," *IRNA*, Almaty, August 18, 1996, at 11:17 hrs.
16. Interview with Bani-Sadr, *Frankfurter Rundschau*, September 10, 1996.
17. "The Mykonos Court Privately Interrogates an Iranian Witness," *IRNA*, October 12, 1996.
18. *Der Spiegel*, October 14, 1996.
19. *Deutschland Funk* (German radio), November 12, 1996.
20. *Deutsche Presse Agentur (DPA)*, February 7, 1997.
21. *Kayhan*, November 15, 1996.
22. "Velayati: German Judicial Branch's Action Took Place Under the Influence of Zionists," *IRNA*, November 21, 1996.
23. *Frankfurter Allgemeine*, November 24, 1996.
24. Official Announcement of the Berlin Prosecutor's Press Department, No. 38/97, April 10, 1997.
25. Press Announcement of the Federal Prosecutor-General, Federal Court, Press Office, May 15, 1997.
26. "Iran's protest to Germany," *IRNA*, April 10, 1997.
27. "Deportation of Four German Diplomats," *IRNA*, April 10, 1997.
28. "Summoning of the German Ambassador to Tehran," *IRNA*, April 10, 1997.
29. *Liberation*, Paris, April 11, 1997.
30. Documents of the Iranian Ministry of Foreign Affairs.
31. *Jomhuri Islami*, April 11, 1997.
32. *Jomhuri Islami*, November 15, 1997.
33. *Guardian,* London, April 8, 1997.
34. *Frankfurter Allgemeine*, March 28, 1996.
35. http://www.iuscomp.org/gla/statutes/StPO.htm#200, article 153C
36. *Der Spiegel*, April 7, 1997.
37. *Frankfurter Allgemeine*, March 15, 1996.
38. Report of the Iranian Embassy in Bonn, April 1996.
39. *Frankfurter Allgemeine*, May 17, 1997.
40. *Al-Hayat*, London, April 15, 1997.
41. *Focus,* November 1, 2000.
42. *Guardian,* April 8, 1997.
43. *Le Monde*, March 17, 1996.
44. Report by Iran's permanent representative at the United Nations in New York, June 1997.
45. *New York Times*, April 11, 1997.

Chapter 5 Analytical conclusions: Foreign policy-making and the management of bilateral relations

1. Sariulqalam, Mahmoud, *Foreign Policy of Iran*, Iranian Institute for Strategic Studies, Tehran, 2001.
2. Allebad, Mostafa, *Alhayat*, London, May 11, 1997.
3. Interview with ex-president Rafsanjani, *Hamshahri*, January 10, 2000.
4. *Sobh-e Emrooz*, January 29, 1999.
5. "Details of Faraj Sarkuhi Case and German Embassy Attack in Tehran," *Fath*, January 2, 2000.
6. *Jahan-e Emrooz*, August 15, 1999.
7. *The Islamic Republic News Agency (IRNA)*, News Item 54, 13:53 local time.
8. *Azadegan*, December 29, 1999.
9. *Sobh-e Emrooz*, August 19, 1999.
10. "Announcement of Iran's Judiciary Organization of Armed Forces (JOAF)," *Resaalat*, July 22, 1999.
11. "The Statements of Head of the JOAF", *Khordad*, November 11, 1999.

12. *Sobh-e Emrooz*, December 4, 1999.
13. *Khorassan*, January 25, 2000.
14. "Disclosure of the Witness About the Western Intelligence Services," *IRNA*, October 22, 2000, 16:32 local time.

Chapter 6   The Middle East as a weapon of mass destruction-free zone

1. David Krieger, "the Most Important Moral Issue of Our Time," www.NuclearFiles.org
2. UN Document, NPT/CONF.2005/wp.40, working paper presented by the State of Qatar on behalf of the States members of the League of Arab States to the 2005 Review Conference of the Parties to the Treaty on the Non-proliferation of Nuclear Weapons. It reads in part:
    13—The outcome of the 2000 Conference was built on the 1995 resolution on the Middle East. The point of departure for the 2005 Review Conference should be based on the cumulative result of the outcomes of those two conferences. Taking into consideration that the outcome of the 1995 Review and Extension Conference of the Treaty on the Non-proliferation of Nuclear weapons represents an integrated package deal, it is important to note that if the 1995 resolution on the Middle East were compromised, all the outcomes of the 1995 Review and Extension Conference would be compromised.
    14—Ten years have elapsed since the adoption of this resolution and five since the last Review Conference, without any serious attempt by the international community at implementing it. There is no mechanism for its implementation or follow-up.
3. "Nuclear treaty in 'crisis of confidence'", *International Herald Tribune*, May 2, 2005.
4. Baumgart Claudia and Muller Harald, "A Nuclear Weapon-Free zone in the Middle East: A Pie in the Sky?," *The Washington Quarterly*, Winter 2004–2005, p. 57.
5. Martine B. Kalinowski, "Steps Towards a Weapons of Mass destruction Free Zone in the Middle East, International Network of Engineers and Scientists against Proliferation," 1999.
6. Baumgart Claudia and Muller Harald, p. 54.

Chapter 7   Iran's nuclear dossier

1. CNN, Interview with Mohamed ElBaradei, Director General of International Atomic Energy Agency, December 13, 2002.
2. Director General's report to Board of Governors on Iran, June 2003.
3. *Los Angeles Times* reported on June 17, 2003, that the American officials have not been able to report Iran's case to the United Nations Security Council. It quoted an expert on weapons of mass destruction as saying that the reconciliatory tone of International Atomic Energy Agency's (IAEA) Board of Governors had amazed him and perhaps Board of Governors thought that the reconciliatory approach will encourage Iran to cooperate more with IAEA.
4. IAEA website, June 19, 2003.
5. Associated Press, Interview with John Bolton, August 13, 2003.
6. Text of his speech in the 47th meeting of IAEA, September 15, 2003.
7. Dr Hassan Rowhani, former secretary of the Supreme National Security Council, "Reports that were given to us at Supreme National Security Council did not reflect such critical conditions. In Mordad 1381 (August 2002) when Iran's underground nuclear activities were revealed by foreign news agencies, officials emphasized that the Islamic Republic of Iran's activities are quite legal and there was no reason for concern. In June 2003 when the Agency presented its first report, officials believed that the dossier contained nothing to concern Iran and said the row will end in the said meeting." Interview with *Daily Iran*, special issue on nuclear crisis, March 2005, p. 9.

8. Hossein Baqerzadeh, "Countdown to Collapse of the Iranian Government Has Started," Akhbar Rooz website, September 26, 2003.
9. ISNA, Tehran Friday Prayer sermons by Ayatollah Hashemi Rafsanjani. The interim Friday Prayer leader emphasized that there is no difference among political groups on signing or rejecting the additional protocol and called rumors as psychological warfare by enemies of Iran, September 12, 2003.
10. The *Financial Times* wrote on June 1, 2003, that Europe should prove that conditional talks with Iran can be beneficial to nonproliferation of nuclear weapons and other weapons of mass destruction. The daily added that the European countries should convince Tehran that Europe and Iran have shared interests and, therefore, they should show Washington and the whole world that more inspections could be useful. The article concluded that if the EU failed to do that, it would be a total failure for the foreign policy of the EU.
11. The *Daily Guardian* reported on October 4, 2003, that concerns stirred by the United States at an international level about Iran carried concerning similarities to the disputes in Iraq. The paper added that the White House had already emphasized the possibility of the use of force against Iran. President George Bush had warned Iranians in late July that it was not in their benefit to build nuclear weapons and noted that the United States was considering all possible options. The *Los Angeles Times* later reported that CIA had informed intelligence services of friendly countries about aerial and missile attacks on Iran's nuclear installations, thus indicating that the countdown had already started.
12. Address by Dr Hassan Rowhani, former secretary of the Supreme National Security Council, to members of the High Council of Cultural Revolution, "All issues on which we reached an agreement with three European ministers had been already determined by the Islamic system. That is, if we had not reached an agreement with the said three ministers, we would have announced unilaterally that we would sign the additional protocol and present full picture of Iran's nuclear activities to IAEA, and we would have declared that Iran would partially suspend fuel cycle. I mean that it had been ratified (in the leaders' meeting) that even if we did not reach an agreement with the said three countries, we would take the above measures unilaterally," *Rahbord Quarterly*, No. 37, p. 10.
13. "… welcomes Iran's decision voluntarily to suspend all enrichment-related and reprocessing activities and requests Iran to adhere to it, in a complete and verifiable manner," part of resolution adopted by IAEA's Board of Governors on November 26, 2003.
14. "Decides that, should any further serious Iranian failures come to light, the Board of Governors would meet immediately to consider, in the light of the circumstances and of advice from the Director General, all options at its disposal, in accordance with the IAEA Statute and Iran's Safeguards Agreement."
15. "Sleuths Patrol Nations for Nuclear Mischief," *New York Times*, December 30, 2003.
16. The *Washington Post* reported on February 24, 2004, that IAEA's inspectors have found out about Iran's experiments with polonium, which is used in atomic explosions. The report called the revelation the latest instance of undeclared nuclear activities by Iran. The paper also noted that information about Iran receiving parts and drawings of P-2 centrifuges to enrich uranium were also disclosed shortly before that. "Neither polonium, nor centrifuges were mentioned in Iran's detailed report and IAEA officials say that discovery of P-2 centrifuge parts and drawings is a hard blow to the Agency's trust in Iran." The paper also quoted an analyst as saying that Iranians describe the omission as a simple ignorance, but IAEA officials do not think so.
17. "Analysis of samples taken from domestically manufactured centrifuge components show predominantly LEU contamination, while analysis of samples from imported components show both LEU and HEU contamination. It is not clear why the components would have different types of contamination if, as Iran states, the presence of uranium on domestically manufactured components is due solely to contamination

originating from imported components," part of the IAEA Director General's report to the Board of Governors, February 2004.

18. *The New York Times* carried a report by William Brod on February 28, 2004, saying that the European diplomats and the American specialists have noted that according to inspectors' findings, part of highly enriched uranium, which has been detected on Iran's nuclear installations, has been imported from Russia. The report also quoted European diplomats as saying that scientists at IAEA's specialized laboratories in Seibersdorf, Austria, have found similarities between atomic properties of Russian uranium and the samples collected by IAEA inspectors from Iranian centrifuges.

19. "As previously reported to the Board of Governors ... the Iranian authorities have stated that none of the imported UF6 had been processed, and, specifically, that it had not been used in any centrifuge tests. It was observed during Agency verification in March 2003, however, that some of the UF6 (1.9 kg) was missing from the two small cylinders. The Iranian authorities have stated that this might be due to leakage from the cylinders resulting from mechanical failure of the valves and possible evaporation due to their storage in a place where temperatures reach 55°C during the summer," part of the Director General's report to the Board of Governors, August 26, 2003.

20. "Iran has estimated that the original amount of plutonium in the solution was approximately 200 μg. Until sample results are available, the Agency cannot verify the accuracy of that estimate. However, based on Agency calculations, the amount of plutonium produced in 3 kg of depleted uranium targets under the declared irradiation conditions should have been substantially higher. The reason for this apparent discrepancy is not yet clear. The matter remains under discussion with Iran," part of the Director General's report to the Board of Governors, February 24, 2004.

21. Dr Hassan Rowhani's address to members of High Council of Cultural Revolution, "The Americans put tremendous pressure on them and they finally withdrew from their commitments. We were first informed about US pressures through political channels before it was revealed by the European press that Bush has contacted Blair and has criticized the agreement signed by three countries with Iran," *Rahbord Quarterly*, No. 37, p. 16.

22. Mehr news agency, "Europe Rejects US Proposed Paragraphs in Draft Resolution," March 7, 2004.

23. "The Non-Aligned Movement is satisfied with increasing cooperation between Iran and IAEA and hopes that cooperation will continue until a complete solution to the issue is achieved in the shortest possible time.... We appreciate role of the European members of Non-Aligned Movement and other countries for bolstering that cooperation and ask other members to support their move and join them," part of NAM statement in Board of Governors meeting, March 10, 2004.

24. "(The Board of Governors) Decides to defer until its June meeting, and after receipt of the report of the Director General referred to above, consideration of progress in verifying Iran's declarations, and of how to respond to the above-mentioned omissions," IAEA's Board of Governors resolution, March 2004, Paragraph 9.

25. The *Financial Times* quoted Nicholas Berns, US undersecretary of state, as warning his European counterparts to be tough on Iran during negotiations and reject any proposal to allow partial resumption of Iran's nuclear program. He added that the US will only support negotiations on the basis of complete cessation of all nuclear activities of Iran; "US Warns EU3," *Financial Times*, May 25, 2005.

26. ISNA news agency, Seyed Mohammad Khatami's press conference, June 17, 2004.

27. "In fact, today we are under no obligation with regard to enrichment and we are sure to make decisions and announce them along with the measures that we are going to take in the upcoming days," Mehr news agency, Dr Hassan Rowhani's press conference, June 20, 2004.

28. Non-Aligned Movement countries noted in their statement on June 19, 2004, that they believed the binding Paragraphs 7 and 8 of the resolution reflected on subjects that lay outside the IAEA's jurisdiction. Non-Aligned Movement member countries also opined

that the two binding paragraphs deprived countries of their undeniable right to produce and use peaceful nuclear energy. They also noted, in addition, that the said paragraphs would reduce the importance and role of safeguards and the reasons for prescribing them.

29. "Also concerned that, at its Uranium Conversion Facility, Iran is planning to introduce 37 tons of yellowcake, as this would run counter to the request made of Iran by the Board in resolution GOV/2004/49," part of IAEA Board of Governors' resolution, September 2004.

30. "Requests the Director General to submit in advance of the November Board:

    • A report on the implementation of this resolution.
    • A recapitulation of the Agency's findings on the Iranian nuclear program since September 2002, as well as a full account of past and present Iranian cooperation with the Agency, including the timing of declarations, and a record of the development of all aspects of the program, as well as a detailed analysis of the implications of those findings in relation to Iran's implementation of its Safeguards Agreement."
    • Part of IAEA Board of Governors' resolution, September 2004.

31. "Despite common notion, Paris Agreement is not a conclusion, but the beginning of true negotiations to reach an agreement. Since Iran had completed its structural facilities regarding fuel cycle at that time, the way was paved to suspend enrichment for a few months without seriously impairing nuclear fuel production plan. Europe had reciprocally accepted to normalize the situation in the meantime to clear the way for overarching talks under a calm atmosphere," part of the report to President Khatami by former secretary of the Supreme National Security Council, July 30, 2005.

32. According to Paragraph 6 of the Paris Agreement, EU3 admitted that suspension was a voluntary, confidence-building measure rather than being legally binding.

33. "Noting specifically the Director General's assessment that Iranian practices up to October 2003 resulted in many breaches of Iran's obligations to comply with its Safeguards Agreement, but that good progress has been made since that time in Iran's correction of those breaches and in the Agency's ability to confirm certain aspects of Iran's current declarations," part of IAEA Board of Governors' resolution, November 2004.

34. "Also noting specifically the Director General's assessment that all the declared nuclear material in Iran has been accounted for, and that such material is not diverted to prohibited activities, but that the Agency is not yet in a position to conclude that there are no undeclared nuclear materials or activities in Iran," part of IAEA Board of Governors' resolution, November 2004.

35. "... welcomes Iran's continuing voluntary commitment to act in accordance with the provisions of the Additional Protocol, as a confidence building measure that facilitates the resolution of the questions that have arisen, and *calls on* Iran once again to ratify its Protocol soon," IAEA Board of Governors' resolution, November 2004, Paragraph 3.

36. Mottaki told NHK on March 6, 2006, that the three European states (Germany, France, and Britain) have agreed to Iran's request for small-scale enrichment.

37. GOV/2005/77, September 24, 2005.

38. GOV/2006/14, February 4, 2006.

39. SC/8679, March 29, 2006.

40. S/RES/1696 (2006), July 31, 2006.

41. "The Security Council shall determine the existence of any threat to the peace, breach of the peace, or act of aggression and shall make recommendations, or decide what measures shall be taken in accordance with Articles 41 and 42, to maintain or restore international peace and security," UN Charter, Article 39.

42. "In order to prevent an aggravation of the situation, the Security Council may, before making the recommendations or deciding upon the measures provided for in Article 39, call upon the parties concerned to comply with such provisional measures as it deems

necessary or desirable. Such provisional measures shall be without prejudice to the rights, claims, or position of the parties concerned. The Security Council shall duly take account of failure to comply with such provisional measures," UN Charter, Article 40.

43. SIRES/1737 (2006), December 27, 2006.
44. Dr Ahmadinejad announced in the First National Festival of Exemplary Entrepreneurs that, "They cannot divide the nation by this worthless piece of paper," *Aftab* newspaper, December 25, 2006.
45. Dr Larijani, secretary of the Supreme National Security Council, told Kayhan that Iran would respond to the resolution by launching 3,000 centrifuges, *Kayhan*, December 24, 2006.
46. Text of "P5 + 1 Nuclear Package of Incentives to Iran," July (2006), www.bilaterals.org
47. Paris Agreement (signed on 15 November 2004), INFCIRC/637, November 26, 2004.

Chapter 8   Human rights

1. European Council of Ministers, Edinburgh, December 11–12, 1992, Conclusions of the Presidency, Doc/92/8, § 15.
2. Indyk, Martin, Speech at the Washington Institute for Near East Policy, May 18, 1993, quoted in Law, John: "Martin Indyk Lays Out the Clinton Approach", *Middle East International*, June 11, 1993, p. 3.
3. Undersecretary Peter Tarnoff, Testimony Before the House International Relations Committee: "Containing Iran," in: *U.S. Policy Toward Iran; Hearing before the Committee on International Relations, House of Representatives*, 104th Congress, First Session, No. 9, 1995. Washington, 1996, pp. 45–54.
4. Rudolf, Peter: *Konflikt oder Koordination? Die USA, Iran und die Deutsch-Amerikanischen Beziehungen* [Conflict or Coordination? The U.S., Iran and German-American Relations], Stiftung Wissenschaft und Politik, Ebenhausen, 1996, p. 18 f.
5. Regelsberger, Elfriede, "Common Foreign and Security Policy," in: Weidenfeld, Werner and Wesseis, Wolfgang: *Europe From A to Z; Guide to European Integration*, (Luxembourg, 1997), pp. 41–46.
6. "Memorandum of the Plenary Session of the 49th UN General Assembly," September 27, 1994, *European Foreign Policy Bulletin*, Doc. 94/228, 1994, Vol. 10, p. 312.
7. Jünemann, Annette: "The Mediterranean Policy of the EU", *France Year Book 1997*, (German–French Institute, Opladen, 1997), pp. 93–115.
8. Hubel, Helmut: "Middle East and Mediterranean Policy", *Year Book of European Integration* (1994/95), Europa Union for the Institut fur Europaische Politik, Bonn, pp. 247–252.
9. "The European Union and Human Rights in the World," *Bulletin of the EU, Supplement* 3/95, Luxembourg, 1996.
10. "Declaration on Human Rights, 21 July 1986," *European Political Cooperation Bulletin*, 1986, pp. 57–58.
11. "Declaration Concerning Human Rights, 28/29 June 1991," *EPC Bulletin*, Doc. 91/194, 1991, Vol. 7, Luxembourg, 1993, No. 46, p. 323.
12. "Declaration Concerning Human Rights, 28/29 June 1991," *EPC Bulletin*, Doc. 91/194, 1991, Vol. 7, Luxembourg, 1993, No. 46, p. 324.
13. "Resolution of the Council and of the Member States Meeting in the Council on Human Rights, Democracy and Development (RHRDD), European Parliament, Committee of Foreign Affairs and Security, Subcommittee on Human Rights," PE 156.345, February 26, 1992, p. 7.
14. Hollis, Rosemary: "Europe and the Middle East: Power by Stealth?" *International Affairs*, Vol. 73, No. 1, 1997, pp. 15–29, here p. 19ff.
15. Duparc, Christiane: *The European Community and Human Rights*, Commission of the European Communities, Luxembourg, 1992, p. 25.
16. Regelsberger, Elfriede: "Common Foreign and Security Policy 1994/95," fn. p. 219 and "Common Foreign and Security Policy 1996/97," n. 39, p. 222.

17. The yearly articles by Rieck Andreas, *Year Book Near and Middle East*, 1987–1996, Deutsches Orient Institut.
18. Ehteshami, Anoushiravan: *After Khomeini: The Iranian Second Republic*, Routledge, London, 1995, pp. xiv f.
19. Hashim, Ahmed: "The Crisis of the Iranian State," *Adeplhi Papers*, 296, London, 1995, p. 36ff.; Ehteshami, Anoushiravan: *After Khomeini: The Iranian Second Republic*, Routledge, London, 1995, No. 63, p. 152f.
20. Hashim, Ahmed: "The Crisis of the Iranian State," *Adeplhi Papers*, 296, London, 1995, fn. 64, p. 37; *EPC Bulletin*, Doc. 90/457, pp. 506–507, Concerning Iran and Human Rights, December 12, 1990.
21. Ehteshami, Anoushiravan: *After Khomeini: The Iranian Second Republic*, Routledge, London, 1995, fn. 63, p. 163.
22. Statement at the 49th Session of the Human Rights Commission, March 1, 1993, *EPC-Bulletin*, Doc. 93/079, p. 147.
23. Nonneman, Gerd (ed.): *The Middle East and Europe*, The Federal Trust for Education and Research, London, 1993, fn. 68, pp. 259–276.
24. Steinbach, Udo: "Ein neues Sicherheitssystem for den Gulf" [A New Security System for the Gulf], *Internationale Politik*, Vol. 50, No. 3, March 1995, pp. 33–40.
25. Steinbach, Udo: "Sicherheitssystem," fn. 72, p. 33f.
26. Personal observation by the author while participating in the meeting.
27. "Reward Increased for Rushdie's Death," *Financial Times*, November 3, 1992, p. 1.
28. "Appeasing Iran: It Doesn't Work," *Economist*, January 15, 1994.
29. Kostiner, Joseph: "The Search for Gulf Security," *Middle East Contemporary Survey (MECS)*, Moshe Dayan Institite, Tel Aviv University, Vol. 166, 1992.
30. Kramer, Martin: "The Global Village of Islam," *MECS*, pp. 193–226.
31. Rieck, Andreas: "Iran 1992," *Nahost-Jahrbuch*, n. 58, pp. 78–85, here p. 80.
32. Fred Halliday: "An Elusive Normalisation: Western Europe and the Iranian Revolution," *Middle East Journal*, Vol. 48, No. 2, Spring 1994, n. 76, p. 326.
33. "European Council of Ministers, Edinburgh," fn. 3, § 15.
34. "European Council of Ministers, Edinburgh," fn. 3, § 16 and § 17.
35. Regelsberger, Elfriede: "Common Foreign and Security Policy 1992/93," fn. 39, p. 226.
36. "Ergebnisse des 'Kritischen Dialogs' mit den Iran," [Results of the Critical Dialogue with Iran], *Deutscher Bundestag, Drucksache* 13/3485, January 16, 1996, p. 4.
37. European Parliament, Written Question No. 2170/92 to European Political Cooperation (September 1, 1992).
38. European Parliament, Written Question No. 3057/92 to the European Communities (December 14, 1992).
39. European Parliament, Oral Questions Nos.: H-519/93, H-535/93, H-537/93 and H-557/93, May 26, 1993, *EPC Bulletin*, 1993, Doc. 93/216, pp. 273–277, here p. 216f.
40. "Mr Van den Broek Meets Salman Rushdie," Press Releases and Declarations, December 9, 1993, IP/93/1080.
41. President Rafsanjani as quoted in: Gerges, Fawaz A.: "Washington's Misguided Iran Policy," *Survival*, Vol. 38, No. 4, Winter 1996–97, pp. 5–15, here p. 10.
42. Declaration by the Presidency on EU–Iran Relations, November 25, 1996, PE SC/96/104.
43. Declaration by the Presidency, Brussels, April 10, 1997, PE SC/97/32.
44. "Ein Dialog ohne Ergebnis' [A Dialogue Without Result], *Die Zeit*, No. 36, August 30, 1996, p. 5.
45. Anthony Parsons: "Iran and Western Europe," in R.K. Ramazani (ed.) *Iran's Revolution: The Search for Consensus*, Indiana University Press, November/December 1995, p. 228.
46. Steinbach, Udo: "Ist der Iran das Reich des Bösen?," *Der Überblick*, Vol. 32, June 1996, pp. 30–32.
47. Foreign Minister Klaus Kinkel on May 19, 1996, in the Bundestag, *Stenographische Bericht*, pp. 9217–9218.

48. Steinbach, Udo: "Der Schöne Schein ist längst verblaßt vom sinn eines Menschenrechtsdialogs mit Tehran," *Frankfurter Allgemeine*, March 28, 1995, p. 11.
49. "Report on Velayati's Trip to Bonn," *Frankfurter Rundschau*, July 25, 1995.
50. "Rushdie's Expectations of Germany," *Stuttgarter Nachrichten*, December 11, 1993.
51. "The Iranian Ambassador in Germany: The West's Support of Rushdie Is an Insult to World Muslims," *Kayhan*, January 31, 1992.
52. "Iranian Ambassador Strongly Protests the European Union's Invitation to Rushdie," *Ettela'at*, September 9, 1994.
53. "Opposition of German State Ministries of Culture to Forming a Cultural Contract With Iran," *Islamic Republic News Agency (IRNA)*, May 7, 1994.
54. "Overhauling the Court of Appeal—Iran opposes the establishment of an appeal court" Navid Kermani, *Frankfurter Allgemeine*, July 20, 1996.
55. Kooroshy, Javad: "Die wirtschaftliche Dimension der Deutsch-Iranischen Sonderbeziehung," *Blätte für Deutsche und Internationale Politik*, Vol. 42, January 1997, pp. 66–73.
56. Müller, Harald: *The New German Export Control Policy*, Peace Research Institute, Frankfurt, 1994.
57. Ziller, Peter: "Ein mustergültiger Schuldner," *Frankfurter Rundschau*, November 26, 1996, p. 4; Schmitz,Gregor: "Milliardenschulden und der Mykonos Prozess," *Rheinischer Merkur*, November 29, 1996, p. 15.
58. "Den Kritischen Dialog Überprüfen," *Frankfurter Allgemeine Zeitung*, April 11, 1997, p. 3.
59. "EU-Botschafter wieder in Iran," *Süddeutsche Zeitung*, November 15, 1997, p. 2.
60. The author was present at the November 1997 meeting of Iran ambassadors with the Leader. The Leader heavily criticized German politicians because of the Mykonos verdict and predicted the final victory of Iran.
61. Commentary in *Kayhan International*, November 23, 1997, p. 2.
62. "France Scoffs at U.S. Protest Over Iran Deal," *New York Times*, September 30, 1997, p. A1.
63. *IRNA*, December 15, 1997.
64. Morgan, T. Clifton; al-Sowayal, Dina; Rhodes, Carl: "United States Policy toward Iran: Can Sanctions Work?" Rice University, 1997, http://www.rice.edu/projects/baker/Pubs/studies/.
65. Law, John: "Martin Indyk Lays Out Clinton Approach," *Middle East International*, June 11, 1993, No. 4, p. 3.
66. Rieck, Andreas: "Iran 1993", *Nahost-Jahrbuch* 1993, No. 58, pp.78–85, here p. 80.
67. "Presidential Executive Order Expands U.S. Sanctions Against Iran," *Middle East Policy*, Vol. 4, Nos. 1 & 2, September 1995, pp. 255–257.
68. Amuzegar, Jehangir: *Iran's Economy and the U.S. Sanctions*, No. 146, pp. 191–196.
69. Hollis, Rosemary: "Europe and the Middle East: Power by Stealth?" *International Affairs*, Vol. 73, No. 53, 1997, p. 28.
70. US Congress, Iran and Libya Sanctions Act, 1996.
71. *Middle East Economic Survey*, November 11, 1996, pp. D1–D3, here pp. D2, D1.
72. EU Declaration, August 21, 1996, PESC/96/72.
73. Debates of the European Parliament, 1996, No. 4-482, p. 279.
74. Hopgood, Steve: Theories of the State and Foreign Policy, School of Oriental and African Studies, Unpublished paper.
75. Halliday, Fred: *Iran: Partner or Pariah?* Paper presented at the conference held by Royal Institute of International Affairs, London, November 14, 1995, No. 127, p. 4.
76. Secretary of State as quoted in Gerges: "Washington's Misguided Iran Policy," No. 103, p. 8.
77. Neff, Donald: "Anti-Iran Fever," *Middle East International*, February 2, 1997, pp. 9–10, here p. 9.
78. Brzezinski, Zbigniew *et al.*, "Differentiated Containment," *Foreign Affairs*, Vol. 76, No. 3, May/June 1997, pp. 20–30.

79. Gerges, Fawaz: "Washington's Misguided Iran Policy," No. 103, p. 9.
80. Conry, Barbara: *Cato Institute Policy Analysis*, No. 258, Washington, August 29, 1996, p. 1.
81. Amuzegar, Jehangir: *Iran's Economy*, No. 146, p. 191–196.
82. Murphy, Richard: "Time to Reconsider the Shunning of Iran," *Washington Post*, July 20, 1997.
83. Brzezinski, Zbigniew; Scowcroft, Brent; Murphy, Richard: *Differentiated Containment*, Brookings Institution, 1997, p. 20f.
84. Fuller, Graham E.; Lesser, Ian O.: "Persian Gulf Myths," *Foreign Affairs*, Vol. 76, No. 3, May/June 1997, pp. 42–52, here p. 52.
85. The list of written and oral questions given in the bibliography and the Debates of *E.P. Journal* No. 4–978 and 4–482 of 1996; 4–464 and 4–461 of 1995; and No. 2–374 of 1989.
86. "Resolution on Iran," February 20, 1997, *Official Journal*, No. C85, March 17, 1997, p. 145.
87. "Resolution on the Incitement to Murder by Iran," *Official Journal*, No. C 158/230–231, June 29, 1989.
88. "Resolution on Iran," May 15, 1997, European Parliament, PE 259–261.
89. Timmermann, Kenneth R.: "Time to End the Critical Dialogue with Iran," *Wall Street Journal*, June 10, 1996; July 24, 1997.
90. "Iran-Politik der Bundesregierung," *Deutscher Bundestag*, 13/3483, January 16, 1996, No. 59, p. 6.
91. Hale, William; Kienle, Eberhard: *After the Cold war: Security and Democracy in Africa and Asia*, London, St. Martins Press, New York, 1998, pp. 153–188.
92. Report of UNSR, Mr Copthorne, Economic and Social Council, E/CN. 4/1997/63, February 11, 1997, § 58–59.
93. "Ergebnisse des Kritischen Dialogs," Deutscher Bundestag, Drucksache 13/3485, 1996, p. 8f.
94. "Iran-Politik der Bundesregierung," *Frankreich-Jahrbuch 1997*, ed. by the Deutsch-Französisches Institut et al., Opladen, 1997, p. 4.
95. United Nations, "Report on Human Rights 1997," No. 114, § 2–4.
96. United Nations, "Report on Human Rights 1997," No. 114, Executive Summary, § 2–4.
97. Reissner, Ute: "Iran on the Way to Becoming a Regional Power," in: *Aussenpolitik und Zeitgeschichte*, No. B., April 18, 1996, pp. 32–39.
98. Halliday, Fred: "*Iran; Partner or Pariah?*" Paper presented at the conference held by Royal Institute of International Affairs, London, November 14, 1995, p. 4.
99. Joffe, George H., (ed.): *Disputes Over State Boundaries in the Middle East and North Africa*, London, New York, 1997, pp. 58–75.
100. Gause III, F. Gregory: "The Illogic of Dual Containment," *Foreign Affairs*, Vol. 73, No. 2, March–April 1994, pp. 56–66.
101. Reissner, Ute: "Iran auf dem weg," No. 124, p. 39.
102. Rieck, Andreans: "Iran 1995," *Nahost-Jahrbuch*, No. 58, 1995, pp. 80–87, here p. 84.
103. *Deutscher Bundestag, Drucksache* 13/2983, November 10, 1995.
104. Steinbach, Udo: "Die Beziehungen Bundesrepublik Deutschland-Nahost 1995," *Nahost-Jahrbuch*, No. 58, pp. 13–16, here p. 16.
105. Geitner, Paul: "Germany Rules on Iran Killing," *Associated Press*, October 10, 1997; "Text of a Death sentence From Tehran," *FAZ*, April 10, 1997, p. 5.
106. "Irans Handelsüberschuß ist im vergangenen jahr spürbar gesunken," *FAZ*, April 14, 1997, p. 15.
107. Fitchett, Joseph: "France Denies Selling Missiles to Iran in Exchange for Peace," *International Herald Tribune*, March 24, 1995, p. 10.
108. Lane, Charles: *Germany's New Ostpolitik*, No. 136, p. 83 f.
109. Aziz, Alkazaz: "Die Wirtschafts Beziehungen zum Nahen Osten," *Nahost-Jahrbuch*, 1995, p. 17.
110. Rieck, Andreans: "Iran 1995," *Nahost-Jahrbuch*, No. 58, 1995, pp. 80–87, here p. 82.

111. Friedman, Alan: "Europe and Iran Guaranteeing $5 billion in Loans, Teheran Reports," *International Herald Tribune*, February 3, 1997.
112. Commissioner Vanni d'Archirafi, European Parliament, Debates, April 22, 1993, No. 3–430, p. 284.
113. Mohammadi, Reza: *EU*, The Organization for Defending Victims of Violence (ODVV), Human Rights Committee, Tehran, spring 2001, p. 56
114. Danesh-Yazdi, Mehdi *et al.*, "*Discrimination and Prohibition of Torture*," The EU–Iran Human Rights Dialogue, December 16–17, 2002, translated by Mina Sinivar, Denmark, 2003, p. 7.
115. "*EU–Iran Human Rights Dialogue*," The Danish Institute for Human Rights, http://www.humanrights.dk/departments/director/iraneu.
116. *A Report on the First Roundtable Under the EU-Iran Human Rights Dialogue, December 16–17, 2002*, The Organization for Defending Victims of Violence (ODVV).
117. Danesh-Yazdi, Mehdi *et al.*, "*Discrimination and Prohibition of Torture*," The EU–Iran Human Rights Dialogue, December 16–17, 2002, translated by Mina Sinivar, Denmark, 2003, p. 11.
118. *A Report on the Second Roundtable Under the EU–Iran Human Rights Dialogue, March 15–16, 2006*, The Organization for Defending Victims of Violence (ODVV).
119. *A Report on the Fourth Roundtable Under the EU–Iran Human Rights Dialogue, June–July 2004*, The Organization for Defending Victims of Violence (ODVV).
120. http://www.bbc.co.uk/persian/iran/story/2005/12/05/1212_fb_eu_iran_hr.shtml.
121. http://www.bbc.co.uk/persian/iran/story/2004/06/040617_a_mb_iran_humanrights.shtml.

Chapter 9   Terrorism

1. Halliday, Fred, 'Iran and the United Kingdom', unpublished report presented to the Foreign Affairs Committee, House of Commons, September 2000.
2. Special Report, Foundation for Democracy in Iran, Maryland, USA, May 6, 1996.
3. Karmon, Ely, "Iran's policy on terrorism in the 1990s," www.ict.org.il/articles
4. The main difference was over the time of using force and the decision-making authority that should determine that time. Most European countries maintained that the United Nations is the authority that should give the go-ahead on the use of force while the United States believed (and still believes) that the decision on the use of force depends on the case. Therefore, on the basis of its doctrine of preemptive strike, the United States considers itself free to launch military action while Europe is insisting on principles of Westphalia by stressing that the use of force should be postponed until after an act of aggression. Out of respect for sovereignty of countries, when a decision is to be made on the internal affairs of a country, it will be based on noninterference and priority should be given to diplomatic efforts. Therefore, the use of force is only justifiable when the UN Security Council has considered a government's measure as blatant breach of international peace and security.
5. Most of the European press maintained that the success of EU3 in getting Iran to implement the Additional Protocol to Non-Proliferation Treaty as "the most important diplomatic achievement of the European Union following Maastricht Treaty." Undoubtedly, the measure was a symbol of adherence of the European states to "soft power" in the face of US preference for 'hard power' in dealing with other countries. Differences between Europe and the United States on how to deal with Iran posed many challenges to the American approach to guarantee international security and order. As put by Brzezinski, those challenges caused the United States to lose face while being the world's superior power. Brzezinski maintains that losing face by the United States had two more dire consequences: loss of international credit and growing international isolation.
6. EU members failed to achieve an agreement on the draft constitution of the EU in Brussels on December 13, 2003. The main difference among member states was over the

right to vote. While Poland and Spain were not willing to have less voting rights than major members of the EU, France and Germany argued that voting right should be handed out according to population of countries. Most experts, however, believed that the new constitution could have improved decision-making and policy making trends of the EU.

7. Sherman, Peter and Sussex, Matthew, *European Security after September 11*, UK, Ashgate, 2004, pp. 4–5.
8. France Has Nuclear Retaliation Option, *Spiegel Online*, January 19, 2006.
9. President Jacques Chirac said in an address about the nuclear policy of France on January 20, 2006, that France was ready to use nuclear weapons against countries that threatened it through terrorist operations. He noted that nuclear missiles of France were ready to hit terrorists; see More, Molly, *Chirac: Nuclear Response to Terrorism Is Possible*, *Washington Post*, Friday, January 20, 2006, P A12.

Chapter 10   The Middle East peace process

1. Ahmad Rashidi, *Peace Process*, Political Sciences Master's Degree Thesis, (Tehran University's Faculty of Political Sciences; Tehran, 1999, p. 79.
2. Ahmad Rashidi, *Peace Process*, Political Sciences Master's Degree Thesis, (Tehran University's Faculty of Political Sciences; Tehran, 1999, p. 80.
3. Seyed Reza Mirtaheri, *al-Aqsa Mosque Intifada*, Ideological and Political Organization of NAJA Press, 2000, p. 26.
4. See http://www.palestine-persian.info/tahlil-e-siasi/2000/tahlil-e-siasi.html
5. *Al-Sharq al-Awsat*, August 12, 2000.
6. Hossein Daheshyar, US Foreign Policy and 1st and 2nd Palestinian Intifada, *Foreign Policy Quarterly*, 15th year, No. 1, spring 2001, p. 158.
7. Katayoun Ansari-Rad, Development of Second Intifada, *Foreign Policy Quarterly*, 15th year, No. 1, Spring 2001, p. 32.
8. Katayoun Ansari-Rad, Development of Second Intifada, *Foreign Policy Quarterly*, 15th year, No. 1, Spring 2001, p. 33.
9. Ahmad Rashidi, *Peace Process*, Political Sciences Master's Degree Thesis, Tehran University's Faculty of Political Sciences; Tehran, 1999, p. 82.
10. Hassan Khodaverdi, Palestinian Authority and Intifada, *Palestine Quarterly*, 2nd year, No. 1, Fall 2000, pp. 103–104.
11. Mohammad Reza Dehshiri, Second Palestinian Intifada, *Palestine Quarterly*, 2nd year, No. 1, Fall 2000, p. 53.
12. Katayoun Ansari-Rad, Development of Second Intifada, *Foreign Policy Quarterly*, 15th year, No. 1, Spring 2001, p. 34.
13. *Kar-o-Kargar*, January 24, 2001, p. 11.
14. *Nida al-Muqawimah*, Political and cultural monthly of Hezbollah Office in Tehran, No. 6, December 2002, p. 16.
15. *Nida al-Muqawimah* periodical, political and cultural monthly of Lebanon's Hezbollah in Tehran, No. 13, June 2003, p. 10.
16. *Islamic Republic Newspaper*, October 22, 2000, p. 12.
17. Seyed Reza Mirtaheri, *al-Aqsa Mosque Intifada*, Ideological and Political Organization of NAJA Press, 2000, p. 117.

Appendices

1. "*Federal Republic of Germany*," Institute of Trade Studies and Research (ITSR) affiliated to the Department of Planing Information Dissemination of Iran's Ministry of Commerce, First Edition, May 1989.
2. "Sarkuhi's Letter," *Tages Zeitung*, Berlin, January 31, 1997 [trans.].
3. "Judiciary Press Department," Ministry of Judiciary of Berlin, Germany, April 10, 1997 [trans.].

Selected bibliography

Books and Articles

Albright, David "An Iranian Bomb?," *Bulletin of the Atomic Scientists*, July–August 1995, pp. 21–26.

Albright, Madeleine, US Secretary of State, Speech before the Asia Society, June 17, 1998.

Amuzegar, Jahangir, "Iran's Economy and the U.S. Sanctions," *Middle East Journal*, Vol. 51, No. 2, Spring 1997.

Beig, Kamal Amir, "Priorities in German Foreign Policy," *Monthly Bulletin, IPIS*, Tehran, No. 140. pp. 15–18.

Berkhout, Frans and Walker, William, *"Plutonium and Highly enriched Uranium 1996: World Inventories, Capabilities, and Policies,"* New York, Oxford University Press/ SIPRI, 1997, pp. 352–363.

Burleigh, Peter, "Lessons of 'Operation Staunch' for future Conflicts," in Eric H. Arnett, *Lessons of the Iran–Iraq War: Mediation and Conflict Resolution*, American Association for the Advancement of Science, Washington DC, 1990, pp. 9–14.

Clawson, Patrick, "What to Do About Iran," *The Middle East Quarterly*, December 1995.

Clawson, Patrick and Eisenstadt, Michael, "Opportunities and Challenges for U.S. Policy," in Patrick Clawson (ed.), *Iran Under Khatami: A Political, Economic, and Military Assessment*, The Washington Institute for Near East Policy, Washington, DC, 1998, pp. 99–114.

Conry, Barbara, "Time Bomb: The Escalation of U.S. Security Commitments in the Persian Gulf Region," Cato Institute Policy Analysis, No. 258, Washington, August 29, 1996, p. 1.

Donfried, Karen, "German–American Relation in the New Europe," Congressional Research Service Brief, Washington, DC, December 5, 1996.

Ehteshami, Anoushiravan, *"After Khomeini, The Iranian Second Republic"*, Routledge, London, New York, 1995.

Eisenstadt, Michael, *Iranian Military Power: Capabilities and Intentions*, The Washington Institute for Near East Policy, Washington, DC, 1996.

European Council in Edinburgh, December 11–12, 1992, conclusions of the presidency, Doc/92/8, §15.

European Parliament, Written Question No. 2170/92, *European Political Cooperation Bulletin*, September 1, 1992.

European Parliament, Oral Questions No: H-519/93, H-535/93, H-537/93, and H-557/93, *EPC Bulletin*, Doc. 93/216, May 26, 1993, pp. 273–277, here p. 216f.

European Union, "Declaration Concerning Human Rights, June 28/29, 1991," *European Political Cooperation Bulletin*, Doc. 91/194, 1991, Vol. 7, Luxembourg, 1993, pp. 322–324.

European Union, "The European Union and Human Rights in the World," *Bulletin of the EU*, Supplement 3/95, Luxembourg, 1996.

European Union, "Role of Europe in the Middle East Peace Process," Speech of Mr. Gerard Collins, former Irish Foreign Minister, October 1997.

European Union, "The Role of EU in the Peace Process," Communication made by Mr. Manuel Marin, Vice President of European Commission, January 26, 1998, pp. 7–9.

European Union, Implementation of the Interim Agreement on Trade and Trade related matters between the European Community and Israel, Communication made by the European Commission, May 1998.

Federal Parliament of Germany, *Ergebnisse des 'Kritischen Dialogs' mit den Iran*, Deucher Bundestag, *Drucksache* 13/3485, January 16, 1996, p. 4.

Foundation for Democracy in Iran, *Special Report*, Maryland, USA, May 6, 1996.

"Government Approves Utilisation of 1% of Carpet Exports for Advertisements and Marketing," *Farshe Iran* [Journal on Iranian Carpets], Germany, January 1993.

Gregory III, Gause F., "The Illogic of Dual Containment," *Foreign Affairs*, Vol. 73, No. 2, March–April 1994, pp. 56–66.

Hale, William and Eberhard Kienle (eds.), *After the Cold War: Security and Democracy in Africa and Asia*, Library of International Relations, Vol. 6. St Martins Press, 1998.

Halliday, "Iran: Partner or Pariah?," Penguin Books, fn. 127, p. 4.

Halliday, Fred, "Iran and the United Kingdom," Unpublished Report to the Foreign Affairs Committee, House of Commons, September 2000.

Hashim, Ahmed, "The Crisis of the Iranian State," *ADELPHI* Paper 296, London, 1995, p. 36 ff.

Hollis, Rosemary, "Europe and the Middle East: Power by Stealth?," *International Affairs*, January 1997.

Hopgood, Steve, "Theories of the State and Foreign Policy," School of Oriental and African Studies, Unpublished Paper, January 10, 1997.

Institute of Trade Studies and Research (ITSR), "*Federal Republic of Germany*," Tehran, May 1989.

International Monetary Fund, *Islamic Republic of Iran—Recent Economic Developments*, September 19, 1995, p. 74; October 5, 1993, p. 38.

Iran Statistics Center, *1984 Activities Report, Iran–German Chamber of Commerce and Industries*, Tehran, 1980.

Iranian government documents (Embassy of the Islamic Republic of Iran in Germany).

Iranian government documents (Embassy of the Islamic Republic of Iran in London).

Iranian government documents (Iranian Ministry of Foreign Affairs).

Joffé, George, "Disputes over Boundaries in the Middle East and North Africa," in Guazzone, Laura (ed.), *The Middle East in Global Change*, London, Macmillan, 1997.

Jünemann, Annette, "The Mediterranean Policy of the EU," in German–French Institut et al. (ed.), *France Year Book 1997*, Opladen, 1997, pp. 93–115.

Karmon, Ely, "Iran's Policy on Terrorism in the 1990s," Paper presented on May 10, 1998, at the International Conference on Terror at the Department of Political Science, Haifa University.

Koch, Andrew and Wolf, Jeanette, "Iran's Nuclear Procurement Program: How Close to the Bomb?," *The Non-proliferation Review*, Fall 1997, pp. 123–135.

Kostiner, Joseph, "The Search for Gulf Security," *Middle East Contemporary Survey*, 1992.

Kramer, Martin, "The Global Village of Islam," *Middle East Contemporary Survey*, 1992.

Lane, Charles, "Germany's New Ostpolitik," *Foreign Affairs*, March–April 1996.

Millward, William, "Containing Iran," Commentary No. 63, *Canadian Security Intelligence Service*, November 1995.

Mohammadi, Manoochehr, *Review of Iranian Foreign Politics During the Pahlavi Period,* Tehran University Publications Institute, Tehran, 1997.

Müller, Harald, *The New German Export Control Policy*, Peace Research Institute, Frankfurt, 1994.

Murphy, Richard, "Time to Reconsider the Shunning of Iran," *Washington Post*, July 20, 1997.

Nonneman, Gerd (ed.), *The Middle East and Europe*, Federal Trust for Education and Research, London, 1993.

OPEC, *Annual Statistical Bulletin*, Vienna, 1982.

Parsons, Anthony, "Iran and Western Europe," *Middle East Journal*, Spring 1989.

Rahmani, Ali, *Reunification of Two Germanies*, Institute of Political and International Studies, Ministry of Foreign Affairs, 1991.

Regelsberger, Elfriede, "*Common Foreign and Security Policy*," in Weidenfeld, Werner and Wesseis, Wolfgang (eds.), *Europe From A to Z: Guide to European Integration*, Luxembourg, 1997.

Reissner, Johannes, "Europe, the United States, and the Persian Gulf," in Blackwill, Robert D. and Sturmer, Michael (eds.), *Allies Divided: Transatlantic Policies for the Greater Middle East*, Cambridge, MA, The MIT Press, 1997, pp. 138–140.

Rieck, Andreas (ed.), *Year Book, Near and Middle East; 1987–1996*, Deutsches Orient Institut, Hamburg.

Riedel, Bruce, "U.S. Policy in the Persian Gulf: Five Years of Dual Containment," *Policy Watch,* The Washington Institute for Near East Policy, No. 315, May 8, 1998, p. 2.

Rubinstein Alvin, "Germans of Their Future," *Orbis*, Winter 1999.

Rudolf, Peter, *Konflikt oder Koordination? Die USA, Iran und die Deutsch–Amerikanischen Beziehungen*, Ebenhausen, Stiftung Wissenschaft und Politik, 1996.

Rumsfeld, Donald H., *Report of the Commission to Assess the Ballistic Missile Threat to the United States: Executive Summary*, Washington, DC, Government Printing Office, 1998, pp. 12–13.

Sariulqalam, Mahmoud, *Foreign Policy of the Islamic Republic of Iran*, Iranian Institute for Strategic Studies, Tehran, 2001.

Steinbach, Udo, "Ein neues Sicherheitssystem für den Gulf," *Internationale Politik*, Vol. 50, No. 3, March 1995, pp. 33–40.

Steinbach, Udo, "Die Beziehungen Bundesrepublik Deutschland-Nahost 1995," *Nahost-Jahrbuch*, fn. 58, pp. 13–16, here p. 16.

Steinberg, Gerald, "The EU and Middle East Peace Process," Jerusalem Centre for Public Affairs, Newsletter No. 418, November 1999.

Tarnoff, Peter, Under Secretary of State, Testimony before the House International Relations Committee: Containing Iran, Hearing before the Committee on International Relations, House of Representatives, 104th Congress, First Session, No. 9, 1995. Washington, 1996, pp. 45–54.

United Nations, "Memorandum of the Plenary Session of the 49th U.N. General Assembly, Sept. 27, 1994," in *European Foreign Policy Bulletin*, Doc. 94/228, Vol. 10, 1994, pp. 312–322.

Zaloga, Steven J., "Third World Ballistic Missiles," *World Missile Briefing*, Teal Group, Fairfax, Virginia, August 1999.

Newspapers and other news sources

German newspapers

Berliner Morgen Post
Deutsche Wochen Zeitung
Deutsche Zeitung
Frankfurter Allgemeine
Frankfurter Rundschau
Focus
General Anzeiger
Handelsblatt
Hannoverische Allgemeine
Kölnische Zeitung
Morgen
Rheinische Merkur
Der Spiegel
Die Stern
Süddeutsche Zeitung
Stuttgarter Nachrichten
Tages Zeitung
Die Welt
Die Zeit

Iranian newspapers

Abrar
Azadegan
Ettelaàt
Entekhab
Fath
Hamshahri
Jahan-e Emrooz
Jomhuri Islami
Kayhan Havai
Khorassan
Khordad
Resaalat
Sobh-e Emrooz
Salam
Sobh-e Emrooz

American newspapers

Christian Science Monitor
International Herald Tribune
Washington Times
Washington Post

British, French, and international Arabic newspapers and journals

The Economist
Financial Times
Guardian
Al-Hayat
Libération
Middle East International

News agencies

AFP
DPA
IRNA
Reuters
UPI

Radio stations

ARD
BBC Radio
Deutschlandfunk (English Service)
NTV

Index

in 1991 Gulf War and impact on 73; Majlis, triple urgency plan 159; March resolution 168–9; Middle East peace process, opposition for 78; Non-Proliferation Treaty (NPT), obligations of 148; November resolution 160–4; nuclear activities, European Union on 154; nuclear dossier dispute 147–8; nuclear weapons acquisition by Pakistan, impact on 73; plutonium tests 166; preliminary negotiations, failure of 159; Rowhani–Chirac agreement 180–2; September 2003 crisis 150–2; Tehran negotiations, achievements for 159–62; United States, on nuclear program 153; US and EU policies against 75–6

Iran and Libya Sanctions Act (ILSA) 206

Iran–Europe relations: and EU's representatives 211; human rights issues affecting 210; strategic conclusions 239–41; in trade 209; Western policies affecting 197–202

Iran–Germany relationship: Abbas Hamadi, release of 29–30; actions detrimental to 84; after Second World War 15–17; agricultural studies, agreements and collaboration 16; and allegations of spying Iranian diplomats 91; arms exports development 17; arrest of officials 88–90; banking sector, agreements and collaboration 54; bilateral influence on 27; bugging devices at Iranian Consulate 92; Bushehr nuclear power plant and 31; cancellation of ministerial visits 114; concerning maritime transportation 56–7; court verdict influencing 107; on debt deferment 32–3; demonstration against German court's verdict 112; Dr Javadi, prosecution of 90–1; economic and commercial agreements 15, 20; espionage equipment 90; on establishment of security relations 28; EU and Middle East peace process influence on 77–8; European aid activity in support of Kurds, influence on 27; exchange between political leaderships 104–6; external actors and foreign policy constraints 3–4; external actors and foreign policy constraints effecting 61; and financial assistance to Israel by Germany 69; first joint economic commission and 49–50; before First

World War 11–13; during First World War 13–14; German ambassador in Tehran, summon of 100; German reunification on 18, 71; German technology acquisition and 133; Germany's position on Iraq's aggression against Iran and UN resolution 27; and granting of DM 4.5 billion credit to 51; Hermes insurance coverage 50–1; human rights, seminar on 30; indictment of Iranian officials by German Prosecutor-General 42–3; intelligence services, cooperation 28; interference of Russia and Britain and influence on 12; Iran–Germany friendship associations, revival of 30; Iranian embassy, allegations against 91–2; Iranian Foreign Minister's trip to Germany and influence on 23–4; Iranian intelligence agents deported from Europe 114; Iranian Minister of Information, subpoena issued to 116–8; Iranian National Football Team, training camp for 44–5; and Iraq invasion on Kuwait 24; Iraqi refugees in Iran, German aid for 25–7; Islamic revolution influence on 18–22; joint cultural meetings 47; kidnappings accusation 83–4; killings at *Mykonos* restaurant 94–5; Kurdish leaders in Berlin, assassination of 4; Kurdish refugees, German aid for 26; letter to President Rafsanjani 101–2; media seminar and 48; on memorandum of understanding in field of judicial cooperation 28; Middle East peace process and human rights 4; moves by German opposition parties against 4; Mr. Ali Fallahian, issue of subpoena to 95; Mykonos trial and influence on 5–7; negative impact on development of 80; oil trade impact on 21–2; Persian language studies 45–6; politics concerning Israel 78; prerevolutionary ties influencing 17–18; prohibition of entry to Germany of Maryam Rajavi 38–9; protest for Mykonos trial 85, 108; railways, agreements and collaboration of 14; recall of ambassadors 112–3; release of German hostages in Lebanon 28–9; and rescheduling Iran's debts 53; and resolution of clashes arising out of "Parchin 6"